THE UNIVERSI
WINCHES

Memory and Power in Post-War Europe

How has memory – collective and individual – influenced European
politics after the Second World War and after 1989 in particular? How
has the past been used in domestic struggles for power, and how have
'historical lessons' been applied in foreign policy? While there is now a
burgeoning field of social and cultural memory studies, mostly focused
on commemorations and monuments, this volume is the first to examine
the connection between memory and politics directly. It investigates how
memory is officially recast, personally reworked and often violently re-
instilled after wars, and above all, the ways in which memory shapes
present power constellations.

The chapters combine theoretical innovation in their approach to the
study of memory with deeply historical, empirically based case studies
of major European countries. The point of stressing memory is not to
deny that interests shape policy, but, with Max Weber, to analyse the
historically and ideologically conditioned formation and legitimation of
these interests. The volume concludes with reflections on the ethics of
memory, and the politics of truth, justice and forgetting after 1945 and
1989.

This ground-breaking book should be of interst to historians of contemporary Europe, political scientists, sociologists and anyone interested in how the political uses of the past have shaped – and continue
to shape – the Europe in which we live now.

JAN-WERNER MÜLLER is a fellow of All Souls College, Oxford. He
is the author of *Another Country: German Intellectuals, Unification and
National Identity* (2000).

Memory and Power in Post-War Europe

Studies in the Presence of the Past

Edited by

Jan-Werner Müller

All Souls College, Oxford

CAMBRIDGE
UNIVERSITY PRESS

CAMBRIDGE UNIVERSITY PRESS
Cambridge, New York, Melbourne, Madrid, Cape Town, Singapore,
São Paulo, Delhi, Dubai, Tokyo, Mexico City

Cambridge University Press
The Edinburgh Building, Cambridge CB2 8RU, UK

Published in the United States of America by Cambridge University Press, New York

www.cambridge.org
Information on this title: www.cambridge.org/9780521000703

© Cambridge University Press 2002

First published 2002

A catalogue record for this publication is available from the British Library

ISBN 978-0-521-80610-7 Hardback
ISBN 978-0-521-00070-3 Paperback

For as at a great distance of place, that which wee look at, appears dimme, and without distinction of the smaller parts; and as Voyces grow weak, and inarticulate: so also after great distance of time, our imagination of the Past is weak; and wee lose (for example) of Cities wee have seen, many particular Streets; and of Actions, many particular Circumstances. This *decaying sense*, when wee would express the thing itself, (I mean *fancy* itselfe,), wee call *Imagination*, as I said before: But when we would express the *decay*, and signifie that the Sense is fading, old, and past, it is called *Memory*. So that *Imagination* and *Memory*, are but one thing...

Hobbes, *Leviathan*

Contents

Part 2 Memory and power in domestic affairs

Contributors

THOMAS BERGER is an Associate Professor in the Department of
International Relations at Boston University. He is the author of
Cultures of Antimilitarism: National Security in Germany and Japan
(1998) and has written extensively on international security,
international migration and political culture. He is currently writing
a book on the dynamics of national identity formation and its impact
on politics in advanced industrial countries.

ILANA BET-EL was Senior Advisor on the Balkans in the UN
Department of Political Affairs (1999–2000), and a senior political
analyst with the United Nations missions in Bosnia-Hercegovina,
both during and after the war there (1995–7). She holds a Ph.D. from
the University of London, has lectured in history at Tel Aviv
University and was a Fellow of the Reuters Foundation Programme,
Green College, Oxford. She has written a number of papers on
history and collective memory in Israel and the UK; her book on the
imagery of conscripts in the First World War, *Conscripts: Lost Legions
of the Great War*, was pubished in 1999.

ANNE DEIGHTON is Lecturer in International Politics at the University
of Oxford, and a fellow of Wolfson College. She has written
extensively on British foreign policy and on European integration.

JULIAN DIERKES is finishing his dissertation in sociology at Princeton
University while on a fellowship at the Japan Centre at the University
of Cambridge. His dissertation, entitled 'Teaching National Identity –
Education in Germany and Japan, 1945–1995', examines the
construction of the nation in post-war history textbooks for
secondary schools in Japan, the Federal Republic of Germany and
the German Democratic Republic. He is also continuing work
examining the organisational structure of large US corporations since
the 1960s.

List of contributors

TIMOTHY GARTON ASH is a fellow of St Antony's College, Oxford. His most recent book is *History of the Present: Essays, Sketches and Despatches from Europe in the 1990s* (1999).

ROBERT GILDEA is fellow and tutor at Merton College, Oxford. His most recent books are *The Past in French History* (1994) and *France since 1945* (1996).

JEFFREY HERF teaches modern European and German history at the University of Maryland at College Park, with a focus on the intersection of political, intellectual and international history. His books include: *Divided Memory: The Nazi Past in the Two Germanys* (1997). The manuscript was awarded the Fraenkel Prize for 1996 by the Institute of Contemporary History and the Wiener Library in London. The book won the 1998 George Lewis Beer Prize of the American Historical Association as the best book by an American citizen dealing with European international history since 1890. His other books include *War by Other Means: Soviet Power, West German Resistance and the Battle of the Euromissiles* (1991) and *Reactionary Modernism: Technology, Culture and Politics in Weimar and the Third Reich* (1984), also published in Italian, Japanese, Portuguese, Spanish and Greek editions.

TONY JUDT is Erich Maria Remarque Professor of European Studies and Director of the Remarque Institute, New York University. His most recent book is *The Burden of Responsibility: Blum, Camus, Aron, and the French Twentieth Century* (1998).

DANIEL LEVY is Assistant Professor in the sociology department at SUNY Stony Brook. His publications revolve around issues of political culture, collective memory studies and the comparative sociology of immigration. His most recent book, *Erinnerung im globalen Zeitalter: Der Holocaust* (with Natan Sznaider), is a comparative study of mnemonic cultures in Germany, Israel and the United States, focusing on how processes of globalisation have affected collective memories in these countries.

JAN-WERNER MÜLLER is a fellow of All Souls College, Oxford. He is the author of *Another Country: German Intellectuals, Unification, and National Identity* (2000).

IVER B. NEUMANN is a researcher at the Norwegian Institute of International Affairs. His latest books are (co-edited with Ole Wæver) *The Future of International Relations: Masters in the Making?* (1997) and *Uses of the Other: 'The East' in European Identity Formation* (1998).

ILARIA POGGIOLINI is Professor of the History of International
Relations at the University of Pavia. She has been a Fulbright Fellow,
a Fellow at the Center for International Studies at Princeton
University and a British Council Fellow at St Antony's College,
Oxford. She is the author of numerous publications on the origins of
the Cold War in Italy and on the transition from war to peace in
Europe and Asia after the Second World War. She is currently
working on a project on the history of European regionalism.

MONROE E. PRICE is Professor of Law at Cardozo Law School in New
York and co-director of the Programme on Comparative Media Law
and Policy at the Centre for Socio-Legal Studies, University of
Oxford. He is the author of *Television, the Public Sphere and National
Identity* (Oxford University Press, 1995).

TIMOTHY SNYDER is an assistant professor in the History Department
at Yale University. His first book, *Nationalism, Marxism, and Modern
Central Europe: A Biography of Kazimierz Kelles-Krauz (1872–1905)*
was published by the Ukrainian Research Institute in 1997. He is
presently completing a study of Poland's relations with its eastern
neighbours since 1939, in which the central issue examined is the
relationship between memory and policy.

Acknowledgements

The editor wishes to thank the Warden and Fellows of All Souls College, Oxford, for giving permission to hold a conference on 'Memory and Power in Post-War Europe' at All Souls on 26–7 June 1998. Especially warm thanks are due to Sir Julian Bullard and Robert O'Neill as co-directors of the All Souls Foreign Policy Studies Programme for intellectually and financially supporting this project throughout. The college staff and Julie Edwards in particular were unfailingly helpful with logistics. For stimulating comments at the conference, thanks to Erica Benner, Kathy Burk, Richard Crampton, Alex Danchev, Michael Ignatieff, Yuen Foong Khong, Ernest May, Jeffrey K. Olick, Alex Pravda, Peter Pulzer and Gesine Schwan. For useful remarks on the manuscript as a whole, thanks also to a number of anonymous readers. Finally, support from Tony Judt, Jair Kessler and the staff at the Remarque Institute of New York University during the conclusion of the project is very gratefully acknowledged.

Material in Jeffrey Herf's chapter first appeared in his *Divided Memory: The Nazi Past in the Two Germanys* (Cambridge, MA: Harvard University Press, 1997). Thanks to Harvard University Press for permission to use this material here. Some of the material in Timothy Garton Ash's chapter has previously been published in his *History of the Present: Essays, Sketches and Despatches from Europe in the 1990s* (London: Allen Lane, 1999). Thanks to Penguin for permission to use this material. Copyright © Timothy Garton Ash, 1999.

Introduction: the power of memory, the memory of power and the power over memory

Jan-Werner Müller

Not ideas, but material interests, directly govern men's conduct. Yet very frequently the 'world images' that have been created by 'ideas' have, like switchmen, determined the tracks along which action has been pushed by the dynamic of interest.[1]

Max Weber

Today Europe rummages through drawers of memories, particularly those which contain the traumatic files of the First World War, the Second World War, fascism and communism.[2]

Dubravka Ugrešić

The best that can be achieved is to know precisely what [the past] was, and to endure this knowledge, and then to wait and see what comes of knowing and enduring.[3]

Hannah Arendt

Memory matters. It matters for the simple reason that memory is an anthropological given, since 'all consciousness is mediated through it'.[4] However, stressing this fact at the current historical juncture risks invoking a cliché, since 'memory', both individual and collective, lies at the intersection of so many of our current concerns and organises many of our current projects. As Ian Hacking has pointed out, memory has become 'a powerful tool in quests for understanding, justice and knowledge'.[5] Yet, for all the present obsession with 'memory thinking' (Hacking), there have been almost no studies of the nexus between memory and political power,

Thanks for memorable comments to Patrick O. Cohrs, Tony Judt and Erika Anita Kiss.

[1] Max Weber, 'The Social Psychology of the World Religions', in H. H. Gerth and C. Wright Mills (eds.), *From Max Weber: Essays in Sociology* (London: Routledge, 1991), 267–301, 280.

[2] Dubravka Ugrešić, *The Culture of Lies: Antipolitical Essays* (London: Phoenix House, 1998), 224.

[3] Hannah Arendt, 'On Humanity in Dark Times', in Hannah Arendt, *Men in Dark Times* (New York: Harcourt Brace & Company, 1995[1968]), 3–31, 20.

[4] James Fentress and Chris Wickham, *Social Memory* (Oxford: Blackwell, 1992), x–xi.

[5] Ian Hacking, *Rewriting the Soul: Multiple Personality and the Sciences of Memory* (Princeton: Princeton University Press, 1998), 3.

especially if one defines politics rather narrowly as the output of political institutions. To be sure, memory is crucial to some of the fields of scholarly inquiry that have been most prominent in recent years: the study of nationalism, questions of ethnic identity and the 'politics of recognition', in which groups are given recognition not least for their past experiences of exclusion and suffering. Moreover, there have been numerous studies of cultural memory as expressed in monuments, memorials and works of art, as well as in school textbooks.[6] But while very few would doubt that memory mattered and exercised power in the Yugoslav wars, even fewer would be able to explain precisely how it mattered. Thus, despite the intense focus on memory in history, sociology and cultural studies, the memory–power nexus remains curiously unexamined.[7] And while it has become a commonplace to stress the imaginary quality of the nation, tradition, and implicitly, memory, that is their sheer 'constructedness', just *how* these imaginations and constructions come to have real political consequences is far from obvious.

The premise of this book is that memory matters *politically* in ways which we do not yet fully understand; its purpose is to clarify the relationship between memory and power. The essays collected here investigate how memory is personally reworked, officially recast and often violently re-instilled, especially after wars. They examine the ways in which memory shapes present power constellations, in particular the way in which collective memory constrains, but also enables, policies. They are not just about political measures explicitly dealing with the past, such as restitution, retribution and amnesty, but also about how memory shapes frameworks for foreign policy and domestic politics.[8] They touch on the relationship between memory and justice, since, as I will argue later in this introduction, the concept of legitimacy inevitably connects memory and normative as well as legal questions. But the main focus of this book is political, not judicial or cultural.

However, how is one to get a handle on a seemingly vague concept such as memory in relation to politics? Can memory be measured, and is it necessarily in competition with material interests? Is it money or memory,

---

[6] See for instance Mieke Bal, Jonathan Crewe and Leo Spitzer (eds.), *Acts of Memory: Cultural Recall in the Present* (Hanover, NH: University Press of New England, 1999).

[7] An important exception is Andrei S. Markovits and Simon Reich, *The German Predicament: Memory and Power in the New Europe* (Ithaca, NY: Cornell University Press, 1997), which correctly chides much of political science for 'reifying measurement as explanation'.

[8] The focus on policies which deal with the past is of course not novel. Some excellent recent studies on post-war Europe include Norbert Frei, *Vergangenheitspolitik: Die Anfänge der Bundesrepublik und die NS-Vergangenheit* (Munich: C. H. Beck, 1996), which is an in-depth study of early West German amnesties for Nazis, and Jeffrey Herf, *Divided Memory: The Nazi Past in the Two Germanys* (Cambridge, MA: Harvard University Press, 1997), which stresses the importance of 'high politics' in preserving a memory of the Nazi past.

as a sceptic of historical studies of memory has asserted?[9] To avoid such false dichotomies and confusions, the contributors to this volume draw a number of important distinctions. At a basic conceptual level – which I shall further explicate below – the essays collected here distinguish between 'collective' or 'national' memory on the one hand, and mass individual memory on the other. The latter refers to the recollection of events which individuals actually lived through. The former establishes a social framework through which nationally conscious individuals can organise their history; it is possible, but perhaps somewhat misleading, simply to call this memory a form of myth. It is this national-collective memory and national identity which are mutually constitutive. This type of memory influences, but also sometimes conflicts with, individual memories. Finally, for the sake of analytical clarity, the contributions also distinguish between national as well as individual memory on the one hand, and the use of memory in the sense of historical analogies on the other – in other words, the use of national or personal memory by individuals in political reflections and decision-making processes. While keeping to these conceptual distinctions, the contributors aim at a nuanced combination of political, sociological and legal perspectives. They insist that it is crucial to identify the relevant political *carriers* of personal and collective memory and the exact historical and sociological locations of these memories – or else memory studies are in danger of deteriorating into a mere enumeration of free-floating representations of the past which might or might not have relevance for politics. The chosen context to test this approach and examine the relationship between memory and power is the period after the Second World War and the very recent past and present, that is, the period after the Cold War. In many of the following chapters, specific parallels are drawn between these two periods.

Two post-war periods

In both periods, the past has not been what it used to be. The relationship between memories and the present, or so it seems, has been stronger and more immediate than at other times. One reason might be that the past returns with a vengeance during times of political crisis. According to John Keane, 'crisis periods . . . prompt awareness of the crucial political importance of the past for the present. As a rule, crises are times during which the living do battle for the hearts, minds and souls of the dead'.[10] But the dead also seem to be doing battle for the hearts, minds and souls

[9] Alan S. Milward, 'Bad Memories', *Times Literary Supplement*, 14 April 2000.
[10] John Keane, 'More theses on the philosophy of history', in James Tully (ed.), *Meaning and Context: Quentin Skinner and his Critics* (Cambridge: Polity, 1988), 204–17, 204.

of the living, as the latter often resort during times of crisis to a kind of mythical re-enactment of the past.

Both patterns of historical action were certainly present in the immediate post-war period: raw individual memories of life during the Second World War, and of occupation and resistance in particular, were overlaid with collective national memories – or myths – which served to legitimate – and stabilise – the political order after 1945. In particular, as Tony Judt argues in chapter 7, a myth of complete common victimisation by the Germans produced social solidarity even among peoples who had in fact benefited from the occupation. But not only memories, also 'instant amnesia', in particular of collaboration, served the purpose of legitimating power.

War itself also seemed to encourage amnesia, or at least a kind of psychological 'numbing'. As Michael Geyer has pointed out with regard to Germany, when the population emerged from an 'extended death zone' during the Third Reich, it entered a state of mind in which a 'permanent numbing of body and soul' was coupled with an effort to pour all energies into reconstruction. 'Instead of sorrow and mourning as an expression of the reaction to mass death', there was 'an exclusion and a quarantine of the dead and of the experience of death among the survivors', and consequently not a simple forgetting or silence, but 'a convulsive closing of injuries as a result of the experience of mass death'.[11] There was no repression of memory *tout court*, as scholars of post-war Germany have too long insisted, but rather selective memories and survival stories.[12] In these memories individual agency became central and broader historical developments – and the Holocaust in particular – as well as the constitutive roles of individuals in them, vanished from the picture of the recent past.[13] Mythmaking and what one might call a radical 'individualisation' or 'disaggregation' of history went hand in hand.

[11] Michael Geyer, 'The Place of the Second World War in German Memory and History', *New German Critique*, 71 (1997), 5–40, 10, 17. For the issue of a 'flight from reality' and the temptation to close all injuries, see also Hannah Arendt's 'Besuch in Deutschland 1950: Die Nachwirkungen des Naziregimes', in Hannah Arendt, *Zur Zeit: Politische Essays*, ed. Marie Luise Knott (Munich: Deutscher Taschenbuch Verlag, 1989), 43–70. For the damage which silence about the past might have done to German democracy, see Gesine Schwan, *Politik und Schuld: Die zerstörerische Macht des Schweigens* (Frankfurt/Main: Fischer, 1997). The Yugoslav wars also seemed to have encouraged a new form of amnesia. See Ugrešic, *The Culture of Lies*, 225.

[12] See also Robert G. Moeller, *War Stories: The Search for a Usable Past in the Federal Republic of Germany* (Berkeley: University of California Press, 2001).

[13] Axel Schildt, 'Der Umgang mit der NS-Vergangenheit in der Öffentlichkeit der Nachkriegszeit', in Wilfried Loth and Bernd-A. Rusinek (eds.), *Verwandlungspolitik: NS-Eliten in der westdeutschen Nachkriegsgesellschaft* (Frankfurt/Main: Campus, 1998), 19–54.

The aftermath of war in 1945 was also fundamentally different from the period after 1918: traditional languages of mourning were no longer available in the face of the Holocaust, the atom bomb and the enormous death toll among the civilian population.[14] But neither did apocalyptic images – and adjacent promises of redemption through historical cataclysms – proliferate in the way they had after the First World War.[15] Instead, it became much more difficult – if not impossible – to extract meaning from the war. What George Mosse has called the 'Myth of the War Experience', that is, the myth of heroism and brotherhood at the front, declined and finally died in most countries after 1945.[16]

Most importantly, memories of the war were themselves instantly caught up in the political constraints and incentives imposed by the Cold War, but also by the projects of constructing socialist societies in the East and European unity in the West. European borders – and identities – were shaped and frozen by the division of the Cold War and the 'desire, common to both sides, to forget the recent past and forge a new continent'.[17] However, as Judt has pointed out, saying that post-war Europe was built on 'founding myths' and forgetting is not necessarily cynical: after all, the myths were often helpful in building a liberal order, and there was much that needed to be forgotten. Some myths arguably contributed to the fact that in 1945 the mistakes of 1919 were not repeated: lessons were drawn from the disastrous inter-war economic policies, the two Germanies were more or less forcibly integrated into Western and Eastern alliances, and potential civil wars in Italy and France were nipped in the bud.[18] But all this came at a price. As Jeffrey Herf shows in his chapter on the memory of the Holocaust in Germany after 1945, memories became divided (and distorted) according to the logic of communism, anti-communism and antifascism. In other countries, the memory of national divisions during the war itself became translated into opposing post-war party political memories, and, as Ilaria Poggiolini argues in her chapter on post-war Italy, also led to deep rifts between state and civil society, in which competing collective memories were cultivated. In that sense, the period of the Second World War was never quite properly closed, there

---

[14] Jay Winter, *Sites of Memory, Sites of Mourning: The Great War in European Cultural History* (Cambridge: Cambridge University Press, 1995), 228.

[15] For the disappearance of redemptive apocalyptical images among German intellectuals after the Second World War, see Anson Rabinbach, *In the Shadow of Catastrophe: German Intellectuals between Apocalypse and Enlightenment* (Berkeley: University of California Press, 1997).

[16] George L. Mosse, *Fallen Soldiers: Reshaping the Memory of the World Wars* (New York: Oxford University Press, 1990).

[17] Tony Judt, ch. 7 below.

[18] Tony Judt, 'Nineteen Eighty-Nine: The End of Which European Era?', *Daedalus*, 123, 3 (1994), 1–19, 1–2.

was no peace treaty as there used to be after conflicts of this magnitude, and despite Nuremberg, there was, overall, no proper justice or reckoning for the guilty.[19] In other words, there was no distinctive framework for the war in time – and memory.[20] Now, after the end of the East–West conflict, the period has arguably been 'closed off', a historical framework is being established and the pressure to mould the past to provide identity and social cohesion has weakened.[21] The recent controversies in Switzerland, Portugal, Norway, the Netherlands and Germany about 'Nazi gold' and Nazi slave labour might at first sight seem to signify a 'return of the past'. But in fact the resolution of these claims and controversies might mean that history can be salvaged from moralising abuse, be judicially dealt with and be laid to rest, before the last survivors of the Second World War and the Holocaust vanish.[22]

After the collapse of communism, memories of the Second World War were 'unfrozen' on both sides of the former Iron Curtain. This is not to say that some pristine, pre-representational memory, free of any political instrumentalisation, could suddenly be recovered. But it is to say that both personal and collective memories were liberated from constraints imposed by the need for state legitimation and friend–enemy thinking associated with the Cold War. In the West, this unfreezing has taken a relatively benign form so far. Memories of the Second World War were omnipresent after 1989, and not just because of the string of half-century anniversaries stretching from 1989 to 1995.[23] In addition, the policies of retribution after the war have increasingly become subject to historical scrutiny. An increasing number of detailed studies have demonstrated how punishment contributed to a myth of expiation and rebirth.[24] These pasts have been 'released' in France and Italy, where local communist parties and the structure of the post-war party systems at least partially collapsed, and also became the subject of major historical controversies in Germany. It was ironically the decline of the communist or at least

---

[19] The prototype of a proper European peace was of course the Westphalian Treaty, where an imperative to 'forget everything' was also imposed.

[20] Judt, ch. 7 below.

[21] Which is of course not to say that the Second World War itself is now beyond historiographical dispute. For some continuing controversies see John Keegan, *The Battle for History: Re-fighting World War II* (London: Pimlico, 1997).

[22] Michael Jeismann, 'Der letzte Feind', *Frankfurter Allgemeine Zeitung*, 2 May 1998.

[23] Of course these commemorations were in one sense a sign that living memory of these events could no longer taken for granted. See John R. Gillis, 'Memory and Identity: The History of a Relationship', in John R. Gillis (ed.), *Commemorations: The Politics of National Identity* (Princeton: Princeton University Press, 1994), 12.

[24] See for instance István Deák, Jan T. Gross and Tony Judt (eds.), *The Politics of Retribution in Europe: World War II and its Aftermath* (Princeton: Princeton University Press, 2000), and Pieter Lagrou, *The Legacy of Nazi Occupation: Patriotic Memory and National Recovery in Western Europe 1945–1965* (Cambridge: Cambridge University Press, 2000).

anti-fascist left in the West which made a more open treatment of the history of fascism in countries like Italy and France possible. Given this overall 'closure', the period after the war now provides an ideal field for case studies on how memory and power interacted in various European countries.

However, the post-Cold War period has supposedly also seen the so-called 'return of history' on yet another, and more immediately political level in the West. In fact, however, as Mark Mazower has pointed out, 'history had never left Europe nor returned to it'.[25] Rather, what has happened is that since international relations have been released from the straitjacket of the Cold War, policy-makers are searching in the 'grab-bag of history' for viable historical analogies and political orientation.[26] Only in this limited sense of a 'rummaging through personal and collective memories' for the purpose of finding analogies has there been a 'return of history'. While postmodern historians and cultural theorists have claimed for years that we now live 'after learning from history', more traditional historians and most certainly policy-makers and their advisers are routinely ignoring the supposed 'depragmatisation' of historical knowledge and the passing of Cicero's *historia magistra vitae* itself into history.[27] Historians saw a particular opportunity in the post-1989 constellation and its supposedly new – and at the same time supposedly familiar, all-too-familiar – geopolitical challenges. They cast themselves as national preceptors by offering parallels with the past. German scholars, for instance, saw unification in 1990 as, above all, the 'chance for the German historians' to offer policy prescriptions based on such rather dubious claims as that the country was 'back in the geopolitical position of the Bismarck Reich'.[28] These self-appointed national preceptors once again seemed to confirm Khrushchev's wary assessment that 'historians are dangerous. They have to be watched carefully'.[29] As Mazower has pointed out, it is often 'easier to dream the old dreams – even when they are nightmares – than to wake up to unfamiliar realities'.[30] And arguably, the historical frameworks employed to interpret post-Cold War

[25] Mark Mazower, *Dark Continent: Europe's Twentieth Century* (London: Penguin, 1998), 402.

[26] Linda B. Miller, 'America after the Cold War: competing visions?', *Review of International Studies*, 24 (1998), 251–9.

[27] Hans Ulrich Gumbrecht, *1926: Living at the Edge of Time* (Cambridge, MA: Harvard University Press, 1997), 413.

[28] Gregor Schöllgen, *Angst vor der Macht: Die Deutschen und ihre Außenpolitik* (Berlin: Ullstein, 1993), 118, and Arnulf Baring, *Deutschland, was nun? Ein Gespräch mit Dirk Rumberg und Wolf Jobst Siedler* (Berlin: Siedler, 1991).

[29] Quoted by Stefan Berger, *The Search for Normality: National Identity and Historical Consciousness in Germany since 1800* (Oxford: Berg, 1997), ix.

[30] Mazower, *Dark Continent*, 403.

Europe – especially the old nightmares – have more often than not been counterproductive. Such resort to analogy instead of argument as a default option for legitimating policies was particularly obvious in the Kosovo war.[31] US observers drew implicit parallels with the Holocaust, while members of a German left-wing government claimed that the correct lesson of history had not been 'Never again War', as the generation of 1968 had previously believed, but 'Never again Auschwitz'. Arguably, the rhetorical resort to such analogies and moral appeals did little to mobilise genuine political support or to illuminate the actual moral and political stakes in Kosovo, but much to ease the *crise de conscience* of the politicians. And, for better or for worse, such facile moralising and analogising was much less present during the 2001 war in Afghanistan. If anything, when support for the war seemed to flag, Tony Blair and other Western leaders attempted to bolster approval by invoking the immediate memory of 11 September and the actual victims. Such appeals easily proved stronger than cautionary distant memories of Afghanistan as the graveyard of empires.

On a more positive reading, however, policy-makers have embarked on a genuine 'historical learning process', which is comparable to the learning of the lessons from the inter-war period which – at least to some extent – took place after 1945.[32] In this context, it is of particular interest how countries which so far have emerged as relative losers of the post-Cold-War world – such as France and Russia – are recasting their memories of the twentieth century, and reorienting their policies on the basis of particular 'lessons from the past'.[33] Often, this recasting has taken a radical turn, and memory has become shorthand for a glorious national past that needs to be regained in the near future (and the 'near abroad'). As John Lloyd has argued, it is the mobilisation of an older collective memory of Russian victimhood and slavophile messianism

---

[31] For the influence of myth and memory in Kosovo itself, see Julie A. Merthus, *Kosovo: How Myths and Truths started a War* (Berkeley: University of California Press, 1999), and Tim Judah, *Kosovo: War and Revenge* (New Haven: Yale University Press, 2000).

[32] Paul W. Schroeder has used the notion of *metanoia*, a 'turning around of the mind', to describe the collective learning process of European statesmen in the eighteenth and the nineteenth centuries, which then resulted in profound change in 'the field of ideas, collective mentalities and outlooks'. See Paul W. Schroeder, *The Transformation of European Politics 1763–1848* (Oxford: Clarendon, 1994), viii. For the collective learning process and attendant policy innovations after 1945, see in particular Michael J. Hogan, *The Marshall Plan: America, Britain, and the Reconstruction of Western Europe, 1947–1952* (Cambridge: Cambridge University Press, 1987). I thank Patrick O. Cohrs for drawing my attention to this.

[33] Tim McDaniel, *The Agony of the Russian Idea* (Princeton: Princeton University Press, 1996).

which has reshaped the Russian right.[34] Is it surprising, then, that its most nasty outgrowth is called *Pamyat*: 'Memory'?

In central and eastern Europe, memory has of course also returned, with a vengeance that the West has been spared. This 'return' has led to yet another temporal fault line across the continent and an unsettling 'contemporaneity of the non-contemporaneous'.[35] As Dubravka Ugrešić has put it, 'in this "post-communist" age it seems that "Easterners" are most sensitive to two things: communality and the past'.[36] The 'return' of memory has taken place on multiple levels: first, the geopolitical 'business' left over from the Second World War is in the process of being 'finished off' – in an often extremely bloody manner, as the most obvious example of Yugoslavia shows. Second, there has been a process of a *nachholende* (catching-up) nation-building, for which collective memories have been mobilised and for which often a more distant past has been invented.[37] Where national collective memories have been increasingly 'desacralised' and democratised in the West, there seems to be a desperate need for founding myths – just as there was after 1945 – in the East (despite – or perhaps because of – the fact that communism had a 'desacralising' effect in many countries). Consequently, historians are busy with excavating national pasts, imagining traditions and writing certain groups out of their history – not surprisingly, primarily minorities and Jews in particular. This nation-building process explains the prominent – and, some might say, pernicious – role of historians in politics, but also why memories have been mobilised in conjunction with 'inflamed' national passions. Equally, the question of memory is often at the heart of issues about national self-determination, arguably *the* most salient political issue in eastern Europe after the end of the Cold War. Third, as in the West, the period during and after the Second World War has been 'unfrozen'. Questions about patterns of complicity, resistance and the

[34] John Lloyd, 'Red Nostalgia', paper presented at 'Memory and Power' conference, Oxford, June 1998, on file with author. For memories of Stalin see Adam Hochschild's fascinating *The Unquiet Ghost: Russians Remember Stalin* (London: Serpent's Tail, 1995), as well as Catherine Merridale, *Night of Stone: Death and Memory in Russia* (London: Granta, 2000).

[35] On the reconfiguration of historical time in post-socialist Europe see Katherine Verdery, *The Political Lives of Dead Bodies: Reburial and Postsocialist Change* (New York: Columbia University Press, 1999), 95–127.

[36] Ugrešić, *The Culture of Lies*, 221.

[37] For an interpretation of '1989' as primarily a catching-up with the West, see Jürgen Habermas, *Die nachholende Revolution* (Frankfurt/Main: Suhrkamp, 1990). The best account of 'inventing traditions' remains Eric Hobsbawm and Terence Ranger (eds.), *The Invention of Tradition* (Cambridge: Cambridge University Press, 1983). See also Michael Ignatieff, *Blood and Belonging: Journeys into the New Nationalism* (New York: Farrar, Strauss & Giroux, 1994).

treatment of minorities such as the Jews have come to the fore. But in addition, there has been the challenge of how to deal with the most recent past under communist rule, and the various possible responses to it: purges, trials, forgetting or 'history lessons', as Timothy Garton Ash puts it in this volume, seem to be the – sometimes tragic – choices on offer.

At the same time, the period under communism itself seems to have been consigned to a 'limbo between history and memory'. As Judt argues, 'in a region whose recent past offers no clear social or political descriptors it is tempting to erase from the public record any reference to the communist era . . . – and in its place we find an older past substituted as a source of identity and reference'.[38] The reconstitution of a national, collective memory, much more so than in the West, has served to shore up social cohesion under conditions of economic dislocation and anomie caused by the move towards market economies. But as in the West, memory has also played a role in foreign-policy-making, both in the sense that policy-makers themselves are casting around for historical analogies, and in the sense that foreign policies are legitimated on the grounds of historical experience. The most obvious example here is the effort of central European countries to enter Western institutions such as the North Atlantic Treaty Organisation and the European Union, based on the collective memories of betrayal by the West before, during and after the Second World War. To this effort the West has responded with a kind of 'selective sentimentality' which in turn served to legitimate NATO expansion.[39] At the same time, as Iver Neumann shows in his chapter on western European collective memories of the 'East' after the end of the Cold War, central European elites have successfully manipulated a collective memory of 'Central Europe' as distinct from 'Eastern Europe' – and an image of Russia as an 'eternal' threat.

Finally, the project of a united Europe will probably require the readjustment of historical narratives – and possibly the recasting of various collective memories from East and West. If East and West are to grow together – and surely this is the prime historical task in Europe today – then one needs not just a politics of enlarging milk quotas and concluding passport agreements, but also what Wolf Lepenies has aptly called a 'politics of mentalities'.[40] Such a politics of mentalities will have to deal with the different national (and imperial) memories of Europe's political

---

[38] Judt, 'Nineteen Eighty-Nine', 8.
[39] John Lewis Gaddis, 'History, Grand Strategy and NATO Enlargement', *Survival*, 40, 1 (1998), 145–51.
[40] Wolf Lepenies, 'Für eine Politik der Mentalitäten: Über das Zeitalter der Revisionen und neuen Identitätsfindungen', *Frankfurter Rundschau*, 22 October 1994.

classes.[41] It will also have to tread the fine line between recognising the dignity of collective historical experiences – and in particular shared suffering – and being sold vindictive myths about 'ancient quarrels' or blessing collective amnesia. As Ilana R. Bet-El shows in her reflections on the international response to the Yugoslav wars, a supranational 'European collective memory', based on the 'Europeanisation' or even 'globalisation' of the Holocaust, might well be in the making – but this does not necessarily have the positive consequences for which one might wish.[42] For now, European memories remain both divided and implicated in each other, which leads to the fierce contestation of historical analogies such as 'Munich', the 'Spanish Civil War' and even the Holocaust, as well as a competitive telling of cautionary tales based on 'lessons from the past'.[43]

This in turn raises the question of how memories of the recent Cold War past which, after all, was one of enmity, will be recast – or not. So far, there has been a fiercely contested 'New Cold War History', but there have been surprisingly few *political* appeals to the Cold war experience – it almost appears as if now for us the entire period had become a 'frozen bloc' between the end of the Second World War and the 'return of history', a meaningless distraction or even a communist tale told by an idiot. One reason might simply be that unlike 'hot wars', the Cold War does not lend itself to memorialisation and, at least in the West, to the tales of suffering and mourning which are familiar from the world wars. Moreover, since the Cold War often blurred the line between war and peace, it became very difficult to define the beginnings and endings of conflicts which are central to the emergence of topographical and temporal sites of memory.[44] And yet, with what has been called a culture of 'endism', with Francis Fukuyama being the most famous – or infamous – example of having declared an 'end' after 1989, one wonders whether *the most recent history* of the Cold War has not faded particularly quickly from our consciousness.[45] Has our inheritance once again not been preceded by any will? As Timothy Garton Ash has put it, the only fact that

---

[41] Larry Siedentop, *Democracy in Europe* (London: Penguin, 2000), 142–3.

[42] See also Daniel Levy and Natan Sznaider, *Erinnerung im globalen Zeitlater: Der Holocaust* (Frankfurt/Main: Suhrkamp, 2001).

[43] For a brilliant exploration of the use of Holocaust images in connection with recent cases of genocide, see Barbie Zelizer, *Remembering to Forget: Holocaust Memory through the Camera's Eye* (Chicago: University of Chicago Press, 1998).

[44] Gillis, 'Memory and Identity', 13. Paradoxically, one reason for the seeming disappearance of the Cold War from memory could of course be that most of us are still living in the Cold War. See Mark Danner, 'Marooned in the Cold War: America, the Alliance and the Quest for a Vanished World', *World Policy Journal*, 14, 3 (1997), 1–33.

[45] Francis Fukuyama, *The End of History and the Last Man* (London: Hamish Hamilton, 1992).

seems to matter about communism in the present is the fact that it is over. Whether or not this period, and its memories, can be 'unfrozen' remains to be seen – it might take another generational interval of forty years before our present returns as a past both present and 'unfrozen'.

And yet new myths, especially east European post-communist myths of nationalist salvation, are clearly in the making.[46] At the same time, the flip-side of mythmaking and nation-building remains a process of more or less forced forgetting, as Ernest Renan first pointed out more than a century ago.[47] This amnesia is particularly obvious in the case of the former Yugoslav republics, where 'nostalgia' is condemned as a form of moral-cum-political depravation. There, as the Croatian exile Ugrešić laments, 'the term Yugo-nostalgic is used as political and moral disqualification, the Yugo-nostalgic is a suspicious person, a "public enemy", a "traitor", a person who regrets the collapse of Yugoslavia, a Yugonostalgic is the enemy of democracy'.[48] Amnesia is once again an indispensable part of nation-building and nationalist exclusion, whether 'catching-up' or not.

It seems, then, that for now we still are in what Judt calls an 'interregnum, a moment between myths when the old versions of the past are either redundant or unacceptable, and new ones have yet to surface' – an interregnum which might or might not have come to an end on 11 September 2001, as only time will tell.[49] Just as the period after 1945, this interregnum presents an auspicious time to analyse the relationship between memory and power, even if the conclusions have to be somewhat more tentative than those about the period from 1945 to 1989. On the other hand, precisely because the relationship between memory and power is to some extent malleable, and because we are witnesses to 'myths in the making', we are faced with not just directly political, but also moral questions: how *should* memory and power be related, lest the new Europe is built on 'shifty historical sands'? How should we treat a difficult past, lest another war of memories turns into a war of shells, as in the former Yugoslavia? In which cases is the opposite of George Santayana's aphorism true that those who do not remember the past are condemned to repeat it? Is there an art of forgetting, an *ars oblivionis*, that sometimes needs to complement the 'art of memory'? Many all-too-glib answers have been offered during the recent 'memory boom'. But if one takes historical learning processes seriously, then historical and

[46] Vladimir Tismaneanu, *Fantasies of Salvation: Democracy, Nationalism and Myth in Post-Communist Europe* (Princeton: Princeton University Press 1998).

[47] Ernest Renan, 'What is a Nation?', in Homi K. Bhabha (ed.), *Nation and Narration* (London: Routledge, 1990), 8–22.

[48] Ugrešić, *The Culture of Lies*, 231.   [49] Judt, ch. 7 below.

social scientific research about memory indeed cannot be entirely separated from normative questions – not least because so many memory tales are shot through with normative claims.

In the remainder of this introduction, I want first to venture an explanation why 'memory thinking' has become so prominent in late-twentieth-century culture and why it seems to have led to a paradigm shift in the humanities, and in history in particular. In addition, I offer a more nuanced view as to why memory seems to have mattered more in politics in recent years, before addressing a number of basic methodological issues at the heart of the memory–power nexus: the definition of collective or social memory, the distinction between history, memory and myth, and finally, the relationship between memory and power. There is clearly scope for fruitful disagreement here. Some of the contributors have taken a slightly different approach and configured these key concepts in other ways, but they all take them as a starting point and lay their methodological cards on the table at the beginning of each chapter. Finally, after having established some of the key parameters of an analysis of memory and power in the context of post-war Europe, I embark on a brief discussion of what one might call the 'ethics of memory'.

Why memory?

There has been an explosion of literature on memory in recent years. Here I can only very briefly sketch some of the larger cultural reasons why memory has led to a paradigm shift in the humanities, and history in particular, and why the theme of memory increasingly pervades the media, political debate and everyday discourse. First, at the most basic level, the profound changes in the technology of data collection and recollection associated with the electronic media constitute a fundamental shift in 'mnemonic techniques', and, possibly, a profound shift in the place accorded to the faculty of memory in our social world – as well as our moral imagination. This shift might be as significant as the invention of the printing press and the eclipse of oral memory and the 'art of memory' after the Renaissance.[50]

Second, with the waning of the generation of Holocaust survivors (as well as slave labourers and soldiers who served in the Second World War), 'communicative memory', that is, living oral memory based on personal recollection, is passing into 'cultural memory' – with 'cultural memory'

[50] Frances A. Yates, *The Art of Memory* (London: Pimlico, 1994), Jacques Le Goff, *History and Memory*, trans. Steven Randall and Elizabeth Claman (New York: Columbia University Press, 1992), and Douwe Draaisma, *Metaphors of Memory: A History of Ideas About the Mind*, trans. Paul Vincent (Cambridge: Cambridge University Press, 2000).

now commonly understood as the cultural representations which lack the immediacy of first-hand recollection.[51] The Holocaust has not only resulted in particularly strong communities of remembrance, it is – tacitly or not – also at the heart of much of the current concern with memory.[52] Pierre Nora has gone so far as to suggest that 'whoever says memory, says Shoah'.[53] There can indeed be little doubt that the Holocaust has been crucial in the shift from a 'history of the victors' or, in Nietzsche's terms, 'monumental history', to a 'history of the victims'.[54] Yet this new critical history of large-scale violence and oppression is sometimes also in danger of turning into a 'monumental critical history', in which lessons are learnt from the past and heroes (anti-heroes) held up for emulation.

Paradoxically, the imminent end of communicative memory has resulted in an unprecedented crescendo of communication about the past, as a final battle over the content of a future cultural memory is waged by witnesses, and as the intellectual legacies to be passed on and the dominant representations of the past are being contested. Why precisely the Holocaust has become so much more prominent in historical consciousness and as a means for political claim-making is itself fiercely debated, as meta-reflections on memory have proliferated alongside representations of the past themselves. In one of the most interesting conjectures, Richard J. Evans has argued that it is in fact the disappearance of communism as a symbol of ultimate political evil which has made the reference to both Hitler and the Holocaust necessary as yardsticks against which the advantages of freedom and democracy can be measured. According to this logic, the West Germans could deal with the 'final solution' earlier than other countries not least because of Ostpolitik.[55]

Equally paradoxically perhaps, efforts to lay the past to rest as in the German *Historikerstreit* (historians' dispute) of the 1980s have merely reinforced its claims on the present. If anything, such controversies have strengthened the feeling among some historians that they are in fact the guardians of collective memory just as much as they are occupying

---

[51] For the distinction between communicative and cultural memory, see Jan Assmann, *Das kulturelle Gedächtnis* (Munich: C. H. Beck, 1997). See also 'Passing into History: Nazism and the Holocaust beyond Memory', special issue, *History & Memory*, 9, 1–2 (1997).

[52] Geoffrey H. Hartman (ed.), *Holocaust Remembrance: The Shapes of Memory* (Oxford: Blackwell, 1994).

[53] Ulrich Raulff, 'Der Augenblick danach', *Frankfurter Allgemeine Zeitung*, 8 July 1998.

[54] The classics on this question remain of course Friedrich Nietzsche, *On the Advantage and Disadvantage of History for Life*, trans. Peter Preuss (Indianapolis: Hackett, 1980 [1874]) and Walter Benjamin, 'Theses on the Philosophy of History', in *Illuminations*, ed. Hannah Arendt, trans. Harry Zohn (London: Pimlico, 1999 [1969]), 245–55.

[55] Richard J. Evans, 'Blitzkrieg und Hakenkreuz', *Frankfurter Rundschau*, 16 September 2000.

professional roles as academics and value-neutral *Wissenschaftler*. Third –
and most obviously – there has been the fin de siècle – and its attendant
exercises in taking stock and remembrance, including the efforts to establish a historiographical framework for the 'short twentieth century'.[56]
Fourth, there is what German sociologist Niklas Luhmann has referred
to as the final disappearance of *Alteuropa* (old Europe), that is a Europe
still steeped in rural traditions, remnants of feudal and aristocratic
life and what in the language of his systems theory amounts to still
'undifferentiated societies'.[57] As students of collective memory have long
recognised, history and memory become central exactly when they seem
'to be losing their salience, their unproblematic presence and importance
for everyday life'.[58] The past is no longer simply present and therefore
unreflected and even peripheral – with further modernisation, it becomes
increasingly central, as its preservation and recovery require explicit and
sustained efforts.[59] Memory and modernisation, then, are not opposites –
they go hand in hand.

There is also a rather vague sense that the preoccupation with memory
is part of the changed structures of temporality at the end of the twentieth
century and the beginning of the twenty-first. Against the 'acceleration'
of time through technical progress, the elimination of distance and the
general blurring of territorial and spatial coordinates in an age of globalisation, the recovery of 'memory' aims at a temporal re-anchoring and
even the much-talked-about 'recovery of the real'.[60] Rather than a simple exhaustion of utopian energies, memory might signify a resistance
to the new utopia of globalisation and to teleological notions of history.

[56] The most prominent attempts have of course been Eric Hobsbawm, *The Age of Extremes*
(London: Abacus, 1993), and François Furet, *Le passé d'une illusion: essai sur l'idée communiste au XXe siècle* (Paris: Robert Laffont, 1995). See also the debate on 'Communisme
et fascisme au XXe siècle', *le débat*, 89 (1996). For an interesting recent contribution,
see Mazower, *Dark Continent*, which decentres communism in favour of fascism from
the European twentieth century, and stresses the contingency of the victory of liberal
democracy after 1989. See also Charles S. Maier, 'Consigning the Twentieth Century
to History: Alternative Narratives for the Modern Era', *American Historical Review*, 105,
3 (2000), 807–31.

[57] Niklas Luhmann, *Soziale Systeme: Grundriß einer allgemeinen Theorie* (Frankfurt/Main:
Suhrkamp, 1984).

[58] Jeffrey K. Olick, 'The Politics of Regret: Analytical Frames', unpublished paper, on file
with author.

[59] See Reinhart Koselleck, *Futures Past: On the Semantics of Historical Time*, trans. Keith
Tribe (Cambridge, MA: MIT Press, 1985), for the idea of an increasing disparity between *Erfahrungsraum* (the realm of experience) and *Erwartungshorizont* (the realm of
expectations) as a hallmark of modernity. The new open-endedness of the future and
the rapid destruction of the past characterising modernity can then be read as the cause
of 'memory crises'.

[60] Andreas Huyssen, *Twilight Memories: Marking Time in a Culture of Amnesia* (London:
Routledge, 1995), 7. See also Hal Foster, *The Return of the Real: The Avantgarde at the
End of the Century* (Cambridge, MA: MIT Press, 1996).

On an alternative reading, globalisation and 'mnemonic particularism' – as long as it can be commodified as ethnically packaged goods – go hand in hand. The cult of memory might be globalised – and yet national memories remain resolutely separate. Moreover, as Charles S. Maier has claimed, 'the surfeit of memory is a sign not of historical confidence but a retreat from transformative politics' in an age of failing expectations, in particular of socialism, and is related to the 'postmodern dissolution of social transparency'.[61] If one cannot change the future, one can at least preserve the past. Or, as Andreas Huyssen has argued, there might even be an implicit hope that the past will redeem the promises which the future has not kept.

Memory, in other words, could thus be read either as a form of contesting the synchronised 'hyper-space' of globalisation – or as a form of neoconservative 'comfort' and 'cultural compensation' for the social and psychological dislocations caused by an 'accelerated' or even 'second' modernity.[62] This is certainly suggested by the fact that the current culture of memorialisation and musealisation has a tendency to shade into a culture of pure sentimentality, in which we have become 'addicted to memory' and where 'excessive memory' leads to 'complacency and collective self-indulgence'.[63] Again, while historians and cultural critics have long diagnosed a 'decidedly anti-redemptory age' alongside the end of any role of history in instructing the living, de facto memory 'on the ground', so to speak, has increasingly acquired a redemptive quality in the last decades.[64]

Finally, there is the rise of multiculturalism, and with it what Jeffrey Olick has referred to as an 'increase of redress claims' and a 'politics of victimisation and regret'.[65] This is, properly speaking, a kind of memory of power, namely the memory of past injustices and traumas inflicted by

---

[61] Charles S. Maier, 'A Surfeit of Memory? Reflections on History, Melancholy and Denial', *History & Memory*, 5, 2 (1993), 136–52.

[62] See for instance Hermann Lübbe, *Geschichtsbegriff und Geschichtsinteresse: Analytik und Pragmatik der Historie* (Basel: Schwabe, 1977). For a critique see Jürgen Habermas, 'Neoconservative Cultural Criticism in the United States and West Germany', in *The New Conservatism: Cultural Criticism and the Historians' Debate*, trans. Shierry Weber Nicholson (Cambridge, MA: MIT Press, 1989), 22–47. The concept of a 'second' or 'reflexive' modernity was coined by German sociologist Ulrich Beck. See for instance his *Risikogesellschaft* (Frankfurt/Main: Suhrkamp, 1986).

[63] Maier, 'A Surfeit of Memory', 140, 137.

[64] See James E. Young, *At Memory's Edge: After-Images of the Holocaust in Contemporary Art and Architecture* (New Haven: Yale University Press, 2000) for the notion of an anti-redemptory age.

[65] It is plausible to argue, as Olick has, that the memory of the Holocaust and the standards of justice established at the Nuremberg trials is also the centre of this 'politics of regret'. See also Elazar Barkan, *The Guilt of Nations: Restitution and Negotiating Historical Injustices* (New York: Norton, 2000), especially 308–49, and Erna Paris, *Long Shadows: Truth, Lies and History* (London: Bloomsbury, 2001).

the state or groups abusing their power. Beyond 'redress claims' in response to the memory of power, minorities have advanced the recovery of unrecorded history, and the social recognition of their particular collective experience. Memory is marshalled as grievance and as a claim on political resources, and groups are eager to have the dignity of their individual historical experience recognised – precisely in the way they have lived through it and present it now.[66] Here memory – like identity – is always in danger of giving rise to absolute moral claims and to becoming non-negotiable. As Bet-El stresses in her chapter on the Yugoslav wars, the claim 'I remember' is sometimes not an exchange, but an authoritative statement, which flows from the stark power of personal conviction. The European culture wars, then, are to a large extent memory wars, and Yugoslavia has horrifically demonstrated what happens when memory wars turn into real wars. At the same time, these real wars were not so much wars over memory, as what Primo Levi once called 'wars on memory'. Memory was literally blown up, as monuments, mosques and other concrete manifestations of collective memory were erased, and mnemonic maps were rewritten as normative maps for an ethnically reconfigured future. The dead, as Walter Benjamin observed as the century's central catastrophe was just about to unfold, are not safe from politics. And, ironically, with the end of actual fighting in the former Yugoslavia, the war over (and on) memory has even intensified further.[67]

All the above mentioned factors have arguably contributed to a fundamental paradigm shift in the humanities, and in history in particular. In Weber's terms, the cultural lights have shifted and the sciences have moved on into new territory. However, this territory has yet again been divided along peculiar national lines, that is the approaches to memory have been significantly different in different national contexts. In France, where a 'self-commemorative' history has so often been instrumentalised to legitimate the national state and its glory, memory could actually serve as a progressive, or even subversive counter-concept.[68] At the same time, there has been a wistful sense in many of the cultural and historical studies of French memory, especially in Pierre Nora's itself monumental project

---

[66] Which is not to say that such memory should be dismissed as subjective. However, as Melissa Williams points out in an important book, memory has to be complemented by history and a 'notion of shared public reason in which empirical evidence, while always contestable, is accepted, in principle, as a valid basis for public decisions'. See her *Voice, Trust and Memory: Marginalized Groups and the Failings of Liberal Representation* (Princeton: Princeton University Press, 1998), 177–8.

[67] For a survey of how schoolbooks have been rewritten in the successor republics, see Wolfgang Hoepken, 'War, Memory, and Education in a Fragmented Society: The Case of Yugoslavia', *Eastern European Politics and Societies*, 13, 1 (1999), 190–227.

[68] Daniel Gordon, 'Review of Patrick Hutton, *History as an Art of Memory*', *History and Theory*, 34 (1995), 340–54, 341.

on the *lieux de mémoire* or 'realms of memory'.[69] After all, examining *les lieux* supposedly only became possible after the disappearance of actual lived and traditional *milieux de mémoire*. As Nora put it, 'we speak so much of memory, because there is so little left of it'. At the same time, examining the *lieux* expressed a national nostalgia for the republican certainties which had vanished and, above all, for a mythical 'Frenchness' lost in the process of modernisation.[70]

Nevertheless, what one might call Nora's 'melancholic' – yet ultimately affirmative – approach to memory has proved enormously fruitful and is now being emulated in other countries.[71] Wherever 'national identity' seems to be in question, memory comes to be a key to national re-covery through reconfiguring the past – including in Britain, where, as Anne Deighton shows in her chapter, the 're-branding' of the country as 'Cool Britannia' has been complemented by imperial nostalgia. It is arguably not least the disappearance of a generation with memories of the Second World War and Empire which has led to the recent spate of – curiously un-English and un-British – books on English and British identity. In Germany, on the other hand, where remembering the Nazi past remains an ethical-cum-political imperative, history, or rather 'historicisation' through memories, both individual and collective, has often been perceived as part of a right-wing agenda aiming at 'normalising' the past through 'historicisation', that is by concentrating on the lived experience of historical actors. Many historians have remained suspi-cious of memory, not just because of methodological reservations but also because studying memory was implicitly equated with conferring le-gitimacy on politically dubious memories. In any case – with or against Nora's approach – across the West as a whole memory has become a cultural buzz word, a memory industry has sprung up, and, many observers worry, the currency of commemoration has been somewhat inflated.[72]

In reaction to this 'memory boom', French historians in particular have charged that memory is beginning to replace history – in the sense that a 'soft', therapeutic concept of memory, even a kind of bound-less mnemonic subjectivism, comes to fulfil the function of conscience, and helps to avoid the confrontation with traditional, 'hard' historical

---

[69] Pierre Nora (ed.), *Les lieux de mémoire*, 7 vols. (Paris: Gallimard, 1984–92).

[70] Jeismann, 'Der letzte Feind'.

[71] For German approaches see Aleida Assmann, *Arbeit am nationalen Gedächtnis: Eine kurze Geschichte der deutschen Bildungsidee* (Frankfurt/Main: Campus, 1993), and, above all, Etienne François and Hagen Schulze (eds.), *Deutsche Erinnerungsorte*, 3 vols. (Munich: C. H. Beck, 2001); for a discussion of Italian perspectives see 'La memoria e le cose', *Parolechiave*, special issue, 9 (1995).

[72] Gordon, 'Review', 352.

approaches – and truths.[73] In this interpretation, memory has turned into a new secular religion, or at least an 'ersatz metaphysics', which feeds on a new emotionalism, and gives rise to endless grievance claims couched in the language of personal memories. The memorialisation of history is at the same time its moralisation, and the stakes of historical inquiry are no longer *wie es eigentlich gewesen* (however flawed Ranke's goal of historicist reconstruction might have been), but the mobilisation of memory to stake out moral claims. Memory and a new international humanitarianism, which takes the memory of the Holocaust and the Second World War as central reference points, feed on each other. What gets lost (and forgotten) are not just the fact that it is always tempting to substitute pious remembrance for actual political action but also older memories – for instance of the inter-war period – which once were instrumental in erecting the post-war European welfare states. Such memories seem to have been crowded out completely by the memories – and moral narratives – of the Holocaust and the Second World War.

It is not surprising, then, that there has been a string of historians' disputes, where historical knowledge and moral claims became inextricably linked. But if Europeans have turned into 'historical animals' with regard to the period fifty, sixty years ago, then precisely what kind of memory is at stake – and what are the stakes, existential, psychological and political? And how should the scholarly inquiry into memory proceed?

Which memory?

The pitfalls in the study of memory and power are numerous. For one thing, the dangers of reification, reductionism and 'collectivisation' loom large. To treat memory as a 'thing' which can be 'shared', 'confiscated', 'repressed' and 'recovered' is suggested by the very language which we use in connection with memory, and by the fact that a 'depth model' of psychology – with all its attendant metaphors of 'mnemonic excavation' – has become deeply ingrained in our cultural vocabulary. So far, only very few historians have managed to use the no doubt sometimes illuminating metaphors drawn from psychology (and pathology) for thinking about memory and politics without lapsing into 'psychologising'.[74] At the same time, against the claim that one can 'recover' some form of 'pristine', pre-representational memory, many scholars have gone towards the other extreme and almost exclusively stressed the malleability and political

---

[73] Ulrich Raulff, 'Marktwert der Erinnerung: Ein Historiker bekämpft den aktuellen Gedächtniskult', *Frankfurter Allgemeine Zeitung*, 5 May 1998.

[74] For instance Henry Rousso, *The Vichy Syndrome: History and Memory in France since 1944*, trans. Arthur Goldhammer (Cambridge, MA: Harvard University Press, 1992).

instrumentalisation of the past. All too often, collective memory is simply collapsed into myth, and important conceptual distinctions are lost. Finally, the more collectivist strands in Maurice Halbwachs's work, especially his contention, or, rather, overstatement, that *all* memory is social and constitutes a Durkheimian social fact, has led to an unwarranted suspicion of the concept altogether by more narrowly empiricist scholars.[75] The latter have a tendency to identify collective memory with some kind of *Volksgeist* or Jungian collective unconscious, because they take what is essentially a metaphor of 'collective memory' literally – when serious students of collective memory are in fact ready to concede that ultimately only individuals can remember. These suspicions have been nourished further by the fact that the study of collective memory has been divided into macro-sociological theory, where seemingly anything goes theoretically, and case studies which fail to offer any general insights into the politics of memory.

Jeffrey Olick has offered a detailed genealogy of the notion of collective memory and the Durkheimian conceptual baggage which it still carries with it.[76] Suffice it to say for now that in order to avoid the numerous pitfalls – or as Olick, following Charles Tilly, has put it, the 'pernicious postulates' – associated with the study of the political effects of memory, the contributors to this volume all draw a fundamental distinction between collective, social or national memory on the one hand, and individual mass personal memory on the other.[77] As Timothy Snyder points out in his chapter, the former is properly speaking *mémoire* or *Gedächtnis*, the latter *souvenir* or *Erinnerung*. It is possible to call it 'myth', as Robert Gildea does, but it is as plausible, and somewhat less normatively charged, to view it as the 'social framework' of memory, or, in Snyder's words, as the 'organisation principle that nationally conscious individuals use to organise their history'.[78] It allows them to place events into a national

---

[75] See also Marc Bloch's review of Halbwachs' work, 'Mémoire collective, tradition et coutume', *Revue de Synthèse Historique*, 40 (1925), 73–83. For the origins (and a critique) of the concepts of collective memory and collective identity, see Lutz Niethammer, *Kollektive Identität: Heimliche Quellen einer unheimlichen Konjunktur* (Reinbek: Rowohlt, 2000).

[76] Jeffrey K. Olick, 'Collective Memory: The Two Cultures', *Sociological Theory*, 17 (1999), 333–48.

[77] The memories of particular groups are an intermediate phenomenon between national and individual memory. They very often are based on living individual memory of members, which then becomes stylised and even standardised when repeatedly told in communities of remembrance, to congeal into a collective framework which then in turn is reinforced through collective rituals. Groups frequently want to have their memories recognised as part of national memory, and make explicit political and material demands on the state. The history of the German expellees which Levy and Dierkes analyse in their chapter is an excellent example of these points.

[78] Robert Gildea, *The Past in French History* (New Haven: Yale University Press, 1994), 10.

narrative, which functions as a matrix of meaning. As Thomas Berger points out, it also endows a collective with emotional and normative underpinning, as well as a 'common language and set of understandings about how the world functions and how it ought to function'. It is this type of memory and national identity which are mutually constitutive, or, to put it differently, there is a circular relationship between collective memory and collective identity.[79]

Identity – understood as a relational concept and as sameness over time – is established by what is remembered, and itself then leads in turn to certain pasts being remembered and others being forgotten: in this sense, and as Renan first pointed out, remembrance and forgetting depend on each other.[80] But, as has been stressed by numerous commentators, neither identity nor memory is ever monolithic. Moreover, neither should be thought of as an unchanging 'possession' or 'property'. There might indeed have been a more 'identitarian' and 'unitary memory-nation' (Olick) during the 'golden age' of nation-building. But even at the height of a process in which collective and national memory served as the 'handmaiden of nationalism' (Erica Benner), the relevant imagined communities were never as homogeneous as historians of nationalism are sometimes prone to suggest.[81] As Berger argues, collective memory is always the outcome of a series of ongoing intellectual and political negotiations; it is never a unitary collective mental act. However, precisely because collective memory is not a property, but an ongoing process, it is also above all collective or national memory which is most susceptible to be influenced by politicians, journalists and historians. 'High politics' understood as presidential speeches and other symbolic gestures by national representatives, the contributors to this volume agree, matters enormously for memory.

Most dangerously, leaders can reconfigure collective memory to present a narrative of victimisation, which then becomes an incentive for aggression. As Bet-El shows in her chapter on the Yugoslav wars, Slobodan Milošević's infamous Kosovo Polye speech in 1987 accomplished precisely that and in itself became part of a nationalist collective memory for Serbs, Croats and Kosovars. On the other hand, politicians can claim to be politically responsible for the past, and apologise, as, most famously, Willy Brandt did in Warsaw, and as, for instance, Croatian president Franjo Tudjman singularly failed to do, despite intense pressure from the West. As Michael Ignatieff has pointed out,

[79] See also Gillis, 'Memory and Identity', and Anthony D. Smith, *Myths and Memories of the Nation* (Oxford: Oxford University Press, 1999).

[80] See also Peter Burke, *Varieties of Cultural History* (Cambridge: Polity, 1997), 43–59.

[81] Erica Benner, 'National Memories and Political Responsibility', paper on file with author.

societies and nations are not like individuals, but their leaders can have an enormous impact on the mysterious process by which individuals come to terms with the painfulness of their societies' past. Leaders give their societies permission to say the unsayable, to think the unthinkable, to rise to gestures of reconciliation that people, individually, cannot imagine.[82]

Jeffrey Herf underscores the point that 'high politics', that is, the speeches presidents and major politicians make, matters crucially – such politics always has a symbolic surplus.[83] Timothy Snyder in turn presents a fascinating case study of how what he calls political 'sovereignty over memory' can prevent the cycles of animosity by politically neutralising certain memories. As Snyder points out, the problem posed by national memory is qualitative: when nations identify with a certain vision of the past, policies which threaten this vision will at first be resisted, and will have to be justified in terms of the larger interest of the nation. In turn, individual memory is a quantitative problem: individuals can be persuaded from interest, but ultimately, if they persist with reranchist claims, for instance, they can also be outvoted. Nevertheless, a reconfigured collective memory will also allow individuals to see their personal experiences differently and place events – and traumas – in a new matrix of meaning. Of course, one could object that this is merely reverse, anti-nationalist manipulation, which is as morally dubious as nationalist manipulation. But since there is no entirely pristine memory beyond any instrumentalisation, it is precisely this ambiguity, the fine line between manipulation and seeking an accurate historical picture that Garton Ash elaborates on, which places such an enormous burden of responsibility on politicians – and historians.

However, apart from the fundamental distinction between national-collective and personal memory, one also has to distinguish between memory and history. While – to some extent – there is obviously a continuum between the two, collapsing one into the other as merely different forms of 'representations' is a pernicious legacy of postmodernism and leads to the loss of a crucial distinction.[84] In fact, collective memory can be seen as ahistorical, even anti-historical, to the extent that it not only

---

[82] Michael Ignatieff, *The Warrior's Honour: Ethnic War and the Modern Conscience* (London: Chatto & Windus, 1998), 188. See also Roy L. Brooks (ed.), *When Sorry Isn't Enough: The Controversy over Apologies and Reparations for Human Injustice* (New York: New York University Press, 1999) and Peter Digeser, *Political Forgiveness* (Ithaca, NY: Cornell University Press, 2001).

[83] For a detailed study of the importance of speeches dealing with the Nazi past in the West German parliament, see Helmut Dubiel, *Niemand ist frei von der Geschichte: Die nationalsozialistische Herrschaft in den Debatten des Deutschen Bundestages* (Munich: Hanser, 1999).

[84] Which is not to deny that postmodern historians have made an important contribution to the 'desacralisation' and even democratisation of national collective memories.

tends to simplify and reduce the ambiguities of the past, but also to insist on its presence and its carrying moral messages in ways which most historians cannot accept.[85] As Snyder points out, history and memory are mutually dependent, and neither can be studied apart from the other, but without separate conceptions the study of neither can proceed.[86] While historical images of the past are often derivative of memory, they are not reducible to it. Or, to put it differently, historians cannot discount memory, but they cannot count on it, either.[87] Instead, historical projects should turn out to be correctives of memory, with historians in the full knowledge that their histories can and will be contested. The past, after all, is an argument, and ideally historians are able to purify public arguments, in the process 'narrowing the range of permissible lies'.[88] History, in other words, can at least sometimes awaken us from the nightmare of memory.

In a similar vein, Henry Rousso has insisted that 'the duty of memory is an empty shell unless it is based on scholarship'. He has added that

memory is a living phenomenon, something in perpetual evolution, whereas history – as understood by historians – is a scholarly and theoretical reconstruction and as such is more apt to give rise to a substantial, durable body of knowledge. Memory is plural . . . [and] at times in a religious or sacred key; history is secular.

Precisely because history and national memory are closely bound up with each other, and in turn serve the project of national identity formation, it is so crucial to distinguish between them. Rousso prominently insisted on the distinction when the French 'Vichy syndrome' which Rousso himself had first identified in the mid-1980s became even more acute in the 1990s. In the middle of *l'Affaire Mitterrand* about the role of the president during the Occupation, Rousso and his collaborator Éric Conan published *Vichy: Un passé qui ne passe pas*.[89] The volume effectively advocated a moratorium on public debate, since serious attempts to understand historical realities were being replaced by 'pseudo-disclosures' and

85 This has been put most forcefully in Peter Novick's fiercely polemical *The Holocaust in American Life* (New York: Houghton Mifflin, 1999), 3–4.
86 Alternatively, one can view history and cultural memory as 'entangled', with the proviso that at least to some extent, they can be disentangled. For this argument, see Marita Sturken, *Tangled Memories: The Vietnam War, the AIDS Epidemic, and the Politics of Remembering* (Berkeley: University of California Press, 1997).
87 For the issue of distortion of memory in general, see Elizabeth F. Loftus, *Eyewitness Testimony* (Cambridge, MA: Harvard University Press, 1996) and Daniel L. Schacter (ed.), *Memory Distortion: How Minds, Brains, and Societies Reconstruct the Past* (Cambridge, MA: Harvard University Press, 1995).
88 Ignatieff, *The Warrior's Honour*, 174.
89 Éric Conan and Henry Rousso, *Vichy: An Ever-Present Past*, trans. Nathan Bracher (Hanover, NH: University Press of New England, 1998).

media frenzy.[90] Subsequently, Rousso went even further. Unlike many other historians, he refused to testify at any of the trials of the Vichy collaborators: the historian is not a witness, and certainly not a 'moral witness' in the way that the victims of atrocity and oppression are.[91]

In short, the conflation of history and memory might have serious political and ethical consequences – for the victims of other victims' memory claims, but also for national public discourse and the parameters of political culture. Justice and 'historicisation' are not necessarily compatible, and even rigorous justice might not satisfy all 'memory claims'.[92] As some opponents of 'memory kitsch' have claimed, history and justice should be liberating, even to some extent be about breaking with the past – and not about creating moral identifications with the past. More importantly, the collapsing of memory and history seems itself often enough to be a perspectivist power claim, an effort to legitimate one's memories (and oneself as a political actor).

Now this is not to deny that there is a shadowy area between history and memory, and not recognising it would be positivist blindness complementing the darkness of postmodernism in which all cows are black. Eric Hobsbawm has called it a 'twilight zone between history and memory', a 'no man's land of time'. And he adds that 'it is by far the hardest part of history for historians, or anyone else, to grasp . . . ', partly, it seems, because the most recent past holds most surprises.[93] But, it seems to me, the fact that this 'recent and relevant past' is not history with the same temporal distance as histories of the Middle Ages does not justify Saul Friedländer's claim that we should call it 'historical consciousness', rather than history.[94]

In a sense, however, memory versus history is something of a false dichotomy to start with; after all, what we are interested in is precisely memory *in* history, the role of the past in history or, for that matter,

---

[90] Richard J. Goslan, 'History and the Responsibility of Memory: *Vichy: Un Passé qui ne passe pas* and the Trial of Paul Touvier', in Richard J. Goslan (ed.), *Fascism's Return: Scandal, Revision, and Ideology since 1980* (Lincoln, NE: University of Nebraska Press, 1998), 182–99. See also Richard J. Goslan (ed.), *Memory, the Holocaust, and French Justice: The Bousquet and Touvier Affairs* (Hanover, NH: University Press of New England, 1996).

[91] For this notion of the 'moral witness', see Avishai Margalit, *Ethik der Erinnerung* (Frankfurt/Main: Fischer, 2000), 59–88.

[92] For the rivalries between historians and judges, see Norbert Frei, Dirk van Laak and Michael Stolleis (eds.), *Geschichte vor Gericht: Historiker, Richter und die Suche nach Gerechtigkeit* (Munich: C. H. Beck, 2000), as well as Carlo Ginzburg, *The Judge and the Historian*, trans. Antony Shugaar (London: Verso, 1999).

[93] Eric Hobsbawm, *The Age of Empire 1875–1914* (London: Pantheon, 1987), 3.

[94] Saul Friedländer, *Memory, History and the Extermination of the Jews of Europe* (Bloomington: Indiana University Press, 1993), viii.

in contemporary politics, and what Jürgen Habermas in the German context once called 'the public uses of history'.[95] It is true that historians 'must reconstruct causal sequences', while 'memories are to be retrieved and relived, not explained' – but this process of retrieval and reliving itself needs to be explained.[96] The point then is not ontologically and epistemologically to 'destabilise' the relationship between memory and history further, as postmodernists would have us do, but to examine carefully the role of memory in past and present politics.

Memory and power: the uses of the past in domestic and international politics

A further distinction needs to be drawn between history, memory and power. One way of understanding the relationship between memory and power is to conceptualise memory itself as a kind of 'symbolic power', which can be marshalled in much the same way as material power and, to use Pierre Bourdieu's terms, economic and cultural capital are marshalled. The essays collected here, however, see 'politics' as strategic public claim-making and struggle over public meanings in specific cultural contexts. They understand 'power' in traditional terms as the output of political institutions, that is, primarily as policies. The question then becomes how memory relates to policy-making, that is, how collective and individual memory influence the present construction and legitimation of foreign policy as well as the contestation of domestic politics.[97] Since the point of this volume is not to focus so much on memories of war as such, or on concrete manifestations of memory such as public commemorations and national monuments, the chapters concentrate on the role national memory plays in political culture, and on the 'lessons' drawn by individuals from the war experience.[98]

---

[95] Jürgen Habermas, 'The Public Use of History', *New German Critique*, 44 (1988), 40–50.

[96] Maier, 'A Surfeit of Memory?' 143.

[97] Such a nominalist and empiricist conception of power would of course be disputed by the majority of theorists of power. See for instance Steven Lukes (ed.), *Power* (Oxford: Blackwell, 1986).

[98] For efforts in this direction see the contributions to Jay Winter and Emmanuel Sivan (eds.), *War and Remembrance in the Twentieth Century* (Cambridge: Cambridge University Press, 1999), Helmut Peitsch, Charles Burdett and Claire Gorrara (eds.), *European Memories of the Second World War* (New York: Berghahn Books, 1999), as well as Martin Evans and Kenneth Lunn (eds.), *War and Memory in the Twentieth Century* (Oxford: Berg, 1997). For the fascinating issue of 'monumental change' and 'dead-body politics' in central and eastern Europe after 1989, see Verdery, *The Political Lives of Dead Bodies*, and on modern 'monumental politics' more generally Reinhart Koselleck and Michael Jeismann (eds.), *Der politische Totenkult: Kriegerdenkmäler in der Moderne* (Munich: Fink, 1994).

One link between memory and power is that of legitimacy: policies are legitimated through appeals to the collective or national memory for social consumption both at home and abroad. As Joshua Foa Dienstag has pointed out, the key connection is

that between the legitimacy of existing institutions, their historical roles and the question of representation. Memory takes on a certain importance when claims of legitimacy rest on claims of representativeness. These, in turn, often rely on historical identification.[99]

This does not imply that all 'mnemonic legitimation' is automatically traditional legitimacy in a Weberian sense. Legitimacy could also be based on a sharp break with the past due to traumatic experiences and disastrous policy failures, from which the appropriate lessons have been drawn. This, in a nutshell, is the case of German foreign-policy-making after the Second World War, which Berger analyses in chapter 3. Memory as the base of legitimacy could also be understood as a kind of 'structural power', that is, the power to define what is put on the political agenda, in what terms political issues are framed and which conflicts get avoided.[100] A focus on legitimacy also draws our attention to memory as a prime factor in political culture, as Jeffrey Olick has pointed out.[101] Olick distinguishes between aggregated individual memories – or 'collected memory' – as a factor in most traditional studies of political culture such as Verba's and Almond's, and collective memory understood as the 'frame' or 'profile' of national memory. The former is relatively easy to 'operationalise' through surveys, and is also easily linked with psychological and even neuro-psychological understandings of memory. The latter, however, symbolically structures the political claim-making which is always both strategic and constitutive of politics, and effectively operates as a constraint in any given political culture by both proscribing and prescribing certain claims. It is not so much that memory is the independent variable determining political culture and ultimately policies, but that memory to some extent *is* political culture. As Olick and Daniel Levy have described this role of memory in political claim-making, mixing metaphors from Marx and Austin, 'people do things with words, but not in circumstances of their own choosing'.[102]

---

[99] Joshua Foa Dienstag, '"The Pozsgay Affair": Historical Memory and Political Legitimacy', *History & Memory*, 8, 1 (1996), 51–66, 60.

[100] On 'structural power', see Steven Lukes, *Power: A Radical View* (London: Macmillan, 1974).

[101] See also Stephen Welch, *The Concept of Political Culture* (Basingstoke: Macmillan, 1994).

[102] Jeffrey K. Olick and Daniel Levy, 'Collective Memory and Cultural Constraint: Holocaust Myth and Rationality in German Politics', *American Sociological Review*, 62 (1997), 921–36, 922.

Alternatively, policy-makers themselves rely on memory – understood here both as collective, national memory and as personal memory – and on historical analogies in particular to decide policy. While it is true that the analogies we draw from the past for present-day analysis often mislead us, it is equally true that policy-makers, journalists and historians cannot resist using them. James Bryce's judgement that 'the chief practical use of history is to deliver us from plausible historical analogies' has yet to deter nationalists, historians and policy-makers from rummaging through the past, even though, as Yuen Foong Khong has shown in a masterful study, analogical reasoning is likely to have poor results, for reasons rooted in cognitive psychology.[103] Mostly, analogies serve to reduce complexity and short-circuit critical reflection, but also to create 'instant legitimacy'.[104] The use of analogies in decision-making by politicians and civil servants directs us to the examination of what Anne Deighton in her contribution refers to as the 'mindsets' of decision-makers. Here the study of relatively homogeneous elites becomes crucial, and Deighton accordingly focuses on the 'imperial mindset' produced by Oxbridge education. However, the discussion of the use of analogies by elites is in fact not divorced from the other aspects of memory analysed in this volume. Analogies are mostly the result of personal memory, but they can also be derived from collective, national memory. In the latter case, in particular, it becomes clear that elite versions of collective memory are not the collective memory per se, but often its dominant version.

Again, one could collapse this notion of memory as historical analogy into 'myth', as Cyrill Buffet and Beatrice Heuser do, when they suggest that myth could be read as 'a shorthand for a particular interpretation of a historical experience or policy, or a policy with some acknowledged historical antecedents, that is invoked in the present to justify certain policies'.[105] But such a collapse risks settling for a vague and yet normatively charged concept like 'myth' on the one hand, and relying on

---

[103] Yuen Foong Khong, *Analogies at War: Korea, Munich, Dien Bien Phu and the Vietnam Decisions of 1965* (Princeton: Princeton University Press, 1992). See also Ernest May, *'Lessons' from the Past: The Use and Misuse of History in American Foreign Policy* (New York: Oxford University Press, 1973).

[104] There is also a distinct ethical question about the use of analogies which has been debated most extensively in connection with extracting 'lessons' from the Holocaust. As Lawrence Langer has pointed out, 'drawing lessons', as laudable as it might be in the abstract, can be part of a strategy of *consolation*, of extracting a comforting meaning from the past, rather than adopting a more painful strategy of *confrontation* with the past. See Lawrence L. Langer, *Admitting the Holocaust* (New York: Oxford University Press, 1995), 5.

[105] Beatrice Heuser and Cyril Buffet, 'Introduction: Of Myths and Men', in Cyril Buffet and Beatrice Heuser (eds.), *Haunted by History: Myths in International Relations* (Oxford: Berghahn, 1998), vii–x, ix.

a mechanistic model of political instrumentalisation of the past on the other. Myth by definition is fictional, whereas analogy is only part or a consequence of personal or collective memory. And memory is more than the invocation of clichés. Once again, an important conceptual distinction – and the possibility of differentiating between different phenomena – is lost.

Introducing the concept of memory into international relations is probably the most controversial (and innovative) part of this volume.[106] The point of stressing memory is not to deny that interests shape policy, but, with Max Weber, to examine the historically and ideologically conditioned construction of these interests. Nevertheless, as Berger points out, there remain serious methodological questions about the measurement of the influence of memory on policies, about the precise relationship between memories invoked and actual behaviour, and, finally, about how the process of change in political culture becomes eventually translated into policy change. A 'realist' outlook would in all likelihood simply dismiss the invocation of memories as pure 'window-dressing' for 'hard' interests. But then the question is why we remain so interested in 'memory matters', if they do not involve our 'interests'.[107] This is not the point at which to get involved in the 'inter-paradigm' debates of international relations, in which even promising newcomers such as 'social constructivism' to some extent remain fixated on their theoretical opponents, and where false dichotomies of paradigms replacing *or* complementing each other lead to ever more 'sterile excitement' (Georg Simmel).[108] Suffice it to say that it is also a false dichotomy to think that rational actor models and an emphasis on socially shared understandings of the world, that is, 'culture', exclude each other – even though some extreme postmodern and positivist epistemologies of course do

---

[106] The case for a link between memory and foreign policy seems strongest in the German case, in the sense both that the Germans drew historical lessons and that the collective memories of other nations constrain German foreign policy. See for instance Thomas Banchoff, 'German Policy Towards the European Union: The effects of Historical Memory', *German Politics*, 6, 1 (1997), 60–76.

[107] Dienstag, '"The Poszgay Affair"', 59.

[108] For the foundational text of constructivism, see Alexander Wendt, 'Anarchy is What States Make of it: The Social Construction of Power Politics', *International Organisation*, 46, 2 (1992), 391–425. For the most sophisticated application yet to a hard core realist topic, see Peter Katzenstein (ed.), *The Culture of National Security: Norms and Identity in World Politics* (New York: Columbia University Press, 1996), and Thomas U. Berger, *Cultures of Antimilitarism: National Security in Germany and Japan* (Baltimore: Johns Hopkins University Press, 1998). For cogent critiques, which nevertheless remain mired in false dichotomies, see Michael C. Desch, 'Culture Clash: Assessing the Importance of Ideas in Security Studies', *International Security*, 23, 1 (1998), 141–70, and Jeffrey T. Checkel, 'The Constructivist Turn in International Relations Theory', *World Politics*, 50 (1998), 324–48.

exclude each other.[109] And it would be equally wrong to see a focus on
memory as necessarily opposed to either neorealism or neoliberalism.
Scholars interested in memory as a factor in foreign policy do not have
to deny that at any given moment the balance of power or the incentives
of international regimes decisively influence behaviour. The point is that
states react to shifts in the balance of power and the evolution of international institutions in ways which have been shaped by political culture –
and memory in particular. While precise causal chains will always be
difficult to establish, one can add memory as a factor in historical and
political analysis – and a focus on memory will not automatically replace
causal analysis by representation, as Maier has claimed.[110] In that sense,
a focus on memory can theoretically and empirically enrich existing analytical perspectives by bringing both states' identity and decision-makers
'back in'.

On the one hand, it has been one of the 'lessons' of the Cold War itself
for scholarship that 'ideas and culture matter' and that power cannot
be calculated in 'monodimensional' material terms; on the other hand,
the 'operationalisation' of this insight has proved much more difficult.[111]
Again, the contributors to this volume take a pragmatic and pluralist
methodological approach to a subject that is, after all, truly 'multidi-
mensional' and needs to be considered from different perspectives. As
Berger argues, for a proper analysis one first needs to trace the origins of
a particular set of collective memories, examine their institutionalisation
and then establish an association between certain types of historically
derived arguments and the underlying core principles on which foreign
policy is based. As Berger explains, 'it then becomes possible to evaluate
the actual strength of the relationship between behaviour and beliefs by
tracing the evolution of both over time, monitoring how they evolved in
response to historical events and pressures'. But it also becomes possible to understand how states 'learn' and how memory establishes what
Berger calls 'cultural parameters' for policy-making.[112] Again, it is crucial to identify the actual social carriers of memory, and explain how they

---

[109] On the impossibility of simply adding methods and epistemologies to each other, see
also John Gerard Ruggie, 'The Past as Prologue? Interests, Identity, and American
Foreign Policy', *International Security*, 21, 4 (1997), 89–125.

[110] Maier, 'A Surfeit of Memory', 141.

[111] John Lewis Gaddis, *We Now Know: Rethinking Cold War History* (Oxford: Clarendon
Press, 1997), 282 and 284. See also Odd Arne Westad (ed.), *Reviewing the Cold War*
(London: Frank Cass, 2000). For attempts to introduce 'culture' into IR theory, see
Friedrich Kratochwil and Yosef Lapid (eds.), *The Return of Culture and Identity in IR
Theory* (Boulder: Lynne Rienner, 1995).

[112] For a promising theory of 'state learning' employing political psychology and rational
choice analysis, see also Andrew Farkas, *State Learning and International Change*
(Ann Arbor: University of Michigan Press, 1998).

related memory to policies. Of course, the notion of 'carriers' is not to imply any passivity on the part of the bearers of memory – on the contrary, the carriers of memory are engaged in a constant process not just of remembering, but also of reshaping. Remembering, after all, *is* a form of action. The contributions in the section on memory and foreign policy show the fruitful application of this research agenda precisely because they aim to be 'meticulously historical, sophisticatedly interpretive and determinedly anti-specialist'.[113] This demonstrates the analytical power of the two 'moves' at the heart of studying memory in international relations: first, a consideration of the part of collective memory in political culture which in turn is constitutive of the 'identity' and the 'interests' of states and, second, the cultural and, so to speak, 'mnemonic' context of decision-making.

In general, distinguishing between the two types of memory on the one hand, and history and policy on the other, allows the contributors to this volume to pay special attention to the ways in which collective memory and mass individual memory interact. Differentiating between the two concepts also makes for a much more subtle treatment of memory and politics than a blanket consideration of all memory and history as equally socially constructed. Above all, it shows that memory, whether national or personal, is neither simply durable nor infinitely malleable; as Olick points out, memory is not a vessel of truth or a mirror of interests, but a process of constructing meaning. Therefore purely 'instrumentalist' or 'presentist' accounts of memory in politics are one-sided and misleading. While present politicians have power over memory, memory also has power over them. And if they do have power over, or even, in Timothy Snyder's words, 'sovereignty over', memory, this is by no means a fact always to be deplored.

Interests, then, are not formulated prior to the uses and abuses of memory in a clear-cut way, but rather, memory and interests become interdependent, as political meanings and interests emerge in the struggle over past and future. As Martha Minow has argued, 'the alternation of forgetting and remembering itself etches the path of power'.[114] Most importantly, there is always a plurality of competing memories at work in the policy-making process. In fact, what makes memories symbolically and politically effective can precisely be their ambiguity, the fact that they appeal to a variety to audiences and evoke many different understandings,

---

[113] Jean Bethke Elshtain, 'International Politics and Political Theory', in Ken Booth and Steve Smith (eds.), *International Relations Theory Today* (Cambridge: Polity Press, 1995), 270.

[114] Matha Minow, *Between Vengeance and Forgiveness: Facing History after Genocide and Mass Violence* (Boston: Beacon Press, 1998), 119.

which then also implies the need to be struggled over to determine one signification.[115] As Katherine Verdery has pointed out, the mark of a good political symbol is that it has legitimating effects 'not because everyone agrees on its meaning but because it compels interest *despite* (because of?) divergent views of what it means'.[116] In that sense, a consideration of the power over memory (and therefore identity) inevitably leads to normative questions of how one *should* treat the past – and how politicians' treatment of the past should in turn be judged.

An ethics of memory?

Through the concept of legitimacy, memory and policy are inevitably linked to normative questions – whether about justice, reconciliation, the quality of democracy or at least, at the most basic level, the question of the identity or sameness of a political unit over time and the obligations to take responsibility for past actions this implies for members of the polity.[117] Therefore no study of memory and power is complete without an explicit consideration of what one might call 'the ethics of memory' – and all authors feel compelled to touch upon it at least indirectly.[118] As Snyder and Herf in particular insist, political elites can play a positive moral role by establishing power over memory, and recasting historical guilt and grievances in such a way that they further rather than hinder the emergence of a democratic political culture. Is there, however, a categorical imperative to remember? And is remembrance possible, or even desirable, without retribution, restoration or restitution? Despite the numerous efforts at general prescriptions for 'transitional justice', it seems exceedingly difficult to make general prescriptions. Not only is every case significantly different, the pasts to be faced and the memories chosen to guide political action are themselves almost always contested and conflicted, which makes reaching political judgements, at least for out-siders, so much more demanding. Studies in 'transitology' have probably clarified the options, but they have not made the judgements any easier.[119]

---

[115] Verdery, *The Political Lives of Dead Bodies*, 29.
[116] *Ibid.*, 31 (emphasis in original).
[117] See also W. James Booth, 'Communities of Memory: On Identity, Memory, and Debt', *American Political Science Review*, 93 (1999), 249–63.
[118] See also Margalit, *Ethik der Erinnerung*.
[119] For a useful systematic, though inconclusive, treatment, see Jon Elster, 'Coming to terms with the past. A framework for the study of justice in the transition to democracy', *Archives Européennes de Sociologie*, 1 (1998), 7–48. For outstanding recent contributions see Carla Hesse and Robert Post (eds.), *Human Rights in Political Transitions: Gettysburg to Bosnia* (New York: Zone Books, 1999), and Ruti G. Teitel, *Transitional Justice* (New York: Oxford University Press, 2000).

Part of the problem is that standard liberal answers to 'difficult memo-ries' might not work. On one level, memory does indeed seem surprisingly similar to religion – it is a shared practice, partially constitutive of identity, and leads to the kind of moral certainty whose dark side is moral abso-lutism. The answer then to our 'memory problems' would be the ancient wisdom of liberalism, namely to privatise and 'neutralise' memory. How-ever, collective memory cannot be privatised by definition, and potentially involves intergenerational, collective obligations with which liberalism – unlike Burkean conservatism – has notorious difficulties. Memory can be either repressed or de-politicised, that is, expressed in civil society, but shorn of its claims on political resources and state power. If it is repressed, or forcibly 'privatised' in families, it might in fact become aggravated and distorted in ways which one day will exact a price. This is essentially the story of Tito's repression of memory in Yugoslavia, the subsequent 'privatisation' and 'proliferation' of memories, and their final unleashing on a 'battlefield of memories' which Bet-El analyses – and where the se-ductive metaphor of a 'return of the repressed' for once seems to be fully applicable. However, it is not at all clear that the reverse of this insight holds true. In other words, it cannot be taken for granted that 'counter-memory', the recovery and recognition of the memories of oppressed groups, is automatically liberating, or that such 'counter-memory' should have legitimacy per se. Counter-memory might contribute to truth, but even if it does, it hardly follows that truth will contribute to reconciliation or justice.[120]

In the end, it is important to recognise that there might be genuinely tragic choices between incompatible or even incommensurable values here, much in the way that Isaiah Berlin described them. In other words, there might be unsolvable dilemmas in attaining truth, justice, reconcil-iation and democracy all at the same time. Justice is necessary and can play a role in finding the truth, but a shared truth might be impossi-ble, as long as political opponents remain trapped in collective memories of trauma and victimhood – or, alternatively, in the defensiveness and self-righteousness of the perpetrators. On the other hand, it is far from obvious that even a shared truth will necessarily lead to reconciliation. As the 'Berliner' Timothy Garton Ash points out, there are two schools of old wisdom facing each other here:

On one side, there is the old wisdom of the Jewish tradition: to remember is the secret of redemption. And that of George Santayana, so often quoted in relation to Nazism: those who forget the past are condemned to repeat it. On the other

[120] See also Robert I. Rotberg and Dennis Thompson (eds.), *Truth v. Justice: The Morality of Truth Commissions* (Princeton: Princeton University Press, 2000).

hand, there is the profound insight of the historian Ernest Renan that every nation is a community of both shared memory and of shared forgetting...And there is the everyday human experience that links 'forgive and forget' in a single phrase. Historically, the advocates of forgetting are many and impressive. They range from Cicero in 44 BC, demanding just two days after Caesar's murder that the memory of past discord be consigned to 'eternal oblivion', to Churchill in his Zurich speech two thousand years later, recalling Gladstone's appeal for 'a blessed act of oblivion' between former enemies.[121]

In the end, however, all contributors considering ethical questions in connection with memory come down on the side of Czeslaw Milosz's injunction that 'those who are still alive receive a mandate from those who are silent forever. They can fulfil their duties only by trying to reconstruct precisely things as they were by wresting the past from fictions and legends'. Garton Ash in particular advocates 'facing history' and a prescription of proceeding to 'find out – record – reflect – but then move on'. In the end, we might have to accept that contested, conflicting and competing memories are an inevitable legacy of transitions to democracy. But that in itself might not be such a bad thing. After all, democracy itself is a form of contained conflict – and as long as memories remain contested, there will be no simple forgetting or repression *tout court*. Rather than aiming for some elusive thick social consensus in which one narrative of the past is enthroned, arguing about the past within democratic parameters and on the basis of what has been called an 'economy of moral disagreement' might itself be a means of fostering social cohesion.[122]

The corollary of this insight, however, is that memory can be equally enabling, rather than simply constraining.[123] After all, if sociologists are right in claiming that collective memory is a prominent part of the stuff that holds societies together, then there is an important link between social solidarity and memory, and between memory and power – as in Hannah Arendt's definition of citizens 'acting in concert' through shared civic understandings.[124] Consequently, Milan Kundera's justly famous remark that 'the struggle against power is the struggle of memory against forgetting' is misleading in at least one sense, since memory can be a

---

[121] Timothy Garton Ash, *The File: A Personal History* (London: HarperCollins, 1997), 200–1.

[122] For an argument against such 'thick social unity', see Jonathan Allen, 'Balancing Justice and Social Unity: Political Theory and the Idea of a Truth and Reconciliation Commission', *University of Toronto Law Journal*, 49 (1999), 315–53. For the idea of an 'economy of moral disagreement', see Amy Gutmann and Dennis Thompson, 'The Moral Foundations of Truth Commissions', in Rotberg and Thomspson, *Truth v. Justice*, 22–44.

[123] See also the excellent treatment of the relationship between 'liberal legality' and collective memory in Mark Osiel, *Mass Atrocity, Collective Memory, and the Law* (New Brunswick: Transaction, 1997).

[124] Hannah Arendt, *On Violence* (New York: Harcourt Brace, 1970).

crucial resource for constituting democratic power.[125] And if, as for instance the German political scientist Gesine Schwan claims, the quality of
democracy can improve through dealing openly with the past, then, conversely, forced silence and forgetting might severely damage democracy.
Democracy, at a basic level, is itself about reiterated acts of accountability – and without facing the past, there can be no accountability.
Ultimately, without facing the past, there can also be no civic trust, which
is the outcome of a continuous public deliberation about the past.

In the end, however, one might well object from a more hard-nosed
institutionalist perspective that 'negotiated memory' is all one can attain
under certain power constellations, and that 'working through the past'
should, as Garton Ash insists, also involve some notion of when to
'move on'.[126] Ideally, liberals would always settle for what has been
called 'cultural strategies', which focus on the creation of genuine liberal–
democratic convictions (and trust), rather than 'institutional strategies' in
which the establishment of democratic institutions and outwardly democratic behaviour receives priority. The first approach puts political 'trust-
as-trustworthiness' first, but the political order and stability which the
second promises is sometimes all we can achieve. As Anne Sa'adah has
pointed out, 'not just democratisation, but also democracy, like so many
other good things in life, may disappoint'.[127] But democratic institutions
might often be not only our best bet, but our only bet, not just for peaceful transitions, but also for the persistence of a plurality of competing
memories which cannot be forced into one shared history for the sake of
'national pedagogy'.[128]

Which brings me to the final consideration of this volume: once an
ethics of memory has been identified, the question becomes how such
prescriptions can be translated into institutional practices. After all, no
consideration of memory and power is complete without detailing the
ways in which, apart from the power of memory to influence the present,
there is also the power of the present to influence memory. The media,
education, public discourse and, of course, the *state*, all play a crucial
role in shaping memory. From a legal perspective, Monroe Price analyses a benign manipulation of the media in Bosnia to calm down inflamed nationalist passions – and as a reaction to the previous abuse of
the 'means of mnemonic production'. He also sheds light on the multiple
connections between law, legitimacy and memory more generally. Daniel

---

[125] Milan Kundera, *The Book of Laughter and Forgetting* (New York: Knopf, 1980).
[126] Anne Sa'adah, *Germany's Second Chance: Trust, Justice and Democratisation* (Cambridge, MA: Harvard University Press, 1998), 2.
[127] *Ibid.*, 9.
[128] Charles S. Maier, 'Doing History, Doing Justice: The Narrative of the Historian and of the Truth Commission', in Rotberg and Thompson, *Truth v. Justice*, 261–78.

Levy and Julian Dierkes, drawing on Halbwachs's original insight that the past is 'stored and interpreted by social institutions', analyse the role of memory in German high school textbooks and citizenship legislation, and the way these institutional practices have shaped conceptions of German nationhood. They re-emphasise that the nation is a contested terrain on which groups with competing memories struggle to generalise their ideal conceptions of society, but they also show that West German educational policies could be read as a successful institutionalisation of the ethical command to remember.

The essays collected here show that memory and power can only be fully understood if domestic and international, social scientific, historical and ethical perspectives are brought together. Neither one-sidedly instrumentalist visions of the relationship between memory and power, nor romantic ideas about a pristine memory to be snatched from the hands of the powerful can do justice to the ways in which politics and memory interact. These differentiated insights will remain relevant as long as 'the political battle is a battle for the territory of collective memory'.[129]

[129] Ugrešić, *The Culture of Lies*, 228.

Part 1

Myth, memory and analogy in foreign policy

1   Memory of sovereignty and sovereignty over memory: Poland, Lithuania and Ukraine, 1939–1999

Timothy Snyder

Revanchism, ethnic cleansing and war are all results of memory; peace in a part of the world where border changes, nationalist murder and bloody conflict are well remembered is at least as interesting. Since the end of the Second World War, Lithuanians have believed that Poland would seize Vilnius if given the chance, while Poles recall Ukrainians (after the Germans) as the greatest and most vicious wartime enemy. Since 1989 Poland and its eastern neighbours Lithuania and Ukraine have successfully negotiated issues of past conflict, in large part because of awareness of the problems memory must pose for statesmen. The question of the importance of national sovereignty to collective memory, and the possibility of gaining sovereignty over memory by way of national policy, involves four theoretical problems.

First, we must distinguish history from memory, while establishing the nature of their mutual independence. Neither can be studied apart from the other, and yet without separate conceptions the study of neither can proceed. Second, we must distinguish two types of collective memory. The first is the recollection of a large number of individuals of events in which they took part. This sort of collective memory we shall call 'mass personal memory'. The second is the organisational principle that nationally conscious individuals use to organise the national history. This is 'memoire' rather than 'souvenir', a 'frame' (Yuen Foon Kong) rather than a picture. It allows us to place events in the national history, whether or not we took part in them.[1] Third, we must account for the influence of communist power upon memory and national historiography, as Iver Neumann points out. Fourth, we must sketch the margins which remain for responsible political leadership, and the circumstances in which free polities may gain a measure of sovereignty over memory.

---

[1] These two sorts of collective memory are easily confused and conflated. There are probably disciplinary and national predilections to giving precedence to one or the other. Empiricists may be drawn to mass personal memory, and students of culture to national memory. It may also be that societies with less to remember are apt to regard the mass personal recollections of others as constructs.

These four problem areas correspond to historical periods. The problem of history and memory, of what is to be remembered, corresponds to the period 1939–47. The distinction between the two types of collective memory, and the character of communist influence on memory, are most saliently put with regard to events of 1947–89. The possibility of sound policy towards memory, of asserting sovereignty over memory, will be investigated with respect to events since 1989. This final section will also serve to elucidate the practical implications of these theoretical problems. History, memory, and policy are separate realms, and the relationship among them is far from straightforward. Good foreign policy does not flow simply from vivid memory or good history, but must address the pressing problems of the day while navigating the straits and passages they define.

History and memory (1939–47)

Memory cannot be studied as memory, at all. Our recollections are always recollections of something, and unless we have an independent source of knowledge about this something, we can learn nothing about how memory works. In experiments on human memory, for example, the psychologist must know what is to be remembered, or her observations of actual recall will be meaningless. This holds whether the researcher is studying memory as our ability to recall information, or memory as a system which organises recollections. The same holds for the historian, even though the historian lacks the expedient of experiments. A historian who studies memory of past events must do so against the background of some picture of these events. The historian's first task, then, must be to use the available sources, including the memories of participants and victims of all sides, to establish such an image. Although this image must be derivative of memory, it is not reducible to it. Indeed, a successful historical project almost always proves to be a corrective of memory.

The section that follows is history, in the important sense that no individual does, and no individual could, remember the events in the way that they will be presented: events can only be seen 'as they really were' with the help of research and retrospect. During the period of wartime conflict between Poles and Lithuanians and Ukrainians (1939–47), the usual problems were posed in severe form. No individual had all of the necessary perspectives; no individual had all of the information; leaders were making life or death decisions rather than seeking truth; several parties believed that massacres here or there should not be allowed to slow the arrival of the greater good; perpetrators of violence often intentionally sowed confusion about their identity and motives; victims of violence were often afraid to press claims; state power was in flux; and the two greatest propaganda machines of all time were at work. With a historical picture of wartime relations between Poles and Lithuanians and Poles and Ukrainians as backdrop, we will be able to pose coherently questions of collective memory.

The Polish–Ukrainian civil war, 1943–7

Polish and Ukrainian memories of the Second World War are extraordinarily different. For Poles, the Molotov–Ribbentrop pact of 1939 was an act of unprecedented treachery. For Ukrainians, its division of Poland allowed all Ukrainian lands to be united into a single political unit.[2] For Poles, the enemies in the Second World War were the Germans and their (sometime) Ukrainian henchmen. Far more Ukrainians, however, fought in the Red Army against the Germans than in the Ukrainian Insurgent Army (UPA) as their allies. The Ukrainian nationalists who did indeed ally with Nazi Germany are regarded by west Ukrainian patriots (and many Ukrainians in Poland) as canny and heroic freedom fighters; for Poles they are usually vicious fascists. Whereas for patriotic Ukrainians the Organization of Ukrainian Nationalists created a moment of Ukrainian sovereign action by declaring a Ukrainian state under Nazi occupation in 1941 and a lasting memory of national heroism by their doomed struggle, for Poles its UPA was the organisation which cleansed Poles from western Ukraine in 1943 and 1944. Ukrainian patriots – even liberals with long experience in the West – are unwilling to accept that the UPA did commit mass race murder in 1943–4. Poles, even those hostile to the communist regime, are apt to believe that the anti-Ukrainian military operations of 1944–7 were a direct result (and a just one) of the UPA's earlier ethnic cleansing. Both views are substantially incorrect. The UPA did indeed brutally murder tens of thousands of Polish civilians in 1943–4. But in 1944–7 the Polish communist regime acted to 'resolve the Ukrainian question in Poland', not only to liquidate the UPA. In both cases, of course, it is fallacious in any event to hold the entire nation responsible for the actions in question. Yet the scale and depth of suffering carry their own truth: in all, some 110,000 lost their lives and 1.5 million their homes in what I call the Polish–Ukrainian civil war of 1943–7, in cleansing actions (the word was used at the time) that were largely independent of the battles of the Second World War, and which was carried out in the name of the Ukrainian nation against Poles

---

[2] See Volodymyr Serhiichyk, *Etnichni Mezhi i Derzhavnyi Kordon Ukrainy* (Ternopil: Vydavnytsvo Ternopil, 1996), 143, for the historical teleology. This view is general and uncontroversial in Ukraine.

and in the name of the Polish nation against Ukrainians. Yet memories of ethnic cleansing provide the sharpest contrast, supply the driest kindling for political conflicts, and evoke the greatest need for historical care. In fact, Poles and Ukrainians each cleansed the other, but in memory each was only the victim of the other. What, then, are the facts?

There is no space here to explain the entire background of the Ukrainian–Polish conflict over Galicia and Volhynia.[3] All that can be shown is that Ukrainian political activity was concentrated in Poland by the 1930s, and that the Second World War enabled its most violent elements to take actions altogether disproportionate to their popular support before the war. During the inter-war period the locus of Ukrainian civil society was Galicia, which had fallen under Polish rule after the conflicts which followed the First World War. Galicia had belonged to Austria: along with Volhynia, which had been ruled by the Russian empire, it was home to the vast majority of Poland's Ukrainian minority. Most of what is now Ukraine was then Soviet Ukraine, but after the reversal of the pro-Ukrainian policies of the 1920s, and especially after the Great Famine of the early 1930s, it no longer supported anything like Ukrainian national activity. Ukrainians in Poland enjoyed enough freedom to organise themselves, but were denied the political options which might have satisfied the ambitions of their elite. In the 1930s Ukrainian political life in Poland was divided among a pro-communist and illegal left, a pragmatically pro-Polish centre, and a violently anti-Polish and illegal right.

This last tendency, the Organisation of Ukrainian Nationalists, was best prepared for the new situation brought by the destruction of Polish state in 1939. As other organisations dissolved themselves, the habitually conspiratorial OUN survived. But it split in 1941 into two fractions, and lost much of its leadership to internecine war, German arrests and, eventually, Soviet attacks. By 1943, when attacks on Polish citizens were initiated on a mass scale, Ukrainian nationalism had been reduced to its youngest and most violent elements. In conditions of enormous stress, they took decisions based upon a changing strategic environment. Some Ukrainian leaders apparently believed that the Second World War would end with the exhaustion of both Germany and Russia, and that Ukraine's final enemy would be a resurrected Poland unwilling to abandon its eastern lands.[4] The formation of sizable units of Polish partisans in the east confirmed this fear. At the time of the establishment of the UPA as a

---

[3] This is the purpose of Timothy Snyder, *The Reconstruction of Nations* (New Haven: Yale University Press, 2003), chs. 7–8.

[4] This is the view advanced in a thoughtful essay by Grzegorz Motyka, 'Od Wołynia do akcji "Wisła"', Więź 473 (March 1998), 110. His *Tak było w Bieszczadach* (Warsaw: Volumen, 1999) is now the major source on this conflict.

fighting force in 1943, the Wehrmacht had lost its momentum in the east. With the Germans forced westward and the Red Army too strong a foe to defeat, Ukrainian nationalists may then have reasoned that the elimination of Polishness from Ukraine was the most that could now be achieved.

At all events, the consequences (and the available documents) point to a firm political decision to prioritise the struggle with the Polish element, and to use violence against civilians as a means of resolving the Polish question in Ukraine.[5] Some of the UPA's soldiers were former German policemen responsible for the murder of Jews in 1941–2, and more generally the example of German nationality policy must have demoralised the Ukrainian population. In any case, the policy of expelling (or even physically liquidating) Poles was popular within the UPA, and found substantial popular support among Ukrainian peasants as well.[6] At least 40,000 Polish civilians were murdered by Ukrainian partisans and peasants in Volhynia in July 1943, and another 10,000 were murdered in Galicia in March 1944. In coordinated attacks on Polish settlements, Ukrainian partisans burned homes and used sickles and rakes to kill those they captured outside. Beheaded, crucified, or dismembered bodies were displayed, in order to encourage remaining Poles to flee. By the time of these attacks, the Polish population in Ukraine had already been thinned by Soviet deportations between 1939 and 1941 and by German executions and deportations since. The enormous majority of remaining Poles who escaped the UPA fled west, some 200,000 before and some 800,000 after the beginning of official 'repatriations' agreed to by Polish and Soviet communist authorities in September 1944.[7] Their flight ended five hundred years of continuous Polish settlement of these lands, and brought to post-war Poland a million first- or second-hand personal memories of atrocities committed in the name of Ukraine.

Meanwhile, news of the slaughter in Volhynia infuriated Poles in Lviv and Galicia, and Polish partisans (of all political stripes) attacked the

---

[5] Petro Balei *Fronda Stepana Bandery v OUN 1940 roku: prychyny i naslidky* (Kyiv: Tekna A/T, 1996), 141; 'Taras Bul'ba-Borovets', undated open letter to the OUN-Bandera., Central State Archive (CDAVOVU) in Kyiv, 3833/1/107, cited in Władysław Filar, *Eksterminacja ludności polskiej na Wołyniu w Drugiej Wojnie światowej* (Warsaw: Zakład Poligrafii, 1999), 85.

[6] Ryszard Torzecki, *Polacy i Ukraińcy: Sprawa ukraińska w czasie II wojny światowej na terenie II Rzeczypospolitej* (Warsaw: PWN, 1993), 238.

[7] A far higher proportion of Poles in Ukraine were willing to be 'repatriated' than Poles in Lithuania and Belarus. Also, Poles in western Ukraine, the site of UPA attacks, were more likely to leave than Poles in central Ukraine. These are reasons to believe that the acceptance of 'repatriation' was a result of wartime experience, and in this sense a result of the UPA's ethnic cleansing.

UPA, assassinated prominent Ukrainian civilians and burned Ukrainian villages. The Polish government-in-exile in London was forced to redirect its limited resources.[8] Although there is no evidence that the Polish government contemplated a policy of revenge against Ukrainian civilians, and in fact explicitly ordered that civilians not be harmed, in the field Polish partisans burned Ukrainian villages and killed Ukrainians found on the roads in Volhynia.[9] Further west, where the demographic balance favoured Poles, the situation was that of a pitiless civil war. Polish partisans (usually but not always formations outside the main command of the Home Army) engaged in the mass killing of civilians. In the eastern half of the Lublin region, Polish partisans of the Peasant Battalions matched the Ukrainians atrocity for atrocity. The testimony of one of these Polish partisans, recently published in English, is worth quoting at length:

We reacted to their attacks, which reached unspeakable levels of barbarity, with a ruthlessness of our own. When we overran a Ukrainian settlement, we systematically took out the men of fighting age and executed them, often by letting them run forty paces ahead of us and shooting them in the back. This was considered the most humane method. Others in the unit, whose actions I will describe, behaved differently and exacted a terrible revenge. No one raised a finger to stop them. While I never saw one of our men pick up a baby or a small child with the point of a bayonet and toss it onto a fire, I saw the charred corpses of Polish babies who had died that way. If none of our number did that, then it was the only atrocity that we did not commit.[10]

Polish communists, the baggage of the Red Army as the front swept across Poland in 1944, knew that in this context the ethnic cleansing of Ukrainians within Poland's new borders would arouse little opposition, and bring much support, from ethnic Poles. Here their interests coincided with orders from Soviet comrades, and the mutual 'repatriations' of 1944–46 were carried out with enthusiasm by both sides. Perhaps 220,000 Ukrainians left Poland of their own volition in late 1944. Many of these

---

[8] Ministerstwo Obrony Narodowej, Biuro Ministra-Wydział Polityczny, L.dz. 1900/ WPol/44, London, 8 January 1944, Oddział VI, sygn. 3.3.3.13.2 (36); Sztab Naczelnego Wodza, Oddział Specjalny, L.dz.719/Tjn.44, London, 28 January 1944, Oddział VI, sygn. 3.3.3.13.2 (37); Sztab Naczelnego Wodza, Oddział Specjalny, L.dz.2366/tjn.43, 17 May 1943, Oddziat VI, sygn. 3.1.3.3.2 (34); Sztab Naczelnego Wodza, Oddziat Specjalny, L.dz.108/Tjn.44, London, 8 January 1944, Oddział VI, sygn. 3.1.1.13.2 (22), all in Studium Polskiej Podziemnej, London.

[9] For examples of such Polish attacks see Michał Klimacki, 'Geneza i organizacja polskiej samoobrony na Wołyniu i w Małopolsce Wschodnej podczas II wojny światowej', in *Polska-Ukraina: trudne pytania* (Warsaw: Karta, 1998), IV, 70, and Roman Stri ka, 'Geneza polskiej samoobrony na Wołyniu i jej roli w obronie ludności polskiej', ibid., 82.

[10] Waldemar Lotnik, *Nine Lives: Ethnic Conflict in the Polish–Ukrainian Borderlands* (London: Serif, 1999), 59.

returned, some by claiming to be ethnic Poles and thus 'repatriating' again in the opposite direction, bringing horrifying accounts of Soviet Ukraine. By 1945 Ukrainians were in general unwilling to resettle, and had organised to appeal for the right to remain. The Soviets requested the use of force in August 1945, and in September 1945 Polish authorities sent in three infantry divisions to resettle forcibly remaining Ukrainians to the Soviet Union. Many of these soldiers hailed from the east and had fought against the UPA, and could be counted on to harbour no tender feelings towards Ukrainians. In April 1946, these divisions, other troops and security forces were organised into Operational Group 'Rzeszów', with the task of completing the expulsion of Ukrainians from Poland. They encircled villages, forced inhabitants at gunpoint into convoys bound for Soviet Ukraine, and moved on. Roughly 260,000 Ukrainians were expelled from Poland in this way.[11]

Polish communist authorities realised in 1947 that more Ukrainians than they had expected had managed to stay. The estimate of August 1946 that 14,000 Ukrainians remained in Poland was increased to 74,000 in March 1947 (a better estimate would have been 200,000). By this time planning had already begun, this time apparently without prompting from the Soviet Union (though of course with Stalin's eventual approval), to disperse remaining Ukrainians in the northern and western territories that Poland 'recovered' from Germany. After a general was murdered by the UPA on 28 March 1947, the politburo decided to 'resettle Ukrainians and mixed families in the regained territories (especially in southern Prussia), not forming any tight groups and not closer than 100 kilometres from the border'.[12] The initial plan, presented on 16 April 1947, began with the words: 'Task: to resolve the Ukrainian problem in Poland once and for all.'[13] No Ukrainians were to be spared: even loyal party members trained in the Soviet Union, even communists who had helped 'repatriate' Ukrainians in the previous wave, were to be forcibly resettled.

Ukrainians were dispersed from south-eastern to north-western Poland (to the territories 'recovered' from Germany) in three waves of operations between April and August 1947. Operational Group 'Wisła' used the same tactics as its predecessor 'Rzeszów', often allowing Ukrainians hours or even minutes to pack their belongings. Some 140,000 Ukrainians

[11] Eugeniusz Misiło, *Akcja 'Wisła'* (Warsaw: Archiwum Ukraińskie, 1993), 15.

[12] 'Z protokołu nr 3 posiedzenia Biura Politycznego Komitetu Centralnego Polskiej Partii Robotniczej': 29 March 1947, Archiwum Akt Nowych, VI Oddział, KC PPR, 295/V-3, reprinted in Misiło, *Akcja 'Wisła'*, 24.

[13] "Projekt organizacji specjalnej 'Wschód'", plan presented by General Stanisław Mossor to Polish politburo 16 April 1947, Archiwum Urzędu Ochrony Państwa, Gabinet Ministra Bezpieczeństwa Publicznego, 17/IX/140, reprinted in Misiło, *Akcja 'Wisła'*, 24.

were packed into trains, and rerouted at either Lublin or Oświęcim (Auschwitz) station to their new places of settlement. Military courts sentenced 178 Ukrainians to death for collaborating with the UPA. A total of 3,936 Ukrainians, including 823 women and children, were taken to the Jaworzno concentration camp, a wartime affiliate of the Auschwitz–Birkenau complex. Brutal torture was routine.[14] Several dozen died in Jaworzno, including two women by suicide. Later in 1947, another operational group finally defeated the UPA – given new life in south-eastern Poland as a defender of Ukrainians who did not wish to leave their homes. Although Polish communist forces never destroyed a UPA battalion, they could and did make it impossible for the UPA to operate in Poland. UPA soldiers escaped across the (sealed) Czechoslovak border and on to the West, or across the (sealed) Soviet border to continue the fight against Soviet power. Some accepted resettlement, and joined the three quarters of the Ukrainian population in post-war Poland which was ethnically cleansed.

The transfer of Vilnius

Whereas Poles and Ukrainians have killed and expelled each other in great numbers, Poles and Lithuanians have fought no major battle in modern times. Rather, Poles and Lithuanians have both claimed the city of Vilnius. Vilnius was the capital of the Grand Duchy of Lithuania, both before and after the duchy was joined with the Kingdom of Poland in 1569 to create the Polish–Lithuanian Commonwealth. As long as the Polish–Lithuanian Commonwealth existed, the Grand Duchy of Lithuania was at once connected to and distinct from the Polish crown lands. Its nobles became citizens of the larger Commonwealth and accepted treated Polish as the language of culture, law and public discourse, but they never ceased to regard themselves as Lithuanian. At this time, therefore, the city of Vilnius was therefore neither 'Polish' nor 'Lithuanian' in a modern, ethnic nationalist sense.[15]

After the Grand Duchy of Lithuania was absorbed by the Russian empire in the partitions of the late eighteenth century, this old identity faced a number of challenges. Over the course of the nineteenth century, traditional multinational Lithuanian patriotism was weakened by failures in practice (the risings of 1831 and 1863), changes in economics

---

[14] This is the conclusion of the investigation of the Polish procurator in 1997. See Leszek Gołowski, 'Dokumenty Javozhna' (excerpts from procurator's report of treatment of Ukrainian prisoners in Jaworzno concentration camp, 1947), *Nashe Slovo*, 28 January 1996, 1, 3.

[15] See Snyder, *The Reconstruction of Nations*, ch. 2.

(the emancipation of the serfs in 1861), and in some measure by Russian policy (which sought to use ethnic Lithuanians as a counterweight to patriotic Poles). As the Lithuanian national movement consolidated along modern ethnic nationalist lines in the late nineteenth century, the reclaiming of Vilnius from Polish culture was one of its major goals – even as most of 'Lithuania' and 'Poland' were ruled by tsarist Russia. After the First World War, Lithuanian leaders struck a bargain with the Bolsheviks for Vilnius, but were foiled when Poland won the Polish–Bolshevik war in 1920. Vilnius was occupied by Polish troops, the local population voted for annexation to Poland, and the victorious powers accepted this frontier arrangement.[16]

Lithuania continued to insist on its legal right to Vilnius, and Lithuania and Poland were technically at war over the city until 1938. The denial of Vilnius determined Lithuanian attitudes towards its neighbours and played an important role in domestic politics. The December 1926 coup and the authoritarian dictatorship that followed were justified in terms of purported Polish interference in Lithuania's internal affairs, and Latvian and British representatives were assured that Poland rather than Russia posed a military threat to the Baltic region.[17] The regime accepted money and favours from Moscow, believing that Poland posed the greater military threat.[18] When the Soviet Union did advance west into Poland on the strength of the Molotov–Ribbentrop pact, Lithuanian representatives pressed claims to Vilnius in Moscow. In October 1939, Lithuania received Vilnius from the Soviet Union in exchange for allowing Soviet military bases on its territory. Lithuanian troops marched unopposed into Vilnius on 28 October, Polish armies having been defeated by the German and Soviet attacks of September.

Lithuanian soldiers were astonished to find that they could not communicate with the local population, and officers were forced to resort to French and German to ask for directions. Even by the official Lithuanian count, only 6 per cent of the residents of Vilnius were Lithuanian. Lithuanian national activists were forced to accept that 'Vilnius, so desired and so dear to Lithuanians, turns out to be entirely non-Lithuanian'.[19]

---

[16] The authoritative account of these events is A. E. Senn, *The Great Powers, Lithuania, and the Vilna Question 1920–1928* (Leiden: E. J. Brill, 1966).

[17] Iver Neumann, 'Poland as a Regional Great Power: the Inter-war Heritage', in Iver Neumann (ed.), *Regional Great Powers and International Politics* (New York: St. Martin's Press, 1992), 134–5.

[18] Tomas Venclova, 'Litwo, ojczyzno nasza', *Lithuania*, 26–27 (1998), 70–82. See also Zenonas Butkas, 'Jei opozicija gauna param iö svetur', *Diena*, 214 (1995).

[19] Algis Kasperovicius, 'Stosunek władz i społeczeństwa Litwy do Polaków na Wileńszczyznie Wrzesień 1939 – Czerwiec 1940', in Małgorzata Giżejewska and Tomasz Strzembosz (eds.), *Społeczeństwo białoruskie, litewskie i polskie na ziemiach poł*

Official propaganda nevertheless spoke of liberating Lithuanians and restoring Lithuanian identity to 'polonised' inhabitants: the consequent policy of suppressing the Polish and Jewish majority population was very popular in Lithuania as a whole, but led to riots in the streets of Vilnius. The 're-lithuanisation' of Vilnius lasted until June 1940, when the Soviet Union invaded Lithuania. The next twelve months saw tens of thousands of Poles, Jews and Lithuanians deported to Siberia, on class grounds. In the first days of Operation Barbarossa, in June 1941, German troops occupied the city, and in 1941–3 the Nazis (and some Lithuanian allies) killed more than 95 percent of Lithuania's Jewish population.[20] Poles organised in the Home Army succeeded in gaining control of the countryside around Vilnius in 1943, and were preparing to seize Vilnius from the Wehrmacht and the Lithuanian police in summer 1944. This they failed to do before the Red Army returned to Vilnius in July 1944, and Home Army soldiers were the first victims of the NKVD (the Soviet secret police) in the months that followed. In all, the Soviets killed, deported to Siberia or 'repatriated' to communist Poland perhaps half of the Polish population in Lithuania as a whole, and the majority of the Polish population of Vilnius. Vilnius was virtually emptied of its two leading peoples, and the border with Poland was pushed westwards, just as Lithuania was incorporated into the Soviet Union. As the Lithuanian joke had it, 'Vilnius is Lithuanian, but Lithuania is Russian'.

During the Second World War, Poles and Lithuanians did little direct harm to each other. Polish soldiers fleeing across the Lithuanian border in September 1939 were well treated by independent Lithuania.[21] Independent Lithuania did intend to eradicate Polishness in the Vilnius region in 1939–40, but its policies were very mild by the standards of the day, and it did not expel or kill Poles. After the German invasion, clashes between the Polish Home Army and Lithuanian police and SS units, as well as attacks on civilians (by Germans and Lithuanians, and in retribution by Poles) brought no more than a few thousand casualties. Poles and Lithuanians did not cooperate against either Nazi or Soviet occupation, but they were not ranged against each other as were Poles

nocno-wschodnich II Rzeczypospolitej w latach 1939–1941 (Warsaw: Instytut Studiów Politycznych Polskiej, 1995), 309; see also Longin Tomaszewski, 'Społeczeństwo Wileńszczyzny wobec władzy Litewskiej i sowieckiej', in ibid., 326–33.

[20] John F. Crossland, 'A Difficult Enquiry Into Lithuania's Holocaust Bears Grisly Fruit', *International Herald Tribune*, 22 March 1994. See also Dina Porat, 'The Holocaust in Lithuania: Some Unique Aspects', in David Cesarani (ed.), *The Final Solution: Origins and Implementation* (New York: Routledge, 1994), 160.

[21] Gintautas Vilkialis, 'Żotnierze polscy internowani na Litwie w latach 1939–1940', in Giżejewska and Strzembosz, *Społeczeństwo białoruskie*, 316–22.

and Ukrainians along the Ukrainian–Polish ethnographic frontiers. As the war ended, and as the Soviet incorporation of the Baltic states was de facto accepted by the great powers, the main disagreement between Lithuanian and Polish elites remained the status of Vilnius, the new capital of the Lithuanian Soviet Socialist Soviet Republic. To the protests of the Polish government in exile, the official Lithuanian reply was that Lithuania had gained no territory, Vilnius having been within its legal borders since 1920.[22]

Two types of national memory (1945–89)

What sort of memory do such experiences leave behind? There are of course numerous legacies of such dramatic events, but the temper of the two conflicts just described is sufficiently different to suggest that two separate types of memory may be usefully invoked. In the case of the Polish–Ukrainian civil war, we contemplate the personal memories of large numbers of Poles and Ukrainians who suffered at the hands of organisations which acted in the name of the other nation. This is an instance of the first sort of collective memory, mass personal memory. By 'mass personal memory' we mean personal recollections held by enough individuals to have national significance. If you and a large number of people of your nation have experienced terrible suffering at the hands of a neighbouring people, this experience will certainly have an irreducibly vivid character unmatched in the generally shared national memory of the rest of your group,[23] and your vivid personal memories (literal flashbacks) can probably be triggered by the reproduction of the emotional state of the original experience.[24] Consider the words one Polish survivor of the Ukrainian massacres, fifty years on, added to a detailed factual account of his own experience of the war: 'Volhynia aflame, the glow of the fires, I see it still, I can't get over it, I can't forget it. I cannot forget my family. What happened in Volhynia will remain in my memory until the end of my days. Although I want to, I can't forget any of it. Everything, as in a film, stands before my eyes.'[25]

---

[22] Krzysztof Tarka, 'Spór o Wilno. Ze stosunków polsko-litewskich w latach drugiej wojny światowej', *Zeszyty Historyczne*, 114 (1995), 64.

[23] Martin Conway, *Flashbulb Memories* (Hove: Erlbaum Associates, 1995), especially 53, 112; Zahava Solomon, Ronald Garb, Avraham Bleich and Daniel Grupper, 'Reactivation of Combat-Related Posttraumatic Stress Disorder', *American Journal of Psychiatry*, 144, 1 (January 1987), 51–5.

[24] See Dawn Macauley, Lee Ryan and Eric Eich, 'Mood Dependence in Implicit and Explicit Memory', in Peter Graf and Michael Masson (eds.), *Implicit Memory* (Hillsdale: Erlbaum Associates, 1993), 75–94.

[25] Wspomnienie II/2110, Archiwum Wschodnie, Ośródek Karta, Warsaw.

In the Lithuanian case, some other phenomenon is clearly at play. Before and during the Second World War, Lithuanians had relatively little reason to fear Poles (as opposed to Russians and Germans), and only historical and mythical (rather than demographic or strategic) reasons to attach such importance to Vilnius. This centrality of Vilnius to the Lithuanian experience of the war (and indeed of the century) suggests that we are dealing with the second sort of collective memory, national memory. This is memoire rather than souvenir: the organisational principle, or set of myths, by which nationally conscious individuals understand the past and its demands on the present. It appears generally true that ideal national histories envision an ancient nation, always present in history as a state, morally at least equal to other states, behaving in the past according to the beliefs of present nationally identifying people. When the state is incontestably absent, nationalists emphasise continuities in culture – in language, in literature, in religion – and the ceaseless political struggle for a new state. If culture is absent, they find surprising continuities, and claim that 'de-nationalised' minorities can be 're-nationalised'. If the political struggle is criticised, they call this propaganda, and say the ends justified the means. In every case, the malevolent neighbour rather than any weakness in the nation is to blame.

For Lithuanians, questions of the continuity of statehood, the survival of national culture and the struggle for independence, and the question of victimhood and moral status all centre on the city of Vilnius. 'To give up Vilnius,' protested a leading inter-war intellectual, 'would break the organic tie which links the present of the Lithuanian nation to its past.'[26] As a Lithuanian scholar put it, fifty years after Lithuania regained its historic capital, 'Poland ruled Vilnius for nineteen years, but in moral terms this act of aggression has remained forever in the eyes of the world a testament to the fact that justice and truth were on Lithuania's side and not with the Poles'.[27] This is not memory as personal experience, as souvenir. This is memory as organising principle, as memoire, which we are calling 'national memory'. If personal memories are the lifelong fate of individuals who have suffered, national memory is the destiny of the dead: to become numbers, facts and events worked into a predictable scheme which 'straightens' the national past and justifies national statehood.[28]

[26] M. Bagdonas, editor of *Lietuva*, cited in Senn, *The Great Powers*, 144.

[27] Kazimieras Graužinas, 'Lithuania's Conflict with Poland over the Territories of Vilnius and Suvalkai', in Algirdas M. Budreckis (ed.), *Eastern Lithuania: A Collection of Historical and Ethnographic Studies* (Chicago: trans. and publ. by the Lithuanian Association of the Vilnius Region, 1985), 509.

[28] 'Straightens' is precisely the word used by Algirdas Budreckis in his introduction to *Eastern Lithuania*.

Then again, as one of the great figures of interwar Lithuanian politics reminds us, 'a nation is composed more of the dead than of the living'.[29]

Communist power and collective memory (1945–89)

If these two sorts of collective memory (mass personal memory in the Ukrainian case and national memory in the Lithuanian case) are indeed different, one would expect to see this difference revealed in the collective memories of Lithuanians, Poles and Ukrainians in the post-war period. For the sake of simplicity, we will limit this part of the study to two cases: Lithuanians in Soviet Lithuania, and Poles in communist Poland (with some brief comment on the position of Ukrainians in Poland). As this demarcation suggests, the most important feature of the context of recollection after 1945 is communist power. It affected both sorts of collective memory in roughly similar ways: emphasising primitive ethnic nationalism, seeking foes other than Russians, isolating nations from one another, and blocking out rival conceptions of nationality emerging in the West. Yet even in this peculiar context, the differences in the two sorts of collective memories remain visible and striking.

The fear occasioned by Polish personal memories of Ukrainian nationalism was directed by the Polish communist regime in a fairly straightforward way. Personal memories of the experience in the east were not encouraged or supported by any organisation subsidised by the state, as the subject of the eastern lands absorbed by the Soviet Union after the shift of Poland to the west was taboo. Nor were the operations of the Polish army and security forces against the UPA and the native Ukrainian population in 1944–7 publicised: only in exceptional circumstances did Poles learn any of the particulars about these operations. The aim was not to draw attention to the concrete, but to promote fear of Ukrainians in the abstract.

To this end, school texts placed the war against Ukrainian partisans at the centre of Polish–Ukrainian relations. Ukrainians were treated as slavic counterparts to the Nazis, bound to them by a wild spiritual kinship. Because some Ukrainian nationalists did cooperate with the Nazis, they could be treated as their mere henchmen. Collaborating Ukrainian units were singled out as such, while collaboration by other nations

[29] The figure is Augustinas Voldemaras, cited in Senn, *The Great Powers*, 55. This view is not entirely unprecedented. Voldemaras did not mean that all of the dead counted: he presumably meant those whom he regarded as Lithuanians. This is not so dissimilar to Auguste Comte's notion of the 'subjective immortality' of individuals who lived in such a way as to leave a historical trace. Given the name, Voldemaras's own ancestors were probably Estonians.

(especially Russians) was ignored or minimised.[30] Ukrainian patriotism was thus reduced to a kind of mindless collaborationism with fascism, which fitted an older Polish prejudice of believing the Ukrainians to be something less than a nation. Meanwhile, the study of history of Ukraine as a political subject in its own right was strongly discouraged.[31]

One aim of this propaganda effort was to deflect attention from the crimes committed by communists during the same period, and here the communists achieved at best mixed results.[32] A second goal was to prevent contact between Polish and Ukrainian oppositionists; by the late 1980s they met regularly. The main success of post-war historiography, literature and propaganda was to move the centre of gravity of the Polish–Ukrainian conflict westwards into Poland: away from Lviv and other areas incorporated into the Soviet Union, and into the Bieszczady mountains, which remained in Poland. The Ukrainian became less a traditional competitor for dominance in certain historically specific regions (Galicia and Volhynia) than a depersonalised object of fear and loathing. One can only speculate how Polish feelings towards Ukrainians would have evolved in other circumstances, and there is no doubt that the simple experience of a million Poles is the fundamental source of Polish disquiet about Poland's great eastern neighbor. Yet the fact that Ukrainians are the first or second most feared nation in public opinion polls taken in the 1990s, half a century after the events in question, is in some measure due to the efforts of communist national policy.[33] In any case, the dominant ethnic definition of the state is a result of communist policy, as is the almost total ignorance of Poles of the suffering of Ukrainians in the Soviet Union, in communist Poland – and in inter-war Poland.

Meanwhile, the mass personal memory of Ukrainians in Poland reminds us of the stubborn force of personal memory even when it is discouraged by the state. Ukrainians were physically dispersed, deprived of

---

[30] John Basarab, 'Postwar Writings in Poland on Polish–Ukrainian Relations', in Peter Potichnyj (ed.), *Poland and Ukraine: Past and Present* (Toronto: Canadian Institute of Ukrainian Studies, 1980), 249.

[31] There were several exceptions. Zbigniew Wójcik attempted to teach his readers that Ukrainians had indeed suffered greatly under Polish rule See his *Dzikie Pola w Ogniu*, (Warsaw: Wiedza Powszechna, 1962), 281–2.

[32] Józef Lewandowski, 'Polish Historical Writing on Polish–Ukrainian Relations During World War Two', in Potichnyj, *Poland and Ukraine*, 232–3, 237–42; Roman Szporluk, 'The Role of the Press in Polish–Ukrainian Relations', ibid., 223.

[33] 'Ukraine Seen as "Most Dangerous Neighbor"', Warsaw PAP in English, 14 February 1992, in *FBIS-EEU*, 18 February 1992, 31; 'Boimy się przede wszystkim sąsiadów', *życie Warszawy*, 1 August 1992, 23. See also Marek Skórka, 'Wspólne sąsiedztwo czy nie chciani intruzi?' *Więź*, 473 (March 1998), 70–81; Michał Strzeszewski, 'Milczenie nie goi ran', *Nashe Slovo*, 21 November 1999, 2.

their national church, and until 1956 prevented from organising themselves in any way. Between 1956 and 1989 they were carefully monitored, and efforts to recall Operation Wisła and the repatriations were criminal offences. Nevertheless, Ukrainians in today's Poland have preserved a memory of their own suffering, and their demands for an official apology for Wisła are as consistent (if not more so) than the demands of Poles for an official Ukrainian apology for the slaughter which preceded it.[34] Young Ukrainians almost without exception recall the UPA as the organisation which defended their families and culture.[35] Ukrainians thus continue to present their nation as innocent victims of the actions of the Polish state, which is a view which requires serious qualification; Poles who remember the UPA see Operation Wisła as the final stage in a struggle against armed Ukrainians, which is politically plausible but historically dubious. Here we see mass personal memories blending into national memories, as each side assumes that it was the innocent victim and the other a simple aggressor.

If the predominant sort of memory in Polish–Ukrainian relations remains mass personal memory, the Lithuanian case illustrates the twists and turns characteristic of national memory. In post-war Polish–Lithuanian relations the issue was not the continuing force of the memories of individuals, but the attitude of Lithuanians as a group to the abstract issue of the right to the city of Vilnius. This continuity of attitudes under Soviet rule requires a word of historical explanation. After Lithuania was absorbed for the second time by the Soviet Union, substantial numbers of Lithuanians took up arms against communist rule. When the last of these courageous resisters were executed or sent to Siberia in the 1950s, Lithuanian intellectuals faced a fundamental choice. The struggle to regain Lithuanian independence through the only political method at hand, armed struggle, had failed. Even more than in Poland, academic and political advancement in the Soviet Union required party membership. As a rule, Lithuanian intellectuals chose to join the Lithuanian Communist Party (or at least to profit from state institutions), but worked to preserve national life. They published a large number of uncensored books and supported a Lithuanian-language university. Intellectuals gravitated towards history, cultivating after the Second World War a historiography

---

[34] To understand the persistence of Ukrainian demands, see the documents collected in Mirosław Czech, *Ukraińcy w Polsce, 1989–1993* (Warsaw: Związek Ukraińców w Polsce, 1993), and compare to 'Menshyny rivni bil'shosti', *Nashe Slovo*, 4 April 1999, 1–2; Natalia Kravchuk, 'Repryvatyzatsiia i politychna bataliia', *Nashe Slovo*, 12 September 1999, 4–5; Eva Pochtar-Shcherba, 'Karta poliaka', *Nashe Slovo*, 17 October 1999, 1, 6; Myroslav Chekh (Mirosłav Czech), 'Shchob ne bulo hirshe', *Nashe Slovo*, 9 January 2000, 1, 6.

[35] Antonina Kłoskowska, *Kultury narodowe u korzeni* (Warsaw: PWN: 1996), 197–9.

which cast the nation as the innocent victim of powerful neighbours. Meanwhile, lack of contact with People's Poland and Soviet propaganda allowed stereotypes about Poles lingering from the inter-war period to survive and flourish.

The Soviet system in combination with the Lithuanian Soviet Socialist Republic's success in preserving Lithuanian culture allowed Lithuanian national memory to flourish in a very pure form. The Lithuanian Soviet Socialist Republic was the first Lithuanian state in modern times with its capital in Vilnius, and Soviet propaganda and educational curricula treated this is a natural state of affairs. The national memory of Vilnius as Lithuania's 'eternal' capital faced no serious challenges, and the demographic changes of the war combined with the Soviet policy of urbanisation eventually (around 1980) allowed ethnic Lithuanians to predominate in the city central to their account of national history. Lithuanian national memory could gloss over just how this correspondence came about (the Molotov–Ribbentrop pact, the Holocaust, and the death or flight of educated Poles). Lithuanians (as a stateless nation) were bound to cherish traditions of statehood – and thus Vilnius as the capital of the only previous 'Lithuanian' state, the mediaeval Grand Duchy. In independent Lithuania, international politics was thus at first curiously dependent upon national history. Even as Poles repeatedly recognised the Lithuanian right to Vilnius, Lithuanians remained unsatisfied that Poles could resist once again seizing the city. This was not a result of personal memory of conflict, but of national memory striving to organise the history of a stateless nation. Lithuanians feared Poles because of enduring stereotypes, their own defensiveness about the acquisition of Vilnius, and the Polish refusal to accept the Lithuanian version of interwar history. For three years after 1991, Lithuania refused to sign an interstate treaty with Poland, on the grounds that Poland should apologise for 'invading' Vilnius in 1920 and 'occupying' the city until 1939.[36] Lithuanian schoolchildren asked after independence to select the most shameful event in the history of Lithuania named the 1569 union with Poland.[37]

Kundera's dictum that the struggle of freedom against power is the struggle of memory against forgetting is not quite right, when the memory

[36] For greater detail see Timothy Snyder, 'National Myths and International Relations: Poland and Lithuania, 1989–1994', *East European Politics and Societies*, 9, 2 (1995), 317–44.

[37] Vytautas Toleikis, 'Historia w szkole litewskiej w perspektywie stosunków polsko-litewskich', in Robert Traba (ed.), *Tematy polsko-litewskie* (Olsztyn: Borussia, 1999), 210–12; for an analysis of school texts see Birute Vareikiene, 'Od konfrontacji do zrozumienia. Stosunków polsko-litewski w podręcznikach szkolnych na Litwie', ibid., 216–25.

in question is national memory. National memory is a means of organising the past such as to preserve the dignity of the group with which we identity, and thus bolsters our pride as individual human beings. The truths which we might find as dispassionate observers must yield to the Truth we need to make our collective story straight and whole. As Nietzsche puts the problem in *Beyond Good and Evil*, 'I have done that, says my memory. I cannot have done that, says my pride, and is unyielding. Memory surrenders at last.' Pride is thus the limit of an impartial investigation of historical truth: when we identify with a nation, our national memory yields to a scheme which, unless and until we learn better, we will try to foist upon others.

Sovereignty over memory (1989-99)

However, a few short years after the collapse of the Soviet Union, Poland's political relations with both Ukraine and Lithuania were excellent. In the teeth of such problems of memory and power, how did this come to pass? The first necessary condition was a Polish eastern programme which took account of the problems posed by memory to relations with these eastern neighbours. The Paris monthly *Kultura* and a number of Polish oppositionists advocated such a programme well before 1989. It sought sovereignty over memory: memory not as individual recollections, not as a collective phenomenon, nor as a reaction to communism, but as a political problem which could be addressed in a future independent Poland by political means. We Poles, their argument ran, may think it natural to reclaim the eastern territories stripped from us by the Soviet Union, but the interest of preserving the Polish state and thus the future of the nation demands that we recognise existing borders. We Poles might think it natural to assert our superiority as the bearers of Western culture in the east, but it would be more profitable to the Polish state to accept our eastern neighbours as equals. We should learn the histories of Lithuania, Belarus and Ukraine, understand that they treated episodes of their pasts with the same sorts of biases Poles applied to their own past, and even appreciate that the eastern neighbours' views of past relations could check Polish prejudices.[38] Statesmanship, above all, is a matter of understanding

---

[38] Key texts are Kazimierz Podlaski, *Białorusini, Litwini, Ukraińcy*, published illegally several times from 1983; Juliusz Mieroszewski, 'Polska "ostpolitik"', *Kultura*, 309 (June 1973); Juliusz Mieroszewski, 'Rosyjski "kompleks polski" i obszar ULB', *Kultura*, 324 (September 1974). This programme was rightfully known as the *Kultura* eastern programme, after the Paris monthly which supported it for decades. On *Kultura*, see Jerzy Giedroyc and Krzysztof Pomian, *Autobiografia na cztery ręce* (Warsaw: Czytelnik, 1996). For evidence of the programme's reception, Andrzej Friszke, *Opozycja polityczna w*

the demands of the future, to which the demands of the past must be subordinated. But to be subordinated, they must first be understood.[39]

The second necessary condition was the realization of this programme. It was implemented, albeit with rough patches here and there, by the post-Solidarity elites who came to power after 1989. Poland began relations with the Lithuanian, Belarusian and Ukrainian republics while the Soviet Union still existed, and gradually earned credibility by its consistent policy: existing borders were to be preserved regardless of historical or other claims, minorities were to be granted cultural rights but treated above all as citizens of the countries they inhabit, historical debate should yield to 'European standards' of international conduct, and history if used at all in international affairs must be understood in instrumental ways: one should make history for the future by protecting the nation now, leave difficult questions of history to historians, and draw examples from the history of post-war western Europe.[40] Poland signed a state treaty with Lithuania in early 1994, just after postcommunists came to power in Poland, but the hard work had been done by their predecessors. By that point Poland's eastern policy had begun to bear fruit, and socialist governments of 1993–7 did not undermine its basic premises. The postcommunist president Aleksander Kwaśniewski, elected in 1995, deserves a great deal of credit for the continuing Polish–Ukrainian political reconciliation.[41]

The third necessary condition was the possibility of a return to Europe. Although the Polish eastern programme of sovereignty over memory had originally been articulated as a means of securing Polish independence by eliminating grounds for Polish–Russian discord, it was attractive in 1989

PRL 1945–1980 (London: Aneks, 1994); Jacek Kuron, *Wiara i wina: do i od komunizmu* (London: Aneks, 1989), 347; Roman Solchanyk, *Ukraine: From Chernobyl to Sovereignty. A Collection of Interviews* (New York: St. Martin's Press, 1992), 59–64; Jerzy Pomianowski, *Ruski miesiąc z hakiem* (Wrocaw: Wydawnictwo Dolnośląskie, 1997); Adam Michnik et al., 'Rozmawiajcie z Prezydentem' (interview with Aleksander Kwaśniewski), *Gazeta Wyborcza*, 3–4 January 1998, 10.

[39] Interview with Jerzy Giedroyc, editor of *Kultura*, Maisons-Lafitte, France, 7 November 1998.

[40] On memory and policy see Krzysztof Skubiszewski, 'Niebezpieczeństwo nacjonalizmu w Europie' (paper delivered in the series 'Nachdenken ber Europa', Frankfurt-am-Oder, 21 February 1992), in Krzysztof Skubiszewski, *Polityka Zagraniczna i Odzyskanie Niepodległości* (Warsaw: Wydawnictwo Interpress, 1997), 197; 'Konkluzja: Pozycja Polski w Europie', ibid., especially 380–1. Skubiszewski was foreign minister during the crucial years 1989–93. The policy documents which describe early eastern policy are Grzegorz Kostrzewa-Zorbas, 'Stosunki Polsko-Litewski: Uwagi i propozycje', Memorandum submitted to the Polish Senate's Foreign Affairs Committee and to the Obywatelski Klub Parlamentarny, 23 October 1989; Grzegorz Kostrzewa-Zorbas, 'Tezy do Polskiej Polityki Wschodniej u Progu Lat Dziewięćdziesiątych', Memorandum submitted to Polish government and parliament, 22 March 1990.

[41] For the full story of Polish eastern policy since 1989, see Snyder, *The Reconstruction of Nations*, chs. 10–14.

as a method of showing west Europeans that Poland was a mature state ready for integration in Western institutions. In the early 1990s, Polish eastern policy neutralised rather than resolved historical problems: it prevented the cycles of animosity that would have inevitably followed had Poland matched historical claim with historical claim, and thereby bought time for political elites in all three countries to learn to think politically about international politics. Such neutralisation was certainly sufficient for Poland's own entrance into Western institutions, but probably insufficient for genuine reconciliation with eastern neighbours. But as the 1990s progressed, the European Union and NATO also became attractive goals for Lithuanian and Ukrainian nationalists and national elites. As Lithuanian elites recognised at the end of 1993, and as Ukrainians seemed to understand all along, the return to Europe involved a Polish waystation. Moreover, programmes such as NATO's Partnership for Peace created an umbrella for institutional cooperation (such as the joint Ukrainian–Polish and Lithuanian–Polish peacekeeping battalions) while Phare and other EU programmes created a cadre of Polish experts now expected to train their eastern colleagues.[42]

Even in this final period of political success, the two types of collective memory remain distinct. Although the goal of Polish eastern policy was to treat memory as a political problem liable to political solution, we may close by noting that in this last period as in previous ones, the character of mass personal memories and that of national memory are significantly different. In Lithuania, where national memory predominates, a moment of national debate and national catharsis was required before reconciliation with Poland could begin. In late 1993 and early 1994, a corner was visibly turned: leading politicians such as the president and foreign minister argued quite explicitly that a secure state was needed to protect the nation and its traditions, and that good relations with Poland were needed to secure the state. The argument for compromise had to begin from the good of the nation, and had to address directly the mental habit of treating international politics as a means of rectifying the national past. In Polish–Ukrainian relations, there have been local conflicts around Lviv and Przemyśl, in the areas of Ukraine and Poland where the bloody war of the 1940s is well remembered by those who suffered and their children. The Polish public fears Ukraine, but in general active opposition to reconciliation is limited to survivors of ethnic cleansing – and even some of them have spoken out for forgiveness and good relations with the new Ukrainian state. By the late 1990s, the two non-governmental

---

[42] For a conceptualisation of the EU's unintended attractiveness, its 'passive leverage', see Milada Anna Vachudová, *Revolution, Democracy and Integration: East Central and South Eastern Europe since 1989* (Oxford: Oxford University Press, forthcoming).

organisations representing opposing Ukrainian and Polish historical claims and the interests of the ethnically cleansed on both sides were jointly sponsoring historical seminars on the Second World War.[43]

Roughly put, the problem posed by national memory is qualitative: when nations identify with a certain version of the past, policy which exposes its incoherence will be at first resisted, and must be justified in terms of the larger interest of the nation. Lithuanian leaders, with the help of Polish policy and the existence of attractive Western institutions, were able to begin such a redefinition. The problem posed by mass personal memory is quantitative: when people have painful recollections of experiences with another nation, they will probably be inclined to oppose reconciliation. These individuals can nevertheless prove to be generous and reasonable, they can be persuaded by arguments appealing to their interests – and in the last instance outvoted. The success of Polish eastern policy on both the Polish public and Lithuanian and Ukrainian elites demonstrated that both sorts of memory can be fruitfully addressed by political means, and that democratic nation-states with good arguments about national interests can exert sovereignty over memory. Democratic nation-states can neither create new memories from nothing nor wish away old ones, but they can conspire with the passage of time to divert personal memories from the issues of the day and coopt national memories in the name of the common good. Although it is too soon to say, the final significance of policy may be at the juncture of these two sorts of collective memory. Policies which bring peace at critical moments when sovereignty is regained and national conflict is expected probably influence the direction of mass personal memories as they flow into the shared national memory. Recollections of the Second World War might have determined, but now probably will not determine, the sense of the these nations' collective memories of one another in the century to come.

[43] I have in mind the Union of Ukrainians in Poland and the World Union of Home Army Soldiers (Volhynia). See the eight volumes of their jointly sponsored *Trudne pytania* (Warsaw: Karta, 1997–2001).

2 Myth, memory and policy in France since 1945

Robert Gildea   ·

In this chapter I hope to show that memory is a key factor in shaping decisions taken in the pursuit of power, but that conversely policy goals have a decisive influence on how memory is constructed. Two different forms of memory should be distinguished for our purposes. First, there are the multitudinous and fragmented memories that individuals may have of events such as the German occupation of France in 1940–5. Such an event may be variously experienced as trauma, loss, hunger, persecution, betrayal, deportation, new-found power or heroic resistance, depending on the individual, and these memories have no unmediated impact on policy-making. Second, there are the myths elaborated by politicians, intellectuals and the media to order and explain those events, and to overcome the pain associated with them. They are myths not in the sense of fictions or fairy-tales but of narratives of the past which serve to give an identity to a collectivity such as the nation, bind it together and legitimate policy decisions taken on its behalf. They constitute what other contributors to this volume refer to as national or collective memory.

Clearly, the main policy objective of a state is security. Among politicians, intellectuals and the media, however, there will be disagreements about the best policy to adopt in order to ensure that security. Some will propose an alliance with a given power, others wariness of it or even war with it. Some will propose the acquisition and retention of colonies, others their abandonment and concentration on securing domestic frontiers. To win the argument and to rally a wider public to their policy position, they will construct different myths of the nation's past and explain the values and aspirations that policy decisions must reflect. History will be rewritten, and rewritten in different ways, to legitimate competing policies.

There is no doubt that the most powerful memories in post-war France were those of the defeat of 1940 and foreign occupation. The French state was almost extinguished, one and a half million soldiers were held in prisoner of war camps, and the Germans (and to a lesser extent the Italians) helped themselves to tribute, raw materials, manufactured

59

goods, transport, labour and Jews. The government of Marshal Pétain, which sued for an armistice and preached collaboration with the Third Reich, told the French people that it was all their own fault, and that they had brought disaster on themselves by paying themselves too much, laziness, alcoholism and not having enough children. In exile in London Charles de Gaulle reminded the French of their long history of heroism and greatness in order to recall them from the path of 'surrender and despair' to that of 'honour and hope'. 'Would Joan of Arc, Richelieu, Louis XIV, Carnot, Napoleon, Gambetta, Poincaré or Marshal Foch,' he asked them, 'ever have agreed to hand all France's armoury to her enemies so that it could be used against her Allies?'[1] After France was liberated de Gaulle showed himself sensitive to the memories of suffering of the French people under the Occupation, which he wove into a story of national humiliation. 'In the last 145 years', he reflected, 'France has been invaded on seven different occasions. Paris has been occupied four times by the enemy. There is not a single power in the universe that has suffered as much. After each of these rapes, in the past, losses suffered and anguish about a renewed attack never failed to provoke deep divisions within the nation.'[2] But against that he set France's vocation of greatness, a history of overcoming defeat and achieving victory, which the French people must never forget and to which they must always aspire. As he famously began his *War Memoirs* in 1954, 'France cannot be France without greatness.'[3]

France and the 'Anglo-Saxons'

One of the perennial debates of French foreign policy was whether greatness was better achieved with the Americans and the British, or without them. On the one hand it was argued that as the Western Allies they had liberated French soil from the Germans in a combat that the French could not have won alone, and that after the war the United States in particular provided both funds for reconstructing a devastated economy and infrastructure and a defence umbrella against the new threat of Soviet aggression. This sense of dependency on the United States inspired a myth of America the liberator. In the autumn of 1945, before his untimely death in a car crash, General George Patton undertook a triumphal tour of French cities, which honoured him with their freedom. To mark the

[1] Charles de Gaulle, broadcast of 2 July 1940, in *Discours et Messages, I. 1940–1945* (Paris: Plon, 1970), 12.
[2] Charles de Gaulle, broadcast of 10 Dec. 1945, in *Discours et Messages I*, 656. The seven occasions he cited were 1792, 1793, 1814, 1815, 1870–1, 1914–18, and 1940–5.
[3] Charles de Gaulle, *Mémoires de Guerre. I. L'Appel, 1940–1942* (Paris: Plon, 1954), 1.

tenth anniversary of the Liberation a sacred flame lit at Arlington military ceremony was landed on the Normandy beaches and carried by American soldiers along a 'Voie de la Liberté' which followed the route of the liberating armies. The presence of American generals and diplomats was much requested at ceremonies in the towns and cities along the route.

An entirely different narrative of the American role, seeing them less as liberators than as conquerors, however, was constructed by General de Gaulle. He deeply resented the way in which President Roosevelt had demonstrated his personal dislike for him during the war, the prospect right up to August 1944 of an American deal with the Vichy government or the subsequent 'bridge' government led by Pétain's prime minister Laval and Herriot, speaker of the Chamber of Deputies, and the threat to impose an Allied Military Government in Occupied Territories (AMGOT) on France as it had on Italy and was to do in Germany. He was angered by the strategic plans of Eisenhower, which involved no French troops in the Normandy landings of June 1944, did not envisage the liberation of Paris and then required the evacuation of Strasbourg, contested between France and Germany since the French Revolution, and which French forces had newly taken. Lastly, he was infuriated that France, which had joined the war against Germany in 1944, was not invited to take part in the summits at which the future of Europe was decided. 'I was not at Yalta' became a constant, carping, refrain. Neither was de Gaulle enamoured of the British, who had given him a base in 1940 and recognised his government-in-exile, but clearly put their special relationship with the United States before any Anglo-French partnership. He frequently told the story of the conversation he had had with Churchill in 1944, on the eve of D-Day. Churchill had summoned de Gaulle from Algiers to tell him that the French would not be taking part in the Normandy landings. When de Gaulle protested that Churchill was simply obeying Roosevelt's orders, Churchill replied that if he had to choose between Roosevelt and de Gaulle he would always chose Roosevelt, and if he had to choose between Europe and the wider world he would always choose the wider world. Perhaps de Gaulle was out of step with the French people and his memory was individual rather than collective. Certainly his resentments were expressed more in private than in public, or took the form of dramatic snubs that were not fully explained. Thus when it became clear that he would not be invited to Yalta he had a row in Paris with Harry Hopkins, President Roosevelt's emissary, telling him that the United States had let France down in 1920 and 1940, that 'the return of France to her rank as a great power' was required for her internal peace and prosperity, and that the United States 'did not seem to appreciate that the very fate of France was tied to her vocation of greatness'.[4] He also refused to see Roosevelt on the latter's way home from Yalta, later telling journalists that this would have been tantamount to approving decisions taken in his absence.[5] However, he was not the only Frenchman to resent American highhandedness. Instructed to evacuate Strasbourg, it was the comander of the French First Army, General de Lattre de Tassigny, who told Eisenhower that 'Strasbourg is a symbol of the resistance and greatness of France ... Its abandonment would cause the French to doubt in victory, and would have world-wide repercussions ... military honour and the prestige of the Allied armies are at stake'.[6] Communists and left-wing Catholics attacked the presence of American forces in France. Graffiti such as 'Yankees go home' graced city walls, while in 1952 the arrival to take command of NATO forces of General Ridgway, who was said to have used biological weapons in the Korean war, provoked riots. Lastly, it was felt that price of American aid was the penetration of French markets by American products, from Hollywood films to Coca-Cola. Communists attacked 'Coca-colonisation' and French drink interests went to the courts in a vain attempt to have the drink banned on health grounds.[7]

Anti-Americanism vied with pro-Americanism among the French public, but after 1958 de Gaulle was in charge of foreign policy and was also equipped to impose the myths that sustained it. The core of his policy was that France must have an independent foreign policy and independent nuclear deterrent in order to hold its own against the superpowers, especially the United States. 'Having lived through great dramas over long centuries', he said in 1961, 'France knows that her army must be hers alone and that no other army will be secure.'[8] In 1964 he refused to attend the twentieth anniversary of the landings in Normandy, rehearsing all the old arguments about the American preference for Vichy, the AMGOT and the exclusion of French forces from D-Day. 'You want me to go and commemorate *their* landing', he asked his advisers, 'when it was the prelude to a second occupation of the country? No, don't count on me.'[9] As a result, US president Lyndon Johnson and Harold Wilson, the UK prime

---

[4] Charles de Gaulle, *Mémoires de Guerre II. Le salut, 1944–1946* (Paris: Plon, 1959), 390.

[5] Charles de Gaulle, press conference 12 Nov. 1947, in *Discours et Messages II. 1946–1958* (Paris: Plon, 1970), 158.

[6] General Jean de Lattre de Tassigny to General Dwight Eisenhower, via General Devers, 2 Jan. 1945, in his *Histoire de la Première Armée Française, Rhin et Danube* (Paris: Plon, 1949), 349–50.

[7] Richard Kuisel, *Seducing the French. The Dilemma of Americanization* (Berkeley: University of California Press, 1993), 48–9, 52–69.

[8] Charles de Gaulle, Strasbourg speech of 23 Nov. 1961, in *Discours et Messages III. 1958–1962* (Paris: Plon, 1970), 368. This was quoted with approval by Michel Debré in *Gouverner: 1958–1962* (Paris: Albin Michel, 1988), 374.

[9] Alain Peyrefitte, *C'était de Gaulle II* (Paris: Fayard, 1997), 85.

minister, did not go, and former US president Dwight D. Eisenhower, who had been supreme commander of the Allied forces in Western Europe in the Second World War, and Viscount Montgomery, the British commander who conducted the Normandy invasion, who were both due to participate, withdrew.

The same resentments lay behind de Gaulle's decision early in 1966 to withdraw from the military command structure of NATO and to require American forces to leave French soil. Aghast at the decision, the US ambassador, Charles Bohlen, sought out Michel Debré, then finance minister, and asked him how the presence of American forces in 1918 and 1944 had infringed French independence. Debré replied that in 1918 the Allied armies were commanded by Marshal Foch while in 1944 'you were the head, the soul and the strength of the coalition which delivered and saved us, but the French people had to force General de Gaulle on you, against your will, in order to avoid the AMGOT'. De Gaulle's decision in 1963 to veto the British request to join the Common Market may also be explained by resentments going back to the Second World War. When Harold Macmillan visited Rambouillet in December 1962 de Gaulle recalled the conversation he had had with Churchill on the eve of D-Day, to the effect that Britain would always choose the United States before Europe.[10] His description of Britain at the press conference where he delivered the veto as 'insular and maritime' betrayed his vision of the Common Market as none other than the Continental System of Napoleon, a customs area serving French purposes and shutting out Britain in order to asphyxiate it. The message was not lost on Macmillan, who complained to President Kennedy that 'De Gaulle is trying to dominate Europe. His idea is not a partnership, but a Napoleonic or Louis XIV hegemony'.[11] Georges Pompidou, who negotiated with Edward Heath Britain's entry into the Common Market in 1972, admitted that 'England could no longer put up with the Europe of Six, which must have reminded her of Napoleonic Europe and the Continental Blockade'.[12]

French presidents after de Gaulle and Pompidou were more aware of the benefits of good relations with the United States. France remained within the NATO alliance and during the presidency of Valéry Giscard d'Estaing the United States began to help the French behind the scenes with nuclear technology. The possession and control of an independent nuclear deterrent underpinned the autonomy of French foreign policy

[10] P. M. H. Bell, *France and Britain, 1940–1994. The Long Separation* (London and New York: Longman, 1997), 196. See also Peyrefitte, who added, 'Ce souvenir est indélébile', *C'était de Gaulle*, 84.

[11] Harold Macmillan, *At the End of the Day, 1961–1963* (London: Macmillan, 1973), 366.

[12] Georges Pompidou, *Entretiens et Discours, 1968–1974* (Paris: Plon, 1975), II, 127.

but also guaranteed France's permanent seat on the Security Council of the United Nations. This enabled France to find the way back to Yalta, in the sense of participating in the decisions of the inner sanctum of great powers. France increasingly became more relaxed about American leadership, and this policy change enabled the French to restore the myth of Americans as liberators. At the D-Day commemoration of 1984 US president Ronald Reagan soothed French amour-propre by insisting that the Americans had landed in 1944 'not as conquerors but as liberators', and he paid homage to the contribution of the French Resistance in which, he said, President François Mitterrand had played his part. Mitterrand himself discovered that seventy-seven French marines had actually participated in the landings of 6 June and unveiled a monument at Ouistreham in their honour.

France nevertheless had two policy reservations concerning the United States which might induce it to swing back to the myth of American domination. One was the threat to its independent nuclear deterrent of superpower disarmament negotiations. As talks between Reagan and Soviet leader Mikhail Gorbachev gathered pace, France's main concern was that they would bargain away its own deterrent. 'We are living at the time of Yalta', declared Mitterrand in 1986, in the sense that the United States and the Soviet Union might settle world affairs to the exclusion of all others. He took his cue from de Gaulle's script when he stated, 'while France favours disarmament, it is not disposed to put its national defence at the mercy of Russo-American negotiation . . . France and France alone will decide the affairs of France'.[13] Referring to another historical taboo subject after Gorbachev accepted the zero option in 1987, the Gaullist defence minister André Giraud rejected what he called a 'European Munich'. From de Gaulle to Jacques Chirac, France's constant position was to maintain a leverage between the superpowers by preserving its independent nuclear deterrent.

The second reservation concerned France's foreign policy in the Middle East, where France had cultivated a special relationship with Arab states from the time of Napoleon's expedition to Egypt and to France's mandate in Syria–Lebanon after the First World War. De Gaulle denounced Israeli aggression during the Six Day War, and after the oil crisis of 1973 France took the view that Arab states must be favoured in preference to Israel to safeguard France's oil supply. Selling arms and nuclear expertise to the Arabs, notably Iraq, was a good way of paying for it. After Iraq invaded Kuwait in 1990, France as a permanent member of the Security

---

[13] François Mitterrand, *Réflexions sur la Politique extérieure de la France* (Paris: Fayard, 1986), 12.

Council was reluctant to break rank and signed up to UN sanctions. But defence minister Jean-Pierre Chevènement, a Jacobin patriot, argued that American belligerence would drag France into a war which would ruin its Arab interests.[14] He then refused to accept the aim of destroying the military and nuclear potential of Iraq – 'the "big stick" applied on a scale never seen before' – and resigned.[15] Pompidou's foreign minister Michel Jobert, who had built up French relations with the Arab states after the 1973 oil crisis, joined the attack on the 'trailer policy' of France, hitched behind the United States while 'lecturing to us about the role and *grandeur* of France'. He praised Chevènement's resignation in the face of 'rampant Atlanticism', and argued that France was repeating the Suez fiasco which 'provoked the hostility of the Third World and buried her in the Algerian war, so that it took ten years to restore balanced relations with a whole range of countries, including Arab ones'.[16] Differences in foreign policy were thus legitimated by appeals to the two rival myths of the United States, one as leader of the free world, the other as an arrogant warmonger who had no concern for French interests and values.[17]

Franco-German relations

The French were agreed that the defeat and occupation in 1940–45 by Germany was impossibly painful and must not be allowed to recur. Policy-makers, however, were divided as to how to go about achieving this. One option was that Germany must be reduced to a position in which its renewed aggression was a military and economic impossibility. The other was that the *delenda est Carthago* attitude was not realistic and that Germany should be contained by the institutions of an ever more integrated Europe. Both of these options developed myths of the past to sustain them. The first held that since unification in 1870 Germany had been a militaristic and aggressive power. The peace imposed on it in 1919 had not been tough enough to prevent a German resurgence, and a modern 'Thirty Years War' between France and Germany had been

[14] Jacques Attali, *Verbatim III. 1988–91* (Paris: Fayard, 1995), entries for 21–2 Aug. 1990 (573–5), and 9–12 Jan. (682–6), 14–16 Jan. (696–702), 18 Jan. (706), 29 Jan. 1991 (715).

[15] Jean-Pierre Chevènement, *Une Certaine Idée de la France m'amène à …* (Paris: Albin Michel, 1991). The title is taken from his letter of resignation of 29 Jan. 1991, continuing 'vous demander de bien vouloir me décharger des fonctions que vous m'avez fait l'honneur de me confier'.

[16] Michel Jobert, *Journal du Golfe, août 1990–août 1991* (Paris: Albin Michel, 1991), 177, 226–7.

[17] This debate was resumed during the Iraq crisis of 1998. See for example the editorial of J.-M. Colombani in *Le Monde*, 26 Feb. 1998.

the result. The clock should therefore be put back beyond 1870, to a Germany as yet divided, and preferably to a Germany dominated by France, as in Napoleonic times. The other myth was that the harshness of the peace imposed in 1919 had in fact provoked German resurgence and that three Franco-German wars in seventy years had been caused by competition for the coal and iron resources of Lorraine, the Saar and the Ruhr. Only the removal of the causes of conflict by Franco-German cooperation within a European framework would ensure peace. These policy differences and these competing myths, feeding off each other, raged from 1945 to Maastricht and beyond.

De Gaulle, as head of the French government in 1944–6, tried to dispose of Germany as had Napoleon himself. German aggression must be made impossible by 'separating the territories of the left bank of the Rhine and the Ruhr basin from what will be the German state or states'.[18] France had to prevent the re-establishment of the unified, centralised Reich that had been 'the instrument of Bismarck, William II and Hitler'.[19] This draconian policy ran directly counter to American policy, which was to build up the federal institutions of West Germany as a buffer against the Soviet Union and made French acceptance of this a condition of Marshall aid. De Gaulle had left office and as foreign minister of the provisional government Georges Bidault had no option but to accept the pro-German terms of the treaty of London (June 1948), arguing that the approach must be 'to build Europe without undoing France'. For many French people, however, memories of the German Occupation were still too painful, and politicians still insisted that Germany must be severely weakened. Bidault was savaged by a parliament of Germanophobes, including Roland de Moustier, a conservative deputy from the Doubs, who compared Bidault unfavourably to Richelieu and suggested that the 'politics of *grandeur* had brought forth very bad fruit', and by Pierre Cot, a former Popular Front minister and resister, who argued that 'our Western allies need to make more of a distinction between the victims and the executioners than they are doing at present'.[20]

Out of the tension between historic French security needs and American Cold War strategy came the European solution of Robert Schuman and Jean Monnet. Natives of the contested borderland between France and Germany, such as Schuman, whose Lorrainer father had fought for France in 1870, while he himself fought for Germany in 1914, tended to favour Franco-German rapprochement as the only way to lasting peace. If

[18] De Gaulle, broadcast of 5 Feb. 1945, *Discours et Messages I*, 518.
[19] De Gaulle, speech at Bar-le-Duc, 28 July 1946, in *Discours et Messages II*, 13–14.
[20] *Journal Officiel de la République française. Débats parlementaires. Assemblée nationale. Séance du 12 juin 1948*, 3462, 3487–8.

German prosperity and power were to be restored as the Americans insisted, then it must be within a framework of European institutions which restricted German sovereignty. But as Schuman told an audience in London in 1953, 'if we wish to make Germany accept these restrictions, we must set her an example... equal treatment means that we cannot retain for ourselves more power... than Germany will have'.[21]

The solution was brilliant, but the question remained: would the French accept limitations on their sovereignty as the price of restraining Germany? The advantage to France of access to Ruhr coal through the European Coal and Steel Community were plain to see. But the European Defence Community (EDC), proposed by Monnet and prime minister René Pleven (in what became known as the Pleven Plan) in response to American pressure to rearm Germany, was more controversial. It raised the issue of the autonomy of the French army, and thus of French sovereignty and French national identity. Debate raged for four years, splitting all political parties down the middle. The trauma of recurrent war, which made cooperation seem the obvious solution for some French people, drove others to insist that a strong, independent national defence was non-negotiable. Supporters of the EDC saw it as rearming the Germans without rearming Germany, under American command. Opponents looked only at the impact on France: an attack on the French army which, the myth ran, had always guaranteed French security and French greatness. 'Why', asked de Gaulle, 'of all the great powers which currently have an army, is France alone to lose hers? What would remain of the prestige of the French nation, given that for centuries, in the eyes of the whole world, the value, greatness and identity of France have never been separated from its army?'[22] In the 1954 National Assembly debate on ratifying the EDC treaty signed two years earlier, Édouard Herriot, the grand old man of the Radical Party, announced that 'the army is the soul of the nation and I would like to know where this army of the European Community will find its soul... it is because the feelings developed by the French Revolution had such depth that the men who fought on the Marne had the courage to die in conditions that we must not forget'. As the treaty was voted down the Assembly rang with the *Marseillaise* and shouts of 'Down with the Wehrmacht!'[23]

The fact that as a result of this the Federal Republic of Germany immediately joined NATO and began to rearm anyway did not trouble the French unduly. Their main concern was that France's own military

[21] Robert Schuman, *French Policy towards Germany since the War*, Stevenson Memorial Lecture, London, 29 Oct. 1953 (London: Oxford University Press, 1954), 21.

[22] De Gaulle, speech at Nancy, 25 Nov. 1951, in *Discours et Messages II*, 479.

[23] *Journal Officiel, Assemblée Nationale, 29 août 1954*, 4468, 4471.

autonomy and national sovereignty should not be restricted. For similar reasons, General de Gaulle, back in office, was prepared to accept the Common Market which came into force on 1 January 1959: Europe would be a 'Europe of states', opposing plans for political unity, while a Europe of Six, based on a Franco-German rapprochement and excluding Great Britain, would be dominated by France as senior partner. In fact it would look very much like the core of the Napoleonic empire in Italy, Germany and the Low Countries. Speaking in Milan in 1959, de Gaulle reminded the Italians that a century before, at Solferino, French armies had sponsored their national self-determination.[24] While Britain continued to be pilloried as the old enemy who had to be kept out of Europe, the myth of an aggressive Germany could now be revised. Welcoming Federal Chancellor Konrad Adenauer in July 1962, de Gaulle praised the Chancellor's opposition to Nazism and proclaimed that he had 'resolutely led [Germany] along the opposite road, that of reason and respect for others'.[25] So long as France remained in the driving seat, it could afford to elaborate the myth of the 'good Germans' who had been taken over and tyrannised by the Nazi regime but were fundamentally committed to freedom, peace and prosperity.

The myth of the good German with whom business could be done was sustained by excellent personal relationships between President Giscard d'Estaing and Chancellor Helmut Schmidt, then between President Mitterrand and Chancellor Helmut Kohl. When the Germans were not invited to the D-Day commemoration of 1984, Mitterrand endeavoured to make up for this by meeting Kohl at Verdun the following September. *Le Monde* considered that the battlefields of the First World War provided a better shrine for Franco-German reconciliation than the sites of memory of the Second World War, since the former had not 'left the same traces in hearts and memories as the occupation of France by a Nazified Germany'. Mitterrand, however, took the opportunity to develop the myth of the good German, arguing that both French and Germans had been victims of the Nazi dictatorship. The enemy in the Second World War, he made clear, was 'not Germany but the government, the system, the ideology that had seized it... Yesterday's enemies are now reconciled and together are building a Europe of liberties... Europe is our common fatherland'.[26]

The famous picture of Mitterrand taking Kohl by the hand at Verdun symbolised Franco-German friendship but also the nervous grip of France on Germany, lest the latter recover its own autonomy and begin to

---

[24] De Gaulle, speech of 24 June 1959, in *Discours et Messages III*, 131.
[25] De Gaulle, speech of 2 July 1962, in *Discours et Messages III*, 432.
[26] *Le Monde*, 25 September 1984.

reassert itself. While France remained the dominant power in Europe and was able substantially to shape it in her own image she was keen to repress the counter-myth of a powerful and aggressive Germany. The fall of the Berlin Wall and the reunification of Germany, however, awakened deep fears in France of a 'fourth Reich' of eighty million Germans wielding 'colossal economic power', leading to a 'Bismarckian Europe'.[27] A Pancho cartoon in *Le Monde* pinpointed the French sense of insecurity about her frontiers: Mitterrand says to Kohl, 'You haven't said anything about the Oder–Neisse line', and Kohl replies, 'Nor about Alsace-Lorraine'.[28] Whereas under the guidance of Jacques Delors the deepening of the European Union by the Maastricht Treaty opened up the vista of continued French domination, now the phenomenon of a resurgent Germany escaping from French control rekindled the anguished debate that had raged about the European Defence Community more than thirty years before. Europhiles took the view that the European Community had to deepen in order to anchor Germany in partnership and prevent a neutralist drift towrds the Soviet Union; Eurosceptics opposed any movement towards federalism on the grounds, as in the 1950s, that any controls imposed on Germany would also be imposed on France and that any limitation of French national sovereignty would render her incapable of protecting her own national interests.

In the debate over the Maastricht Treaty each side fought to appropriate historical myths to underpin its case and to discredit that of its opponents. Opening the debate in the National Assembly, prime minister Pierre Bérégovoy announced that he had lived through the débâcle of 1940 as an adolescent and (without acknowledging it) using the formula of Bidault, that he wished to 'build Europe . . . without undoing France'. He quoted Victor Hugo's panegyric on the the United States of Europe, interrupted by an ironic Jean-Louis Debré, 'the Bébête Show is better!'[29] The left was far from united, however, and Chevènement drew different conclusions from the fact that France had been 'wounded body and soul twice in one century'. He argued that it had lost confidence in its ability to influence events and was 'melting into the new Holy German-American Empire of capital'. Instead of the 'Lilliputian strategy of binding herself in order to bind Germany better', it must 'reinvent the Republic' and build Europe alongside Germany as two nation-states with a grip on

---

[27] Claire Tréan on Foreign Minister Dumas's 'ostrich policy' in *Le Monde*, 14 Oct. 1989. See also Alain Peyrefitte in *Le Figaro*, 11 Nov. 1989, Michel Colomès in *Le Point*, 26 Nov. 1989, and Dave Berry and Martyn Cornick, 'French Responses to German Unification', in *Modern and Contemporary France*, 49 (April 1992), 42–55.

[28] *Le Monde*, 10–11 Dec. 1989.

[29] *Journal Officiel. Débats parlementaires. Assemblée nationale*, 5 May 1992, 840.

themselves and their pasts.[30] The Gaullists too were divided, with Alain Juppé arguing that the Maastricht Treaty was in the direct tradition of Robert Schuman, while Philippe Séguin led the charge against Maastricht by wheeling out the old argument that under the Declaration of Rights and the Constitution of 1958 national sovereignty belonged to the people and could not be alienated. He argued that from the Hundred Years War to the battle of Valmy in 1792 national sovereignty had been secured by national independence, and that national identity itself was at stake: the treaty would leave the French 'our cheeses and a few of our customs . . . perhaps the *Marseillaise* too on condition that we change the words'.[31] Gaullists in the one camp argued that the General would have supported the treaty, Gaullists in the other asserted that he would have attacked it. Jacques Chirac, speaking near Strasbourg, declared that 'Maastricht is the prolongation of a policy endorsed by General de Gaulle'.[32] Michel Debré *père*, campaigning against Maastricht as he had once campaigned against the EDC, attempted to force the issue by framing it in terms of collaboration and resistance: 'Laval would have said yes to the Maastricht agreement', he asserted, 'de Gaulle would have said no'.[33] In the game of historical leapfrog, however, few could match the confidence of one poster in Paris which announced, 'Napoleon would have voted for Maastricht'.[34]

France and empire

In the years after the Second World War France, like other west European countries, was absorbed by the debate about whether to retain or to give up her empire. Given the paralysis of state power during the war France in fact had to regain its empire in 1945 before it could decide what to do with it. The policy issue was shaped by and helped to shape two rival myths: one of France's vocation of greatness, of which the empire was both an expression and a guarantee, the other of France's liberating mission, as defined in the constitution of 1791, essentially repeated in that of 1946, that 'the French nation renounces the undertaking of war with a view to conquest, and will never use its strength against the liberty

---

[30] *Le Monde*, 8 May 1992. For fuller arguments see his *France-Allemagne: Parlons franc* (Paris: Plon, 1996).
[31] *Journal Officiel, Assemblée Nationale*, 5 May 1992, 863–78. His speech was published separately as *Discours pour la France* (Paris: Grasset, 1992).
[32] *Le Monde*, 9 Sept. 1992.
[33] Michel Debré, *Combattre toujours, 1969–1993* (Paris: Albin Michel, 1994), 175–6, 221.
[34] Robert Gildea, *The Past in French History* (New Haven and London: Yale University Press, 1994), 110.

of any people'.[35] Addressing the French Consultative Assembly in May 1945, Gaston Monnerville, an assimilated black from French Guiana and future president of the French upper house, tried to reconcile the two myths. 'Without the Empire, France would not be a liberated country', he said, reflecting on the crucial rallying of the French empire in Africa to de Gaulle, but adding, 'thanks to its Empire France is a conquering power.'[36]

In reality it was more difficult to reconcile the two strands. Thus on 8 May 1945, when victory against the Third Reich was being celebrated in Europe, in Algeria French troops were massacring rioters, with even French communists claiming that the rioters were inspired by Hitlerian agents.[37] But at the level of myth, some reconciliation was possible through the claim of France's civilising mission. Embedded deep in Enlightened thought was the notion that liberty could only legitimately be enjoyed by peoples who had been brought to a certain level of civilisation. The 1946 constitution of the Fourth Republic declared that 'faithful to her traditional mission, France intends to guide the peoples for whom she has taken responsibility to freedom of self-administration'. This meant raising them materially and mentally to a level at which they might administer themselves, but always within the framework of the French Union. By subordinating liberty to civilisation the French mind found a seductive way of holding on to its empire in order to preserve great-power status, and legitimating the repression of national movements for self-determination that were regarded as premature. Thus the bombardment of Haiphong in November 1946 killed about six thousand Vietnamese, while the insurrection in Madagascar in 1947 was put down at a cost of up to 200,000 lives.

These contradictions came to a climax, of course, over the Algerian war. At stake was the myth of French greatness, for after the loss of Indochina in 1954 Algeria was the principal remaining guarantee of that greatness. Pierre Mendès France, who was attacked as a 'capitulator' for ending the war in Indochina, was for this reason keen to 'maintain the unity and indivisibility of the Republic, of which Algeria is a part.'[38]

---

[35] Jacques Godechot, *Les Constitutions de la France depuis 1789* (Paris: Flammarion, 1979), 65.

[36] Charles-Robert Ageron, 'La Survivance d'un mythe. La Puissance par l'empire coloniale (1944–1947)', in René Girault and Robert Frank (eds.), *La Puissance française en question, 1945–1949* (Paris: Publications de la Sorbonne, 1988), 32.

[37] Grégoire Madjarian, *La Question coloniale et la Politique du Parti Communiste Français, 1944–1947* (Paris, Maspéro, 1977), 103.

[38] Pierre Birnbaum, *Anti-semitism in France: a political history from Léon Blum to the present* (Oxford: Blackwell, 1992), 289–90; Pierre Mendès France, *Dire la Vérité: Causeries du Samedi, juin 1954–février 1955* (Paris: Julliard, 1955), 60.

His governor-general in Algeria, the tough former Resistance leader, Jacques Soustelle, argued that 'It is precisely *because* we have lost Indochina... that we must not, at any price, in any way and under any pretext, lose Algeria.'[39] Algeria also formed part of France's liberation myth, having in 1943–4 been the seat of France's government-in-exile, the Committee of National Liberation. However, the civilising mission, which historically provided a bridge between the two myths, proved increasingly unable to fulfil its task as French intellectuals divided about what precisely liberty and civilisation meant in this context.

Whereas it might be supposed that most French intellectuals would take the side of Algerian nationalists, in fact former Dreyfusards, anti-fascists and resisters took the side, by and large, not of the freedom-fighters but of the French police and army, whom they saw as upholding French values of individual liberty, democracy and secularisim against fanaticism and barbarism. Albert Bayet, an ex-Dreyfusard, and Paul Rivet, one of the founders of the Vigilance Committee of Anti-Fascist Intellectuals in the 1930s, signed a petition denouncing the rebels as 'instruments of a theocratic, racist and fanatical imperialism', by which they meant Islam, and asked, 'who, if not the *patrie* of the Rights of Man, can clear a human way to the future' for the populations of Algeria?[40] Albert Camus, whose roots were in Algeria, condemned the terrorism that might one day strike down his mother and told students, 'I believe in justice, but I would defend my mother before justice.'[41] Bidault, who had chaired the National Council of the Resistance which had grouped resistance movements and political parties in France in 1943–4, set up another one in 1962 to oppose the idea of Algerian independence and saw himself moving logically 'from one resistance to another'.[42] A minority of intellectuals, however, took the view that the ideology of the Resistance required support for a people fighting for its freedom and that by their brutality the French were betraying their claims to have a civilising mission. When it became known that French police and paratroopers were using torture against Algerian nationalists in order to elicit information, they provoked a violent debate and crisis of identity by suggesting that what the Gestapo had done to the French, the French were now doing to the Algerians. The human rights activist and journalist Claude Bourdet denounced 'Your Gestapo in Algeria', while Jean-Paul Sartre argued that 'if fifteen years are enough

---

[39] Jacques Soustelle, *Le Drame algérien et la décadence française* (Paris: Plon, 1957), 68.

[40] *Le Monde*, 21 April 1956, cited by Jean-François Sirinelli, 'Guerre d'Algérie, Guerre des Pétitions? Quelques jalons', in J.-P. Rioux and J.-F. Sirinelli (eds.), *La Guerre d'Algérie et les intellectuels français*, Cahiers 10 (Paris: Institut d'Histoire du Temps Présent, 1988), 189–90.

[41] Interview of 13 Dec. 1957, cited by David L. Schalk, *War and the Ivory Tower* (New York and Oxford: Oxford University Press, 1991), 65.

[42] Georges Bidault, *D'une Résistance à l'autre* (Paris: les Presses du Siècle, 1965).

to turn victims into executioners, it must be opportunity alone which decides ... anyone, any time, can become either victim or executioner'.[43] One of the key French organisations opposing the war in Algeria called itself Jeune Résistance, while the Manifesto published in 1960 by 121 intellectuals headed by Sartre enunciated the radical, relativist doctrine that 'the cause of the Algerian people, which contributes decisively to undermining the colonial system, is the cause of all free peoples'.[44] In the *Damnés de la Terre*, for which Sartre wrote a preface, moreover, Frantz Fanon attacked colonialism not as the vehicle of liberty or civilization but as the purveyor of violence, torture and genocide.[45]

The Algerian war has been described as the 'impossible memory', blocked off and repressed because it in fact undermined the imperatives of greatness, liberation and the civilising mission. It was never in fact referred to as a war, but as 'the events', a problem of public order in French territories. Songs such as Boris Vian's 'Le Déserteur' (1954) and Jean-Luc Godard's film, *Le Petit Soldat*, were banned during the hostilities.[46] The rebels, headed by General Salan, who resorted to the military putsch and the terrorism of the OAS to prevent the 'abandonment' of Algeria were put on trial, but the 'abandonment' was not allowed to tarnish France's self-image. De Gaulle announced in Guadaloupe in 1964 that 'the international situation of our country is more brilliant, more assured than it ever was. We are a great nation.'[47] The 'police pogrom' against Algerians demonstrating in favour of Algeria for the Algerians, directed by Maurice Papon, then Paris prefect of police, on 17 October 1961, was long hushed up until brought into the open by SOS-Racism, an organisation representing the 'Beurs' or French-born Algerians. Conscripts organised in the National Federation of Veterans of the Algerian War were not recognised fully as veterans until 1974, and their attempts to have 19 March 1962, the date of the Evian agreement which ended hostilities, officially commemorated, aroused the hostility of the main veterans' association, which demanded 'Do you celebrate Waterloo or Agincourt?', and of professional soldiers who refused on principle to drink Evian water.[48]

---

[43] Pascal Ory and Jean-François Sirinelli, *Les Intellectuels en France, de l'Affaire Dreyfus à nos jours* (Paris: Armand Colin, 1986), 199; Jean-Paul Sartre, *La Victoire* (Paris: Pauvert, 1966), 100.

[44] Jean-Pierre Vittori, *Nous les appelés d'Algérie* (Paris: Stock, 1977), 286–8.

[45] Frantz Fanon, *Les Damnés de la Terre* (Paris: Maspéro, 1961).

[46] Benjamin Stora, *La Gangrène et l'Oubli. La Mémoire de la Guerre d'Algérie* (Paris: Éditions de la Découverte, 1991), 40.

[47] Charles de Gaulle, speech of 20 Mar. 1964, in *Discours et Messages IV, 1962–1965* (Paris: Plon, 1965), 200.

[48] *Le Monde*, 18 Mar. 1992; interview with General Yves de Sesmaisons, Nantes, 16 July 1997.

Not only have many French been unwilling to come to terms with the loss of Algeria, they have also seized on recent events to suggest that they were right to try to hold on to it. The rise of the Islamic Salvation Front, its election victory cut short by the Algerian military government in 1991, and the consequent escalation of Islamist terrorism have re-opened the controversy as to where freedom and civilisation lie. 'Today', said François Bayrou, general secretary of the Union pour la Démocratie Française (UDF), on the fortieth anniversary of the end of the war, 'people realise that Camus was right.' Seeing the conflict in terms of secu-larism and fundamentalism, the Gaullist deputy Elizabeth Hubert stated that she 'felt solidarity with the lay, modernist élites. You simply can't negotiate with fundamentalists'.[49] After a wave of massacres in 1997 in-tellectuals such as Bernard-Henri Lévy and Alain Finkielkraut rehearsed the 'Enlightened' view of the 1950s that while the Algerian government was reaching out for democracy and building up oil wealth, 'savage' Islamist fanatics had a 'massacre strategy' and hundreds of emirs were is-suing *fatwas* ordering the 'extermination of civilians'.[50] On the other side Pierre Vidal-Naquet, who had published *La Torture dans la République* in 1983, riposted, arguing that most of the massacres in Algeria were the work of militias armed by the Algerian military. He put the case of the 'latter-day Dreyfusards' against those who argued simply that 'The Algerian throat-slitters kill in the name of Islam, therefore Islam is the killer. There is nothing else to understand: the religious madness that has perpetrated mass killings in history is once again at work in Algeria.'[51]

Conclusion

All myths are artificial constructs, but some are more artificial than oth-ers. A distinction may be proposed between myths elaborated to support a particular policy which have a relatively weak connection with collec-tive memory, and myths that may be used to support particular policies but have a powerful connection with collective memory. Myths that are essentially driven by policy, it may be argued, will have difficulty over-riding those that are founded on powerful and deep-seated collective experiences.

The myth of the United States as a world bully having no understand-ing of or concern with French national interests still holds some sway, as illustrated over the Gulf War. But it has not triumphed over the myth of

[49] *Le Monde*, 18 Mar. 1992.
[50] *Le Monde*, 8 and 9 Jan. 1998; *Libération*, 21 Jan. 1998.
[51] François Gèze and Pierre Vidal-Naquet, 'L'Algérie et les Intellectuels français', *Le Monde*, 4 Feb. 1998.

the United States as France's liberator in 1944, a myth that has become reinforced over the decades by the myth that America has shown the way to freedom and prosperity. The myth of the good German developed to lay the basis of Franco-German rapprochement has certainly made progress, but it has not seen off the myth of Germany as a large, aggressive power which is founded on painful collective memories of the Occupation. For that reason, policy moves towards a more integrated Europe, while that Europe appears to be dominated by Germany, will always have trouble rallying a reliable majority of public opinion in France. By the same token, the myth that French conduct during the Algerian war could be equated to that of the Germans in France during the Second World War never unseated the myth of France's liberating and civilising mission. Though this took a hammering in the Algerian crisis, the way in which Algeria subsequently fell prey to Islamist terrorism has given comfort to those who argued that the liberty and civilisation offered by France was genuine and that Islam could only ever offer repression and barbarism. The only myth that seems have survived intact whatever the vagaries of collective experience is that of French *grandeur*. Frequently it has borne little resemblance to the reality of French power but it has always been multifaceted, cultural as much as military. On 14 July 1998 the traditional display of military hardware on the Champs-Elysées was eclipsed by the guests at the Elysée Palace garden party greeting the victorious World Cup football team with a rendering of 'We are the champions!'

3 The power of memory and memories of power: the cultural parameters of German foreign policy-making since 1945

Thomas Berger

The study of post-1945 German foreign policy has been distinguished by the perennial debate between those experts who claim that the Federal Republic is on the brink of a major transformation in the way it approaches defence and national security, and other experts who insist with equal vehemence that the very little change is in the offing. At the core of this debate is the issue of German historical memory. To what extent have Germans learned lessons from their history? How deeply rooted are those memories in the institutions and collective consciousness of the nation? Even analysts who deny that such factors as memory or culture have any real causal force in world affairs typically sift through German debates over the past for evidence that a shift in behaviour is under way.

During the 1970s, for instance, many observers warned that Germany's pursuit of its own version of détente with the Soviet Union, Ostpolitik, signalled a return to the traditional German policy of balancing the East against the West and could lead to an unravelling of Germany's commitment to the Atlantic alliance.[1] Defenders of the Brandt government, on the other hand, insisted that Ostpolitik represented an adjustment to the American policy of détente and an increased German willingness to live up to its responsibility to the victims of the Nazi regime, the majority of whom lived in Eastern Europe. The stormy political battles over the deployment of a new generation of theatre nuclear weapons in the 1980s called forth similarly contradictory reactions. Critics on the German left warned that the missile deployments heralded the revival of German Realpolitik thinking and represented a perfidious cooption of the Federal Republic into the belligerent foreign policy stance of the administration of US president Ronald Reagan. More conservative analysts for their part claimed that the Christian Democratic government was standing up to Soviet provocations and that it was the left that represented

---

[1] See for instance Walter S. Hahn, 'West Germany's Ostpolitik: The Grand Design of Egon Bahr', *Orbis*, 16 (Winter 1973).

the rebirth of a romantic German nationalism that would undermine the Western alliance.[2]

In retrospect it would appear that both the prophets of change as well as the prognosticators of continuity overstated their case. Ostpolitik and the deployment of an intermediate nuclear force (INF) were in fact significant policy decisions, with far-reaching implications for both German domestic politics and the international system. At the same time, they neither led to a fundamental transformation of German foreign policy nor signalled the re-emergence of a more nationalist German approach to foreign affairs. In fact, what is remarkable is the extent to which arguably the basic features of the foreign policy course that the Federal Republic had charted in the 1950s have remained unaltered for nearly five decades, despite the tumultuous events of the past half-century. The Federal Republic continues to be firmly committed to the institutional structures of the Western alliance, it has eschewed increasing its military power beyond the minimum held to be necessary for the defence of its territory, and in general it has pursued conciliatory policies towards its neighbours. At the same time, since the 1960s Germany has shown an admirable resolve to confront its troubled past and in doing so it has shunned all expressions of the intense nationalism and power politics thinking that characterised German politics and foreign policy in the past.

Today, analysts across a broad spectrum of political and theoretical positions once again argue that Germany is set on a course that will lead to fundamental shifts in its foreign and national security policies. The reasons cited in support of such a view appear at first glance clear and compelling: the end of the Cold War and German reunification has fundamentally altered Germany's geo-strategic environment. No longer a divided nation on the front line of the East–West conflict, it finds itself at the heart of an expanding European union faced with a range of options as well as a score of challenges that were virtually inconceivable a decade earlier. As these momentous changes in Germany's international settings are taking place, domestically the debate over Germany's national identity has once more burst on to the political stage with great fanfare. As in the past, this debate is tied *nolens volens* to the country's troubled political past. Leading analysts and politicians, once more, are drawn into debates about the lessons of history. While such debates are not new by any measure, their scope and vitriol appear to be without precedent. From the perspective of many observers, the timing and character of these debates

---

[2] Jeffrey Herf, *War by Other Means: Soviet Power, West German Resistance and the Battle over the Euromissiles* (New York: Free Press, 1991).

lends further credence to the view that a fundamental change is under way.[3]

Germany's participation in the 1999 NATO military campaign in Kosovo may be seen as the final proof that the new Berlin Republic has shed the ghosts of the past and is prepared to act unfettered on the world stage. For the first time the armed forces of the Federal Republic flew combat missions over a territory that had been occupied by the German Wehrmacht during the Second World War. German armoured columns were shown on German television rolling across the green fields of Macedonia. German flight commanders, cool and self-confident, were interviewed in the media. All this, it might be added, occurred under a Social Democratic–Green coalition government, acting without a UN mandate, with hardly a trace of the sort of massive popular protest that had accompanied the Gulf War less than a decade earlier.

This chapter will argue that such fears regarding a deeper tectonic shift in post-Second World War German political culture are misplaced. While important shifts in the international environment have indeed led to significant changes in German foreign policy-making, the underlying principles that have informed German foreign policy-making and national security for close to half a century remain intact. These principles include most importantly a commitment to multilateralism, a preference for non-military instruments of foreign policy, and a defence strategy based in equal measure on deterrence and reassurance. While this approach to foreign policy represents a calculated response to the political exigencies faced by the Federal Republic in the 1950s and 60s, it has taken on a dynamic of its own. Rather than a merely tactical calculation aimed at maximising 'objective' German national interests, the new multilateralism and the emphasis on non-military instruments of diplomacy are rooted in a distinctive interpretation of the German past and of German national identity that has come to permeate the entire German political system. Consequently, while German foreign policy undoubtedly will continue to evolve in the future, German leaders in the new 'Berlin Republic' will seek to adhere to the same principles that had guided their predecessors in Bonn, and predictions of dramatic change, once again, will remain unfulfilled.

One of the main reasons why analyses and commentaries on German foreign policy, both academic and non-academic, frequently have been off the mark is that the major theoretical models used in the study of international relations by and large fail to deal systematically with the political

---

[3] Regarding the debate provoked by the Chancellor Gerhard Schröder's comments regarding a new, unburdened German relationship to its past, see Werner A. Perger, 'Wir Unbefangenen', *Die Zeit*, 12 November 1998.

culture and historical memory. Researchers studying German foreign policy encounter a superabundance of references to historical issues in the German public discourse on defence and national security. The general tendency has been either to ignore the role of collective memory or to factor it in on an ad hoc basis, as an addition to models of foreign policy-making based on such factors as the distribution of power in the international system or the existence of formal international institutions.[4] To compensate for this gap this chapter will begin by explicating a theoretical model of collective memory that addresses some of the central issues in its analysis and the ways in which collective memory may influence foreign policy-making. The subsequent two sections then apply this framework to show how post-war Germany's domestic political debates evolved in response to pressures emanating from the country's external political environment. In conclusion I examine the likelihood of fundamental changes in the Federal Republic's post-war political culture occurring and whether and to what degree parallel shifts in foreign and national security policies are likely to follow.

Memory, political culture and foreign policy formation – a theoretical model

Memory exists on a variety of levels: the individual, the generational and the collective. For the individual, memories are recollections of events that have been directly experienced by that individual at an earlier point in time, regardless of whether these recollections are accurate, or whether these events actually occurred at all. On a generational level memories are recollections of the past shared by large numbers of its members. Entire generations of people bear with them certain common recollections – for instance of the Kennedy assassination, which was a defining moment for most adults living in the United States at the time. Likewise German Federal Chancellor Willy Brandt's famous *Kniefall* before the monument to the Warsaw ghetto uprising, broadcast on television news

---

[4] In recent years, however, there has been a spate of literature that takes the issue of historical memory and its impact on German foreign policy more seriously: Andrei S. Markovits and Simon Reich, *The German Predicament: Memory and Power in the New Europe* (Ithaca, NY: Cornell University Press, 1997); John S. Duffield, *World Power Forsaken: Political Culture, International Institutions and German Security Policy after Unification* (Stanford, CA: Stanford University Press, 1998); Peter J. Katzenstein (ed.), *Tamed Power: Germany and the New Europe* (Ithaca, NY: Cornell University Press, 1998); Thomas Banchoff, 'German Policy towards the European Union: The Effects of Historical Memory', *German Politics*, 6, 1 (April 1997); Gunther Hellmann, 'The Sirens of Power and German Foreign Policy: Who is Listening?' *German Politics*, 6, 2 (August 1997); and Thomas Berger, *Cultures of Antimilitarism: National Security in Germany and Japan* (Baltimore, MD: Johns Hopkins University Press, 1998).

shows and plastered across the front pages of newspapers and magazines around the world, became an image that was seared in the minds of virtually every German adult of the time. Such shared societal memories define a political generation. They provide that generation with a sense of identity and serve as common reference points. They also may create profound fault lines in social, political and economic values between different age cohorts in a given society.[5] Collective memory differs from the other two forms in that it is based not on the direct experiences of individuals or groups of individuals in a society, but rather the memories of the collectivity as a (necessarily fictitious) whole. At the most basic level collective memory exists as various types of communication – in the form of official histories taught in schools and institutions of higher learning, in the written accounts produced by historians, novelists and film makers, in the rhetoric of political leaders and parties. Collective memory is embodied physically in such symbols as the flag and the national anthem, and is passed down as oral lore from one generation to the next in the context of the church, the work place and the family.[6]

Like individual and societal memories, collective memories serve an important practical function. They provide the collectivity with an identity and a common myth of origin. They endow it with emotional and normative underpinning. They simplify the task of organising collective action by providing its members with a common language and set of understandings about how the world functions and ought to function. Political leaders who seek to mobilise societal resources for some common goal typically invoke collective memories to explain and legitimise their policies. Likewise, political leaders' understanding of the world is shaped by collective memories, often in subtle ways.

All three levels of memory are necessarily interlinked. Intersubjective understandings of the society and the collectivity may reinforce or alter the individual's memories of his or her own experiences. By the same token individual memories can undermine shared and collective memories when the level of dissonance becomes too great – as evidently occurred on a massive scale in Eastern Europe under communism. At the same time, these different levels of memory are analytically distinct – existing at different levels of society and responding to often quite different forces.

---

[5] A classical analysis of the question of political generations is Karl Mannheim, 'The Problem of Generations', in Karl Mannheim, *Essays on the Sociology of Knowledge*, ed. Paul Kecskemeti, 5th edn (London: Routledge & Kegan Paul, 1972 [1952]).

[6] For an interesting application of the concept of collective memory to the study of German foreign policy, see Markovits and Reich, *The German Predicament*, especially the discussion on pages 14–20. The definition of collective memory given here differs from Markovits and Reich insofar as it lays a heavier emphasis on the cognitive as well as the normative and legitimation functions of collective memory.

All too often, however, they are confounded with one another. For instance, with respect to the Federal Republic it is often claimed that once the generation of leaders with direct experience of the war disappears, Germany's inhibitions regarding the use of force are likely to fade.[7] What this all too facile analysis overlooks is the way in which one form of memory can turn into another, and thus have consequences that far outlast the lives of individuals or groups of individuals.

Collective memories are part of the larger political culture of a country. As such they are of greater durability than either individual or generational memories.[8] Like cultures, however, historical memory is subject to change. In the history of a nation certain events which were once salient in the collective fade, to be displaced by other, more recent, events. Sometimes these changes are the result of deliberate manipulation by various political and cultural elites.[9] At other times memories change naturally, as each generation inevitably translates the past in the light of their own experiences.[10]

The analysis of the impact of collective historical memory on foreign policy poses a number of serious methodological obstacles. Three in particular require special attention. The first is the problem of measurement. Since culture is intangible and immaterial it can only be measured indirectly and imprecisely. As the German political scientist Max Kaase put it, trying to nail down culture is like trying to nail pudding to the wall.[11] Second, there is the problem of establishing the relationship between culture and actual behaviour. Are the particular historical memories and historically grounded norms and values invoked by leaders in connection with their decisions actually motivating factors, or are they merely empty rhetoric added on in a post-hoc fashion? Alternatively, might not the lessons of history influence policy-making even when they are not invoked?[12] Third, and finally, there is the problem of specifying the

---

[7] See for instance, Timothy Garton Ash, 'Germany's Choice', *Foreign Affairs*, 73, 4 (July/August, 1994), 74.

[8] For a good overview of the evolution of the concept of political culture, see Stephen Welch, *The Concept of Political Culture* (New York: St. Martin's Press, 1993). Note that collective historical memory is only one form of culture, and there may be many others that originate in different societal processes. For a more extended analysis, see Berger, *Cultures of Antimilitarism*, 9–11.

[9] See for instance David D. Laitin, *Hegemony and Culture: Politics and Religious Change among the Yoruba* (Chicago: University of Chicago Press, 1986).

[10] For a classic example of this view of history see, Theodor Mommsen, *A History of Rome under the Roman Emperors* (London: Routledge, 1996).

[11] Max Kaase, 'Sinn oder Unsinn des Konzepts "politische Kultur"', in Max Kaase and Hans D. Klingemann (eds.), *Wahlen und Politisches System* (Opladen: Westdeutscher Verlag, 1979).

[12] For a discussion of this problem see Donald Elkins and R. Simeon, 'A Cause in Search of its Effects or what does Political Culture explain?' *Comparative Politics*, 11 (1979). See also Welch, *The Concept of Political Culture*.

conditions under which cultures change. Obviously cultures do change, but if they change in response to every shift in their external environment, or change in a random and arbitrary manner, they become either epiphenomenal or impervious to systematic analysis.[13]

These problems are not unique to the study of political culture. It is just as difficult, if not more so, for a rational-choice theorist to deduce the preference structures of individual actors and relate them to group behaviour as it is to nail down historically grounded beliefs and values.[14] Analyses in the historical–institutionalist mode suffer from the same problems as cultural theorists when dealing with the problem of change.[15] Nonetheless, in order to demonstrate and track the actual impact of historical memory on state behaviour it is incumbent upon the analyst carefully to craft a research strategy for analysing the relationship between historical memory and foreign policy behaviour.

The first step in such a research strategy is to trace the origins of a particular set of collective memories and investigate the ways in which such memories became embedded in the culture and the political system. Since events do not speak for themselves, the analyst must explore the ways in which pivotal events in a nation's history are addressed by different groups in a society, especially political leaders and intellectuals. The method used is necessarily an interpretative one, requiring the investigator to engage in an in-depth analysis of the statements of the chief participants in the opinion-forming segments of society. Public opinion data, popular culture and other reflections of popular attitudes can be used as supplements for investigating the way in which collective memory becomes institutionalised in the society, although political scientists may wish to focus in the first instance on the political debate.[16]

---

[13] For a discussion of the problem of change, see Harry Eckstein, 'A Culturalist Theory of Political Change', in Harry Eckstein, *Regarding Politics: Essays on Political Theory, Stability and Change* (Berkeley: University of California Press, 1992).

[14] In this sense the charge that cultural explanations are inherently post-hoc rationalisations of whatever has occurred can just as easily be levelled against rational choice theory or any other theory of human behaviour that relies on some model of actor motivation. See Brian Barry, *Sociologists, Economists and Democracy* (London: Collier-Macmillan, 1970), and Carole Pateman, 'Political Culture, Political Structure and Political Change', *British Journal of Sociology*, 1, 3 (July 1971).

[15] Sven Steinmo, Kathleen Thelen and Frank Longstreth (eds). *Structuring Politics: Historical Institutionalism in Comparative Perspective* (New York: Cambridge University Press, 1992), esp. 13–22.

[16] Various other forms of data, including literature and films and other forms of popular culture, can be used as well to investigate the construction of historical memory. For an innovative exploration of collective memory as reflected in debates over the construction of public monuments, see Rudy Koshar, *Germany's Transient Pasts: Preservation and National Memory in the Twentieth Century* (Chapel Hill, NC: University of North Carolina Press, 1998).

The main point of such an exercise is not to delineate some unified, modal understanding of history. On the contrary, the aim is to identify the different, often contending, views of history and the types of lessons that are drawn from the past.[17] Collective historical memory is not simply a record of past events; it is the intersubjective outcome of a series of ongoing intellectual and political negotiations. The products of these negotiations may achieve a certain degree of stability for a period of time, but they are constantly subject to challenges and alternative interpretations.

Having pinpointed the main parameters of historical debate in a given political system at a particular point in time, the next step is to investigate the policies that emerged out of the political process and to analyse the ways in which they are legitimated. Although it is impossible to prove definitively that historically grounded legitimations and arguments were the actual causes of the policies that emerged, the analyst can at least establish an association between certain types of historically derived arguments and the underlying core principles on which foreign policy was based. It then becomes possible to evaluate the actual strength of the relationship between behaviour and beliefs by tracing the evolution of both over time, monitoring how they evolved in response to historical events and pressures.

Of central importance to the analysis is determining the degree of consistency between behaviour and expressed historical memory over time. If the beliefs and values of the actors shift without any corresponding changes in behaviour, there is reason to question the posited relationship between the two. Likewise, if behaviour changes without shifts in the expressed beliefs associated with earlier policies, then again we have reason to doubt that the two factors influence one another. In other words, expressed historically grounded beliefs and values should develop in tandem with defence and national security policy. When there is a disjuncture between the two – between the existing norms and values and the kinds of new policies that political actors are attempting to implement – an appropriate degree of tension should be observable in the political system.

Finally, it is necessary to identify the conditions under which a culture is likely to change. Here it may be suggested that cultural systems, including the types of lessons drawn from history, remain plausible only insofar as

[17] In contrast to earlier generations of scholarly work on political culture, contemporary theorists focus on culture as complex, fractured and defined as much by the boundaries that it draws between itself and others as by its actual content. For a brief review, see Yosef Lapid, 'Culture's Ship: Returns and Departures in International Relations Theory', in Yosef Lapid and Friedrich Kratochwil (eds.), *The Return of Culture and Identity in IR Theory* (Boulder: Lynne Rienner, 1996), esp. 6–9.

they help actors make sense of the world around them and enable them to achieve the objectives they have set for themselves. When a cultural system no longer serves this function, actors are likely to begin to defect and find some alternative way of dealing with the world.[18]

The formation of German historical memory and foreign policy, 1945–89

The end of the Second World War was a pivotal event in German history, and it created a rupture in the way in which Germany understood itself and its outside world. In the wake of the catastrophic defeat an extreme mood of war-weariness and disillusionment swept the country, displacing the extreme nationalism and emphasis on power politics that had exercised such a powerful hold on the nation's mind in the pre-war period. Whereas before 1945 the German people had been possessed by what Friedrich Meinecke called the 'Demons of Power', after the war they developed a profound aversion to nationalist themes, especially when expressed in connection with foreign policy goals.[19]

In the early post-war period the average German was overwhelmed by the task of trying to survive in the midst of the chaos and misery the war had left behind. There was little public appetite for confronting the past or drawing lessons from it. German leaders, however, could not afford to avoid these issues. As a divided nation on the front line of the emerging Soviet–US confrontation, they were under intense pressure to face up to the issue of military security and with it the anxieties that possible German rearmament provoked, among both the German people and Germany's neighbours.

Inevitably the issue of how to interpret the recent past, and what lessons to draw from it, became the centre of a fierce political debate that would rack German politics for the first twelve years of the Federal Republic's

[18] In this sense cultural systems evolve and develop in a way quite similar to the ways in which scientific theories are said to develop according to the philosopher of science Imre Lakatos. See Imre Lakatos, 'Falsification and the Methodology of Scientific Research programs', in Imre Lakatos and Robert Musgrave (eds.), *Criticism and the Growth of Knowledge* (New York: Cambridge University Press, 1970).

[19] For a brief overview of pre-1945 militarism, see Volker R. Berghahn, *Militarism: The History of an International Debate 1861–1979* (Oxford and New York: Berg, 1981), esp. ch. 3. On the extreme disillusionment of the post-1945 era and its long-term consequences for German national identity, see Helmut Schelsky, *Die Skeptische Generation: Eine Soziologie der deutschen Jugend* (Düsseldorf-Köln: Eugen Diederichs Verlag, 1963); Martin and Sylvia Greiffenhagen, *Ein Schwieriges Vaterland: Zur politischen Kultur Deutschlands* (Munich: List Verlag, 1979); and Elisabeth Noelle-Neumann and Renate Koch, *Die Verletzte Nation: Über den Versuch der Deutschen, ihren Charakter zu ändern* (Stuttgart: Deutsche Verlags-Anstalt, 1988).

existence. Out of the welter of rival views of the past swirling around the post-war political and intellectual scene there emerged two sharply divergent interpretations, one associated with the left end of the political spectrum and the other with that of the right.[20]

On the right a coalition of conservative forces came together under the leadership of Konrad Adenauer and the Christian Democratic parties, the CDU and CSU. The conservatives attributed the failure of pre-war German democracy and the nation's involvement in two world wars to Germany's uneasy geopolitical and spiritual position between the liberal, democratic West and the totalitarianism of the East. Unable to commit themselves fully to the ideals of liberal democracy, and threatened by the Bolshevik menace from the Soviet Union, the German people had blindly supported a totalitarian solution of their own, Nazism, with catastrophic consequences.

The principal practical implication that conservatives drew from this interpretation of the past was that Germany had to anchor itself solidly in the Western camp by joining the Western alliance centred on NATO. In this way Germany would side with the values of liberal democracy and Christian humanism in opposition to the godless totalitarianism that reigned in the East. Such a commitment to the West, the conservatives argued, would both ensure German national security and solidify the fledgling democracy of the Federal Republic. Eventually, they hoped, it would pave the way for German reunification on favourable terms.

Opposing Adenauer and the Christian Democrats was an alliance of left-leaning political forces assembled under the banner of the Social Democratic Party (SPD). In contrast to the Christian Democrats, the left attributed the collapse of the Weimar Republic and Germany's involvement in two world wars to primarily domestic political factors as opposed to external factors. In particular they blamed the anti-democratic elites of the pre-war era for stoking overweening nationalism and militarism. These elites, the left argued, had exploited nationalism and militarism for their own purposes, and they had tolerated the rise of Hitler in order to resist the rising tide of working-class activism. Integration with the West, they feared, would reinforce the power of these same elites and prevent the kind of root and branch reform that they felt Germany needed. Instead of rearmament and entry into the Western alliance system, the Social Democrats and the left maintained that a socialist Germany should strive for a position of lightly armed neutrality between East and West. Germany could then act as a bridge between the East and the West, tempering the

[20] For a more extended discussion of the domestic political debate of the period, see Berger, *Cultures of Antimilitarism*, ch. 2 and 3.

potentially disastrous geopolitical competition between the United States and the Soviet Union and serving as a model for a 'third way' between the oppressive socialism of the East and the destructive capitalism of the West.

In the fierce political battles of the 1950s the conservatives enjoyed the upper hand, helped in no small measure by the powerful incentives the United States offered for joining the Western alliance. However, although the conservatives won out in the struggle to lay the foundations of post-war German foreign policy, they were unable to avoid making at least some concessions to the left, particularly in the areas of civil–military relations and arms control. In order to shore up support for rearmament and the reintroduction of conscription, Adenauer and the Christian Democrats were compelled to accept the uniquely liberal model of civil–military relations associated with the doctrine of *Innere Führung* (internal leadership).[21] Likewise, in the late 1950s the Adenauer government was obliged to reassure the German public that war was not imminent by pursuing arms control talks with the Soviet Union, even though at the time it was thought that such talks were likely to prove fruitless.[22]

The German conservatives' acceptance of arms control and a liberal model of civil–military relations involved far more than merely tactical concessions to the opposition. Adenauer and his ministers were compelled to accept the motivating logic and values behind these policies as well. *Innere Führung* was adopted as a way of creating a new, more democratic military, one that broke decisively with the authoritarianism of the German military establishment of the past. Likewise, the combination of deterrence with arms control was portrayed as a new, cooperative approach to diplomacy, aimed at preserving the peace rather than achieving maximum national security. Once legitimated in these terms these policies became far more costly, politically, to change. In other words, along with the usual give and take of the political arena a parallel process of cognitive bargaining took place in which the two political camps were forced to accept not only some of the other side's policies but also elements of their world view as well. Reality as well as policy was subject to negotiation.

Over the course of the next thirty years this process of negotiating reality was to continue. The first and most dramatic shift came at the SPD conference at Bad Godesberg in 1960, when the SPD shifted towards acceptance of rearmament and the alliance with the West.[23] Later, in the

---

[21] For an overview see Donald Abenheim, *Reforging the Iron Cross* (Princeton, NJ: Princeton University Press, 1988).

[22] Mark Cioc, *Pax Atomica* (New York: Columbia University Press, 1988).

[23] On the transformation of the Social Democrats' vew of national security see Joachim Hütter, *Die SPD und Nationale Sicherheit: Internationale und innenpolitische*

early 1980s, the CDU in turn was compelled to accept the SPD policy of establising diplomatic ties with the Soviet Union and Eastern Europe, Ostpolitik.[24] Undoubtedly these shifts in policy were influenced by hard-nosed calculations of how to win votes and gain power. Without acceptance of the Christian Democrats' policy of integration with the West, it is unlikely that the SPD could have joined the government in the latter half of the 1960s. Likewise the CDU was compelled to embrace Ostpolitik in order to form a coalition with the Free Democrats. Yet once these changes in policy had been institutionalised they led to gradual shifts in the world view of both camps. For instance, although initially only a small minority within the SPD may have been genuinely committed to integration into the West in the 1960s and 70s, by the 1980s members of the SPD had increasingly come to take integration with Europe for granted. Some Social Democratic leaders, such as Horst Ehmke and Karsten Voigt, even began to embrace the European Community as a bulwark that could enable Germany and other European countries to resist the belligerent security policies of the United States.[25]

The net result of this process was a narrowing of the gap between the different political camps on certain key aspects of German foreign policy. This is not to say that a clear consensus on security policy emerged. On the contrary, ferocious debates over foreign policy erupted periodically, accompanied by anguished debates over Germany's past and the moral as well as practical implications. Brandt's diplomatic opening to Eastern Europe was linked explicitly to confronting the ghosts of the Holocaust and to renewing German democracy.[26] Similarly, the deployment of Pershing II missiles on the territory of the Federal Republic was closely linked to heated debates over Germany's past and national identity.[27]

Despite these sporadic tempests, however, the different parties gradually came to favour a general approach to foreign policy that centred on

Determinanten des Wandels der Sozialdemokratischen Sicherheitspolitik 1959–1961 (Meisenheim: Anton Hain, 1975); Lothar Wilkes, *Die Sicherheitspolitik der SPD 1956–1966: Zwischen Wiedervereinigung und Bündnisorientierung* (Bonn Bad Godesberg: Verlag Neue Gesellschaft, 1977). For a revisionist view, see Thomas Enders, *Die SPD und die äussere Sicherheit* (Melle: Knoth, 1987).

[24] See Clay Clemens, *The Reluctant Realists: The Christian Democrats and West German Ostpolitik* (Durham, NC: Duke University Press, 1989).

[25] See Horst Ehmke, 'Eine Politik zur Selbstbehauptung Europas', *Europarchiv* (10 April 1984), and Karsten Voigt, 'Die Vereinigung Europas – westeuropäische Integration und gesamteuropäische Kooperation', *Europarchiv* (10 July 1989).

[26] See for instance Brandt's famous inaugural speech in which he linked Ostpolitik to the renewal of German democracy. Presse- und Informationsamt der Bundesregierung, *Bundeskanzler Brandt: Reden und Interviews* (Bonn: Presse- und Informationsamt der Bundesregierung, 1971), 14.

[27] For a discussion of the fierce domestic political debates that surrounded the decision to deploy the Pershing II missiles, see Herf, *War by Other Means*.

three core principles.[28] The first was a general strategy of *Einbindungspolitik*, or encouraging other countries to join Germany in ceding sovereign decision-making power over a broad range of issues to multilateral institutions. Rather than building up its military power to match that of its many potential rivals, Germany's post-war leaders sought to encourage its neighbours to join it in forgoing the pursuit of independent national power and to pool sovereign authority instead.[29] Ironically, it was the very threat of German potential power that made this policy so successful. Germany's Western neighbours were willing to join the Federal Republic in sacrificing autonomy precisely because they feared the potential consequences of German power untrammeled by institutional restraints. *Einbindungspolitik* was also attractive for many on the German left because it was couched in anti-nationalist rhetoric. Having been burned twice by the fires of hypernationalism, the German people were to join the rest of Europe in rejecting the nation-state as a political form.

The second core element of the post-1945 German approach to national security was what has been termed its 'culture of restraint' in military affairs. The Bundeswehr was closely integrated into NATO and had no independent military staff apparatus of its own, relying instead on the joint Western headquarters to coordinate military operations in the event of hostilities. Legally, German forces could not be dispatched for missions outside the area covered by the Atlantic alliance. Moreover, whenever the Federal Republic joined in taking steps to strengthen the military side of its alliance with the West, it insisted that concurrent efforts be made to reassure the Soviet Union that these new measures were non-offensive in nature. Once again, this principle of combining reassurance with deterrence fitted in well with the general rejection of power politics as it had been practised by German and other European statesmen in an earlier era.

Finally, the third pillar of the post-war West German approach to national security was the integration of the new military establishment

---

[28] For a similar listing, see Thomas Berger, 'The Past in the Present', *German Politics*, 6, 1 (April 1997), 48–9.

[29] A growing number of analysts have come to see this penchant for multilateralism as the distinguishing feature of German foreign policy. See for instance, Simon Bulmer, 'Shaping the Rules? The Constitutive Politics of the European Union and German Power', and Jeffrey Anderson, "Hard Interests, Soft Power and Germany's Changing Role in Europe', both in Katzenstein *Tamed Power*; Duffield, *World Power Foresaken*; Gunther Hellmann, '"Einbindungspolitik". German Foreign Policy and the Art of Declaring "Total Peace"', in Jörg Calliess (ed.), *Die Zukunft der deutschen Aussenpolitik* (Rehburg-Loccum: Evangelische Akademie Loccum, 1995); and Michael Staack, 'Die Entwicklung der Internationalen Beziehungen und die Bundesrepublik Deutschland', in Werner Süss (ed.), *Die Bundesrepublik in den achtziger Jahren: Innenpolitik, Politische Kultur, Aussenpolitik* (Opladen: Leske+Budrich, 1991).

into broader society through the democratisation of its armed forces and the creation of new image of the German soldier as 'a citizen in uniform' (*Staatsbürger in Uniform*). Here again the lessons of the past loomed large. Post-war German military reformers were determined that the armed forces should never again become the font of authoritarian, anti-democratic values that it had been in the pre-1945 period. Even Social Democratic critics of rearmament such as Fritz Erler were convinced that the left during the Weimar Republic had committed a fatal error by failing to reach out to the armed forces and integrate them into a democratic polity.[30]

These three principles emerged during the 1950s and became the template on which all subsequent German foreign policy was based. While initially controversial, gradually this approach to foreign policy was accepted by all the major political players in Germany and enjoyed considerable popular support. By most criteria German foreign policy was remarkably successful. The Federal Republic rose from the ashes of the defeat in the Second World War and was reintegrated as a central player in European affairs. Militarily Germany enjoyed an unprecedented degree of security, while economically it grew and became immensely prosperous. The two major causes of concern from the German point of view were the continued partition of the German state and a relative lack of room for independent manoeuvre. With the fall of the Berlin Wall in November 1989 both of these situations came to an abrupt end.

German foreign policy and historical memory after the fall of the Berlin Wall

The effective end of the Cold War in 1989 and the formal reunification of Germany in 1991 transformed the German domestic political system and its international political environment. Domestically the sudden addition of seventeen million new citizens from East Germany dramatically altered the electoral landscape and imparted a profound shock to the German economy from which it has yet to recover. Accompanying these wrenching changes was an initial upsurge in nationalist feelings, reflected in the outburst of a mood of popular exuberance in the immediate aftermath of reunification and, more ominously, in the rise of xenophobic violence directed against asylum seekers and foreign residents in Germany.[31]

---

[30] See Abenheim, *Reforging the Iron Cross*, 123–5.

[31] For an expression of the kinds of concerns that these developments created, see Reinhard Kühnl, 'The German Sonderweg reconsidered: Continuities and Discontinuities in Modern German History', in Reinhard Alter and Peter Monteath (eds.), *Rewriting the German Past: History and Identity in the New Germany* (Atlantic Highlands, NJ: Humanities Press, 1998).

Internationally, the collapse of the Soviet Union freed Germany from the threat of a military invasion that had hung over its head for forty years like the sword of Damocles. Reunification with the eastern third of Germany ended the partition of the nation that had preoccupied German leaders since 1945. In the new European landscape the reunified Germany towered above its neighbours economically, demographically and in military potential. At the same time, Germany was confronted with new diplomatic challenges and security threats. The most obvious of these was the conflict in the former Yugoslavia, which sent hundreds of thousands of refugees over German borders and brought the Federal Republic into conflict with its Western allies over the recognition of the new, breakaway republics of Croatia and Slovenia.[32] Equally dramatic were the intense pressures that the United States and other allies placed on the Federal Republic to participate in the allied war effort against Saddam Hussein in the Gulf in 1991.[33]

The Federal Republic thus found itself in a situation more fluid than at any point since the late 1940s. Outside Germany, many observers predicted that the new logic of Germany's altered geostrategic environment would compel it to reduce its reliance on multilateral security arrangements and seek to increase its capacity to conduct an independent foreign and security policy, including the acquisition of its own nuclear deterrent.[34] Such expectations were hardly confined to the halls of academe, and anxiety over German power was expressed by a number of European leaders at the time of reunification, beginning with the British prime minister Margaret Thatcher and French president François Mitterrand.[35] For the most part these views were peculiarly far removed from the way in which most Germans interpreted their situation.

[32] See Beverly Crawford, 'German Foreign Policy and European Political Cooperation: The Diplomatic Recognition of Croatia in 1991', *German Politics and Society*, 13 (Summer 1995).

[33] Michael J. Inacker, *Unter Ausschluß der Öffentlichkeit: Die Deutschen in der Golfallianz* (Bonn-Berlin: Bouvier, 1992).

[34] John Mearsheimer, 'Back to the Future', *International Security*, 15, 1 (Summer 1990); Christopher Layne, 'The Unipolar Illusion: Why New Great Powers will Rise', *International Security*, 17, 4 (Spring 1993), esp. 41–5; Kenneth Waltz, 'The Emerging Structure of International Politics', *International Security*, 18, 2 (Fall 1993).

[35] Margaret Thatcher, *The Downing Street Years* (New York: HarperCollins, 1993), 790–9, 813–15; Jacques Attali, *Verbatim III, Chronique des années 1988–1991* (Paris: Seuil, 1995), 354; Stanley Hoffman, 'French Dilemmas and Strategies in the New Europe', in Robert E. Keohane et al. (eds.), *After the Cold War* (Cambridge, MA: Harvard University Press, 1992), 130; Anne-Marie Le Gloannec, 'The Implications of German Unification for Western Europe', in Paul B. Stares (ed.), *The New Germany and the New Europe* (Washington, DC: Brookings Institution, 1992), 252. The Germans were well aware of their allies' misgivings. See Horst Teltschik, *329 Tage: Innenansichten der Einigung* (Berlin: Siedler, 1991), 37–38, 59–61, 95–102.

As in the 1950s, there swirled a host of different views on how Germany might respond. Predictably, on the left there were those, like Brandt's former adviser Egon Bahr, who called for the dissolution of the Western military alliance and its replacement with more cooperative, multilateral security structures embracing the former Soviet Union and other east European nations.[36] Reinforcing the left's traditional rejection of power politics was the belief – derisively referred to as 'Genscherism' by many observers in the United States – that Ostpolitik and German support for continued dialogue with the Soviet Union had helped bring about the Gorbachev revolution and hastened the end of the Cold War. In this way the experience of the Cold War merely reinforced the German left's traditional penchant for pursing a cooperative, demilitarised approach to national security.

Not surprisingly, the German right had a rather different perspective on recent history. In their view Ostpolitik, while valuable, had not been the key to ending the Cold War. Instead, the conservatives maintained that the Federal Republic's solidarity with its NATO partners, and in particular Chancellor Kohl's willingness to deploy Pershing II missiles in the face of strong opposition, had helped convince the Soviet leadership that political–military victory was out of their reach and had encouraged them to seek a negotiated solution. Thus, like the left, the right interpreted history in ways that suited its purposes, and which reinforced its existing inclinations.

In short, reunification and the end of the Cold War, far from obliterating the memory of the Second World War and the lessons drawn from the experiences of the 1930s and 40s, in many ways reinforced them. Cleavages between the different political currents remained, they merely had been given new fields of memory upon which they could contest. At the same time, despite these differences, in contrast with the post-1945 period, both the left and the right agreed that the nation had been on the right course. As a result, support for the three core principles of German foreign policy remained as strong as ever and the underlying aversion to nationalism remained as strong as ever. Whereas defeat in the Second World War had shaken the German world view to the core, the end of the Cold War reaffirmed it.

As a result, in the decade following the fall of the Berlin Wall there has been a considerable degree of continuity both in the German approach to security policy and in domestic debate on security issues. Some significant adjustments were made in response to the pressures placed by the

---

[36] See Harald Müller, 'German Foreign Policy after Unification', in Stares (ed.), *The New Germany and the New Europe*, 132–5.

international environment on Germany, above all in the area of peace-keeping and out-of-area military missions. These changes in foreign policy behaviour, however, have come relatively slowly and remain consistent with the three core principles of German foreign policy that had developed during the Cold War period. Internally, while there have been renewed discussions of national identity and of the lessons to be drawn from German history, the basic contours of the debate remain quite familiar to the student of the pre-1989 debate.

In the years following the fall of the Berlin Wall the Federal Republic has reaffirmed its commitment to multilateralism in a variety of ways. Instead of seeking to dismantle or weaken the institutional bonds that bind it to the West, Germany has sought to broaden and deepen the multilateral frameworks in which it is embedded, and, where possible, to adapt them to the new challenges of the post-Cold War era. NATO remains the central pillar upon which Germany relies for military security and has been adapted to serve not only its main mission of territorial defence but also as the chief instrument for dealing with regional security crises.[37] Likewise, instead of diluting the European Union, the Federal Republic has played a central role in both expanding and deepening the integration process. German politicians took the lead in pushing for the expansion of the European Union to include both the former EFTA countries as well as the countries of east–central Europe. At Maastricht in 1991 Helmut Kohl agreed to an epochal deepening of the integration process, even at the cost of sacrificing that most potent symbol of post-war German economic process, the Deutschmark.[38] Although within the context of the European Union the Federal Republic has become more willing to pursue positions that are at odds with the interests of other members, there is little evidence that any serious political party in Germany would consider reversing the nation's commitment to multilateralism.[39]

The Federal Republic also has continued to to exercise a relatively high degree of restraint in military matters. Instead of building up its forces, the German forces shrank in size, from over 650,000 in 1989 (including the forces of the defunct East German army) to 340,000 in 1999. Concomitantly German defence spending fell to among the lowest levels in the OECD at 1.5% of gross domestic product (GDP). The

[37] See Dieter Mahnke, 'Wandel im Wandel: Bundeswehr und europäische Sicherheit', *Aus Politik und Zeitgeschichte* B 15–16, 9 April 1993, 40–6.
[38] On the politics behind Germany's decision, see Dorothy Heisenberg, *The Mark of the Bundesbank: Germany's Role in European Monetary Cooperation* (Boulder, CO: Lynne Rienner, 1998).
[39] See Jeffrey A. Anderson, *German Unification and the Union of Europe* (New York and London: Cambridge University Press, 1999).

Bundeswehr is perhaps more closely integrated with the forces of its allies than ever, with a profusion of multinational units modelled on the Franco-German corps being formed as a way of reassuring Germany's neighbours of its benign intentions. And within the context of the alliance German policy-makers in general tend to counsel in favour of diplomacy over the use of force.[40]

The chief point of departure from Germany's previously resolutely anti-militarist stance has been the Bundeswehr's participation in military missions outside of the area covered by the NATO alliance. Since the end of the Cold War German forces have participated in a number of peacekeeping and peace-making operations, first in Somalia and then in the former Yugoslavia. In July 1995 German forces were authorised for the first time since the Second World War to use force if necessary in order to separate the warring parties in Bosnia.[41] This new policy, however, can hardly be viewed as evidence that Germany is seeking to assume the role of a great military power. The German Constitutional Court ruled that such missions could only take place in a multilateral framework, and a tremendous debate has ensued over what sort of multilateral frameworks may be acceptable. Moreover, the decision to use German forces abroad was achieved only after tremendous internal political struggle.[42]

Finally, the Federal Republic continued to adhere to the doctrine of *Innere Führung* and, despite the disappearance of the threat of a massive conventional military invasion from the east, to military conscription. Conscription, while much criticised by some, retained strong support among political elites as well as the general populace.[43] According to one public opinion study in 1997, only 4.6 per cent of the population favoured complete abolition of conscription, although a plurality

[40] To take only one example, the new German foreign minister encouraged the United States not to resort to air strikes in response to Iraqi provocation over UN-supervised arms inspections. See *Süddeutsche Zeitung*, 4 November 1998, 1, 9.

[41] On the original German debate over out-of-area missions after the Gulf War, see Clay Clemens, 'Opportunity or Obligation? Redefining Germany's Military Role Outside of NATO', *Armed Forces and Society*, 19, 2 (April 1993). On the decision to allow German forces to participate in peace-making missions in Bosnia, see *Frankfurter Allgemeine Zeitung*, 1 and 2 July 1995, *Der Spiegel*, 26 June 1995, 22–5, and *Die Zeit*, 7 July 1995.

[42] See *Der Spiegel*, 5, 12 and 19 April 1993; *Frankfurter Allgemeine Zeitung*, 25 March, 8 April 1993.

[43] See the published version of a special parliamentary commission's report on the future of the Bundeswehr, Hans-Adolf Jacobsen and Hans-Jürgen Rautenberg (eds.), *Bundeswehr und Europäische Sicherheitsordnung* (Bonn: Bouvier, 1991), 50–1, 55–9; and Jürgen Kuhlmann and Ekkehard Lippert, 'Wehrpflicht Ade? Argumente für und wider die Wehrpflicht in Friedenszeiten', in Gerd Kaldrack and Paul Klein (eds.), *Die Zukunft der Streitkräfte angesichts weltweiter Abrüstungsbemühungen* (Baden-Baden: Nomos Verlagsgesellschaft, 1992).

indicated that they might favour some sort of modification in favour of civil over military service.[44]

The continuity in actual foreign policy behaviour is mirrored and reinforced by an underlying continuity in the domestic political debate over national identity and foreign policy. The past continues to loom large in the ways in which German leaders try to legitimate their policies. During the Maastricht debate, for instance, Chancellor Kohl warned time and again that the only alternative to European integration was war.[45] Similar sentiments have been expressed by the foreign minister of the new SPD/Green coalition government, Joschka Fischer.[46] Underlying much of the German commitment to multilateralism and non-military solutions to foreign policy dilemmas remains a continued and profound suspicion of nationalism and power politics, on both the left and the mainstream right.[47]

The basis of these suspicions remain the disastrous experiences of the Second World War, as reinforced both internally and externally by popular histories, films and the entire elaborate system of political and cultural rituals that commemorate the events of 1933 to 1945. More than fifty years after the end of the war, the German media are periodically dominated by debates over the proper portrayal of the Holocaust – as reflected in the Martin Walser–Ignatz Bubis controversy of 1998. Political careers can be damaged by ill-considered remarks concerning the Nazi era – as occurred with Stefan Heitman, Helmut Kohl's candidate to replace Richard Weizäcker as the federal president in 1994. And, improbably, Daniel Goldhagen's *Hitler's Willing Executioners* became the number one bestseller in the Federal Republic, with many German tourists apparently selecting that particular harshly anti-German tome as their preferred summer reading material to peruse while sunning themselves on the beaches of Majorca. However much one may decry the ritualisation of German guilt, and however many instances one can find of German leaders choosing to ignore the potentially negative symbolic consequences of their actions – such as moving the capital from Bonn

---

[44] Bernhard Fleckenstein, 'Warum wir die Wehrpflicht (noch) brauchen', *Aus Politik und Zeitgeschichte* B29/1997 (July 11, 1997), 19.

[45] Thomas Banchoff, 'German Policy Towards the European Union: The Effects of Historical Memory', *German Politics*, 6, 1 (Spring 1997), 61–5.

[46] See interview with Fischer in *Der Spiegel*, 23 November 1998, esp. 86.

[47] For instance, Fischer rejected seeking to form an axis with either Britain or France within the framework of the European Union precisely because he feels that such bilateral special relationships are rooted in anachronistic nineteenth-century power politics – 'Nationalstaatsdenken' – which led to the First and Second World Wars (*Der Spiegel*, 2 November 1998, 38).

to Berlin – it is hard to maintain that the horrors of the Nazi past have been forgotten.[48]

To be sure, there has been the emergence of a small but vocal group of New Right intellectuals who advocate a more nationalist approach to German foreign policy and espouse a revisionist view of German history.[49] Yet, despite the considerable attention this group has attracted both within Germany and abroad,[50] such arguments have had little discernible impact on the political mainstream or public opinion.[51] Likewise, on the left there are those who advocate the major downgrading of NATO and the military components of the German approach to national security. Yet, to date at least, they too have had little influence on either the national debate or the making of foreign policy.

In this light the German decision to participate in NATO military operations in Kosovo should be seen as part of an evolutionary process spanning many years. The mission represented an important shift in German policy in a number of respects. For the first time Bundeswehr air units participated in combat missions, albeit on a small scale. In addition, in contrast to the mission in Bosnia, this time German forces were acting without a mandate from the United Nations, something which earlier the left had insisted should be an absolute prerequisite for Bundeswehr participation in military operations outside the area covered by the Atlantic alliance.

At the same time, it is important not to over-emphasise the degree of discontinuity that Kosovo represented. German policy-makers continued

---

[48] For a subtle discussion, however, of how the legacy of the Nazi period has been ritualised, see Jeffrey Olick, 'What does it mean to normalize the Past? Official Memory in German Politics since 1945', *Social Science History*, 22, 4 (Winter 1998).

[49] See Rainer Zitelmann, 'Position und Begriff. Über eine neue demokratische Rechte', in Heimo Schwilk and Ulrich Schacht (eds.), *Die Selbstbewußte Nation*, 3rd ed. (Berlin: Ullstein, 1995); Karlheinz Weissmann, ' "Der Westen" in der Historgraphie nach 1945', in Rainer Zitelmann, Karlheinz Weissmann, and Michael Grossheim (eds.), *Westbindung: Chancen und Risiken für Deutschland* (Frankfurt/Main: Propyläen, 1993). The New Right is hardly a uniquely German phenomenon, and there are comparable developments throughout Europe. For good overviews, see Hans Betz and Stefan Immerfall (eds.), *The New Politics of the Right: Neopopulist Parties and Movements in Established Democracies* (New York: St. Martin's Press, 1998); and Herbert Kitschelt, *The Radical Right in Western Europe* (Ann Arbor, MI: University of Michigan Press, 1997).

[50] For overviews, see Olick, 'What does it mean to normalize the Past?'; Jacob Heilbrunn, 'Germany's New Right', *Foreign Affairs*, 75, 6 (1996), 80–98; John Ely, 'The *Frankfurter Allgemeine Zeitung* and Contemporary German national-Conservatism', *German Politics and Society*, 13 (Summer 1995).

[51] As persuasively argued by Hans Betz, 'Perplexed Normalcy: German Identity after Unification', in Alter and Monteath, *Rewriting the German Past*. See also Jan Müller, 'From National identity to National Interest: The Rise (and Fall) of Germany's New Right', *German Politics*, 8, 3 (December 1999).

to stress the importance of multilateralism. Indeed, without a multilateral framework it would have constitutionally been impossible for the Federal Republic to act militarily. The chief reason given by the Schröder government for the dispatch of the Bundeswehr to Kosovo was *Bündnistreue* – the need for Germany to fulfill its obligations to the Atlantic alliance. Moreover, in keeping with its anti-military traditions, Germany was at the forefront of the movement within the alliance seeking a diplomatic solution.[52] At the same time the Federal Republic pressured the United States and its Western allies to hold off on launching a ground campaign, reportedly going so far as to threaten to use its authority inside NATO to veto such an operation.[53]

There were good reasons for Schröder's eagerness for the war to end quickly and with a minimum of violence. Much as the model of political culture described earlier predicts, tremendous domestic political tensions developed in response to Germany's assumption of a larger military role. First and foremost these tensions manifested themselves inside the coalition government as foreign minister Joschka Fischer desperately struggled to retain control over his fractious Green party, many of whose members were desperately unhappy with what they viewed as an immoral militarisation of German foreign policy. The launching of a NATO ground campaign was widely believed to be the point at which the Green party would either leave the coalition or face a split within its own ranks. In either case the Schröder government would have fallen.[54] Public opinion data also indicated that support for the war would evaporate if ground forces were sent in to attack the Serbian army in Kosovo.[55] In sum, Kosovo may have represented a watershed event in the development of German foreign policy. It did not, however, signify a transformation of the Federal Republic into a 'normal nation', if normalcy is taken to mean the same sort of relatively unfettered approach to the use of military power as a tool of foreign policy exhibited by other European powers such as France or the United Kingdom.[56]

Ironically, as the structural parameters of German foreign-policy-making have expanded to allow for a greater measure of initiative than Germany has enjoyed at any point in the preceding forty odd years, the

[52] See *Die Welt*, 19 May 1999.

[53] See *The New York Times*, 20 May 1999, A1, A14. Whether the Federal Republic in fact would have risked such a rupture with its allies remains open to question.

[54] See news item, *Tagesspiegel*, 21 April 1999, also ibid., Bernd Ulrich, 'Die Grünen und der Krieg'.

[55] Renate Köcher, 'Das Kosvo spaltet Deutschland Ost und West', *Frankfurter Allgemeine Zeitung*, 16 June 1999, 5.

[56] For an elaboration of this argument, see Thomas Berger, 'A Perfectly Normal Abnormality: German Foreign Policy after Kosovo', *International Relations of the Asia–Pacific* (2002).

German domestic political willingness to pursue a more independent foreign policy has probably never been weaker. After more than forty years during which a consensus in favor of the moderate foreign policy course slowly coalesced, it can hardly come as a surprise that Germany's leaders have been unwilling to contemplate a change in course. While other countries, such as France or Britain, might have found the lack of national profile galling and the lack of independent policy-making capability disturbing, Germans feel that all their major policy objectives had been fulfilled. Even the goal of reunification of the German nation has been achieved, albeit it perhaps twenty years later than Adenauer had hoped. Thus, although in the eyes of many foreign observers the German approach to foreign policy seems terribly idealistic and naive, Germans can point to the successes of the past fifty years and argue that theirs has been the most reasonable policy after all. Germans are pragmatic realists, but not in the sense of Realism as understood in the international relations theory. Their particular interpretation of the historical record makes theirs a profoundly anti-Realist Realism.

Conclusions

How much longer is the new Federal Republic likely to continue to cleave to this moderate course of foreign policy? Although the social sciences cannot be employed to predict the future with anywhere near the degree of accuracy that is possible with the natural sciences or engineering, there are good reasons to expect that for the foreseeable future dramatic changes are quite unlikely. The German domestic political consensus in favour of multilateralism, military restraint and a democratised military establishment is as firm as it ever was. The underlying German view of history – the perception that power politics and nationalism are fundamentally incompatible with democracy and pose a threat to peace – likewise remains unshaken and if anything enjoys greater credibility than ever.

This approach to foreign policy and this view of history continues to receive positive reinforcement from the international system. Despite some misgivings, Germany's key west European partners, including most importantly France, remain willing to pursue the European integration project. The United States remains committed to maintaining European security and played a key role in defusing the tensions that emerged among its Western allies during the German reunification process.[57]

[57] For an authoritative account of the US role in the reunification process see Philip Zelikow and Condoleeza Rice, *Germany Unified and Europe Transformed: A Study in Statecraft* (Cambridge, MA: Harvard University Press, 1995).

Likewise, Germany's neighbours to the east, especially Poland and the Czech Republic, have sought to establish closer ties to the Federal Republic and embarked on a reconciliation process aimed at healing, if not forgetting, the wounds of the past.[58] Even were Germany to encounter difficulties in one of the many and overlapping fields of multilateral institutions in which it is embedded – say the Atlantic alliance with the United States, the European Union or the Partnership for Peace – unless this led to a collapse in its entire set of external relationships, there is no reason for the Federal Republic to see its basic strategy of *Einbindungspolitik* as having been discredited.

There are two, more or less plausible, if somewhat improbable, scenarios under which the German approach to foreign policy could be undermined. One would involve a failure of the extended deterrence system – say as the result of a terrorist attack using weapons of mass destruction on a German population centre. Another might result if the United States were to withdraw its security commitment to Europe and at the same time a serious new security threat were to emerge, perhaps in eastern Europe, to which the major west European countries were unable to coordinate an effective response. Either of these two scenarios would represent a fundamental challenge to the entire post-1945 German approach to national security and the political culture on which it is founded. Either one would force German elites to reconsider the way in which they understand the international system operates and the kinds of objectives Germany can achieve.

Even were such catastrophic scenarios to be realised, however, it is far from self-evident how German policy-makers would respond. As in the wake of the Second World War, there would be fierce debates over how to interpret recent events, and a multitude of different perspectives, each informed by its own peculiar experiences and motivated by different sets of interests, would be likely to emerge. The end result of such a process would, as in the 1940s and 50s, be determined by a large number of historically contingent factors that cannot be predicted in advance.

Barring such dramatic developments, German foreign and national security policies are likely to continue to evolve in the same sure but gradual way in which they have over the past ten years. Similarly, German collective memories of the Second World War and the Third Reich will

[58] On Germany's relationship to the countries of central Europe, with special reference to the critical issue of dealing with the legacies of the past, see Markovits and Reich, *The German Predicament*; Ann L. Philips, 'The Politics of Reconciliation: Germany in Central-East Europe', *German Politics*, 7, 2 (August 1998); and Dieter Bingen, 'Bilanz deutscher Politik gegenüber Polen 1949–1997', *Aus Politik und Zeitgeschichte* B53/97, 26 December 1997.

slowly change as the past is reinterpreted in the light of new societal experiences. Historical memories and in particular of the catastrophic human, political and moral consequences of the unconstrained pursuit of power continue to exercise an almost startling hold on the national consciousness of the reunited Germany. As a result the basic cultural parameters within which the Federal Republic's foreign policy is embedded appear likely to endure for some time to come.

4 The past in the present: British imperial memories and the European question

Anne Deighton

In the second half of the twentieth century, Empire has been both re-membered and portrayed by successive British governments as a pos-itive phenomenon, despite a relentless decline in the British Empire's reach. Britain's imperial inheritance conveyed strong images of a seafaring nation with an effective global span and with great global responsibil-ities, of a stable monarchy and of a secure, legitimate and respected constitution. These memories have been closely inter-twined with hero-ism, and success in war in the twentieth century, as Britain, its empire and its dominions contributed to victory in two world wars.[1] Received images of war promoted national British solidarity and emphasised the resilience of the British constitution as well triumph on the battlefield: these were truly memories *of* power. Such memories of power in turn contributed to enduring suspicions of post-war continental European supranational integration, a sense of superiority compared to other Europeans, and a notion that the United Kingdom's role in European international politics was still that of a balancer of other continental powers.

One facet of what has remained of Britain's post-imperial political cul-ture is a deep craving for a leadership role, or to 'punch above our weight' as former Foreign Secretary Lord Hurd once put it. This has been impor-tant in the context of image projection at home and in continental Europe,

---

[1] In the early twentieth century, colonies with substantial white European populations were granted dominion status, with a high level of self-government. These changes were acknowledged in the 1931 Statute of Westminster, and in 1939 these dominions made their own declarations of war. The phrase British Commonwealth of Nations was used until 1946, when the word 'British' was dropped. India and Pakistan both joined the Commonwealth when they became independent republics. By 1999, thirty-three mem-bers of the Commonwealth were republics, sixteen had the Queen as the official head of state, and five had national monarchs. This makes it clear that inherited memories, personal memories and the continued impact of a still existing empire–Commonwealth cannot be satisfactorily disentangled for analytical clarity. For a suggestive and compelling comparative analysis of empires, see Dominic Lieven, *Empire: The Russian Empire and its Rivals* (London: John Murray, 2000), and in particular on the British empire, 89–120, 366–78.

as well as on the wider international stage.[2] 'Leadership' appears to be a key way in which the memory of an imperial past that did not terminate in disastrous humiliation in war has been captured and cherished in Britain. It runs like a thread through the policies of successive governments. As a rhetorical device for British political leaders to secure domestic support for foreign policy, it has been particularly successful, and has retained a remarkable appeal with British electorates. As well as memories of global power, the memory of these imperial obligations has also given successive British governments a real sense of national duty and responsibility, whatever the political complexion of the government. To project the image of leadership has been both a temptation and a trap, from which no British political leader has escaped. To deliver as post-imperial leaders in international politics, successive governments have been obliged to spend vast sums on military weapons, nuclear and non-nuclear. When Britain has not in practice been able to lead, or even to agenda-set in continental Europe, the fall-back position has been either to assert conditionality for participation in European projects or to present alternative schemes from the wings, neither of which has had positive political results. This preoccupation with leadership therefore merits further investigation as a marker of at least one specific feature that has passed from imperial history and success in twentieth-century warfare into both the rhetoric and the policies of successive British post-war governments.

This chapter develops this idea of the British instinct to project leadership in the context of its post-war policy towards European supranational integration. The first part of the chapter is a brief and introductory examination of some of the manifestations of the reality and the memory of empire among instinctively Eurosceptic post-war British political elites. This is necessarily a partial and suggestive exercise, made harder by the fact that Empire has still not completely disappeared, which means that memories are at once received, and personal or 'actual'. The second part of the chapter will deal with how these ideas which were derived from the past experience of empire have played themselves out in political decision-making over European integration since 1945, with particular emphasis upon Labour and New Labour policy.[3] As Jan-Werner Müller

---

[2] Willy Brandt recalled of Labour's attempt to join the EC in the 1960s, that, 'When I met George Brown [the British Foreign Secretary] . . . he told me, "Willy, you must get us in, so we can take the lead".' Willy Brandt, *My Life in Politics* (London: Hamish Hamilton, 1992), 420.

[3] Obviously, this analysis is not intended to imply that Britain's imperial past alone explains Britain's policies towards European integration: the intention is, rather, to explore one facet of a complex of reasons for the policies of successive governments. For a general overview, see P.J Marshall, 'Imperial Britain', in P.J. Marshall (ed), *The Cambridge Illustrated History of the British Empire*, (Cambridge: Cambridge University Press, 1996).

says in the introduction to this volume, 'memory shapes present power constellations... [it] constrains, but also enables policies. [This is] ... not just about political measures explicitly dealing with the past, such as restitution, retribution and amnesty, but also about how memory shapes frameworks for foreign policy and domestic politics.'[4] Both Labour and Conservative governments first strongly resisted, but then made applications – driven by immediate economic and political expediency – to join the European Communities. Neither Labour nor Conservative leaders were able easily to take their parties with them in accepting a different role for Britain in Europe. 'Europe' thus shipwrecked both parties at different times, while no effective ruling 'European' party was ever created. So, as European integration has proceeded, the British public has been dragged along, often largely unknowingly and always reluctantly. The debate about Britain and the Continent has had a unique quality that has set 'Britishness' and the baggage of Britain's imperial legacy and global role as a counterpoise to the 'European' enterprise, even as the United States was taking over the mantle of 'imperial' hegemon.[5] An examination of how far this has changed under New Labour will conclude the chapter.

To explain how memories are sustained and manipulated is necessarily complicated, but it is clear that, in the British case, this has been a process whose suggestive traces we can catch in certain public commemorations, in popular culture and in education. It is 11 November, the day of the armistice in the First World War, that is still used in the annual commemoration of the two world wars, creating a blurred myth of imperial endeavour and martial victory over time. On 11 November 1998, eighty years after the end of the First World War, the Queen commemorated Armistice Day 1918 in Paris, as well as unveiling a statue of Winston Churchill, who, as prime minister during the Second World War, had himself commemorated Armistice Day in the Champs-Elysées in 1944, while France was still only partially liberated. By comparison, 'Europe Day' is barely noticed in the United Kingdom.[6]

The European Economic Community (EEC) was created in 1957. In 1967 the Merger Treaty created the European Communities (EC) with the merging of the institutions of the European Coal and Steel Community (ECSC), the EEC, and EURATOM. In 1993, the European Union (EU) was created from the EC, with the Second and Third Pillars established under the Maastricht Treaty.

[4] Jan-Werner Müller, 'Introduction: the power of memory, the memory of power and the power over memory', above, 2.

[5] D.C. Watt, *Succeeding John Bull: America in Britain's Place, 1900–1975* (Cambridge: Cambridge University Press, 1984); Lieven, *Empire*, ch. 3.

[6] David Cesarani has written of the partial nature of memories of the Second World War, 'Lacking in Convictions: British War Crimes Policy and National Memory of the Second World War', in Martin Evans and Ken Lunn (eds.), *War and Memory in the Twentieth*

In a recent essay the historian Philip Bell has examined the work of three leading English historians who were widely known and respected in the early post-war period. They were George Macaulay Trevelyan, Herbert Fisher and Arthur Bryant, all of whom were the 'products of the highest form of English intellectual and cultural life'. Their histories sold in vast quantities. Trevelyan's *History of England*, first published in 1926, had sold 200,000 copies by 1949. Herbert Fisher's *History of Europe*, first published in 1935, was reprinted nineteen times. Arthur Bryant's *Years of Endurance* and *Years of Victory* appeared during the 1940s as 'patriotic' manifestos, and were hugely popular with book clubs well into the post-war period. Bell concludes that these three historians emphasised the 'separateness' of Britain, a country of unique flexibility and stability, that had only found its true destiny when it turned away from continental Europe. They did not just tap into a mass-market readership. Prime ministers Winston Churchill, Clement Attlee and Harold Wilson have remarked that Bryant was their favourite historian, and Bell concludes that 'it is safe to say that the mental baggage of many Englishmen, including many who passed into political life and the civil service, was heavily stocked with the ideas of these historians ... these ideas were still firmly established in the minds of educated Englishmen as they considered the question of European integration, and in most cases rejected it.'[7] Imperial images, reinforced by a common language, permeated the fabric of British society, and this was reflected in ignorance of and relative indifference to European questions in opinion polls: as Francis Boyd put it in 1964, 'The multi-racial Commonwealth is still so new and tender that the British may look upon it with astonishment as well as pride, but this does not weaken the strength of the feeling which binds many British families to the older members of the Commonwealth ... [with] the shared experience of two World Wars. No estimate of the British attitude towards the Commonwealth should undervalue the living bond between the British and their kinsmen overseas.'[8]

Imperial images and Britain's global role have also been reinforced through the national education system, especially in private schools.

Century (Oxford: Berg, 1997), 27–42, especially 35, when he cites former prime minister Edward Heath as arguing that it was foolish to delve into the past when the new Europe was being born. Joanna Bourke, *The Second World War: A People's History* (Oxford: Oxford University Press, 2001), also talks of selective recitals of the past, and significant silences. She recounts that in Britain, the end of the war was remembered as a time of rejoicing: see ch. 13, 'The Memory of War'.

[7] Philip Bell, 'A Historical Cast of Mind: Some Eminent English Historians and Attitudes to Continental Europe in the Middle of the Twentieth Century', *Journal of European Integration History*, 2, 2 (1996), 5–19.

[8] Francis Boyd, *Politics in Transition* (London: Pall Mall, 1964), 210.

Jon Stallworthy, poet and professor of English Literature, sums this up succinctly in a recent memoir. As a young New Zealander being educated in a leading British 'prep' school in the 1940s, he realises now, but did not know at the time,

and our teachers may not have known, that our curriculum had been shaped by imperial priorities. It was no accident that the expansion of the British public school in the second half of the nineteenth century coincided with the expansion of the British Empire: the role of the one was to provide proconsuls for the other. Rome was the model, and Latin the means whereby its values were transmitted... Looking back through a post-colonial telescope, it is surprising to see how determined were the descendants of colonised Britons to remember only the commendable achievements of the conquerors and colonisers: their laws, their mosaics, their roads. The reason, of course, was that these achievements of the Roman Empire were held to justify our own.[9]

The conservative nature of British society has, further, enabled traditional ways of thought and reflexes of action to be sustained over time within decision-making circles. Well into the post-war period, the dominant mindset of British decision-makers was still imperial: for example, London University's School of Oriental and African Studies was established to train colonial administrators. The Whitehall machinery of the British civil service further reflected the conservative, elitist and rather narrow educational base of the British system, typified by the public schools and Oxbridge.[10]

However, these memories and reflections tend to reflect and reinforce in the United Kingdom existing images of an imperial past, but alone do not give a strong clue about the relationship between memories of the past and actual political decisions. Perhaps the clearest starting point for this period is none other than Winston Churchill, who, both for the public and for many decision-makers and politicians of both parties, epitomised success in war. He was leader of the Conservative opposition between 1945 and 1951, and then prime minister again between 1951 and 1955. He wrote, gave speeches and personally interpreted Britain's immediate and more distant history to a huge audience. Churchill's public statements, most notably to the Conservative Party conference in 1948, reflect a continuing ambition about Britain's current place in the world. This ambition

---

[9] Jon Stallworthy, *Singing School: The Making of a Poet* (London: John Murray, 1998), 39–41.

[10] Keith Robbins, *History, Religion and Identity in Modern Britain* (London: Hambledon Press, 1993); Anne Deighton, 'British Foreign Policy Making: the Macmillan Years', in Wolfram Kaiser and Gillian Staerck (eds.), *British Foreign Policy, 1955–64: Contracting Options* (Basingstoke: Macmillan, 2000), 3–18; N. Piers Ludlow, 'All at Sea: the Meaning of Europe in British Political Discourse', unpublished paper, London School of Economics, 2000.

derived largely from its past, and came to be echoed over time by both Labour and Conservative leaders:

'As I look out upon the future of our country in the changing scene of human destiny I feel the existence of three great circles among the free nations and democracies. The first for us is naturally the British Commonwealth and Empire with all that that comprises. Then there is also the English speaking world, centring upon the United States, in which we, Canada, and the other British Dominions play so important a part. And finally there is a United Europe... These three majestic circles are co-existent, and if they are linked together there is no force or combination which could overthrow them, or even challenge them effectively. Now if you think of the three interlinked circles you will see that we are the only country which has a great part in every one of them. We stand in fact at the very point of junction, and here in this island at the centre of the seaways and perhaps of the airways also, we have the opportunity of joining them all together... Over and above all special questions there rises before us the dread and solemn issue of the survival of Great Britain and her Empire as a united power in the first rank among nations.'[11]

Churchill captured the essential dilemma of a declining, but not defeated, imperial power, but one whose history and pride now meant that it was confronted with the quandary of either remaining a player in all arenas or deliberately scaling down its operations. Churchill's clear preference was for Britain now to use all the advantages of its history in the service of protecting the free world from the inroads of communism. But, as he said in 1951, 'I never thought that Britain or the British Commonwealth should, either individually or collectively, become an integral part of a European federation, and have never given the slightest support to the idea... We help, we dedicate, we play a part, but we are not merged and do not forfeit our insular or Commonwealth-wide character. I should resist any American pressure to treat Britain as on the same footing as the European States, none of whom have the advantages of the Channel and who were consequently conquered.'[12] Neither Conservatives nor Labour thinkers deviated far from this stricture until the pressures became too great: the 'founding myths' of integration on the Continent were not necessary for the British, given their different experience of empire and

---

[11] W. S. Churchill, *Europe Unites: Speeches, 1947 and 1948* (London: Cassell, 1950). The Labour Foreign Secretary Ernest Bevin also referred indirectly to the three circles concept in 1948, when he called for a Western democratic system with the backing of the Americas and the dominions to counter the communist threat. Likewise, Anthony Eden was very much influenced by Winston Churchill's aphorism, talking of the three unities.

[12] Public Record Office, Kew, London: C(51), 32, CAB 129/48, quoted in Silke Skär, *The British Conservative Party and Supranational European Integration, 1948–1955*, DPhil thesis, University of Oxford, 2000, 211.

war. Those on the left and the right used his theme in different ways, yet Britain's continuing global aspirations were common to those at both ends of the political spectrum: Euro-indifference and Euroscepticism did not develop simply as a matter of ideological or constitutional distaste for supranational integration.

In the Conservative Party, some – those in the Suez group, as well as others – transferred loyalty to the Commonwealth as the offspring of Empire.[13] Enoch Powell reflected in graphic but engagingly self-deprecating terms in 1991 that

When I resigned my chair in Australia in 1939 in order to come home and enlist, had I been asked 'What is the state whose uniform you wish to wear and in whose service you expect to perish?' I would have said, 'The British Empire'. I would have had no doubt in giving that reply. It was a worldwide power that had decided to face its enemies upon the battlefield. And this gigantism, this delusion that big is great, the bullfrog mentality, has haunted Britain ever since 1945...I also know that on my deathbed I shall still be believing with one part of my brain that somewhere on every ocean of the world there is a great grey ship with three funnels and 16-inch guns which can blow out of the water any other navy which is likely to face it.[14]

Margaret Thatcher was faced with the traditional British politician's dilemma of the competing pressures of her ideology and world view, and the need to compete. These drove her at once to public hostility to the Communities, best expressed in her Fontainebleau speech of 1984, and towards the Single Act – on ideological grounds. She was at her most comfortable with the pursuit of the Falklands War, and the consensus she received from the House of Commons as the British navy put to sea was a powerful reminder of the imperial reflex that remained across British society. Robert Conquest, a conservative scholar of the Soviet Union, has most recently observed the emergence of this reflex. He has encapsulated the post-imperial dream in his proposal for an English-speaking Oceanic Association, of Britain, the White Commonwealth and the United States, to which he feels Britain more 'naturally' belongs. The EU is, as he sees it, divisive for the West, and for Britain is in contradiction to the principles of firm leadership and light rule based upon law and liberty that characterise British political activity.[15] Thus, for some, Britain's 'relationship

---

[13] See, generally, Nicholas Mansergh, 'The Historical Experience', in Nicholas Mansergh (ed.), *The Commonwealth Experience* (London: Weidenfeld & Nicolson, 1969). Preservation of the constitution and sovereignty have been two other dominant themes of Euroscepticism on the right.

[14] Enoch Powell, 'Commentary' to 'Never Again', in Brian Brivati and Harriet Jones (eds.), *What Difference did the War Make?* (Leicester: Leicester University Press, 1993).

[15] Robert Conquest, *Reflections on a Ravaged Century* (London: W. W. Norton, 2000), chs. 14, 15. This grouping would be weaker than a federation but stronger than an

with the European Union is haunted by the hankering for a lost empire. Euroscepticism has built been on the scepticism of a nation unwilling to own up to the present.'[16]

In the Labour Party, many who opposed supranational integration also emphasised the inheritance of Britain's traditional internationalism and its global reach. This was best transmitted through the post-imperial Commonwealth, and one of the most articulate proponents of this view was Douglas Jay, who wrote and debated extensively against British membership of the European Communities during the 1960s. He went on to be a leading campaigner for the 'No' vote in the 1975 referendum, having suggested as early as 1968 that a referendum might be held on Britain's membership. 'Britain's whole future', he wrote in 1968, in a Penguin Special,

depends on our preserving and strengthening our world links and our close relations, political and economic, with very many countries in all continents and of various political allegiances, colours and creeds. Neither economically, politically, culturally nor sentimentally are we a merely European power – if indeed 'Europe' can be said to exist as anything more than a stretch of land from the Urals to the Atlantic coast. The British public just does not feel itself more closely allied to Poles or Spaniards than to the people of Australia or New Zealand.

Membership of the EC might look superficially like a step to a more united Europe and a move towards world organisation and a wider international outlook for Britain, but, actually, 'it would reduce our influence'. The political kinship of Britain, Canada, Australia and New Zealand was something of the greatest value and overwhelmingly worth preserving, and Britain's influence in the world would be far greater if it could act as a bridge between the old and new Commonwealth in the interest of democratic institutions and racial harmony, rather than simply pursuing the aim of 'the merging of independent countries in one continent'. Indeed, 'if the federalists had their way, the UK would cease, I suppose to be a member of the UN; while Ghana, Nigeria, Romania and Formosa [Taiwan] would still belong.'[17]

alliance, and 'could become the foundation for a full unity of the democratized world', 281. The present Echelon signals intelligence network of more than 120 satellites is based on cooperation between the five larger English-speaking, Anglo-Saxon powers. This has caused considerable hostility from EU partners who are excluded: European Parliament Civil Liberties Committee, September 1998; *Le Monde*, 23 February 2000. See also Max Beloff, *Britain and the European Union: Dialogue of the Deaf* (London: Macmillan, 1996).

[16] Philip Stevens, *Financial Times*, 25 April 1998. Euroscepticism should here be interpreted as negative opinions about both the viability, and the desirability, of the continental European supranational integrative enterprise, either with or without the participation of the United Kingdom itself.

[17] Douglas Jay, *After the Common Market: A Better Alternative for Britain* (Harmondsworth: Penguin, 1968), 13, 102, 125.

The leader of the Labour Party, Hugh Gaitskell, largely shared these views at the time of the first British application. He made his outspoken appeal against the EEC at the Labour Party conference of 1962. If the thrust of what he said was intended to unite left-wingers and the centrist anti-EEC factions at a moment when he believed that the British application would fail anyway, his appeal was also couched in a rhetoric that was blatantly nationalist and in which membership of the EEC could only be accepted for Britain if the whole nature of the project was changed out of all recognition. Membership of a federal Europe would mean 'the end of Britain as an independent European state. I make no apology for repeating it. It means the end of a thousand years of history . . . And it does mean the end of the Commonwealth. How can we seriously suppose that if the mother country, the centre of the Commonwealth, is a province of Europe (which is what Federation means) it could continue to exist as the mother country of a series of independent nations? It is sheer nonsense.' He went on to invoke the Commonwealth contribution at Vimy Ridge and Gallipoli (as well as the merits of tea-drinking), and was met by an extraordinary ovation from the Party.[18]

Perhaps the best evidence for the continued presence of the imperial overhang in British politics is that, soon after coming to power in May 1997, New Labour itself made an effort to draw a line under this remembered past, with its campaign 'Cool Britannia' during the early months of 1998. Here, emphasis was laid upon youth (those who would have no direct memories of world wars or of the management of empire), civilian virtues and the brand values of Britain as a clever and creative island and one of the world's pioneers, rather than as one of its museums, despite the deeply – deliberately? – ironic imperial connotations of the word 'Britannia'. In *Britain TM: Renewing our Identity*, an entertaining, yet analytically shrewd effort was made to re-brand Britain, with the strategy of projecting a renewed national identity for greater economic prosperity and confidence. It was suggested that, to draw a line under the past, the monarch should visit all those major sites of the world 'where there is still bitterness over Britain's past, [to heal] . . . memories of everything from the Opium Wars in China to the legacies of Empire, from Africa to the Caribbean to Iran and Ireland. Both Germany and Japan have been

---

[18] For a full account of Gaitskell's thinking in 1962, see Brian Brivati, *Hugh Gaitskell* (London: Richard Cohen Books, 1997), ch. 17. The response to this kind of argument from the Labour pro-Europeans was well summarised by Roy Jenkins: 'Are we happy at the thought of marching into battle [against the EEC] at the head of a motley crew composed of Beaverbrook imperialists, little Englanders, defenders of inefficient vested interests, and plain straightforward xenophobes?' Roy Jenkins, *Common Market Debate* (London: Fabian International Bureau, 1962). By the 1980s these arguments had been reinforced by ideological, nationalistic and sovereignty arguments within the Labour Party.

forced into actions of this kind, but precisely because decolonisation was relatively untraumatic for Britain, there has been no thoroughgoing signal that Britain is no longer an imperial power.'[19] This suggests that collective memories that have largely been sustained as positive experiences could be erased by in fact treating them as negative experiences. Blair's own view was that 'we cannot pretend that the Empire is back because it isn't. My generation has moved on beyond all that. My generation has come to terms with its history. When I see the pageantry in Britain I think that's great, but it does not define where Britain is today. The whole idea of a modern British identity is not to displace the past, but to honor it by applying its best characteristics to today's world.'[20] But as we shall see, in reality Blair too is driven by the quest for post-imperial European and global leadership, both as a means to influence policy and as a representational device.

How, in practice, has the reality and then the memory of Empire, and the resilience of the notion of leadership that is bequeathed to the British decision-making classes played out in Britain's European policy? British policy towards the European Communities was, and remains, the most contentious foreign policy issue for British politicians since the 1950s. Both major parties have realised that the lure of the past, and the strength of the image of Britain's independent great power role in the world, have worked against the need to downgrade, adapt to and participate in European integration projects.

The European foreign policy of the first post-war – Old Labour – government between 1945 and 1951 was, naturally, deeply affected by memories of empire/dominion and war, and it was during these years that the framework of post-war British foreign policy was established. In 1945, memories were direct and personal, as well as institutionalised, for, as the war ended, Britain's great power status was not contested. However in practice, as one Foreign Office official put it, alongside the United States and the Soviet Union, it was more a case of the Big Two-and-a-Half, than the Big Three. Throughout subsequent decades, the direct memory of Empire and Britain's global role was to be changed into a collective historical memory that was easily and subconsciously sourced by individual politicians as well as Whitehall. Resistance to 'Europe', an unhappy alternative to great powerdom, remained a powerful force in British politics.[21]

---

[19] Mark Leonard, *Britain TM: Renewing our Identity* (London: Demos, with the Design Council, 1997), 70.

[20] *Time*, 27 October 1997; the cover was titled 'Renewed Britannia' and showed a stained Union Jack flag being pulled away to reveal a pristine one beneath – plus ça change?

[21] Clement Attlee 'would frequently half in earnest, half in jest, make such remarks as "can't trust the Europeans – they don't play cricket". He admired and liked Frenchmen,

In 1945, Empire and the white dominions were living entities as well as a direct memory, and the post-war Commonwealth was an issue of practical politics. Under the first post-war Labour government there were early attempts to reinvent the global reach that the old empire had represented so that Britain could reoccupy the 'middle of the planet' as a 'third force' or 'third world power' in world politics, rather than focus upon Europe.[22] A Labour Party pamphlet of 1947 made it clear that 'our interests are too widespread, our principles are too international, for us to restrict ourselves to the idea of regional blocs, however constructed'.[23] Of more lasting practical importance were decisions taken, first to engage the United States in British and European politics, and second, to develop a British atomic bomb. Whilst it was known that Britain's financial position was desperate after the war, the expectation was that Britain's old position could be recovered and that, as Oliver Franks implied in the 1954 Reith lectures, Britain's global status, and with it sterling, had taken only a temporary battering in the war.[24] Meanwhile, the old world could work with the United States to the mutual advantage of both. The 'special relationship' had its origins in the wartime period and it was hoped that this relationship would continue to enhance British influence as a global power, as the Churchill speech suggested, for, as the deputy under-secretary of state in the Foreign Office wrote in 1945, 'we must be prepared for the United States to falter from time to time when called upon to pull their weight in Europe ... We must have a policy of our own and try to persuade the United States to make it their own'.[25] At the same time, the Labour government's decision to develop its own atomic bomb was in the interests of Britain's role as a great power, its passport to continuing great power status, and the programme was driven through despite US scepticism about the British project: 'We have got to have this

---

Germans and Italians, but did not approve of the way they ran their countries': Keith Harris, *Attlee* (London: Weidenfeld & Nicolson, 1982), 315. On the 1940s see also Antonio Varsori, 'Is Britain Part of Europe?: the Myth of British "Difference"', in Cyril Buffet and Beatrice Heuser (eds.), *Haunted by History: Myths in International Relations* (Oxford: Berghahn Books, 1997).

[22] See John Kent, 'The British Empire and the Origins of the Cold War, 1944–1949', in Anne Deighton (ed.), *Britain and the First Cold War* (London: Macmillan, 1990), 165–84; Public Record Office, Kew, London: Bevin to Attlee, 16 Sept. 1947, FO800/444; John Darwin, *Britain and Decolonisation: the Retreat from Empire in the Post-War World* (London: Macmillan, 1990), 126; *Feet on the Ground: A Study of Western Union* (London: Labour Party, 1948); Avi Shlaim, *Britain and the Origins of European Unity, 1940–1951* (Reading: Graduate School of European Studies, Reading University, 1978).

[23] *Cards on the Table*, London, 1947, Archives of the British Labour Party, Series II, Bodleian Library, Oxford.

[24] The Reith lectures were published as Oliver S. Franks, *Britain and the Tide of World Affairs* (London: Oxford University Press, 1955).

[25] 'Stocktaking memorandum', 1945, *Documents on British Policy Overseas*, 1st Series (London: HMSO, 1984), 181ff.

thing over here whatever it costs . . . We've got to have the bloody Union Jack flying on top of it', said Ernest Bevin in 1947.[26]

Between 1948 and 1949 the British did in fact manage to find a temporary leadership position for themselves in Europe. The creation of the Brussels Treaty Organisation (1948) and the Council of Europe (1949) both owed much to Britain in terms of their structures and institutional framework. The NATO Treaty of 1949 helped to fulfil Britain's desire to balance the power of the Soviet Union (and to guard against the possible resurgence of German power) by engaging the United States on the Continent. However, after 1949, British attitudes towards Western Europe became increasingly those of the defensive outsider. The concept of an Atlantic Community as a global Western alliance appealed to British decision-makers, and it was, and has remained, a means of engaging British interests in continental Europe, but was inadequate to deal with developments in Europe after France seized the initiative and leadership in Europe in 1950. The Labour government deliberately chose not to take the risk of participation in the first experiment in supranational, sectoral integration, the European Coal and Steel Community (ECSC). This reluctance was most clearly expressed on the conclusion of a factfinding exercise, conducted during 1951, into the character and direction of the integration movement. The Permanent Under-Secretary's Committee (PUSC), established by the Eurosceptical PUS William Strang concluded thus:

The United Kingdom cannot seriously contemplate joining in European integration. Apart from geographical and strategic considerations, Commonwealth ties and the special position of the United Kingdom as the centre of the sterling area, we cannot consider submitting our political and economic system to supranational institutions . . . Nor is there, in fact, any evidence that there is real support in this country for any institutional connection with the Continent. Moreover, although the fact may not be universally recognised, it is not in the true interests of the Continent that we should sacrifice our present unattached position which enables us, together with the United States, to give a lead to the free world.[27]

Leadership of the continental Europeans was now not considered as attractive a prize as the global alternatives. Many 'pro-Europeans' have also argued that the 1950 decision was wrong, but for leadership reasons:

[26] Peter Hennessy, 'Never Again', in Brivati and Jones, *What Difference did the War Make?* 13. Evidence is also emerging of efforts in the 1950s to develop a dominion axis in the nuclear domain: Matthew Hill, 'The Great Leveller?: the 1951–55 Churchill Government, Atomic Energy and Thermonuclear weapons', unpublished paper, University of Oxford, 2000.

[27] *Documents on British Policy Overseas*, Series II, Vol. II, no. 20. Pro-Europeanists derided the Commonwealth argument as a myth. See, for example, Edward Beddington-Behrens, 'The Myth of the Alternatives', *Is There any Choice?: Britain must join Europe* (Harmondsworth: Penguin Special, 1966). On Strang, see entry in *New Dictionary of National Biography* (Oxford: Oxford University Press, forthcoming).

Europe needed Britain's leadership. Oliver Franks is reported to have said that the failure to join the ECSC 'cost us the leadership of Europe which we had enjoyed from the end of the War until May 1950'.[28] Indeed, a major study by Edmund Dell (himself a successful Labour politician) on the ECSC is actually called *The Schuman Plan and the British Abdication of Leadership in Europe.* Dell argues that the 'British reaction to the Schuman Plan was the failure to perceive that British participation in it was consistent with Britain's view of itself. It could be a global power, and at the centre of the Commonwealth and sterling area, and still participate in the Schuman Plan.'[29] Recent research makes it clear that, in the discussions about the Schuman Plan, the British cabinet was peeved that the idea had been brought forward by the French and Germans without their knowledge and, indeed, that the Americans had seen the draft plan before the British. When the British government then tentatively suggested that they might sit in on the planning committees, this was to be on the condition that they would do so without commitment. When the French then set the British a deadline for unconditional participation, the British deliberately withdrew, fully aware that they were abandoning leadership on the Continent in favour of a global role.[30]

By 1951, when Labour left office, a framework of continuing great power status was in place, despite Britain's parlous financial state. It was built upon the memory of Britain's past imperial world role, which was now to be symbolised by the atomic bomb; a close bilateral and multilateral (NATO) alliance with the United States which reinforced their shared successes in war; the creation of the Commonwealth to deal with decolonisation and change in the empire/dominions; and continued attachment to sterling as a global currency, despite the 1947 and 1949 sterling crises. Attachment to the Commonwealth (particularly the white dominions), to the United States and NATO, and indeed to the possession of nuclear weaponry appear to have reflected very well the images of former imperial status, and have become largely internalised into the British body politic. None of these characteristics of British foreign policy have yet been seriously contested in Britain. However, this architecture of Britain's international role was to prove a severe constraint in the face of the reconstruction and reinvention of a West European power bloc.

---

[28] Alex Danchev, *Oliver Franks: Founding Father* (Oxford: Oxford University Press), 1993, 75.

[29] Edmund Dell, *The Schuman Plan and the British Abdication of Leadership in Europe* (Oxford: Clarendon Press, 1995), 4. This view is very close to that held by the 'Strasbourg' Conservatives at this time, see Skär, *The Conservative Party*, passim.

[30] *Documents on British Policy Overseas*, Series II, Vol. II, No. 33. The French were aware of this, too: Janne Taalas, 'Leadership in Western European multilateral diplomacy, 1947–1951: Britain in the Marshall Aid negotiations and France in the Schuman Plan negotiations', D.Phil. thesis, University of Oxford, 1999.

In 1955 the British decided not to involve themselves in the projects to create a European Atomic Energy Community (EURATOM) and a European Economic Community (EEC). In the debates that took place in 1955–6, at the time of the negotiations about a West European customs union, the empire/Commonwealth trading system remained the key reason for Britain's refusal to participate in the negotiations which established the EEC.[31] There was a widespread reluctance to move away from a long-established and well-tried system that still seemed to enhance Britain's world diplomatic and trade position, although, militarily, it was quite clear that even by 1950, empire and Commonwealth security could not be guaranteed by Britain alone. The ANZUS Pact of 1951, between Australia, New Zealand and the United States, was evidence of the increasing fragmentation of the Commonwealth, as was the growing dependence of Canada on the United States. Economically, Britain knew that Commonwealth countries were looking increasingly for dollar assistance for their development, and that they were forming new trading partnerships. The GATT (General Agreement on Tariffs and Trade) regulations, by forbidding any new preferences, put a brake on the development of special trading links that had been established through the inter-war system of Imperial Preference. The pattern of the United Kingdom as the supplier of manufactured goods in exchange for food and other raw materials was not reflecting the dynamic of economic development in the empire/Commonwealth.[32] Likewise, the sterling area (which extended beyond the Commonwealth) became a policy block for successive British governments, and, despite its image of representing Britain's global trading links, contributed to financial crises until it was wound up in 1972. The symbolic value of the empire/Commonwealth thus became far more important than its practical value. As a Permanent Under-Secretary's Committee paper privately admitted as early as April 1950, the Commonwealth 'has no central authority . . . its members are increasingly framing their policies on grounds of regional and local interests . . . [although] substantial identity of views among Commonwealth countries is undoubtedly an important influence for world peace.' Indeed, the granting of independence to India and Burma was a truer reflection of declining British power. Lorna Lloyd has argued that investing time and energy in developing the Commonwealth was largely an ineffectual

---

[31] For a general history that provides insight into how it was that the Foreign Office, in its quest for a leading role within Whitehall, espoused 'Europe' more ardently than the Treasury: Hugo Young, *This Blessed Plot: Britain and Europe from Churchill to Blair* (London: Macmillan, 1998). The British bureaucratic mind and the imperial/ historical reflexes it brought to the European question merits a full study.

[32] See generally Catherine Schenk, *Britain and the Sterling Area: From Devaluation to Convertibility in the 1950s* (London: Macmillan, 1994).

exercise, although Britons 'continued to draw emotional comfort and diplomatic kudos from the Commonwealth and Britain's still-special role in it'.[33] But to join the EEC would have meant Britain abandoning one of the three Churchillian circles of its influence, and accepting the end of its role as an imperial and global power, and this it still could not do, despite the Suez fiasco of 1956. Instead, Britain unsuccessfully offered the continental Europeans an alternative scheme, the Free Trade Area, that better fitted Britain's own perceived interests and in which it would play a leading role.

In 1961 Prime Minister Harold Macmillan finally decided to apply for membership of the European Communities – a 'grim choice', he said.[34] This decision was based on the palpably evident decline in Britain's influence after 1960. Further, a report written by Frank Lee, a very senior civil servant, had argued that Britain could no longer hope to have greater global influence outside, rather than inside, the communities. Lee's worst-case analysis was that Washington would look to Brussels before London.[35] But it was not until 1972, after two rejections by de Gaulle of its membership application, that Britain finally joined the EC. Despite the provocative manner in which these vetoes were executed, it was clear that de Gaeulle's arguments about Britain's 'semi-detached' position, its attachment to its global role and to sterling had some good reason.

After its return to power in 1974 the Labour government held a referendum on the basis of very minor renegotiated 'conditions' for British membership. But opposition within the party was building fast, and by 1983 the Labour Party was committed to a withdrawal from the European Communities. Its manifesto stated that the decision to withdraw did not represent a weakening of a commitment to internationalism, only to the Treaty of Rome, but, however, that Labour 'attached a special significance to the Commonwealth – a unique forum of nations, cutting across ethnic, cultural and ideological barriers'.[36] So, by the 1980s, British Conservatives were led by a belligerent Thatcher, and the British Labour Party had a manifesto commitment to leave the EC. Labour's European policy,

---

[33] Lorna Lloyd, 'Britain and the Transformation from Empire to Commonwealth: the Significance of the Immediate Post-War Years', *The Round Table*, 345 (July 1997), 333–360; see Stephen Howe, *Anticolonialism in British Politics: The Left and the End of Empire, 1918–1964* (Oxford: Clarendon Press, 1993), ch. 4, for an interpretation that reveals that consensus was portrayed as being deeper than it actually was.

[34] Harold Macmillan, *Pointing the Way* (London: Macmillan, 1972), 316.

[35] Public Record Office, Kew, London: Lee Report, CAB 134/1853, 1960; Anne Deighton and Piers Ludlow, ' "A Conditional Application": Britain's first application to the EEC', in Anne Deighton (ed.), *Building Postwar Europe, 1948–1963* (London: Macmillan, 1995), 107–26.

[36] *The New Hope for Britain*, Labour Party Manifesto, 1983.

such as it had been, was thus in tatters, and a decade of reformulation of policies and outlook has resulted in the creation of New Labour, whose very title implies a break with the past.

But under New Labour a residue of these earlier memories remains, despite a genuine, deliberate effort to reinvent the party. The need for New Labour to portray the global 'leadership' image continues to permeate its thinking about Europe and beyond, and continues to create friction between the demands of government and general perceptions about European integration and Britain's role. The collective historical baggage of the past has been added to, not replaced, by New Labour thinking. How far this has been done consciously or unconsciously remains an intriguing question.

After eighteen years of Conservative governments, any change was bound to be widely trumpeted and closely observed. New Labour raced to a spectacular victory on 1 May 1997, basing its policy proposals on a manifesto which was up-beat on Europe but which still reflected a traditional desire to lead and to change Europe itself. 'We will give Britain leadership in Europe', one manifesto headline screams. It is accompanied by a symbolic full-colour picture of Labour leader Tony Blair in full flow, with French president Jacques Chirac looking on, open-mouthed, in apparent amazement. The manifesto draws on Britain's historic role as a 'leader of nations'. It is nationalistic, if not messianic in tone, as Blair pledged a 'bond of trust I set out at the end of this introduction, in which ten specific commitments are put before you. Hold us to them. They are our covenant with you.' Britain would be 'resolute in standing up for its own interests', but would make a 'fresh start' with a leading role. The effect of this appears to be intended to reinforce Europe as a vehicle for the restoration of a natural global leadership role for Britain, harnessed to the instinctive sense of moral responsibility and internationalism that characterises the Labour Party. The EU is, as it were, now taken for granted as a part of the British overseas landscape, although a federal Europe is explicitly rejected in the manifesto.[37]

New Labour has strongly promoted the idea of a new 'Third Way', in both domestic and, increasingly, foreign policy. Indeed, Blair has equated New Labour with the Third Way. Policy associated with the European Union was perhaps the most difficult question facing those trying to devise a 'Third Way' in foreign policy, as it directly confronts positive memories of an imperial past. Blair told the French National Assembly in March 1998: 'There is a sense in which there is a third way in EU development also. We integrate where it makes sense to do so; if not, we

[37] *New Labour because Britain deserves better*, Labour Party Manifesto, 1997.

celebrate the diversity which subsidiarity brings.'[38] But what is striking about this speech is that it is nevertheless permeated by the desire to change and to lead. The European Third Way is presented as a project to lead Europe in a new direction, and to change the EU with a new agenda, new priorities and the creation of a people's Europe. Indeed, the guru of the Third Way, Anthony Giddens, explicitly 'reinvented' the EU as an instrument to deal with globalisation, which is a novel interpretation of the Communities.[39]

New Labour can argue with good reason that there has been a real shift in Britain's priorities.[40] But the desire for leadership and the need to change Europe to fit Britain's interest has remained a central part of the rhetoric, if not the practice, of European politics.[41] The caution surrounding the economic and monetary union (EMU) project is the clearest example of this. In the run-up to the election it was clear that, in private, many senior members of the Labour Party felt that the EMU issue would evaporate. After all, a project for economic union had been proposed in 1970, for completion by 1980. The British gut reaction was that this continental initiative would not run, much as was thought about the Messina talks in 1955, which set up the EEC. Yet the EMU question has starkly exposed the gap between the rhetoric of leadership and the inability to carry this out while outside the system. There remain grave doubts about the EMU project, but the government has been forced to try to move closer to membership, and to persuade British opinion that this is the right thing to do, as it is clear that broader 'leadership' arguments will otherwise founder. Ironically, it has once again set up conditions for membership, although it could be argued that all except one – the convergence of British and continental economies – are devices for domestic consumption, rather than 'real' conditions.

New Labour now sees the EU as a means for projecting military power out into the wider world. During the air strikes over Kosovo in 1999, and the invasion of Afghanistan in 2001, Blair's personal role was dramatic – and was dramatically presented to the domestic as well as world press as an exercise in global leadership in war which also required his skills of leadership of both European and global allies. He was portrayed as

---

[38] Speech by Tony Blair to the French National Assembly, 24 March 1998; http://www. fco.gov.uk

[39] Anthony Giddens, *The Third Way: The Renewal of Social Democracy* (Cambridge: Polity Press, 1998), 141–2.

[40] For a full account of EU policy during Blair's first term see Anne Deighton, 'European Union Policy', in Anthony Seldon (ed.), *The Blair Effect: The Blair Government, 1997–2001* (London: Little, Brown, 2001), 307–30.

[41] Charles Grant, *Can Britain Lead in Europe?* (London: Centre for European Reform, 1998), 1.

leading the Americans over the Kosovo crisis, and standing 'shoulder to shoulder' with them over Afghanistan.

As a parallel to the EMU debate, Blair – and by every account, the initiative is a very personal one – has set up an alternative trajectory for British leadership in the EU, with the proposals to give the Union a military capacity to act collectively in non-Article 5 situations.[42] Although much of what was proposed in the Anglo-French Declaration agreed in St Malo in December 1998 had been debated by Britain's continental partners for some while, it was presented as an arena in which the United Kingdom was leading a new initiative.[43] The timing and place of the declaration – in France and by a joint statement with the French – was skilful, for, as Blair had reminded the French in his National Assembly speech, 'we are both nations that are used to power. We are not frightened of it or ashamed of it. We both want to remain a power for good in the world.'[44] The so called St Malo project for an EU Rapid Reaction Force is based on the premise that the inter-governmental *sine qua non* will hold over time, and that Britain will secure a new policy arena for the EU without caving into the forces of supra-nationalism (this means keeping the European Commission with a minimal role). The project is designed to enable Britain and its EU partners to work, with NATO (read United States) backing, in arenas of conflict that stretch beyond the European mainland, and to project power in the interests of values and security. Thus British officials privately talk of the capacity of this ad hoc force to be applied across the world, particularly in Africa, and indeed, Blair is reported even to have considered some kind of Commonwealth peacekeeping force before December 1998.

While emphasising the capacity of the government to project hard power through the EU, it has not tried to shake off the trappings of great powerdom that the first post-war Labour government established. The Commonwealth Heads of Government Meeting (CHOGM) in Edinburgh in 1997 revealed that the Labour government wished to play a continuing leadership role with regard to the Commonwealth. It was an exceptional occasion, and the government was determined to extract maximum benefit from it. Blair told the meeting:

[42] The initiative pre-dated the air strikes over Kosovo in the early summer of 1999, but was given additional intensity by the glaring inadequacies in European (including British) capabilities that the NATO action revealed. NATO Article 5 joint actions are in territorial self-defence, and the Blair/ Chirac proposal concerned security operations (including peacemaking and peacekeeping).

[43] For the St Malo Declaration of 4 December, 1998, see http://www.amb-grandebretagne.fr/decl/discs/

[44] Blair speech to the French National Assembly, 24 March 1998, http://www.fco.gov.uk/

The perceptions of Britain are changing, too. I cherish the ties of history, sentiment and culture that hold us together ... We are again becoming a central player
in Europe. Our relationship with the United States is stronger. Across a range of
international bodies from the UN to the G8 we are playing our true role again.
Our aim is to be pivotal ... We will be measured by what we are and what we stand
for, not for what we were. We use the strength of our history to build our future.
One of those strengths is the Commonwealth ... I believe that the Commonwealth
is needed more today than at any time in its history.[45]

Equally, in an important speech to the South African Parliament,
Blair deliberately linked the foreign policy 'Third Way' to the need for
continued British leadership: 'Any project of transformation calls for
energy and leadership. It calls on people like us to give the leadership ...
A nation that is led not drifting, leadership that takes the tough decisions
and does not flinch when the going gets tough.'[46] By early 1998 the
Labour government had also devised a new approach to the remaining
British Dependent Territories, 'a source of pride to Britain ... because
there is a family bond'. The government's approach has been to rename
the territories as 'British Overseas Territories', and it has acknowledged
Britain's duty to defend them, while asserting that they should also be
prepared to rally round Britain in its times of need. These two dimensions
of Labour's policy reveal a concern with the actual residue of the imperial legacy, and a desire to exploit the opportunity to show leadership in
a context beyond Europe.

New Labour has, conservatively, not wished to shake the consensus
on nuclear weaponry or on close ties with the United States. In a discussion with 'outsiders' about the far-reaching Strategic Defence Review
which was attended by both the Foreign Secretary and the Minister of
Defence, it was made quite clear that there were two issues which simply were not up for discussion by New Labour: one was the continued
possession of nuclear weapons, the other was the NATO alliance.[47] This
inheritance from Old Labour of 1945–51, which was itself born of what
Peter Hennessy has called 'of course' decisions to recast Britain's former
imperial greatness, has survived the Third Way largely intact.

It is clear that the memory of Empire, and the way that this has played
into the determination to develop the Commonwealth, the retention of
nuclear weaponry, and the cleaving to the only superpower, the United
States, has continued to affect the management of British foreign

---

[45] Blair speech at the CHOGM Opening Ceremony, 24 October, 1997; http://www.
chogm97.org/

[46] http://www.fco.gov.uk/news/speechtext.asp?1895

[47] This was a deliberate, political judgement, as New Labour did not wish to stir memories
of Old Labour's debates on nuclear weaponry; private information from FCO minister.

policy under New Labour. Positive memories of imperial greatness, reinforced by success in two world wars, have been sustained over the Cold War and post-Cold War periods.[48] Continuity has been more powerful than change, despite the ending of the Cold War, and the reconfiguration of the European continent. Blair's 1998 speech to the Press Association admirably reflects the power of the memory of the past, and the way that this has played out in a need to lead and shape others' destinies, and, extraordinarily, it carries within it (deliberate?) echoes of Churchill's Three Circles speech of 1948 quoted earlier. Blair said that 'though Britain will never be the mightiest nation on earth, we can be pivotal. It means building on the strengths of our history . . . It means realising once and for all that Britain does not have to choose between being strong with the United States, or strong with Europe . . . To be a country of our size and population, and to be a permanent member of the UN Security Council, a nuclear power, a leading player in NATO, a leading player in the Commonwealth, gives us huge advantages which we must exploit to the full.'[49]

As Kenneth Morgan has commented, 'the rapidity and lack of tension with which Britain shed her imperial domain is perhaps the most notable of tributes to national stability and, possibly, maturity in the post-war world . . . Britain shed her imperial role between 1947 and 1970 (Rhodesia excepted) with much skill and humanity. It was decolonisation without traumas and without tears.' In his excellent study, *The Pursuit of Greatness*, Robert Holland argues that shaking off the memories of imperial strength may take a generation.[50] I suggest that the timeframe may be longer. Indeed, because imperial memories have been portrayed as being so positive, they have not yet played themselves out in British politics, despite an increasing acceptance, in day-to-day life, of Britain's role in the EU. These direct manifestations of the old are mixed but still obvious – ranging from the rabid, but short-lived, nationalism engendered by the Falklands War, to the acceptance of a quasi post-imperial role concerning Kosovo, Sierra Leone and Afghanistan, and the low-key, but self-congratulatory, ending of empire in Hong Kong.[51]

Empire has now virtually vanished. Dominc Lieven is right to point out that the 'transition from British to American global leadership was

---

[48] For an interpretation that places even greater emphasis on a continuing 'imperial order' and continuity over time, see Mark Curtis, *The Great Deception: Anglo-American Power and World Order* (London: Pluto Press, 1998), Parts 1, 2.

[49] Blair speech to the Associated Press, London, 15 December 1998: http://www.fco. gov.uk/. 'Pivot' was also used to the CHOGM.

[50] Robert Holland, *The Pursuit of Greatness: Britain and the World Role* (London: Fontana, 1991).

[51] Christopher Hill, 'Foreign Policy', in Seldon (ed.), *The Blair Effect*, 331–54.

managed peacefully, and by historical standards, with astonishing amity' after the Second World War.[52] However, Britain's genuine imperial sway has long since ended. But the memory of imperialism has not evaporated. Britain's need to portray itself, especially at home, as a great global power with an instinct to show leadership has proved to be remarkably resilient, although British leadership rhetoric is now shrouded in a moral, rather than imperial, hue. Blair, like most prime ministers before him, has continued to try to sustain the great British balancing act in its three circles of influence: Empire–Commonwealth, the United States, and Europe. To do this, he has continued to construct a post-imperial, and contrived leadership role to bind these circles together, consistently constructing them as complementary, and not as alternatives. The extent to which imperial memories, and their adaptation by Old Labour between 1945 and 1951, have been consciously or unconsciously retained or constructed by New Labour is not clear. What is clear is that liberation from 'decolonisation without trauma and tears' appears to be as hard, but in different ways, as liberation from trauma. Thus New Labour's Third Way in foreign policy has been bolted on to, and has not replaced, received memories of Britain's imperial past and the concern for global powerdom and 'leadership' through which these memories have been nurtured, and well beyond the end of the Cold War.

[52] Lieven, *Empire*, 68.

5   Europe's post-Cold War memory of Russia: *cui bono?*

Iver B. Neumann

In the course of the last ten years, a sizable chunk of territory which we used to refer to as 'Eastern Europe' has changed social, political, economic and alliance allegiances and reincarnated itself as 'central Europe'. How could this happen so quickly? Inasmuch as this shift has been imbricated in changing power relations in the area, the event calls for political analysis. In partial answer to this call, the chapter points to two mnemonic factors. First, during the 'Eastern European' years, a discourse was kept alive by dint of which this territory was also remembered as something else, namely as 'central Europe'. Thus, an alternative memory was already available to the local political elite, even as the Cold War era was coming to a halt. This memory was used in order to differentiate this territory from the former Soviet Union, and also from the Balkans. Second, if it was possible for this alternative memory of the territory as qualitatively different from the former Soviet Union to be accepted by 'the West', it was because the dominant memory of Russia in Western discourse was informed by memories of Russia as a backward country and a potential military threat. These memories emanated from periods which antedated communism, and so the fall of communism was not in and of itself enough to erase them. Central Europeans used these memories as a manipulable resource of symbolic political power in order to gain political advantages such as membership of NATO and of the European Union (EU). All this was possible because Russia is liminal to European identity itself. By making up a spatial grey area towards China and a chronological grey area towards Europe's own past, Russia is the boundary which tells us who we are and where we belong, in space as well as in time. This chapter offers an account of how elites have handled what Tim Snyder in chapter 1 calls 'national memory' or *mémoire*. In other words, I am dealing with collective representations of the past at the level of overall political discourse. The chapter has nothing to say about the material and communicative transmission of memory, nor does it offer anything on the individual memory of others than intellectuals and politicians.

Cold War discourse on central Europe: a memory of something else

In its present incarnation, the discourse on central Europe dates back to the 1950s, when Czeslaw Milosz and other intellectuals re-initiated it under the new post-Yalta conditions. Milan Kundera has summed up its major themes as follows.

As a concept of cultural history, eastern Europe is Russia, with its quite specific history anchored in the Byzantine world. Bohemia, Poland, Hungary, just like Austria, have never been part of eastern Europe. From the very beginning they have taken part in the great adventure of Western civilisation, with its Gothic, its Renaissance, its Reformation – a movement which has its cradle precisely in this region. It was here, in central Europe, that modern culture found its greatest impulse: psychoanalysis, structuralism, dodecaphony, Bartók's music, Kafka's and Musil's new aesthetics of the novel. The post-war annexation of central Europe (or at least its major part) by Russian civilisation caused Western culture to lose its vital centre of gravity.[1]

This marking of western Europe as being as it were outside itself as long as central Europe remained in the custody of the Soviet Union, also re-veals the very positive moral assessment of 'the European idea'. Indeed, most traits ascribed to 'central Europe' can be refound in the rhetorical armoury of European federalists. Moreover, the positive assessment also extends to western Europe, warts and all. In order to highlight the broad significance of the debate under scrutiny, one could reproduce two Hungarian insertions into the international security debate:

the countries of West Europe have been the 'core' of the world system as the most advanced and powerful countries of the world. They almost always dominated their neighbours to the East which by the twentieth century were generally very small and, at most, semi-developed countries. Furthermore, these small countries (although many of them were packed into the Habsburg empire for several centuries) suffered from the pressures of Western modernised and industrialised states on one side and the Eastern empires (Russian and Ottoman) on the other. They have been swinging through history between long waves of Westernisation and Easternisation. After the last five decades of Easternisation, there appears once more to be a fundamental turn in the other direction and so their Westernisation begins again.[2]

Again,

---

[1] Quoted in Ladislav Matejka, 'Milan Kundera's Central Europe', *Cross Currents*, 9 (1990), 127–34, 131.

[2] Attila Ágh, 'After the Revolution: A Return to Europe', in Karl E. Birnbaum, Josef B. Binter and Stephen K. Badzik (eds.), *Towards a Future European Peace Order?* (London: Pinter 1991), 83–97, 84–5.

For Hungary, the notion of 'European identity' expresses an awareness of Europe as the 'common cultural homeland', of the fact that Europe is, despite its political division, a single cultural whole, with a diversity of links that even the Cold War years could not wholly dissever.[3]

The controversy is not so much about the western European other, which is perceived ambiguously as both self and other at the same time, but about the other to the east. It is not a matter of different moral assessments of the Soviet Union as a *political* entity, which is seen almost universally as morally inferior to 'central Europe'. It is, rather, about whether the other is simply confined in time to the Soviet political system, or whether the other is 'eternal Russia'. Moreover, it is about whether Russia is wholly other, or whether there is the same kind of ambiguity between self and other in the case of 'central Europe' and Russia, as there is between 'central Europe' and the West. In his essay, Kundera was very clear about this – the other was not simply the Soviet Union, but eternal Russia: 'Russia is not just as one more European power but as a singular civilisation, an *other* civilisation . . . totalitarian Russian civilisation is the radical negation of the modern West'.[4] The central European discourse naturalises a memory of Russia by insisting that it springs from an 'eternal' fount, it departicularises the communist experience by making it into one more variant of a Russian political tradition, and it demonises Russia by suggesting that this tradition is unchangeable. These practices in turn serve to naturalise, departicularise and idealise central Europe as a counterpoint to the posited Russian tradition.[5]

The break-up of Yalta: who lost eastern Europe and who won central Europe?

As the Soviet Union lost its grip on its Warsaw Pact allies and those countries began to look west, there followed a short but intense Russian debate about who lost eastern Europe. A number of leading military men came to the fore with accusations against the Gorbachev leadership for having desecrated the memory of those Soviet soldiers who fought in the

---

[3] László J. Kiss, 'European Security: Hungarian Interpretations, Perceptions and Foreign Policy', in Ole Wæver, Pierre Lemaitre and Elzbieta Tromer (eds.), *European Polyphony: Perspectives beyond East–West Cooperation* (London: Pinter, 1989), 141–53, 145.

[4] Milan Kundera, 'The Tragedy of Central Europe', *New York Review of Books*, 26 April 1984. The argument was not new, but had been set out by academics such as Tibor Szamuely, *The Russian Tradition* (London: Fontana, 1974).

[5] See Jeffrey K. Olick and Joyce Robbins, 'Social Memory Studies: From "Collective Memory" to the Historical Sociology of Mnemonic Practices', *Annual Review of Sociology*, 24 (1998), 105–40, 126.

Great War of the Fatherland by frittering away the prize of that war. To them, eastern Europe was lost in territorial terms.[6]

If the debate in the Soviet Union was about a loss of something which was presented as something which was rightfully 'ours', the events of 1989 were greeted enthusiastically by the participants in the discourse on central Europe. New contexts in which this discourse could be introduced sprang up. Whereas before, two memories contested one another from inside contexts which maintained a rather static relationship, now one of those memories could be introduced in contexts from which it had previously been banished. If eastern Europe was a Soviet-occupied political project which was now disappearing, this was the hour of rebirth for central Europe. Central Europe could be presented as yet again becoming what it once was. In January 1990, Václav Havel once again gave voice to the idea that central Europe was a cultural concept in search of realisation when he told the Polish Sejm that

there is before us the real historic chance to fill with something meaningful the great political vacuum that appeared in Central Europe after the break-up of the Habsburg Empire. We have the chance to transfer Central Europe from a phenomenon that has so far been historical and spiritual into a political phenomenon. We have the chance to take a string of European countries that until recently were colonised by the Soviets and that today are attempting the kind of friendship with the nations of the Soviet Union which would be founded on equal rights, and transform them into a definite special body, which would approach Western Europe not as a poor dissident or a helpless, searching amnestied prisoner, but as someone who has something to offer.[7]

Moreover, in keeping with the cultural image presented by most Czechoslovak, Hungarian, Polish, Slovene and Croatian participants in the debate, there was indeed a clear-cut difference in electional behaviour between these lands and other parts of the 'Eastern Europe' of the bygone postwar era. In these lands, non-communists were voted into power, and a regime change was initiated. Elsewhere, sections of the old ruling groups were voted in, and regime changes were much slower or failed to emerge altogether.

However, what also failed to emerge was the 'central European' co-operation which should, in Havel's words, transform central Europe into a political phenomenon – that is, actualise the memory of central Europe in tangible and operative political institutions which could

---

[6] Suzanne Crow, 'Who lost Eastern Europe?' *Report on the USSR*, 3 (15): 12 April 1991, pp. 1–5; Irina Kobrinskaya (1997) *Rossiya i Tsentral'naya Vostochnaya Evropa posle 'kholodnoy voyny'* Moscow: Carnegie Endowment for International Peace.

[7] 'President Václav Havel's Speech to the Polish Sejm and Senate, 21 January 1990', *East European Reporter*, 4, 2 (1990), 55–7, 56–7.

actualise central Europe in even more contexts. Two summit meetings between Czecho-Slovak, Hungarian and Polish heads of state and substantive and repeated Polish and third-party initiatives notwithstanding, concrete cooperation and institutions generally failed to emerge. Even where interests and strategies were perceived to dovetail, as in the case of policy vis-à-vis the European Communities (EC), cooperation was not entered into, but had to be imposed by what was effectively the third party, the EC: 'the competition among the three states to be the first to enter Europe is held in check by the Western political community's inclination to treat the new democracies of central Europe as a unit'.[8] The programme of Havel the participant in the debate about 'central Europe' was thwarted by, among others, Havel the president. However, the 'central European' project continued to operate as a political project in the way it always had – as a moral appeal and reproach addressed to western Europe. Indeed, this is yet again set out programmatically in the second half of Havel's insertion, together with a new proposal for relations with that other external other – the crumbling Soviet Union. Contrary to what was often implied by participants such as Václav Havel, it appeared that although the 'central European' project did not result in institutionalised contacts between societies and/or states in the area, it could still be used politically vis-à-vis western Europe and Russia. In terms of identity politics, the project's reality was actually unimpaired by the failure of political structures to emerge; its dynamics had from its very inception lain on the interface between the imagined region and its external others, Russia and western Europe, and continued to do so.

The attempted external differentiation of 'central Europe' from, and at the expense of, Russia, continued as before. Perhaps the most concrete and striking example of this practice was an October 1991 self-proclaimed appeal to the EC's Maastricht summit which argued that

though we should do our utmost to promote democracy in the new Russia, this should not obscure the more immediate and manageable challenge of central Europe... Historically and culturally, Poland, Hungary, and Czechoslovakia belong to Europe. A Europe which contains Crete but not Bohemia, Lisbon but not Warsaw, is historical nonsense... Yet where would this leave the rest of post-communist Europe?... It makes plain, practical sense to start with those that are nearest, and work out to those which are farthest. Poland, Hungary, and Czechoslovakia are nearest not only geographically, historically, and culturally,

---

[8] Rudolf L. Tökés, 'From Visegrád to Kraków: Cooperation, Competition, and Coexistence in Central Europe', *Problems of Communism*, 40 (November–December 1991), 100–14, 113. This pattern, which could also be seen where Polish entry into the Pentagonal was concerned, is analysed in Iver B. Neumann, 'Poland as a Regional Great Power: The Interwar Heritage', in Iver B. Neumann (ed.), *Regional Great Powers in International Politics* (London: Macmillan, 1992), pp. 141–59.

but also in the progress they have already made on the road to democracy, the rule of law, and a market economy.[9]

So, the three co-authors conclude, 'Following the suggestion originally made by the Czechoslovak Foreign Minister, Jiří Dienstbier, some of the aid to Russia and the other post-Soviet republics should be made in a form which both enables and obliges them to spend it in east central Europe.' Moreover, all other EC concerns should be streamlined to the overriding priority of catering to 'Poland, Hungary and Czechoslovakia': 'All proposals for a deepening of the present EC of twelve through closer integration must be workable by extension in a community of twenty'. Finally, it is asserted that all good things may come together. Privileging 'central Europe' will turn it into 'a magnet for south-east Europe, for the Baltic states, the Ukraine, and, yes, for the European parts of Russia', and the broadening of the Communities it entails will 'help in deepening' the EC's integration process as well. All this is presented by *The New York Review of Books* under the title 'Let the East Europeans In!', which yet again stresses that what is good for 'central Europe' is good for 'eastern Europe' as well as for Europe.

Far from being a peripheral part of the discourse, these formulations have already found their way into the rhetorical armoury of people like the Polish minister of foreign affairs. In a *tour d'horizon* of the state of European relations in spring 1992, Polish foreign minister Krzysztof Skubiszewski held that

as a consequence of the end of the Cold War, contemporary security relations on our continent have lost their simplicity and may be geographically described as concentric circles progressing from the stable nucleus of the countries of the European Communities, the western European Union and the North Atlantic Alliance, to the most unstable peripheries... The most important danger zone in Europe, with regard to possible military conflicts, is the area extending between Russia, the Ukraine, and Romania... The association of the three countries [i.e. Czechoslovakia, Hungary and Poland] with the European Community is relevant to their security but also to that of the West: the hard core of Europe will comprise a bigger territory.[10]

The memory of Russia

How could the memory of central Europe come to dominate political discourse so easily? One may of course treat this as a clear-cut case of

---

[9] Timothy Garton Ash, Michael Mertes and Dominique Moïsi, 'Let the East Europeans In!' *The New York Review of Books*, 24 October 1991, 19.

[10] Krzysztof Skubiszewski, 'The Challenge to Western Policy of Change in Eastern Europe', paper presented at the Conference on Britain and the Future of Eastern Europe and the Former Soviet Union, All Souls College, Oxford, 10–12 April 1992.

power politics, whereby Western institutions such as NATO and the EU take advantage of the central European discourse for their own ends, and assimilate these willing areas as a *Vorderland* or *antemurale* to Russia. But this Realpolitik answer simply begs the next question, which is what kinds of memories which made it possible to construct central Europe as a friend, and Russia as a foe.

One immediately notes the ease with which Russia is discussed as a seemingly timeless entity in 'Western' discourse, for example in the frictionless references to the present president as a 'tsar'. Where Russia is concerned, the legitimacy and relevance of discussing how the handling of day-to-day questions of policy are influenced by references to the past are seldom questioned. Neither does one need an excuse for drawing parallels between sixteenth- and twentieth-century rulers. By extension, one should also expect there to be a scholarly debate about how European and Western metaphors of the past colour the handling of the question of where Russia fits in. Very few politicians and diplomats, and only the most ardent positivist scholar, would object to the general argument that the way in which a political question has been variously discussed in the past will impinge on the political business at hand. And yet, when it comes to the question of where Russia fits in, there is little by way of scholarly reflection on how this complex of issues has been handled previously.

At the present juncture, the discussion about Russia concerns its future more than its present. Russia is often seen as a learner of European economic and political practices. Economically, it has emerged from the ruins of a failed modernisation strategy and is now in the process of getting in place the prerequisites of a capitalist economy: a market with supporting institutions, and a middle class to run it. Politically, it is beginning to develop a differentiated elite structure with supporting institutions and a legal system based on the idea that written laws bind all actors. Thus, it is seen as substituting the successful modernisation strategy for the unsuccessful one that it embodied before. However, to a degree unheard of in contemporary Europe, political power is bound to the bodies of persons, and not to the bodies of institutions. Hence the importance of a European policy of supporting the leader (Gorbachev, Yeltsin) rather than the emerging system *in abstracto*. To the extent that this is contested, and that is not a very large extent, the question is not whether this is what is happening, but what and how important the role of Europe and the West was in bringing about this change.

Competing memories do exist. The Estonian politician Tiit Made, for example, went on record in 1989 with the view that, because Russian women had for centuries been raped by Mongol and Tatar men, the people were untamed and wild, and tended to spread like a blot all over the territory they could find.[11] During and immediately after the breakdown of the Soviet Union, other Baltic politicians frequently spoke in the same terms on lecture tours in Scandinavia, and presumably elsewhere as well. At present, however, this memory has to some extent been suppressed by the other just given, but it remains what one Lithuanian ambassador to a Scandinavian country once referred to in conversation with fellow diplomats as 'common folk wisdom' in the Baltic states. It will be demonstrated below that such biologically based or essentialist memories have a rich genealogy.

The idea of Russia as a learner does of course imply that Russia is becoming more like 'us', less 'different'. In accordance with what was said earlier about the impossibility of fixing any one identity, I will not dwell on the fact that this 'us' to which Russia is presumably growing more similar is forever changing by context, and may be 'the West', 'Germany', 'the Baltics' as well as Europe. The main point is that, as Russia is 'learning' successfully, it is expected to become less of a threat. What is heavily disputed is whether the idea that it is a learner will remain a dominant identity in Russian political discourse itself. The idea of learning, after all, presupposes a disequilibrium, and so for Russians there is an obvious tension between accepting the role as 'learner' from Europe and maintaining the notion that Russia is a European great power, a notion which presupposes some kind of equilibrium with (other) European great powers.

Whereas politicians such as Strobe Talbott and academics such as Anders Åslund have stressed that the market is already in place and the rest will therefore quickly follow, even that Russia is a place for a possible capitalist *Wirtschaftswunder*, a competing and perhaps even more widespread view has it that the learning process may quickly be discontinued. Aggressive nationalists may take over, and a military threat to Europe may follow (the reader is referred to the last ten years' worth of NATO country defence reviews for examples of this view). It is sometimes stressed how Russia's being a poor learner in one particular but crucial area, namely that of human rights in general and minority policy in particular, shows that the possibility of an aggressive nationalist policy vis-à-vis Europe may be imminent. Russia's seeming inability to treat its ethnic minorities such as Chechens and also the 'near abroad', perhaps even the Baltics, as nations on a par with the Russian nation itself, suggests insecurity about its sense of self which may also result in an aggressive nationalist policy vis-à-vis Europe (see, for example, the influential writings by Zbigniew Brzezinski in *Foreign Affairs* and elsewhere).

[11] Quoted in *Svenska Dagbladet*, Stockholm, 24 July 1989.

Learners should pass tests, and in Europe Chechnya was made a test of Russia's prospective European policy. Less conspicuously, Russian reactions to expansions of the EU and NATO are seen as tests of the extent to which Russians have learned that these particular institutionalisations of European and Western selves are not and cannot be potential threats to Russia. Thus, European discourse validates central European discourse by validating its memory of Russia as a threat, and at the same time insists that Russia, too, should validate the central European memory of itself as a threat. The most interesting thing is perhaps not how European discourse thus usurps the power to inculcate Russia with a particular memory of self, but how it does so without stopping to reflect what it is really doing, and how that which it does may impinge on Russian discourse on Europe.

A memory of Russia which stresses a learning aspect and, to a lesser extent, a potential military threat, dominates contemporary European discourse. By putting itself forward as a teacher who has the right to sanction bad learning behaviour, Europe creates one dominant problem for its Russia policy. As every teacher knows, there is a clear limit to the amount of sanctions she can mete out before the pupil will respond by challenging her authority, and the teaching will simply have the effect of underlining the difference between the two parties. In order effectively to shape the pupil not as different but as similar, a teacher needs at least some degree of recognition from her pupil. The version which is being reiterated over and over in Europe by people holding positions which add weight to their statements, attempts to solve this problem by recognising Russia not as a fully fledged great power, but as a great power by courtesy. There is a focus on human rights, and particularly minority rights. These are areas which also figure prominently in other European discourses, such as that on the institutionalisation of European integration. Russia is seen as part of Europe in the sense that it is its apprentice and thus a potential apostate. The discourse on Russia is prominent among political discourses, but hardly dominant. It is, for example, a disputed point whether the actualisation of a Russian threat is the most immediate challenge to the configuration of the international system, or whether that role is played by the posssibility of a change in Chinese or even Indian foreign policy, by Islam, by the possibility of a worldwide ecological crisis, and so on.

Although there has been a lack of reflection about how European discussions of Russia have changed, things *were* rather different only a handful of years ago, during what may be called the short twentieth century (from the outbreak of the First World War to the end of the Cold War). The memory of the Soviet Union as an actual military, and to some extent also a political, threat was so pervasive that it was and is ubiquitously used in the delineation of a period of European history: the Cold War. The Other inscribed itself in the temporal dimension of the European self's identity by giving name to a period of its history. Indeed, the Soviet initiative to end the Cold War was made among other things by means of issuing an application to join Europe – recalling the slogan of the Common European Home. European reactions to these applications varied from bafflement that such an application should be necessary, to assertions that the Soviet Union was (mostly) 'in Europe but not of Europe', to wariness that the intention was to decouple (Western) Europe from the United States.[12]

These reactions mirrored the pervasive memories of the Soviet Union of the Cold War period, which were two. One was of an Asiatic/barbarian political power which had availed itself of the opportunity offered by the Second World War to intrude into Europe by military means. In 1945 Churchill is said to have maintained, with reference to the Soviet Union, that the barbarians stood in the heart of Europe, and the following year Konrad Adenauer wrote to William Sollmann that 'Asia stands on the Elbe'.[13] These interventions are interesting, not least because they serve to exile the memory of the alliance against the Nazis into political irrelevance by foregrounding other dimensions of the relationship. One may even argue that the question is not why this memory was not stronger, but why this memory was not allowed to become politically relevant in the first place.

The view of Russia as barbaric was also widespread in academic literature. For example, in a book series on the formation of Europe published in France in 1950, the first paragraph of the first chapter of the volume on Russia is called 'La Russie est asiatique'. Here, one reads that Russia cannot be judged by European measures, that there exists a primordial geographical antithesis between Europe and Russia, and that the former is sedentary and thus civilised, while the latter is nomadic and thus barbarian.[14] One notes the ambiguity of these statements given their inclusion in a book series on *European* history. We have here the theme of the barbarian at Europe's gate, which may be traced throughout the period and which was kept alive in the discourse on 'central Europe'.

---

[12] Günther Nonnenmacher, 'Gorbachev's message for Europe a dangerous, phoney metaphor', in *The German Tribune*, 15 March 1987 (trans. of *Frankfurter Allgemeine Zeitung*, 9 March 1987).

[13] Konrad Adenauer, *Briefe, 1945–1947*, ed. Hans Peter Mensing (Berlin: Siedler, 1983), p. 191; Churchill quoted by Sir Ian Jacob in Michael Charlton, *The Eagle and the Small Birds. Crisis in the Soviet Empire: from Yalta to Solidarity* (Chicago: University of Chicago Press, 1984), 43.

[14] Gonzague de Reynold, *Le monde Russe*, La formation de l'Europe 6 (Paris: Librairie Plon, 1950), 25–8.

A competing memory of the Soviet Union, one which did make the alliance experience relevant and built on it, saw this state not only as the deliverer of Europe from the scourge of Nazism (the 'halo of Stalingrad'), but also as a model for Europe to emulate.[15] The major point for our purposes is that this memory dominated memory less and less as the Cold War came to its close. Furthermore, at the end of the Cold War, very little was left of the idea of Soviet Russia as a political threat, which had been the main dimension of threat in the inter-war years.

During the inter-war period, with the radical exception of Nazi discourse, Russia was seen as part of Europe, but a somewhat errant part. Perhaps Carl Schmitt, who spent a lifetime theorising about the delineation of friend from foe, encapsulated this best: he held that 'We in *Mitteleuropa* live *sous l'oeil des Russes*', and that Russia was 'a state which is more, and more intensely, statist [*staatlich*] than any state ruled by an absolute monarch'. This, he maintained, was because Russia could be seen as Europe's radical brother, 'who took the European nineteenth century at its word'.[16] Schmitt's memory of Russia was shot through with fear not only of that particular state as a factor external to Europe, but also of the possibility that Russia's present should be Europe's future. This memory of Soviet Russia as a political threat has not been reactivated in post-Cold War discourse, where the stress has been on Russia as a learner, but also as a chaotic challenge and a potential military threat. These are memories which may be traced back to the nineteenth century.

The Napoleonic Wars brought Russian soldiers to Paris. Russia was confirmed as a great power, and, on the defeat of Napoleon, in 1815, with the other great powers (Austria, Britain and Prussia) renewed the Quadruple Alliance, first formed in 1813, to prevent the recurrence of French aggression. Russia remained a fully fledged player in European politics throughout the period. Bismarck summed up a century of geopolitical thinking and practice with his adage that one must always try to be *à trois* in a world of five great powers. There was a debate about Russian intentions, with Russian fortunes in its wars with Turkey and Persia (and in 1904–5 with Japan) being the main factor to influence assessments of its strengths and intentions. It should not be forgotten, however, that the question of a possible Russian hegemony in Europe was not allowed to dominate – within the discourses of other great powers, Russia was not

---

[15] In this they could draw on widely held views from during the war. For example, 'A report by the [British] postal censorship authorities in March 1942 stated that "The majority of writers seem to pin their faith almost entirely on the Russians – 'the chaps who don't talk but keep on killing Huns'"'; P. M. H. Bell, *John Bull and the Bear: British Public Opinion, Foreign Policy and the Soviet Union 1941–1945* (London: Edward Arnold, 1990), 88.

[16] Carl Schmitt, *Der Begriff des Politischen: Text von 1932 mit einem Vorwort und drei Collarien* (Berlin: Duncker & Humblot, 1963), 79–80.

alone in being suspected of such intentions. Similar things were being said about France, particularly at the beginning of the period, about Germany as the period drew to a close, and about Great Britain throughout.

There was, first, the tendency to view Russia not only as a power grasping for hegemony, but also as doing this in the manner of a barbarian at the gate (as opposed to being seen as launching the attempt from inside). And then there was the tendency to try to refashion the idea of the European balance of power itself, so that the Europeanness which inclusion in it conferred on Russia could be relativised. It is hardly surprising that both these themes were particularly pronounced among Napoleonic French writers. Napoleon at one point held that Europe and the rest of the world would soon be enmeshed either in the American republic or the Russian universal monarchy. After his fall, he is reported to have held that Europe would become either cossack or republican.[17]

The theme of the barbarian at the gate has already been described in its Cold War version.[18] As part of the preparations for his Russian campaign, Napoleon had issued orders that the Ministry of Foreign Affairs should orchestrate the publication of articles to show that 'Europe is inevitably in the process of becoming booty for Russia' (if it did not become republican, that is, dominated by Napoleonic France). One of the upshots of this was the publication, in October 1812, of a meticulously researched and annotated book by Charles Louis Lesur, *Des progrès de la puissance russe*. This contained a modified version of a document written for the French Directory by the Polish general Michael Sokolniki fifteen years previously, which was now passed off as the testament of Peter the Great. The alleged testament was nothing short of a recipe for attaining European hegemony:

Hold the state in a system of continual warfare, in order to maintain strict discipline among the soldiers and in order to keep the nation on the move and ready to march at the first signal . . . At any costs involve yourself in the quarrels of Europe either by force or by ruse . . . All these divisions will then provide total latitude for the soldiers of the front lines, so that they may with vigour and all possible certitude conquer and subjugate the rest of Europe.[19]

---

[17] Michel Cadot, *L'image de la Russie dans la vie intellectuelle française (1839–1856)* (Paris: Fayard, 1967), 516.

[18] As noted at the outset, the level of generality works to the detriment of focusing on spatial variation at any one point in time. For example, Bruno Naarden, *Socialist Europe and Revolutionary Russia: Perception and Prejudice, 1848–1923* (Cambridge: Cambridge University Press, 1992), 32, notes that, even in the first half of the nineteenth century, when Russophobia reached a height in other parts of Europe, it was absent in Holland.

[19] Translation from Raymond T. McNally, 'The Origins of Russophobia in France 1812–1830', *American Slavic and East European Review*, 17 (April 1958), 173–89, 174. The testament was republished by, among others, Louis Napoleon and Hitler.

Throughout the period, the theme of the barbarian at the gate was reinforced by focusing on the existence of Muslim and therefore presumably Asiatic national minorities inside Russia, and using these as a *pars pro toto* to underline the Asiatic nature of Russia as a whole. It is a small step from this to the idea that, if one scrapes a Russian, the Tatar will emerge. Take away the borrowed feathers of European civilisation and military might, and the barbarian (or even a savage if one scraped hard enough!) would emerge in the raw.

Going hand in hand with the memory of the barbarian at the gate, however, was an auxiliary attempt to disrupt the idea that Russia has a place inside the European balance of power by changing that memory itself. The crucial name here is l'abbé Dominique-Georges-Frédéric de de Pradt, who in a series of books exhorted Europeans to close ranks and gates against the Russians:

Russia is built up despotically and Asiatically . . . Europe must draw closer together and as she shuts herself up, Europe should cooperate in outlawing all participation in her affairs by any power which does not have a direct interest in them and which has the force to weigh down the balance to suit her own interests.[20]

In a number of works published in the aftermath of the Napoleonic Wars, de Pradt, who was an archbishop and Napoleon's former confessor, went on to develop the thesis that 'l'Angleterre règne sur la mer, la Russie sur la terre: tel est la partage actuel du monde'. Russia must be kept from Europe, and the way to do it was to expand the idea of the balance of power to include America! Here is the genesis of the idea that Europe is situated between America and Russia, and that European power politics must be conducted on the basis of this fact. Crucially, by changing the balance of power from an intra-European to a European-focused phenomenon, this idea negated the dictum that inclusion in the balance of power in and of itself should confer Europeanness on a particular power. Since it came at the exact time when there could no longer be any doubt about Russia's pivotal role in the European balance of power, this was indeed a crucial move. Since, after the nineteenth century, the relevance of inclusion into the balance of power for inclusion into Europe clearly faded, it was also a move which was to prove productive in the long run.

The idea of the barbarian at the gate, then, lent a particular flavour to European strategic discourse on Russia. Russia was depicted as an ambiguous presence on the border, which could be associated with Europe, but also with China. It is, then, not surprising to find as the central

[20] Quoted in McNally, 'Origins of Russophobia', 182; also Dieter Groh, *Russland und das Selbstverständnis Europas: Ein Beitrag zur europäischen Geistesgeschichte* (Neuwied: Hermann Luchterhand, 1967) 128–31.

metaphor in the perhaps most widely read book of the period, the Marquis de Custine's *Lettres de Russie: La Russie en 1839*, the idea that Russia was cordoned off from western Europe by a 'Chinese Wall'.[21] What should be particularly noted, however, is where the Marquis de Custine located this wall, namely on the Vistula. For de Custine, it was the military reach of Russia which determines where this wall was to be found, and not the cultural traits of the particular peoples who happened to live in the relevant territories. Bearing in mind the very recent debate about the delineation of 'eastern' from 'central' Europe, this problematique is not without contemporary relevance.

Conclusion: Europe's pangolin

In a minor anthropological classic, Mary Douglas discussed the taxonomic practice of the Lele, and fastened on to their problems in categorising the pangolin (a scaly ant-eater to some): 'The pangolin is described by the Lele in terms in which there is no mistaking its anomalous character. They say: "In our forest there is an animal with the body and tail of a fish, covered in scales. It has four legs and it climbs in trees"'.[22] The pangolin is seen to have properties that do not go together, and so it threatens the very principles of Lele taxonomisation, and, by extension, taxonomisation as such. Since taxonomy is at the core of the world view and thus identity of the Lele themselves, this is an extremely serious matter: 'They would never say, "We avoid anomalous animals because in defying the categories of our universe they arouse deep feelings of disquiet." But on each avoided animal they would launch into disquisitions on its natural history.'[23]

For this reason, the pangolin is constructed as a monster, but also by some as the totem animal of a fertility cult. One could argue that Russia is Europe's main pangolin. Being a pangolin which does not fit in is, however, still very much being part of the taxonomy, and a very important part at that. Since the time of Peter the Great, Russia has been seen as a pupil and a learner, be that a successful one (the Enlightenment), one who should learn but refuses to do so (the nineteenth century), a truant (the twentieth century), or a gifted but somewhat pigheaded one (the present). It is therefore deeply appropriate that, for the last decade or so, the main metaphor used in European discussions of Russian

---

[21] Cadot, *L'image de la Russie*, 540, 173.

[22] Mary Douglas, 'Animals in Lele Religious Symbolism' in her *Implicit Meaning: Essays in Anthropology* (London: Routledge & Kegan Paul (1975 [1957]), 27–46, 33.

[23] Mary Douglas, *Purity and Danger: An Analysis of the Concepts of Pollution and Taboo* (London: Ark, (1984 [1966]), 173.

politics and economics has been that of *transition*. The dimension of European identity formation along which Russia stands out is not first and foremost the spatial one, but rather the mnemonic one: Russia is trapped in a time which (the rest of) Europe is forever leaving.

Danger resides on the borders, Mary Douglas argues, and so, as long as Russia is constructed as a border case, it will also be inscribed with danger. Anne Norton has suggested that identities are at their most transparent when they are at their most ambiguous, and that the most rewarding place to study them is, therefore, in their attempted delineation from what she calls their liminars.[24] Russia, in whatever territorial shape, by whatever name, as whatever memory, has a history as Europe's main liminar. The uncertainty of self with which memories of it are associated throughout the periods given here is, therefore, highly interesting, not only when the issue is Russia, but also when it is European identity. There are uncertainties surrounding its Christian status in the sixteenth and seventeenth centuries, uncertainties about to what extent it could succeed in internalising what it learned from Europe in the eighteenth century, uncertainties about its military intentions in the nineteenth century and military–political ones in the twentieth century, and now again uncertainties about its potential as a learner: uncertainties everywhere.

Once asked about the patronage of the EEC, Paul-Henri Spaak answered that Stalin was its father, inasmuch as fear of the Soviet Union had provided the impetus to hang together rather than hang separately.[25] To wheel out another and perhaps overused quote, the first secretary-general of NATO, Lord Ismay, held that the job of NATO was to keep the Americans in, the Russians out and the Germans down. Regardless of degree of institutionalisation, then, Europe is tied to the idea of the Russian other. Since exclusion is a necessary ingredient of integration, this is in itself no problem. The temptation remains, however, to play up the alterity of Russia *in order to* increase the integration of the European self. This is an ingredient of a number of contemporary debates which are to do with the expansion of the EU and NATO: trade policy, arms control, and so on. Since these issues are tied up with half a millennium's memory of Russia as barbarian, Asiatic and so on, they seem to call for rather more sensitivity to the question of how the memory of Russia enters into them than seems to have been shown so far. It lies close at hand to remember Russia as a learner, as half Asiatic, as having despotic political institutions, as riding roughshod over its Muslim minorities and

---

[24] Anne Norton, *Reflections on Political Identity* (Baltimore: Johns Hopkins University Press, 1988).
[25] Paul-Henri Spaak, *Combats Inachevés: De l'Indépendance à l'Alliance* (Paris: Fayard, 1969).

potentially over 'central Europe'. For a start, all these ideas and more are part of Russian selves as they emerge in its attempted delineation of Europe.[26]

In conclusion, I suggest that, if in our ongoing discourse on Russia we do not allow for more reflection of how the deeply entrenched patterns discussed here remain a more or less unacknowledged factor of memory, we will add our voices to the chorus that confirms the memory of Russia as a learner which is forever and already just about to make the transition into Europe. The success of the discourse of central Europe demonstrates not only that memory may be successfully activated as a resource of symbolic political power, but also how this success is predicated upon a very modern way of thinking, by means of which Russia is relegated to a past from which first western Europe and now central Europe has escaped. Russia, then, is represented as the living memory of our own past, a past to which we must see that we do not return.

[26] See Iver B. Neumann, *Russia and the Idea of Europe: A Study in Identity and International Relations* (London: Routledge, 1996).

6   Memory, the media and NATO: information intervention in Bosnia-Hercegovina

Monroe E. Price

If collective or social memory is power, then those engaged in the contest for control will seek to manage its production. One of the most important ways in which public or national memories have been nourished, shaped and limited in the twentieth century has been through broadcasting and, in the period since the late 1950s, more specifically through television. Television is one of the prime means by which to establish what Timothy Snyder in his chapter calls 'sovereignty over memory', and to provide both a national framework for collective memory and to shape individual memories of national events. In this chapter, I want to explore an important episode in the management of memory as an instrument of conflict prevention or resolution, namely the role played, in Bosnia-Hercegovina in the late 1990s, by the US-led NATO Stabilisation Force (Sfor) and the Office of the High Representative (OHR). As Ilana R. Bet-El shows in her chapter, the Bosnian context was one in which, for generations and centuries, memories were articulated, projected and raised as flags of combat. Television gave a whole new force to such articulations.

The narrative of control of information in Bosnia can be linked to the history of efforts by one state, or a group of states, to influence the articulation or suppression of particular narratives within the borders of another state. More than that, it is the precursor of a fairly radical and important area of potential change, given new media technologies, in the way in which governments treat the information space of other countries in times of crisis. Already, 'information warfare' is the subject of increased focus by military strategists.[1] Increasingly, there are examples of media

I want to acknowledge the considerable editorial assistance of Stacy Sullivan who was my research assistant at the Media Studies Center in New York. An extended treatment of this subject can be found in Monroe E. Price, 'Information Intervention: Bosnia, the Dayton Accords and the Seizure of Broadcasting Transmitters', *Cornell International Law Journal*, 33 (2000), 67.

[1] Information warfare has been defined as follows: 'Action taken in support of national security strategy to seize and maintain a decisive advantage by attacking an adversary's information infrastructure through exploitation, denial, and influence, while protecting

restructuring in the wake of conflict, part of the general effort (often an element of peacekeeping) to alter forces tied to historical animosities reflected in narratives of identity. Information warfare – dealing with the jamming of enemy military communications technology and command and control functions – is beyond the scope of this essay. I am interested, here, rather, in interventions to shape ideas, news, public perceptions of past and present events, and the relation between an infrastructure of memory that undergirds a fierce or combative patriotism and one that turns a people against their government or one another. In this respect, information warfare includes 'public diplomacy measures, propaganda and psychological campaigns, political and cultural subversion, deception of or interference with local media, infiltration of computer networks and databases and efforts to promote dissident or opposition movements across computer networks'.[2]

Studying the seizure of transmitters in Bosnia in 1997 helps in exploring what role law has in affecting memory in the adjustment of power. In Bosnia-Hercegovina; the international governmental organisations that used military authority to structure the space of memory contended that they were acting pursuant to law. There can, of course, be efforts to shape memory by the use of force alone without legal justification. That was not, however, what the Office of the High Representative and NATO contended as they sought to limit Serbian television's broadcasts – promulgations of memory-prodding rhetoric which had been deemed destructive to the peace process. The case of Bosnia, like other similar cases, demonstrates how those in power, faced with the opportunity or need for propaganda, use electronic media to play on memories, sometimes to contrast the painful present with a glorious past, sometimes to create or reinterpret a past to justify aggressiveness in the present, often to change perceptions of the present through manipulation of a sense of history. These events demonstrate problems in the way in which legal systems authorise or prohibit particular modes of invoking, controlling or inventing memory.

This case study tracks an international peacekeeping effort in which the tactical significance of power over media and the invocation of memory was fully recognised. The primary skirmish described in this chapter concerned not a point of traditional military advantage, but rather control over a series of regional broadcast towers. In a strategy involving memory, it is the modes of affecting speech and perception that are the

---

friendly information systems', United States, Office of the Chief of Naval Operations, Department of the Navy, OPNAVINST 3430.26 1 (18 January 1995).

[2] John Arquilla and David Ronfeldt, 'Cyberwar is Coming!' *Comparative Strategy*, 12 (1993), 141, 144.

battleground, not bridges or physical terrain. The territory over which both the international governmental organisations (IGOs) and historic political forces sought power was not just physical but psychological. Through control of broadcasting media, both the competing forces within Bosnia and the peacekeeping administration that entered hoped strategically to invoke and suppress particular memories, and thereby to shape loyalties and behaviours of the viewing population. Of course, there is nothing new in this. Collective memory of defining events shapes and sustains national identity. Even in times of peace, states maintain – or even construct – such memories as sources both for shared national identity and for the legitimacy of state power. Conventional state mechanisms for emphasising particular histories and strengthening selected memories include things as relatively innocuous (except when they are points of turmoil) as designation of national holidays or days of remembrance and construction of monuments and memorials. Primary education, too, provides an opportunity to instil in children reverence for bygone national struggles or heroes, contempt for historic enemies and particular conceptions of the role of the state. In the past century, regulation of the media has emerged as another powerful mechanism for state control over memory construction and maintenance. Placing broadcasting in government hands, requiring that programmes reflect a predefined national identity, or establishing rules for the treatment of subjects such as Holocaust denial – these are all efforts to control who, and under what circumstances, will have the power to reinforce or alter those memories that affect the distribution of power within the society.

The narrative of Bosnia also underscores the fact that actors other than states participate in the formation of collective memory. Within the state, disempowered populations may articulate counter-histories, emphasising events elided in dominant versions of national history or offering alternative constructions of famous events. Disputes over the proper significance of Columbus's 'discovery' of the Americas reflect rival memories of this sort, as do Irish folk-songs condemning Oliver Cromwell. Similarly, outside actors, including other states or international organisations, may put forth their own version of events as the authentic one, and so seek to reshape memories within national boundaries. For these actors, both legal and technical challenges arise as they attempt to bring new influences to foreign information space.

As it happens, a surprising amount of law can be read as affecting the shaping of memory. Governments have used the power of the state as they seek to legitimise themselves by reinforcing their version of the past. Domestic law, even in the relatively pedestrian field of rules of evidence, may deal with the shaping of memory. The relation of memory to law is particularly strong in laws and structures regulating electronic media. It is in large part because radio and television have such inherent power to alter perceptions of time, place and history, that their regulation has been the province of government. Still, there has not been a systematic analysis of how international norms are adjusted to allow or forbid the use of force to shape memory, or how international law is invoked to regulate memory in which memory is employed in the service of power. Yet, looking at international covenants and conventions, an underlying concern with the role of memory in the legitimate and illegitimate uses of power can be discerned. Paragraph 2 of Article 10 of the European Convention for the Protection of Human Rights and Fundamental Freedoms, dealing with limitations on freedom of expression, stands as a tacit recognition of the power of rhetoric, fuelled by memory, to provoke violence and threaten 'national security, territorial integrity or public safety'. Even in those instruments aimed at preventing violations of human rights, such as the Genocide Convention, it can be said that the shaping of memory has been a subject of international legal discussion. The Genocide Convention's concern with destructive attempts against groups based on ethnic and national identities is reiterated in more positive terms by the Convention on the Rights of the Child (CRC). Article 30 of the CRC expresses a positive right of children of indigenous ethnic minorities to be raised within that group and to 'enjoy his or her own culture' – in other words, to share the collective memories and perspectives of the particular group.[3]

While invocations of false memory may be the most obvious point of concern to international law, this is not the only significant issue. Indeed, in certain circumstances, invocations of inflammatory and all-too-real memories can trigger genocidal activities, and promote racism and war. Certain symbols – a burning cross or flag of the Confederacy in the United States, a swastika in much of the world, pictures of a mosque in India in the process of destruction, the very voice of a person designated a terrorist – these alone can be powerful and dangerous triggers of memory. Law sometimes has the function of mediating between permitted and prohibited expression of such flashpoints of nationalist emotion.

---

[3] Convention on the Rights of the Child, Article 30. The requirement that children be raised within their own culture is reiterated in Art. 20 Par. 3, concerning state child care, and Art. 29 Par. c 1, concerning education. The Universal Declaration of Human Rights' guarantee of freedom of thought, conscience and opinion, and the International Covenant on Economic, Social and Cultural Rights' guarantee of peoples' right to self-determination can also be seen as considerations of cultural identity, as shaped by shared memories of historic and current events.

For more than six months in late 1997 and 1998, Sfor, the NATO troops playing the peacekeeping role in Bosnia, held key broadcast transmitters under 'security protection' to ensure that information transmitted to Bosnian Serbs through the media avoided the signals of conflict deemed dangerous by the IGOs' so-called Contact Group, the United States, the United Kingdom, France, Italy, Russia and Germany. Sfor also used its control of the media space to promote a more positive image of itself and of the Dayton Accords. Members of the Contact Group sought to create an entire new mechanism for the licensing of radio and television stations throughout Bosnia, establishing standards for their operation and providing enforcement mechanisms (including fines and closures) against what the Office of the High Representative deemed transmissions of propaganda undermining the peace process. This active, directed and explicit intervention in Bosnia, including the seizure of transmitters, has raised to a new level an international debate, one that began in earnest after the Rwanda massacres, about the appropriate role of media policy in the prevention of ethnic conflict and preservation of peacekeeping processes. Bosnia represents the whole gamut of foreign assistance to remould an indigenous media and the narratives it carries. Everything from professional training to the closing down of stations was employed – all with the goal of systematically altering representations about the past and the present.

Background on Bosnia and the role of the media in the conflict

Much has been written about the way in which the media were used by nationalist leaders to manipulate the collective memory and alter the framework of power in the former Yugoslavia. Several months before anyone in the region bore arms, agitators in the various Yugoslav republics began laying the groundwork for war by planning media campaigns that would draw from a repertoire of inflammatory memories. As an example, the then president of Serbia, Slobodan Milosevic, who is widely blamed for instigating the war in Bosnia, sent paramilitary troops and technicians to seize a dozen television transmitters in the northern and eastern parts of Bosnia-Hercegovina in spring 1992. These were the areas closest to Serbia which also had substantial Serb populations. As a result, more than half the people in the territory of Bosnia-Hercegovina began receiving the television signal controlled by Belgrade rather than the usual television from Sarajevo.

With these important transmitters under Milosevic's control, the formerly unified Bosnian information space, once centred on a national signal emanating from Sarajevo, was fractured. The stage was set for a fierce war of propaganda and mobilisation of remembered hostilities that would precede any actual fighting. With the airwaves firmly in Milosevic's hands both in Serbia and in more than half of Bosnia-Hercegovina, his television began broadcasting fictitious reports that Serbs in Croatia and Bosnia-Hercegovina were being massacred by 'Croatian fascists' and 'Islamic fundamentalists'. The propaganda drew on one thread of collective memory, that of past hostility between ethnic groups. Audience members' perceptions of these reports were inevitably shaped by their own 'memories' of Croat or Muslim acts in the past – memories in part historical, in part apocryphal. Of course, neither individual nor collective memory is necessarily uniform in its ideological significance. Mobilisation of one powerful memory often requires the suppression of others. In this case, Milosevic's broadcasts emphasised conflict while obscuring fifty years of peaceful coexistence by Muslims, Croats, and Serbs. Widespread Serbian embrace of this bellicose propaganda was particularly remarkable given the 30 per cent intermarriage rate in Bosnia-Hercegovina, and perhaps reflects the emotional power of remembered, older hostilities.

There are varying, though unsatisfactory, interpretations of why the propaganda was so effective (some commentators point to historic ethnic divides arising out of the two world wars, others to the tradition of media always controlled by the state). False reports drew heavily on collective memories and suspicions. They were laden with Serb symbolism and historical references to Serb struggles against Ottoman Turks and the Bosnian Muslims who cooperated with them, as well as against German Nazis and Croat fascist collaborators. This appealed to many Serbs on an emotional level; for some, even questioning the truthfulness of the news reports was seen almost as treason against Serb culture. Some independent journalists in Belgrade wrote about the pernicious and dangerous potential of Milosevic-controlled television, but their publications did not have mass readership and could hardly combat the powerful nationalist television. Whatever the reason, this nationalist and inflammatory propaganda struck fear into the Serb population. So, when Belgrade television encouraged Serbs to arm themselves against the 'enemies of the Serb people', many Serbs in both Bosnia-Hercegovina and Croatia did as they were told.

The Serbs were not the only ones who understood that a key to power and influence lay in television and the invocation of memory. Well before any fighting began in Bosnia, the Croats of Hercog-Bosna, the area in Bosnia-Hercegovina that is closest to Croatia and has the largest population of Croats, seized nearby television transmitters and began receiving Croatian television broadcasts. Like its Serbian counterpart, Croatian television inflamed remembered hostilities with its broadcasts, claiming that Serbs intended to exterminate the Croat population in order to form a 'Greater Serbia'. These incendiary programmes suggested to Croats that they were in mortal danger from the Serbs and that they should arm themselves before it was too late.

In early 1992 the Bosnian Serb leadership left Sarajevo for the nearby village of Pale, which would later become their self-styled capital. Almost immediately, in April 1992, they began broadcasting their own television channel, Serb Radio and Television (SRT). Firmly under the control of the nationalist leaders who would lead the war, SRT used the same tactics as Belgrade television before the war. They recognised the importance of reinforcing a particular set of memories to maintaining support for those then in control. Falsified reports of Serbs being slaughtered by Islamist fundamentalists (Turks) and Croatian fascists (Ustashe) were the norm, as were false reports about Western conspiracies against the Serb nation. But no matter how preposterous the broadcasts, they were successful in stirring up hatred against Muslims and Croats. Ample coverage was also given to the Serbs who were killed or interned by the Croats allied with the Nazis during the Second World War, lending credence to reports of new atrocities by reference to real, remembered ones. Ordinary Serbs came to believe that the 'Turks' and the 'Ustashe' were waging a war of aggression and that the Serbs needed to fight for the survival of their nation. They became convinced that if they did not begin 'cleansing' Muslims and Croats from 'their territory', the Muslims and Croats would do it to them.

For the first year of the war, the Muslims and Croats were allied against the Serbs. But once the Serbs were pushed back from Croat territory in 1993, the Croats turned against their former Muslim allies and began fighting them. Again, television played a key role. The Croats, like the Serbs, wanted to carve out a piece of Bosnia-Hercegovina for themselves to create a 'Greater Croatia'. Again playing on memories of past hostilities, Croatian television from Zagreb began broadcasting reports about Islamist fundamentalists trying to create a state in which Roman Catholic Croats would be oppressed and subjugated. Muslims were portrayed as dirty and anti-Christian, intent on depriving the Catholics of their religion and heritage. The strategy was effective, encouraging a sufficient number of Croats to fight against their Muslim neighbours and increase the carnage.

The Dayton Accords and the media

The war in Bosnia was a brutal combination of psychological manipulation and physical violence, which ended with the 1996 US-brokered

Dayton Peace Accords. Bosnian President Alija Izetbegovic, Serbian President Slobodan Milosevic and Croatian President Franjo Tudjman were summoned to Dayton, Ohio, where diplomats worked through the nights to hammer out a compromise and redraw the boundary lines on the map. It was finally agreed that Bosnia-Hercegovina would remain one country, but divided into two entities: Republika Srpska, and the Muslim-Croat Federation. That structure satisfied the Serbs because they were, in a sense, given their republic, even though it was an 'entity', not a state. The agreement satisfied the Muslims because it, in a sense, kept Bosnia-Hercegovina whole. It offered less to the Croats, except that, as part of the Muslim-Croat Federation, they were able to form special ties with neighbouring Croatia. A critical question was who would control the information space, who would determine which memories were repeated and reinforced, what narratives of the future would be created. How history was presented, including the very recent history, would affect the possibility of elections, the potential for resettlement of refugees and the success, if that word were possible, of the Dayton Accords themselves.

The civilian aspects of Dayton were not so well thought out as its military provisions and led to divided and complex sources of authority. The accords stipulated that the Organisation for Security and Cooperation in Europe (OSCE) would organise elections, that the United Nations would create an unarmed civilian police force to supervise the entities' police forces and that the United Nations High Commissioner for Refugees would oversee the return or resettlement of displaced peoples or refugees. A High Representative chosen by the Contact Group would coordinate the activities of the different organisations. Together, these organisations aimed, in a sense, to reconstitute Bosnia-Hercegovina's former multi-ethnic nature and create a Bosnian national identity against a backdrop of continuing ethnic hatred and loyalties. Each element – elections, domestic security and the return of refugees – implied a kind of reconstruction of consciousness that implicates the reformulation of memory. Each element, if it were to be perceived as organic and evolved, and not as an artificial creation of an alien occupation, had to find part of its justification in a practice or ethos of the past. The elections, which were designed to reverse ethnic cleansing, would be the IGOs' most crucial task, and also the most rigorous test of Dayton's success in altering the relationship of past to future.

The accords were signed in Paris in January 1996 and were immediately put into force. It was not possible, as part of the initial accords, to dislodge the recently conflicting entities from control of the media; Serb and Croat leaders clung to their party-controlled television and radio outlets to maintain and extend existing power. The Serb-held parts of

Bosnia-Hercegovina were still strictly under the influence of the rabidly nationalist Serb Radio and Television (SRT), and the Croat-held parts of Bosnia-Hercegovina under the equally nationalist influence of Croatian Radio and Television. The Bosniak-controlled part of the country received broadcasts from Bosnia-Hercegovina Radio and Television, which had become increasingly nationalistic over time, although committed to the cause of integration and the success of the Dayton experiment.

All three groups vied for use and control of the airwaves both within and beyond their geographic spheres of influence. Croats, Serbs and Muslims set about repairing war-damaged television transmitters on mountains within their respective territories, seeking the means to broadcast as far and wide as possible. Belgrade set up a television transmitter in Serbia, near the border with the newly created entity of Republika Srpska, to broadcast Serbian television throughout Serb-controlled territory, and also aided the Bosnian Serbs in repairing transmitters damaged by NATO bombing. Zagreb put up additional transmitters in Croatia, near the border with Bosnia, to broadcast Croatian television into Bosnian territory, and aided the Bosnian Croats in repairing existing transmitters, as well as adding additional transmitters to increase the coverage of Bosnian Croat television. The Bosnian government received outside assistance from the Norwegian government to renovate and repair some twenty-one television transmitters to enhance the multi-ethnic voice that would have the capacity to facilitate reconciliation. Each entity used broadcasting power to continue sending its own messages, reinforcing its own preferred threads of collective memory, and influencing viewers' sense of ethnic and national identity.

Implementation of the accords

Just days after the Dayton agreement was signed in Paris, Robert Frowick, the American who headed the OSCE mission in Bosnia, arrived in Sarajevo to begin planning for the elections. Frowick and the other European and American diplomats who were implementing the Dayton Accords were keenly aware of the role the media played in the war, and the role it would continue to play in peace. The diplomats feared that as long as rival broadcasters saturated the airwaves with invocations of divisive memories and tropes of conflict, the unified country envisioned by Dayton could not be realised. If alternative sources of information were not provided across the country, the same nationalist leaders who waged the war and controlled the airwaves were sure to be voted back into power. The international community recognised that it needed to play a role in adjusting media practices.

The refashioning of memory became part of the context of administrative vocabulary as it was translated into the field of bureaucratic operation. The template for election reform demanded objectivity and impartiality (as defined by the IGOs) – and failure to sustain this perspective in representations of past and present issues rendered political parties and broadcasters vulnerable to official complaint. The OSCE established a Media Experts Commission (MEC) within the Provisional Electoral Commission. It issued a set of rules and regulations, charging the media with duties including 'providing true and accurate information', 'refraining from broadcasting incendiary programming', and running OSCE and international election-related statements and advertisements. It also set up a monitoring group which could cite violations of these rules. Truth and accuracy could have reference to the past as well as to the present.

In addition to rules designed to restrain the existing media, the OSCE pioneered another technique of intervention, helping to finance a special broadcast network that would positively influence the mix of narratives and images transmitted to the public. The Free Elections Radio Network (FERN), was initially started by the Swiss government to provide 'objective and timely information on the elections' to the people of Bosnia-Hercegovina in all entities. This project provided a less incendiary news source, avoiding the national broadcasters' constant emphasis on recent hostilities and tragedies – content which the OSCE found inconsistent with the reconciliation and democratic process envisioned by Dayton.

The seizure of transmitters

The existence of a highly nationalistic ethnically homogenous and intensely focused political party, coupled with a virtual monopoly of the media, posed a threat to the Office of the High Representative and the operation of the Dayton bureaucracy as it went about its rebuilding efforts. Regulation of the electoral process by the OSCE was not enough to reduce the harsh bias by which divisive memories were nourished. And, in spite of all the efforts to create alternative sources of information across Bosnia-Hercegovina, in spring 1997 the media remained divided into three mutually antagonistic components in Republika Srpska, Bosniak-controlled Federation territory and Croat-controlled Federation territory. The party-controlled television stations remained the most influential media outlets and the main source of news for all of Bosnia-Hercegovina's ethnic groups. Other, internationally sponsored, efforts to break a tradition of dependence on official programming was not sufficiently successful. Clearly, the attempts by the IGOs to create an alternative to the party-controlled media had not been sufficient to combat the nationalist television stations, which continued to stir up hostility, not only towards each other, but also towards the IGOs themselves. Much of Sfor's and the other international organisations' work towards reconciliation was perceived by Sfor and the OHR as being jeopardised by the news and propaganda of nationalist television and radio.

Over the summer of 1997, conflict over the content and control of broadcast media intensified. The Steering Board of the Peace Implementation Council of the Contact Group, distressed by the continuing divisiveness of party-controlled media, issued the Sintra Declaration, a document considered by OHR to be an extension of the Dayton Accords, although neither Bosnian signatories of Dayton nor current elected Bosnian officials signed the Declaration. This instrument dramatically asserted OHR's right both to demand airtime for its own broadcasts and to suspend broadcasts which contravened the letter or spirit of Dayton. The Sintra Declaration was later to be cited in justification of Sfor's seizure of broadcasting towers.

Within Republika Srpska struggles for media control intensified as US-backed Biljana Plavsic announced that the SRT station in her power base of Banja Luka would cut ties with the central SRT Pale station, broadcasting from the seat of her rival Radovan Karadzic. The Pale broadcast had drawn heavily on viewers' memories and associations of conflict, openly comparing Sfor to the occupying Nazi forces of a generation before. The broadcast played on recollections of previous atrocities, and featured alternating images of Sfor soldiers and Nazi storm troopers.

On 22 August US troops acted on the Sintra Declaration and, claiming that they moved to prevent possible clashes between Plavsic and Karadzic, seized the SRT broadcast tower in the north-eastern town of Udrigovo. This move cut off SRT Pale broadcasts to the region, temporarily suspending the flood of inflammatory invocations. Ten days later, American soldiers guarding the tower were attacked by a mob of 300 Serbs, presumed to be supporters of Karadzic. Pale radio broadcast that Sfor had 'occupied' the SRT transmitter and claimed that Sfor was a 'heavily armed military force threatening courageous unarmed citizens'.[4]

The resulting negotiation between the Sfor and the Pale authorities produced a document that became known as the Udrigovo Agreement. Sfor handed back the tower to the SRT authorities in Pale, and in return the Pale authorities agreed to certain conditions for resumed broadcasting. Pursuant to the Agreement, the media of the Serb Republic would stop producing inflammatory reports against Sfor and the other international

---

[4] Bosnian Serb Radio, Pale, in Serbo-Croat, 1 Sept. 1997.

organisations implementing the Dayton Accords; SRT would regularly provide an hour of prime-time programming to air political views other than those of the ruling party; and SRT would provide the Office of High Representative with half an hour of prime-time programming daily.[5]

The Agreement required SRT to transmit alternate representations of both current events and the history that had led up to them. In the wake of the Udrigovo Agreement and the formation of the international Media Support Advisory Group (MSAG), the Serb leadership appeared to take a more conciliatory tone towards the Western diplomats implementing Dayton. But that cooperation was short-lived. On 8 September the OHR and Sfor sent a letter to SRT in Pale, demanding ninety minutes of airtime to broadcast an OHR programme that same evening and an hour of airtime the following day, among other time demands. SRT Pale refused to broadcast the material, and instead, further angering international officials, charged OHR and Sfor with violating 'freedom and human rights'. The SRT Pale newscaster read a statement from the SRT Pale editorial board stating: 'We publicly announce that under no conditions would we implement these requests. By doing this, we would trample on our moral integrity and our profession. In our radio and TV broadcast, we shall continue to ridicule orders like the one saying that video material must be broadcast in its entirety and with no changes...[6] Against this background of increased conflict on the airwaves of Republika Srpska, and raised stakes for political control of the entity as the election drew nearer, US government opinion increasingly favoured jamming SRT Pale's broadcasts. In fact, the United States dispatched three air force EC-130 Commando Solo aircraft capable both of broadcasting information and jamming existing radio and television signals. US officials claimed that the primary role of the electronic warfare aircraft would be to 'broadcast fair and balanced news and information to the local population';[7] but Voice of America (VOA) broadcasts to Bosnia-Hercegovina also stated that the aircraft had the capability to jam pro-Karadzic transmissions. VOA also

---

[5] The Media Support Advisory Group (MSAG) consists of the OHR, Sfor, the OSCE and the UN, the four principal organisations responsible for the implementation of Dayton. Established in late September 1997, its function was essentially to monitor and govern the media in Bosnia-Hercegovina to the extent that it could according to the Sintra Declaration and the OSCE's Media Experts Commission (MEC). The MSAG declared itself 'the body that provided the executive mechanism to demand the level and type of access required in an outlet deemed in violation of the ... MEC'. If such demands were not complied with, the MSAG would then recommend escalation 'as necessary' using the par. 70 powers of the Sintra Declaration giving the High Representative authority to 'curtail or suspend' any media network or programme whose output is in violation of the Dayton Accords.

[6] Radio B92, Belgrade, in Serbo-Croat, 8 September 1997.

[7] Voice of America, Washington, English, 13 Sept. 1997.

reported the US belief that Karadzic supporters had violated the Udrigovo Agreement's mandate that they soften their rhetoric against Plavsic and NATO peacekeeping troops, and broadcast a US Defense Department spokesman's claim of Sfor's legal authority to block broadcasts.

As the local elections loomed nearer, with the battle for the Republika Srpska's airwaves becoming increasingly bitter, Western diplomats feared that the media conflict could lead to more violence. Milosevic (the real power broker among the Serbs) was urged to summon Plavsic and rival leader and broadcaster Momcilo Krajisnik to the bargaining table in Belgrade, where the internationally brokered Belgrade Agreement was hammered out. This document established a 'fairness doctrine' for SRT Banja Luka and SRT Pale, in which the two leaders agreed that the unified media environment of the Republika Srpska and free access to media by all participants in elections was 'vital' for a democratic process. They agreed that news programmes be broadcast daily from studios in Pale and Banja Luka alternately.[8]

Hope for a harmonious implementation of the Agreement were immediately dashed. Only a day after it was signed, the MSAG 'expressed concern about the editorial policies'[9] of SRT Pale. A news release from the OHR said that SRT Pale was continuing to broadcast political announcements as news, 'devoid of any balance or alternative opinion'.[10] The news release might have been taken as a warning by SRT Pale. But, characteristically, SRT Pale refused to soften its editorial content, and continued to structure its representations of both Sfor and domestic rivals to invoke memories of conflict, and sustain ongoing hostilities.

On the following day, 26 September, the chief prosecutor of the International Criminal Tribunal for the Former Yugoslavia, Louise Arbour, gave a press conference in Sarajevo, which was covered by SRT. In a commentary, the SRT Pale announcer reiterated the Bosnian Serb leaders' long-held position that the tribunal was a political instrument and that it was prejudiced against the Serbs. The United Nations, which is a member of the MSAG, considered this a breach of prior understandings, including the Udrigovo Agreement, and demanded that SRT Pale make a public apology on television. On 30 September SRT Pale did so, and broadcast unedited footage of the news conference.[11] In spite of SRT Pale's apology, Sfor troops seized control of four SRT transmitters the next day (1 October), thereby preventing SRT Pale from transmitting its broadcasts. In addition to asserting that SRT Pale's blunder was a violation of the Sintra Declaration, Western governments also claimed

[8] Belgrade Agreement, point 3, Belgrade, 24 Sept. 1997.
[9] Beta News Agency, Belgrade, in Serbo-Croat, 25 Sept. 1997.   [10] Ibid.
[11] Beta News Agency, Belgrade, in Serbo-Croat, 30 Sept. 1997.

that the station's repeated broadcast comparing Sfor troops to Nazis constituted a threat to the safety of the Sfor troops and, therefore, needed to be silenced. SRT Pale's appeal to memories of oppressive occupation, these governments recognised, could have very real consequences in the responses of viewers.

Sensitive to the potential for condemnation of the seizure, Sfor and OHR announced that SRT Pale could regain access to the transmission network and resume operations, but only if strict conditions were met. SRT Pale would be obliged to agree to 'criteria for its reconstruction and reorganisation, as well as for editorial control of broadcasting, as suggested by the Office of the High Representative in Bosnia-Hercegovina and the international community'.[12] On 6 October, several days after NATO seized the transmitters, the major international power broker, US special envoy for the Balkans Robert Gelbard appeared in the region. In a statement two days later, the High Representative said that a 'transitory international director-general' and two deputies would be appointed by the OHR to head SRT Pale, that the OHR would draft a statute and editorial charter for the station, that SRT Pale would be obliged to broadcast programmes requested by officials from other international organisations without editing or commentary, and that a team of journalists and editors would be brought in to train personnel and supervise the programming of SRT Pale. He added further that the SRT journalists and editors would be evaluated by the international representatives and that 'only those who are positively evaluated will be able to get a job again'.[13] This was an extraordinary assertion of power by the High Representative and it infuriated the Bosnian Serb leadership in Pale, possibly drawing on a history of associations with official interventions in the Soviet period.

At the Peace Implementation Council's meeting in Bonn in December 1997, the Contact Group members agreed to reinforce efforts to 'break the political control of the media', and restructure the media landscape 'according to internationally recognised standards'.[14] The OHR said that the idea was to create an interim media regulation board to intervene in editorial content, restructure the media and regulate its content. The board would provide training to journalists, but it would also have the power to shut down media and to pick and vet journalists – in other words decide who could and could not work as a journalist. OHR would establish two commissions, one to 'ensure that media standards are respected and would issue licenses. The other would be of an appellate nature and would deal with complaints on media treatment or media

[12] Radio Bosnia-Hercegovina, Sarajevo, in Serbo-Croat, 3 Oct. 1997.
[13] Beta news agency, Belgrade, in Serbo-Croat, 9 Oct. 1997.
[14] OHR Media Strategy paper, Background, point 2, April 1997.

behaviour in the communications process.'[15] In a neat reversal of SRT Pale's Nazi comparisons, the officials noted that the foundation for the new media strategy in Bosnia-Hercegovina was based on the Allies' post-war experience in Germany. Here, the power of Second World War memories was mobilised against the broadcasters, rather than against the Western powers.

Information intervention, memory and the marketplace for loyalties

Bosnia-Hercegovina is an institutionally and legally complex case study of the phenomenon newly christened as 'information intervention'. In the world of ethnic and regional conflict, whether it involves Zapatistas in Mexico, Kurds in Turkey, separatists in Angola or Tamils in Sri Lanka, terrestrial transmitters and signals direct from satellites can serve to shape public perception of current events, often drawing on collective memory of previous conflict or injustice. These resurgent memories can be fuel for campaigns of violence by or against the state and among communities with different views of the public order – often shaped by their different versions of past events. Not only the United States as superpower, but the international community as a whole, increasingly sees potential for countervailing use of the media as a therapeutic tool, including the affirmative use of a more pluralistic media to reduce or prevent conflict or increase the possibility of democracy.

Because of the importance of this phenomenon of information intervention, it is crucial to understand the basis on which the international community can intervene in a way which, on one level, seems to violate free speech principles, and which had such a comprehensive effect on media and information space in Bosnia-Hercegovina. If the international parties intervening were not acting pursuant to legal authority themselves, their moral claim that those in conflict follow the rule of law loses some of its credibility. NATO, the OSCE and the OHR acted as law-makers and enforcers: they required that their statements be broadcast; they established standards for existing stations; they closed stations down; they put into operation a mechanism wholly to revise the licensing and administration of radio and television. What occurred was one of the most comprehensive possible catalogues of the exercise of authority. Various groups within Bosnia-Hercegovina questioned whether the United Nations or NATO or others had valid power to engage in these activities, and outside groups, including the World Press Freedom Committee,

---

[15] Dveni Avaz, Sarajevo, in Serbo-Croat, 30 Oct. 1997.

expressed grave reservations as to whether these steps were consistent with international norms.

The law of media intervention in Bosnia-Hercegovina is nowhere clearly stated, and it is not necessarily true that the United States and other parties sought a legal justification at each step as opposed to responding to practical realities. But the source of law matters. For example, if the United States and its Western allies were acting as occupiers, then their powers and the limits on them would be governed by a particular body of international norms.[16] If they were acting, on the other hand, under a consent regime, then the shape of their authority would be governed, in large part, by the conditions of their entry. One could ask whether the peacekeeping forces were functioning as occupiers, although under current norms (norms that, themselves, are subject to debate), occupation – and certainly 'belligerent occupation' – does not best describe the status of the international presence in Bosnia. This is important because occupiers have the capacity to act in lieu of a sovereign, although those actions are constrained by the duty to serve as a surrogate for the local sovereign and to do so in accord with internationally established standards.

[16] Another source of law – either authorising the actions of NATO and the OHR or establishing limits to those actions – involves what might be called the law of occupation. There has been a debate about the use of the term 'occupation' in describing the activities of the international community in Bosnia and a debate, as well, over the use of the power of the occupier to justify media and information intervention there. After the Second World War, the United States and its allies made it a major objective to refashion totally the radio broadcasting systems in Germany and Japan. One of the important elements of the occupation was to construct or reconstruct a democratic society. To do that required a transition and an imposed architecture that would have transformative capabilities. A focus on changes in radio seemed especially appropriate given the key role of propaganda in fuelling the war, both at home and abroad.

In Germany, the future structure of broadcasting was changed for ever by the Allies, who forced a splitting up and decentralisation so as to prevent a dominant national voice. In Japan, the US government sought to eradicate all elements of militarism and nationalism, as it was there understood. The first Memorandum of the Allies, in somewhat Orwellian phrases that are invited by this kind of situation, claimed to be reestablishing freedom of speech and of the press, but at the same time required that news be true to facts, be faithful to the policies of the Allied Powers and refrain from sceptical criticisms of the Allied forces. None of this history, of course, necessarily serves to justify the actions of the OHR or Sfor. Bosnia-Hercegovina is not Japan or Germany, and the accoutrements of occupation are not exactly present there.

In Japan and Germany, the Allies were 'belligerent occupiers', and a framework of international law has developed to articulate standards for such an occupation. Less well developed is what might be called a 'non-belligerent occupation', one that is more characteristic of the Bosnian context. (The question of whether there is such a status as non-belligerent occupier and what powers such an occupier has comes down to consent. And in that sense, the issue of the powers and limitations of this non-belligerent occupier are governed by the Dayton Accords, since is that is the foundational consent of that agreement.)

Perhaps at the heart of the Dayton Accords was some understanding, at least by the parties, that memory and its exploitation was as important an element of peacekeeping as more traditional military and quasi-military undertakings. The maintenance of an intensely partisan, politically controlled, monopoly media, strongly contesting the integrity, goals and competing narrative of Sfor and the IGOs simply could not long be tolerated. If a plural, multi-party Bosnia-Hercegovina was to emerge from Dayton, then, at least in the eyes of the OHR, a morphological unity between political party, ethnic group and dominant channel had to be broken. The media structure symbolised a Bosnia-Hercegovina that was seen as antithetical to a multi-ethnic future polity. Breaking the hold of the Bosnian Serbs' nationalist party on the media and the electorate was part of the basis of seizing the transmitters that serviced SRT Pale. In establishing the machinery for elections, the parties agreed to have put in place a set of election principles and a mechanism for deciding when those principles were violated.

Conclusion

'Information intervention' describes efforts by those in power – an international force or local authority – to use media to shape collective memory of the past so as to influence present and future activity. Media regulation and exploitation is commonly used by the controlling group or groups to reinforce its ideal notion of identity and history. As in a market for goods, competitors in the 'market for loyalties' seek to use force or the force of law to seize and maintain power over media. A narrow funnel for expression, created by controlling which viewpoints have access to the means of mass communication, is often used either to function as an integrating, assimilating influence, subtly reinforcing a vision of cohesion, or to support and exacerbate existing cultural divisions in society.

Law has been used to protect domestic producers of national identity from international competition. For most of the twentieth century, the international order believed that radio transmissions should be contained primarily within the boundaries of one nation; the international function was to dispense frequencies so as to ensure that conditions of market division along national borders could be realised and enforced. International regulations and arrangements were built to implement the policy of limiting broadcasting, in large part so that these internal monopolies over memory could be preserved. For example, an early document of the League of Nations provided that 'The High Contracting Parties mutually undertake to prohibit and, if occasion arises, to stop without delay the broadcasting within their respective territories of any transmission which to the detriment of good international understanding is of such a character as to incite the population of any territory to acts incompatible with the internal order or the security of a territory of a High Contracting Party.' And in the debate in the 1970s over the use of direct broadcasting satellites, a draft agreement provided that state parties 'undertake to exclude from television programmes transmitted by means of artificial earth satellites any material publicising ideas of war, militarism, Nazism, national and racial hatred and enmity between peoples as well as material which is immoral or instigative in nature or is otherwise aimed at interfering in the domestic affairs or foreign policy of other States.'

In Bosnia-Hercegovina NATO and Sfor, managing what I have called a market for loyalties, used media law to establish the parameters of what memories could and could not be articulated. A market for loyalties implies one in which entry is highly regulated, essentially to reinforce the mix of accounts of the past and present that maintains the existing power structure. In fact, the function of government in a market for loyalties ordinarily goes far beyond its role as regulator and enforcer for a cartel of identity producers. The government is frequently a participant in the market for loyalties in its own right, also trying to insert and promulgate its own version of historical narrative. The relationship between the state as censor and the state as generator of images is important. Not only have governments historically sought to exclude a range of destabilising narratives, but they have also ensured that a reinforcing sense of national identity is available and, if possible, prevails. The actions of Sfor and the OHR are in this tradition of state control of memories. The nature of the peace process and the qualities of those elected offices would be a direct function of the images of the past that received the extraordinary imprint of television. For that reason, intervention became the desired option. If there is a market for loyalties, the Bosnian example illustrates how external powers' forcible control of information space alters the functioning of the cartel and redefines the relationship of memory to power.

Part 2

Memory and power in domestic affairs

7   The past is another country: myth and memory in post-war Europe

Tony Judt

> Fifty years after the catastrophe, Europe understands itself more than
> ever as a common project, yet it is far from achieving a comprehensive
> analysis of the years immediately following the Second World War. The
> memory of the period is incomplete and provincial, if it is not entirely
> lost in repression or nostalgia.
>
> Hans-Magnus Enzensberger

From the end of the Second World War until the revolutions of 1989,
the frontiers of Europe and with them the forms of identity associated
with the term 'European' were shaped by two dominant concerns: the
pattern of division drafted at Yalta and frozen into place during the Cold
War, and the desire, common to both sides of the divide, to forget the
recent past and forge a *new* continent. In the West this took the form of
a movement for trans-national unification tied to the reconstruction and
modernisation of the west European economy; in the East an analogous
unity, similarly obsessed with productivity, was imposed in the name of
a shared interest in social revolution. Both sides of the divide had good
reason to put behind them the experience of war and occupation, and a
future-oriented vocabulary of social harmony and material improvement
emerged to occupy a public space hitherto filled with older, divisive and
more provincial claims and resentments.

In this chapter I want to propose some reflections on the price that
was paid for this deliberate and sudden unconcern with the immediate
European past and its replacement by 'Euro-cant' in its various forms.
I shall argue that the special character of the wartime experience in continental Europe, and the ways in which the memory of that experience was
distorted, sublimated and appropriated, bequeathed to the post-war era
an identity that was fundamentally false, dependent upon the erection
of an unnatural and unsustainable frontier between past and present in
European national memories. I shall suggest that the ways in which the
official versions of the war and post-war era have unravelled in recent
years are indicative of unresolved problems for both western and eastern
Europe, though in distinctive ways. Finally I shall note some of the new

myths and mis-memories attendant upon the collapse of communism and the ways in which these, too, are already shaping, and mis-shaping the new European 'order'.

The Second World War was a very particular, and in certain respects novel experience for most Europeans. It was in the first place horribly, unprecedentedly destructive, especially in its final months. In particularly badly hit countries like Yugoslavia, something like 66 per cent of all livestock, 25 per cent of all vineyards, most railway rolling-stock and all major roads were destroyed. Western countries too suffered terrible material loss – during the fighting of 1944–5, France lost the use of some 75 per cent of its harbours and rail yards and half a million houses were damaged beyond repair. Even unoccupied Britain is calculated to have lost some 25 per cent of its entire pre-war national wealth as a result of the war.[1]

But the scale of material destruction pales in comparison with the human losses, in central and eastern Europe in particular. There is no need here to go through the familiar statistics of death, suffering and loss. On the one hand the human cost has to be calculated on an industrial basis, so efficient was the machinery of extermination elaborated and operated by Germans and their associates; on the other side, the war saw an unanticipated return to older terrors – in the weeks following the Soviet army's capture of Berlin some 90,000 women in the city sought medical assistance for rape. In Vienna, the Western allies recorded 87,000 rape victims in the three weeks following the arrival of the Red Army. From the Volga to the Elbe the Second World War constituted an experience whose special combination of efficiency, fear, violence and deprivation was comparable to nothing in local memory (though Armenians and Spaniards had been afforded a brief foretaste a few years earlier).

And yet... The Second World War was not the same for everyone. Some places had quite a 'good' war, at least until the very last months. Bohemia and Moravia, for example, did relatively well under Nazism, favoured for their natural and industrial resources, their skilled and pliant workforce and their proximity in manner and outlook (if not race) to their German neighbours. Most Czech workers and peasants were coddled by the Germans, securing high wages, full employment, good rations and so forth – only resisters, communists and Jews, here as elsewhere, were seriously at risk and exposed to the constant threat of harassment, loss and deportation. Slovaks and Croats finally got their own 'independent' states,

---

[1] See figures given in Gerold Ambrosius and William H. Hubbard, *A Social and Economic History of Twentieth-century Europe* (Cambridge, MA: Harvard University Press, 1989), *passim*; Kenneth Morgan, *The People's Peace: British History, 1945–1989* (Oxford: Oxford University Press, 1990), 52.

albeit run by collaborators, and many were pleased with the achieve-ment. Germans and Austrians suffered badly only towards the latter part of the war, their economies sustained until then by the forced extraction of materials and labour from the occupied territories. Even France, per-haps especially France, did not do so badly – most of French wartime losses and some of the worst acts of collective punishment came only after the Allies landed (which accounts for mixed French memories on that subject, as Robert Gildea also points out in his chapter). Overall, it was clearly not good to be a Jew, a Gypsy or a Pole in the Second World War; nor was it safe to be a Serb (in Croatia), a Russian (until 1943) or a Ukrainian or a German (after 1943). But if one could stop the clock in, let us say, January 1944, most of occupied Europe would have had little of which to complain by contrast with what was about to come.

Another way of putting this is to say that most of occupied Europe either collaborated with the occupying forces (a minority) or accepted with res-ignation and equanimity the presence and activities of the German forces (a majority). The Nazis could certainly never have sustained their hege-mony over most of the continent for as long as they did had it been otherwise: Norway and France were run by active partners in ideological collaboration with the occupier; the Baltic nations, Ukraine, Hungary, Slovakia, Croatia and Flemish-speaking Belgium all took enthusiastic advantage of the opportunity afforded them to settle ethnic and terri-torial scores under benevolent German oversight. Active resistance was confined, until the final months, to a restricted and in some measure self-restricting set of persons: socialists, communists (after June 1941), nationalists and ultra-monarchists, together with those, like Jews, who had little to lose given the nature and purposes of the Nazi project. Such resisters were often resented, opposed and even betrayed by the local population either because they brought trouble by attracting German retaliation, or else because the indigenous ethnic and political majority disliked them almost as much as the Germans and were not unhappy to see them hunted down and removed.

Not surprisingly, then, the war left a vicious legacy. In the circum-stances of the Liberation, everyone sought to identify with the winners – in this case the Allies and those who had sided with them before the final victory. Given the nature of the war, which by its end had mutated into a whole series of brutal local civil wars, it was for most Europeans a matter of some urgency that they emerge on the correct side. This in turn entailed distinguishing and distancing oneself from those who had been the enemy (within and without), and since the actions of this enemy had been without precedent in their brutality and scale, there was univer-sal agreement that it should be punished. Even those like Albert Camus who came to doubt the possibility of identifying 'war criminals' with any accuracy or justice recognised the emotional and political necessity of such a judicial purge and retribution. The question was who and how.[2]

At this point we leave the history of the Second World War and begin to encounter the myth of that war, a myth whose construction was undertaken almost before the war itself was over. Everyone had an interest in this affair, the context of which ranged from private score-settling to the emerging international balance of world power. Indeed, it was the years 1945–8 which were the moment not only of the division of Europe and the first stage of its post-war reconstruction but also, and in an intimately related manner, the period during which Europe's post-war memory was moulded.

I want to list briefly the most salient factors which contributed to the official version of the wartime experience which was common European currency by 1948. The first was the universally acknowledged claim that responsibility for the war, its sufferings and its crimes, lay with the Germans. 'They' did it. There was a certain intuitive logic to this comforting projection of guilt and blame. After all, had it not been for the German occupations and depredations from 1938 to 1945, there would have been no war, no death camps, no occupations – and thus no occasion for the civil conflicts, denunciations and other shadows which hung over Europe in 1945. Moreover the decision to blame everything on Germany was one of the few matters on which all sides, within each country and among the Allied powers, could readily agree. The presence of concentration camps in Poland, Czechoslovakia and even France could thus readily be forgotten, or simply ascribed to the occupying power, with attention diverted from the fact that many of these camps were staffed by non-Germans and (as in the French case) had been established and in operation before the German occupation began.[3]

Moreover, this focus on Germany made it possible to resolve by neglect certain tricky subjects such as the post-war status of Austria. Beginning with the Moscow Declaration of 1943, Austria was established as the 'first victim' of Nazi aggression, something which suited not only

---

[2] For an extended discussion of Camus's shifting position on the dilemma of revenge and retribution in post-war France, see my *Past Imperfect: French intellectuals 1944–1956* (Berkeley: University of California Press, 1992).

[3] In addition to the concentration camp established by the Nazis at Struthof in Alsace, there were several internment camps in southern France. Some of these had been set up in the last months of the Third Republic to handle Republican refugees from Spain; under Vichy they served as holding pens for Jews, refugees and other undesirables prior to their deportation, in most cases, to the East. See Anne Grynberg, *Les camps de la honte: Les internés juifs des camps français, 1939–1944* (Paris: La Découverte, 1991), as well as the haunting memoir by Arthur Koestler, *The Scum of the Earth* (London: Victor Gollancz 1955).

Austrians but also the prejudices of someone like Churchill, for whom Nazism was a natural extension of Prussian militarism and expansionist ambitions.[4] If *Austria* was guiltless, then the distinctive responsibilities of non-German nationals in other lands were assuredly not open to close inspection. Hence the achievement of Nuremberg, where *German* guilt was in turn distilled into a set of indictments reserved exclusively for German *Nazis,* and then only a select few. This was a matter of some concern to the Soviet authorities involved in the war crimes trials; they wished to avoid any discussion of broader moral and judicial questions which might draw attention to the Soviet Union's own practices, before and during the war. That the Nuremberg trials served an important exemplary and jurisprudential function is beyond doubt; but the selectivity and apparent hypocrisy with which the Allies pursued the matter contributed to the cynicism of the post-war era, while easing the consciences of many non-Germans (and non-Nazis) whose activities might easily have been open to similar charges.

Next there was the issue of denazification. Within a very short time after the Liberation it became clear that Germany (and Austria) could not be returned to civil administration and local self-government, even under Allied supervision, if the purging of responsible Nazis was undertaken in a sustained and consistent manner. Moreover, the local Social Democratic and Christian Democratic parties in both countries could not be expected to ignore the votes of former Nazis, once these were allowed to re-enter public life; thus the 1948 amnesty in Austria, which returned their full civil rights to some 500,000 former registered Nazis, inevitably resulted in a sort of instant amnesia, whereby all sides agreed that these men and women were henceforward no different from the rest. Even the remaining 'more incriminated' Nazis, some 42,000 of them, were nearly all amnestied within the following seven years, as the Western Allies sought to minimise the risk of alienating Austrians and Germans from the Western bloc through any excessive emphasis on their past and its price. In a process that would have been all but unthinkable in 1945, the identification and punishment of active Nazis in German-speaking Europe had effectively ended by 1948 and was a forgotten issue by the early fifties.

The association of wartime responsibility with Germans, and of Germans with Nazism, sat all the more comfortably with non-German nations in that it provided a context and an excuse for a 'final solution' to the nationality problem in continental Europe. Woodrow Wilson and the Treaties of Versailles notwithstanding, the sixty million Europeans

---

[4] A view shared by de Gaulle, which helps to explain his occasional inability to grasp the essential distinction, when it came to post-war retribution, between Prussian 'barbarism' and Nazi genocide.

living under an 'alien' jurisdiction in 1914 had not all achieved self-determination after the First World War: there were still some twenty-five million persons living in 'someone else's state'. The Nazi occupation had gone some way to resolving this perennial European problem by killing most of the Jews and some of the smaller stateless groups. After the war, the liberated states took the occasion to further this process by removing the Germans themselves. As a result of the shifting of Poland's frontiers agreed at Potsdam, the expulsion of the *Volksdeutsche* from the Balkans and the collective punishment visited upon the Sudeten Germans, some fifteen million Germans were expelled in the post-war years: seven million from Silesia, Pomerania and East Prussia, three million from Czechoslovakia, nearly two million from Poland and the USSR and a further 2.7 million from Yugoslavia, Romania and Hungary. After some two million died in flight or during the expulsions the majority ended up in West Germany (especially Bavaria), where as late as 1960 some 28 per cent of the federal government employees were *Vertriebene* (expellees).[5]

Beyond its significance for post-war German domestic politics (which were considerable) this process had a marked impact upon the states whence these Germans came. Poland and Hungary (as well as West Germany itself) now became ethnically homogeneous states as never before. Others felt free to indulge in further exercises in ethnic purification: the Czechoslovaks especially took the opportunity to expel or transfer hundreds of thousands of ethnic Hungarians from Slovakia (in some cases forcing them to occupy the vacated Sudeten regions), the liberal Benes announcing the day after his country's liberation that Czechs and Slovaks 'did not want to live' in the same state as Germans and Hungarians.[6] It might be thought that such actions, and the sentiments they reflected and aroused, would have caused misgivings in a Europe so recently liberated from similarly motivated collective miseries brought upon the continent by the occupier. On the contrary: a clear and quick distinction was made between the sorts of collective violence and punishment visited on these lands by German war criminals, and the mass, racially motivated purges represented by these expulsions and undertaken by freely elected or newly liberated national authorities.

---

[5] For a somewhat partial, but well-documented account of the expulsion of the Germans, see Alfred M. de Zayas, *Nemesis at Potsdam: The Expulsion of the Germans from the East* (Lincoln, NE: University of Nebraska Press, 1989).

[6] On the unhappy history of post-war, pre-communist Czechoslovakia's treatment of some of its national minorities, see Radomir Luza, *The Transfer of the Sudeten Germans: A study of Czech-German relations, 1933–1962* (New York: New York University Press, 1964); Petr Pithart, 'Let us be kind to our History', *Kosmas*, 2 (winter 1984); and Kalman Janics, *Czechoslovak policy and the Hungarian minority 1945–1948*, Social Science Monographs (New York: Columbia University Press, 1982).

Two sorts of memories thus emerged: that of things done to 'us' by Germans in the war, and the rather different recollection of things (however similar) done by 'us' to 'others' after the war (taking advantage of a situation the Germans had obligingly if unintentionally made possible). Two moral vocabularies, two sorts of reasoning, two different pasts. In this circumstance, the uncomfortably confusing recollection of things done by us to others *during* the war (i.e. under German auspices) got conveniently lost. It was in these circumstances that the 'Resistance' myth emerged. If there was to be a reference point in national memory for the years between 1939 and 1945 it could only be the obverse of that now firmly attached to Germans. If Germans were guilty, then 'we' were innocent. If guilt consisted of being German or working for Germans and their interests – and it could hardly be denied that in every occupied country such persons had been present and prominent – then innocence had to mean an anti-German stance, after 1945 but also before. Thus to be innocent a nation had to have resisted, and to have done so in its overwhelming majority, a claim that was perforce made and pedagogically enforced all over Europe, from Italy to Poland, from the Netherlands to Romania.

Where the historical record cried out against this distortion – in France, in Italy where the anti-fascist resistance came late and was confined to the north, in the Netherlands where grossly exaggerated accounts of heroic farmers rescuing downed British airmen became part of the post-war national mythology – national attention was consciously diverted, from the very first post-war months, to examples and stories which were repeated and magnified ad nauseam, in novels, popular histories, radio, newspapers and especially cinema.

It is understandable that former collaborators, or even those who simply sat it out, should have been happy to see the wartime tale thus retold to their advantage. But why did the genuine resisters, who in most cases were also those in power in the immediate post-war years, agree to retouch the past thus? The answer is twofold. In the first case, it was necessary somehow to restore a minimal level of cohesion to civil society and to re-establish the authority and legitimacy of the state in countries where authority, trust, public decency and the very premises of civil behaviour had been torn down by totalitarian government and total war. Thus de Gaulle in France, De Gasperi in Italy and the various communist-dominated National Front governments in eastern Europe all found it necessary to tell their citizens that their sufferings had been the work of the Germans and their handful of traitorous collaborators, that they had suffered and struggled heroically and that their present duty, the war now over and the guilty suitably punished, was to address themselves to post-war tasks, place their faith in constitutional regimes and *put the war behind them*. Seeing little option but to concur, the domestic resistance movements abandoned their plans for radical domestic renewal and went along with the priority accorded to the search for stability even if (as in the Italian case) it entailed signing the Rome Protocols of November 1944 which effectively secured the continuity of the Fascist state apparatus into the post-war era.[7]

Second, the communists, whose agenda was of course distinctively different from that of their allies in the domestic resistance, nevertheless had reasons of their own to recast the wartime record of their fellow citizens in their own heroic image. In the west, they could hope to capitalise on their war record by claiming to have spoken for the nation in its time of trial, and thus seek the authority to speak for it still. For that reason the Parti Communiste Français (PCF) in France or the Partito Communista Italiano (PCI) in Italy had no objection to exaggerating the resistance record of the mass of the French or Italians, so long as they could themselves inherit the benefits of this illusion at the voting booth and in the national memory. It was thus ironically appropriate that it should be Togliatti, the Italian communist leader, who drafted the 1946 amnesty which ended the foreshortened and selective post-war Italian purges (see also Ilaria Poggiolini's chapter for the long-term effects of the PCI's cultivation of particular memories on Italian political culture).

In the east, where communism everywhere except in the special cases of Yugoslavia and Albania had returned to the country not through the heroic efforts of the local resistance but in the baggage train of the Red Army, the communists had an interest in flattering the recalcitrant local population by inviting it to believe the fabrication now deployed on its behalf by the USSR – to wit, that central and eastern Europe was an innocent victim of German assault, had played no part in its own downfall or in the crimes perpetrated on its territory, and was a full partner in the work of liberation led by Soviet soldiers abroad and communist partisans at home. This story, which found its way into forty years of school texts in the 'People's democracies' was actually even less credible than the fibs being told in Paris and Rome, and few in central and eastern Europe believed it, even among those who had strong motives to do so. But since no-one had an interest in denying it – and within two years to do so was anyway no longer possible – the story took root.

Moreover, the communists' emphasis in Eastern Europe on identifying and punishing those few 'traitors' who had betrayed the otherwise heroic

[7] See Paul Ginsborg, *A History of Contemporary Italy, 1943–1988* (Harmondsworth: Penguin, 1990), 53 ff.

local people offered them the occasion to indict, try and imprison or execute a lot of people whom they feared might impede their path to power. Thus in January 1945 'people's courts' were set up in Hungary to try war criminals. Initially these functioned with reasonable integrity, but later on the crimes of 'sabotage' and 'conspiracy' were added to their remit, with sombre consequences; something similar happened in Romania and especially Bulgaria, where the Fatherland Front settled post-war scores with thousands of real or potential political rivals, making no distinction between pro-German, pro-Western and anti-communist candidates for punishment, all in the name of the nation and its wartime sufferings. Meanwhile the construction of war memorials was undertaken, all of them with the same pedagogical message: the Second World War had been an 'anti-fascist' war in which the Nazi Germans had served capitalist and imperialist ends and been opposed by the undifferentiated 'people' whose lands they occupied. Atrocities were described as perpetrated by 'fascists' (foreign and domestic) against the local population, and no mention was *ever* made of the sufferings of national, ethnic or religious minorities, whether at the hands of Russians (of course), the local population or even the Germans themselves. This process reached its purest form in the officially approved version of the wartime experience and post-war character of *East* Germany, a land of workers and peasants hitherto oppressed by and now liberated from a handful of Nazi capitalists from the West.

Most of the acts of retributive punishment which took place in this period happened before the countries in question had been liberated, or else at the very moment of that liberation, as German authority lapsed and new powers had yet to be installed. Of the approximately 10,000 summary executions in France which marked the transition from Vichy to the Fourth Republic, about a third were carried out before D-Day and a further 50 per cent during the battles of the following weeks. Similarly in Italy, most of the 12–15,000 persons shot for fascist or collaborationist activities at this time were dealt with before or during the weeks of final liberation. In other words, the majority of the most severe 'punishments' meted out for wartime activities were completed *before* formal or official tribunals had been set up to pass judgement.[8] The same is true in eastern Europe (Yugoslavia included), where partisan score-settling was the primary form of semi-official retribution for collaboration and war crimes.[9]

---

[8] *Ibid.*, 64–70. On later charges levelled at the partisans for their acts of summary justice, see Luca Alessandrini and Angela Maria Politi, 'Nuove fonti sui processi contro i partigiani, 1948–1953', *Italia Contemporanea*, 178 (1990), 41–62.

[9] As in the case of the massacre of Hungarians in the Vojvodina by Tito's partisans, revenge for the Hungarian military's activities there in January 1942.

Thus at least two of the functions of retributive jurisprudence – the administration of natural justice and the canalisation of private violence – had been coopted and largely dispatched before legitimate post-war institutions came into force. What remained were the establishment of public security to protect new political institutions, symbolic acts of justice to legitimise the new authorities and public words and deeds designed to shape and circumscribe the moral regeneration of the nation. Here the post-war European experience of justice was universally unsuccessful and inadequate. Of denazification I have already spoken. But even when it came to dealing with serious criminals, the exercise was half-hearted. The Austrian and French instances are exemplary (the eastern European experience was distinguished by the abuse of court procedures already noted). 130,000 persons were investigated for war crimes; of these 23,000 were tried, 13,600 found guilty, 43 sentenced to death (about the same number as were condemned to death in Denmark) and 30 actually executed. In France, 791 death sentences were carried out, of the 2,640 passed by the courts. More telling were the overall figures: whereas in Norway, Belgium and the Netherlands the number of persons sentenced for collaboration varied between 40 and 64 per 10,000 inhabitants, in France the numbers were just 12 per 10,000.[10]

In both France and Austria, then, the emphasis was clearly placed on the need to reduce to the minimum the number of convictable and convicted persons, reserve for this select few a sort of symbolic and representative function as criminals and traitors, and leave the rest of the social fabric untouched or, where this was not possible, to repair the damage as soon as possible through a process of benign collective neglect.[11] It should also be noted that in many countries those who were in the end punished were more likely to have been chosen for the egregious nature of their activities – the record left by their writings – or for their pre-war prominence than for the extent or consequences of their actions, a basis for selection which did not pass unnoticed and helps to account for the public scepticism of the era.[12]

---

[10] For the Austrian figures I am indebted to Dr Lonnie Johnson of the Institut für die Wissenschaften vom Menschen in Vienna. For France, see Henry Rousso, 'Les élites économiques dans les années quarante', in *Le elites in Francia e in Italia negli anni quaranta, Mélanges de l'Ecole française de Rome*, 95 (1982–3), 29–49; but also Marcel Baudot, 'L'épuration: bilan chiffré', *Bulletin de l'Institut d'Histoire du Temps Présent*, 25 (Sept. 1986), 37–53.

[11] In which the French at first proved remarkably adept. In July 1951 one observer wrote of their 'alarming' success in putting Vichy out of mind. See Janet Flanner, *Paris Journal 1944–1965* (New York: Atheneum 1977), 153.

[12] For the benign and limited character of the purge of economic collaborators, see e.g. Rousso, 'Les élites économiques'.

The last point to note in the context of the post-war years concerns the international arena. With the exception of a series of imposed agreements with minor belligerents, signed in Paris in 1946, the Allies never resolved their post-war dealings with former enemy states by any final peace treaty. In contrast to the experience after the First World War, the Second World War petered out in a string of ever more contentious and unproductive meetings of foreign ministers, culminating in those of 1947 and 1948 in Paris, Moscow and London which saw an end to the wartime Allied collaboration and the onset of the Cold War. The main issue was of course disagreement over the division of Germany; the formal creation of the Federal Republic and its Eastern *doppelgänger* in 1949 was thus the effective end of the immediate post-war era, with the Western Allies nonetheless waiting until July 1951 to declare that their 'state of war' with Germany was now over. The significance of the absence of any peace treaty of the kind traditionally signed after major European conflicts was this: the Second World War lost its original and particular meaning as a struggle between Germany and its Allies and became instead a sort of bloody prelude to other arrangements and new confrontations, a situation which produced different configurations and thus further confused an already obscure memory of the war itself.

Thus Western Europeans, having begun the post-war era by thrusting all responsibility for the war upon Germany found themselves in a short period of time having to think of Germany, or at last some part of Germany, as an ally in a different sort of struggle whose meaning could not easily be related to that which had been given to the world war. In Eastern Europe a war of national liberation from Germans became the overture and starting point to a domestic revolution which forced inhabitants of the region to describe the wartime years in a way which made no sense and could only be achieved by an act of voluntary amnesia. It was necessary to forget everything one had known not only about Germans and Russians and Americans, but also about one's neighbours, one's friends and even oneself. A peace treaty would not of course have changed this outcome very much, if at all. But it would have ended the Second World War and thus given it a distinctive framework, in time and in memory. Until such a treaty came along, Europeans (governments and peoples alike) postponed any collective effort to come to terms with the memory of the war it would have rounded out. When it never happened, they simply left the matter unresolved, buried, neglected and selectively forgotten.

Up to this point, I have treated the experience of Eastern and Western Europe as one. Despite the obvious differences in the wartime and post-war history of Europe's two halves, in the respects relevant to this chapter they had much in common. But from 1948 their histories diverge in ways which are also directly pertinent to the theme of memory and national mythology. Only in the later process of recollection and awakening do their paths again converge. From 1948 the Western states of Europe waved goodbye to the immediate past and embarked on the 'European adventure' to which their national energies and prospects have been officially attached ever since (with the exception of Britain, for whom the story begins distinctly later, for reasons not unconnected with its good fortune in missing the sorts of experiences continental Europeans were in a hurry to forget). In the course of this new-found Europeanism, Western Europeans settled for some twenty-five years into a comforting 'collective amnesia' (the phrase is Enzensberger's), resting their half of the continent on a number of crucial 'foundation myths'.

These myths were in essence the obverse of the wartime and post-war histories noted above. They required common acceptance of the claim that Nazism was a strictly German phenomenon, that West Germany had been effectively de-Nazified and that those who ought to be punished had been, with certain notorious individual exceptions. France's Vichy interlude was treated as an aberration in the national history, brought about by the circumstances of war and occupation and foisted on an unwilling country by the treasonable activities of a minority. Italy's experience with Fascism was left largely unrecorded in public discussion, part of a double myth: that Mussolini had been an idiotic oaf propped into power by a brutal and unrepresentative clique, and that the nation had been purged of its Fascist impurities and taken an active and enthusiastic part in its own liberation. Norway, Denmark, the Netherlands and Belgium were accorded full victim status for their wartime experience, and the active and enthusiastic collaboration and worse of some Flemings and Dutch struck from the public record. Austria, returned to full independence by the 1955 State Treaty, extracted from the Allies an agreement to relieve it of any responsibility for its years under Nazi rule, and thereby relieved its citizens in their turn of any last remaining need to remember those years or the enthusiasm with which *all* sides (many Social Democrats included) had greeted the idea, if not the reality, of *Anschluss*.[13] Sweden and Switzerland too managed to share in this Era of Good Feelings, of Franco-German reconciliations and economic miracles, purged of any vague abiding memories of Sweden's economic dealings with wartime Germany and the Swiss insistence on distinguishing

[13] See William B. Bader, *Austria between East and West, 1945–1955* (Stanford: Stanford University Press, 1966) and Robert E. Clute, *The international legal status of Austria, 1938–1955* (The Hague: Martinus Nijhoft, 1962).

Jews from non-Jewish Germans and returning the former to the Nazis whenever they attempted to make their way across the border.[14]

It is not easy today to recall this particular Europe, the one which held sway from the Marshall Plan to the early seventies. It, too, is another country. It was characterised by an obsession with productivity, modernity, youth, European economic unification and domestic political stability. Symptomatically, it was largely the creation of politicians who came from the geographical margins of their respective nations – Schumann, De Gasperi and Adenauer – and who encouraged their more typical countrymen to think beyond their traditional terms of national and local reference. While the accumulation and relatively radical redistribution of wealth and services displaced national traumas and unhappy memories, the idea of 'Europe' was refurbished as a substitute for the kinds of national identitification which had caused such wounds in the recent past. I say 'refurbished' because the notion of a united Europe was not new. The very phrase 'Etats-Unis d'Europe' was first used in the Paris journal *Le Moniteur* as early as February 1848, and the concept of a European identity had in fact flourished in certain circles during the inter-war decades and in the war itself. But the problem was that it was the right, specifically the fascist right, which had made much play with the idea in that time, contrasting a New European Order with the anarchic and febrile democracies of the liberal era, and proposing it as a bulwark against the imperialist challenge of the 'Anglo-Saxon–Jewish plutocracies' which threatened the old continent from the West and the 'Judaeo–Communist–Slavic' danger from the East. Thus after 1945 'Europe', too, remained to be invented, benefiting from a line drawn under the past and dependent for its credibility on a refusal to acknowledge its own provincial, defensive and exclusive roots.

The revenge of history

The revenge of history has been slow, and remains partial. For many years the teaching of modern history in West Germany did not pass beyond Bismarck, and it is well known that the French government refused for more than a decade to allow Marcel Ophuls film *Le Chagrin et la Pitié* to

---

[14] See Rudolf Bindschedler, Hans Rudolf Kurz, Wilhelm Carlgren and Sten Carlsson, *Schwedische und Schweizerische Neutralität im Zweiten Weltkrieg* (Basel: Helbing & Lichtenhahn, 1985), notably the contributions by Carlsson, Bindschedler and especially Samuel Werenfels ('Die Schweizerische Praxis in der Behandlung von Flüchtlingen, Internierten und entwichenen Kriegsgefangenen im Zweiten Weltkrieg', 377–405). Also Sven-Olof Olsson, *German Coal and Swedish Fuel* (Göteborg: Institute of Economic History, Gothenburg University, 1975).

be shown on national television. But in both France and Germany a new generation began to ask embarrassing questions, prompted in Germany especially by the series of trials of concentration camp administrators held in the years 1963–5. These, together with the trial in Jerusalem of Adolf Eichmann, in turn prompted the passage in France, on 26 December 1964, of a law making crimes against humanity imprescriptible. Despite this evidence of a growing concern with the crimes committed in France under the auspices of the German occupation, it was often left to foreign scholars to raise and investigate the hard questions; the 'Vichy Syndrome' which can stand for similar historical mystifications throughout western Europe, has only really begun to unravel in the 1980s and 1990s.[15]

The forms of that unravelling have been various. In France, and to a lesser extent in the Netherlands and Belgium, it has been the work of professional scholars working in relative obscurity, their conclusions and evidence surfacing into the public realm only when a particularly egregious case – those of René Bousquet, Maurice Papon and Paul Touvier in France being the best known – caught the headlines. In Germany the *Historikerstreit*, a much publicised argument among professional historians over the proper way to interpret and contextualise the Nazi years, did not so much reveal new material about Nazism (for the reasons noted earlier the sins of the Germans had been widely advertised) as open for the first time a discussion of the relative status of Nazism in the context of other contemporary state crimes, notably those of Stalin's Soviet Union. In Austria it took the presidential candidacy and election of Kurt Waldheim to shake the nation (or some of it) from its historical complacency and the widely held opinion that 1945 was 'Year Zero' in Austrian history, with all that preceded it dismissed as being of no consequence.[16]

---

[15] Henry Rousso, *Le Syndrome de Vichy, de 1944 à nos jours*, 2nd edn (Paris: *Editions dn Seuil*, 1990). Examples of the seminal contributions of foreign scholars include Eberhard Jäckel, *Frankreich in Hitlers Europa* (Stuttgart: Deutsche Verlags-Anstalt, 1966), of which a French translation finally appeared in 1988; Robert O. Paxton, *Vichy France: Old Guard and New Order, 1940–1944* (New York: Knopf, distrib. Random House, 1972); Dennis Mack Smith, *Italy: A Modern History* (Ann Arbor: University of Michigan Press, 1959) and *idem.*, *Mussolini* (London: Weidenfild & Nicolson, 1981). Note, too, the work of Gerhard Hirschfeld. His *Nazi rule and Dutch collaboration: The Netherlands under German Occupation 1940–1945* (Oxford and New York: Berg, distrib. in United States and Canada by St. Martin's Press, 1988), a translation of *Fremdherrschaft und Kollaboration: Die Niederlande unter deutscher Besatzung 1940–1945* (Stuttgart: Deutsche Verlags-Anstalt, 1984), provided a much-needed corrective to even the best Dutch historiography on the subject. See also Nanda van der Zee, 'The recurrent myth of "Dutch heroism" in the Second World War and Anne Frank as a symbol', in G. Jan Colijn and Marcia S. Littell (eds.), *The Netherlands and Nazi Genocide* (Lewiston, NY: E. Mellen Press, 1992), 1–14.

[16] For the Waldheim presidency and its ramifications in Austria, see the new book by Richard Mitten, *The Waldheim Phenomenon in Austria: The Politics of Antisemitic Prejudice* (Boulder: Westview Press, 1992).

The common theme of these uncomfortable revelations and discussions has been the degree of *refoulement*, of public and private denial, upon which democratic Western Europe was reconstructed. Older Europeans still cling to this alternative past – polls in France suggest that the majority of persons over fifty would rather the matter just went away. They see little benefit in rehashing the atrocities committed by Vichy even when they themselves bear no possible personal responsibility for them. In Austria, the Waldheim experience has exacerbated the generation gap: in a March 1988 poll, Austrians under thirty were evenly divided on the question of whether Austria was a victim of the *Anschluss* or its accomplice, whereas for those over fifty the status of victim was selected by nearly twice as many as those who assigned blame.

A further element in the opening up of the past has been the steady decline of communism. Once the French and Italian Communist Parties lost their stranglehold on some of the electorate and much of the political imagination of their countries, it became easier to ask hard questions about their role in the Resistance and the real dimensions of the latter itself. Now that everyone is jumping on this bandwagon and a virtual sub-discipline of critical Resistance historiography has emerged, it is sometimes difficult to remember that until just recently the dispassionate analytical studies of historians such as Claudio Pavone or Henry Rousso would have been unthinkable – and in certain circles unpublishable. It is a curious irony that it should be the decline of the anti-fascist *left* which makes it possible to acknowledge the true dimensions of domestic fascism and collaboration in an earlier era. Yet there is some logic in this: few in France wished to acknowledge the elements of continuity between Vichy and the preceding and subsequent republics, both because of the implicit downgrading of the 'break' of 1945 and the apparent 'normalising' and relativising of the Vichy years that such an acknowledgement might entail.[17] Similar constraints impeded close attention to continuities in modern Italian history.

Because so much of this troubled and troubling renegotiation with the past is directed towards the public rather than the scholarly community (few of the debates alluded to above have added much to our knowledge of past events, any more than the seminal impact of the *Gulag Archipelago* depended upon the new information it imparted, which was minimal), it has had its most important impact only in the countries directly concerned. But even in France, Italy and West Germany the impact of the newly acknowledged past, bubbling its half-digested way back into the throats of politicians and journalists whose real attention is elsewhere, has been

---

[17] See the reflections on this theme by Rousso, Daniel Lindenberg, Stanley Hoffmann and others in 'Que faire de Vichy?' *Esprit* (May 1992), 5–87.

as nothing compared with the dramatic implications of the recovery of memory in central and eastern Europe.

If the problem in western Europe has been a shortage of memory, in the continent's other half the problem is reversed. Here there is too much memory, too many pasts on which people can draw, usually as a weapon against the past of someone else. Whereas the west European dilemma was confined to a single set of unhappy memories located in the occupation years 1940–44/45, the East Europeans have multiple analogous reference points: 1918–21, 1938, 1939, 1941, 1944, 1945–8, 1956, 1968 and now 1989. Each of these moments in time means something different, and nearly always something contentious and tragic, to a different nation or ethnic group, or else to succeeding generations within the same group. For eastern Europeans the past is not just another country but a positive archipelago of vulnerable historical territories, to be preserved from attacks and distortions perpetrated by the occupants of a neighbouring island of memory, a dilemma made the more cruel because the enemy is almost always within: most of these dates refer to a moment at which one part of the community (defined by class, religion or nationality) took advantage of the misfortunes of another to help itself to land, property or power. These are thus memories of civil wars, and in a civil war the enemy is still there once the fighting stops – unless some external agency has been so helpful as to impose a final solution.

The coming of communism seemed to put an end to all this. Soviet power appropriated national myths for its own ends, banned all reference to uncomfortable or conflictual moments save those which retroactively anticipated its own arrival and enforced a new 'fraternity' upon the eastern half of Europe. But it did not just abolish the past, of course, it also re-invented it. We have already seen how and why communist regimes inflated the myth of wartime anti-fascist resistance. More subtly, the communists de-emphasised the revolutionary nature of Nazi occupation – the fact that Eastern Europe's social revolution, completed under the Soviet aegis after 1947, was in fact begun by the Germans, sweeping away old elites, dispossessing a large segment of the (Jewish) urban bourgeoisie and radically undermining faith in the rule of law. But the historical reality, that the true revolutionary caesura in modern eastern Europan history came in 1939 and not 1945, could not be acknowledged. The continuities between Nazi and Soviet rule were necessarily denied and the alternative myth of revolutionary *post-war* transformation took their place.

From Bulgaria to Poland this process was more or less similar. In East Germany, as Jeffrey Herf also notes in his chapter, a special national history was conceived, whose emphases varied with the needs of Soviet foreign policy, but whose consistent impact on the local population was disastrous. After an initially aggressive pursuit of denazification, the communists reversed their strategy and announced to the East Germans that their own history was unsullied. Meanwhile significant numbers of low-ranking Nazis pursued their careers in police and bureaucracy under the new regime. East Germans, all too knowledgeable about their real past and the initially violent way in which the Russian had extracted revenge for it, were now invited to sit back in officially mandated approval while the essential characteristics of the Nazi state apparatus were reconstructed before their eyes. The consequences of what Peter Schneider has called the 'double zombification' of East Germany are now clear to all.[18]

The silence which fell across eastern Europe was unbroken for forty years. The revolts of 1956 and the reforms of 1968 did not crack this frozen past; on the contrary, the memory of them, and the fact that it could not be acknowledged except mendaciously, added to the strata of public mythology. In private many people of course scorned the official version of the past; but having only their personal or communal recollection to put in its place and pass on to their children, they contributed inadvertently to the double crisis of history which now afflicts eastern Europe. On the one hand cynicism and mistrust pervade all social, cultural and even personal exchanges, so that the construction of civil society, much less civil memory, is very, very difficult. On the other hand there are multiple memories and historical myths, each of which has learned to think of itself as legitimate simply by virtue of being private and unofficial. Where these private or tribal versions come together, they form powerful counter-histories of a mutually antagonistic and divisive nature.

After 1989, there have been certain chronically intertwined themes which have been reshaping and further distorting the Eastern European past. The first is guilt over the communist era itself. No matter how many times people proclaim that 'they' did it to 'us', the fact is that very few people could or did object to communist power (in some places, notably Czechoslovakia, it was even initially welcomed in free elections by a large minority of the electorate). It was in the nature of 'real existing socialism' in Eastern Europe that it enforced the most humiliating, venal kinds of collaboration as a condition for rendering daily life tolerable. And most people, sooner or later, collaborated: intellectuals, priests, parents, managers, workers, shoppers, doctors and so on. It is not for any real or imagined crimes that people feel a sort of shame at having lived in and under communism, it is for their daily lies and infinite tiny compromises. Until the coming of Solidarity this pattern was unbroken, and even the uniform heroic picture of Polish resistance in the eighties is not without

---

[18] Peter Schneider, *The German Comedy: Scenes of Life after the Wall* (New York: Farrar, Straus & Giroux, 1991).

its self-serving mythological dimension. In Czechoslovakia, just 1,864 persons in a population of fifty million signed Charter 77. Even in June 1989, with the repressive apparatus relatively relaxed and well into the Gorbachev era, only 39,000 signed 'A Few Sentences', the first manifesto of what would become Civic Forum.[19]

It is this sense that whole nations share a dirty little secret which accounts for the post-1989 obsession in eastern Germany, in Czechoslovakia and to a lesser extent elsewhere with retribution, purification and purge – the consequences of which Timothy Garton Ash analyses in his chapter. The analogy here with 1944 in France is striking. There is an epidemic of finger-pointing and blame, with all opinions represented, from those who wish to restrict guilt, indictment and punishment to a representative or egregious few to those who would have whole nations atone for their past. What is getting lost in all this is any dispassionate appreciation of the communist era in Europe. Few dare to point out that communist rule differed from previous regimes in most of the region mostly by virtue of its cynical exploitation of national resources for a *foreign* (Soviet) interest. As governments, regimes and elites, post-Stalinist communists were not always so very unlike what had gone before – and will thus have to be absorbed and included in any understanding of the history of these lands. They cannot just be written out and written off.

Here too the analogy with Vichy, or with Italian Fascism, is perhaps appropriate. The Soviet-imposed regimes of eastern Europe are part of their respective national histories; they continued in certain local traditions, pursued pre-established patterns of economic policy, and have contributed to the post-Communist character of their societies. As with Pétain and Mussolini, so with the puppet authorities of the 'People's Democracies': however tempting it may be, they cannot be eliminated from their country's history, nor 'bracketed' from it, as an alien and passing aberration. In addition, the arrival of the Red Army saved what remained of certain minorities (Jews, notably); this was an important strand in the arguments of some of the protagonists in the German *Historikerstreit*; but in a region where antisemitism remains endemic it is hardly a popular argument in defence of regimes which were often themslves charged (in private) with being the work of Jews. My point here is not to attempt any sort of a balance sheet for Soviet rule, but to note that the communist experience did not come from nowhere, did not disappear without leaving a certain record, and cannot be written out of

---

[19] See Tony Judt, 'Metamorphosis: the Democratic Revolution in Czechoslovakia', in Ivo Banac (ed.), *Eastern Europe in Revolution* (Ithaca, NY: Cornell University Press, 1992).

the local past, as it had earlier sought to extrude from that past those elements prejudicial to its own projects.

The mis-memory of communism is also contributing, in its turn, to a mis-memory of anti-communism. General Antonescu, the wartime Romanian leader who was executed in June 1945, defended himself at his trial with the claim that he had sought to protect his country from the Soviet Union. He is now being rewritten into Romanian popular history as a hero, his part in the massacre of Jews and others in wartime Romania weighing little in the balance against his anti-Russian credentials. Anti-communist clerics throughout the region, nationalists who fought along-side the Nazis in Estonia, Lithuania and Hungary, right-wing partisans who indiscriminately murdered Jews, communists and liberals in the vi-cious score-settling of the immediate post-war years before the commu-nists took effective control, are all candidates for rehabilitation as men of moderate and laudable convictions; their strongest suit, of course, is the obloquoy heaped upon them by the former regime.[20]

The most telling crisis of all concerns the theme of restoration of property. In most of eastern Europe there has been legislation to restore land and buildings to those who lost them in 1948. But this raises hard questions. Why 1948, just because it was the communists who at that point began a programme of expropriation? What of those whose homes, farms and businesses were expropriated in the years 1945–8? Or the millions whose possessions were illegally taken during the war itself and, in the Czech and Slovak cases, after 1938? If the communist regime alone is to be treated in this way, what of those who benefited from the expulsion of the Sudeten Germans, the forced transfers of Hungarians in Slovakia, the deportation and murder of the Jews everywhere? Was illegal expro-priation, collective punishment and loss of material goods and livelihood wrong in itself or only if undertaken by communists?

The complication here of course is that there are many in all these coun-tries who benefited from the sufferings of others in the years 1938–48. This is not something on which the communists laid any emphasis af-ter 1948, and it is not something the beneficiaries, their heirs and their fellow-countrymen want to hear about today. It explains why so many Czechs and Slovaks resented Havel's apology to Germany for the expul-sion of the Sudeten Germans (almost his first public act on entering the presidency), and it is also part of deeper complexes and silences about

---

[20] More problematic still is the case of someone like the Romanian writer Mircea Eliade, a liberal intellectual nowadays much admired for his prescient critiques of Stalinism in the fifties and after. It is all too easy to forget that before the Second World War, like much of the intelligentsia of central and eastern Europe, Eliade was a supporter of the extreme nationalist right.

wartime and post-war collusion and worse in the treatment of minorities. The problem of Poles and Jews in Polish history, including the traumatic experiences of Jews in Poland *after* the war, is the most dramatic and best-known of these issues, but it is far from unique.[21] Finally there is another, utterly unresolvable dilemma: what good does it do to restore *property* when you cannot return to tens of millions of people the loss of opportunity and liberty they suffered after 1948? Is there not something wrong in an outcome whereby the Schwarzenberg family gets back its palaces, and long-departed émigrés are paid for a loss which their descendants have turned to advantage, while those who had nothing get nothing and watch bitterly as their own and their children's lost chances go for nought? It may or may not be just but it certainly does not look very fair and it is politically most imprudent.

These and other ironies of present attempts to resolve unhappy memories help explain the resurfacing of older sentiments and allegiances in post-1989 eastern Europe. This was in some measure predictable, of course. The communist era did not forge new ways of identifying and describing local and national interests, it merely sought to expunge from public language all trace of the old ones. Putting nothing in their place, and bringing into terminal disrepute the socialist tradition of which *it* was the bastard product, it left a vacuum into which ethnic particularism, nationalism, nostalgia, xenophobia and ancient quarrels could flow; not only were these older forms of political discourse legitimated again by virtue of communism's very denial of them, but they were the only real terms of political communication that anyone could recall, with roots in the history of the region. Together with religious affiliation, which in pre-1939 eastern Europe was often itself the hallmark of nationality, they and the past they describe and represent have returned to haunt and distort post-communist politics and memory.

This has to be understood on its own terms. Unlike France or Britain, for example, the little nations of eastern Europe have lived for centuries in fear of their own extinction. It is truly tragic that on those occasions when they were afforded a measure of autonomy or independence it was usually at the expense of someone else and under the protection

---

[21] In the pogrom at Kielce on 4 July 1946, forty-one Jews died. There were many similar, lesser outbursts of antisemitism in post-war Poland. But there are some grounds for thinking that these atrocities (like the murder of two Jews at Kunmadaras in Hungary on 21 May 1946), were provoked by the communist police, who had an interest in exacerbating already strained relations between Jews and non-Jews. See Alexander Smolar, 'Jews as a Polish problem', *Daedalus*, 116, 2(1987), 31–73, and Yosef Litvak, 'Polish-Jewish refugees repatriated from the Soviet Union to Poland at the end of the Second World War and afterwards', in Norman Davies and Antony Polonsky (eds.), *Jews in Eastern Poland and the USSR, 1939–1946* (New York: St. Martin's Press, 1991). I am indebted to Professor Istvan Deák for his observations on this point.

of an authoritarian foreign interest. Many Slovaks still speak enthusiastically of Father Tiso, the Slovak leader hanged in April 1947 for his
collaboration and war crimes during the years of Slovak independence
from 1939 to 1944. This helps explain both the Slovak drive for separation and the refusal by some Slovak representatives to vote for ratification
of the accords with Germany which declared Munich null and void. The
cruel fact is that for many Slovaks, then and now, Munich *was a good
thing*.[22]

Croats by contrast are largely unenthusiastic about the brutal rule of
the Ustashi regime which took advantage of the German-protected independent Croatian state to exterminate Jews and Serbs on a massive scale;
but they can hardly be blamed for a degree of confusion when they are
asked to disassociate utterly from that brief memory of autonomous national existence. Polish national sentiment can be an ugly thing, rooted in
an unhealthy Catholic exclusivism. Jews and Ukrainians have good reason
to fear it (as do Czechs, who know something of Poland's opportunistic
land grab after Munich). But Polish memory has for two generations been
force-fed a counter-intuitive affection for Russian-imposed internationalism, and it would be surprising indeed were the nation to have turned
directly from a 'fraternal socialist Europe' to the cosmopolitan (Western)
Europeanism of optimistic dissident imaginings without passing through
some such nostalgic engagement with a properly *Polish* past.

Of all the old languages which have rushed in to fill the space left by
communist discursive power, antisemitism is the most striking. It is almost irrelevant that there are hardly any Jews left in contemporary eastern
and central Europe.[23] Antisemitism in this part of Europe has long had
a central political and cultural place; it is as much a way of talking about
'them' and 'us' as it is a device for singling out Jews in particular. What is
striking, though, is the discomfort aroused by any suggestion that eastern
Europeans today need to come to terms with their *past* treatment of Jews.
That particular past has been so profoundly buried, by communists and
non-communists alike, that attempts to disinter it are resented by everyone, including Jews. Indeed, the Jewish intelligentsia of Budapest and
Warsaw (which includes a goodly portion of the dissident intellectuals of
the past twenty years) does not like to be reminded (i) that its own and its
parents' recent past was closely tied to that of the communist movement;

[22] The Treaty on Cooperation and Friendship between Czechoslovakia and Germany was
signed on 27 February 1992 and ratified in the Czecho-Slovak Federal Assembly on
4 April 1992, by 226 votes to 144. Deputies from the communist, social democratic
and Slovak nationalist parties voted against, the Slovaks objecting to the phrase which
affirmed the 'continuity of the Czechoslovak state since 1918'.

[23] Only in Hungary is the Jewish presence significant. It numbers about 100,000 persons,
most of them in Budapest.

and (ii) that Jews in eastern Europe who survived the war and chose not to emigrate often made considerable efforts to hide their Jewishness – from their colleagues, their neighbours, their children and themselves. They are often the first to insist that antisemitism ended in 1945 – indeed they will sometimes claim that its earlier presence in countries such as Poland, Czechoslovakia, Hungary and even Romania was much exaggerated.[24]

The special difficulty of coming to terms with the treatment of Jews, especially during the war, is that it is hopelessly imbricated with other buried histories already mentioned. For some time now there has been an interesting debate among Hungarian historians over whether the extermination of the Hungarian Jews could have been prevented. Certain of the historians involved in this debate were Jews, from different generations. The older scholars (including Jews) were often very reluctant to concede that Hungarians could have done more to prevent the deportation of their Jewish community in 1944; what was at issue was less the fate of Hungarian Jews than the responsibility of Hungarians for their own dealings with the Nazis in the last stages of the war.[25]

Curiously, this syndrome has its close equivalents further west – even though there are also important exceptions, as Jeffrey Herf's chapter on Germany demonstrates most clearly. Post-war Austrians – Jews and non-Jews alike – preferred to think of Hitler's Austrian victims as a single undifferentiated category: Jews, social democrats (and Jewish social democrats), Christian socialists and so forth were conflated after 1945 into a single memory of the oppression of the Austrian nation by Prusso-German Nazis. In Austria as in its eastern neighbours, this misrepresentation of history and memory (which in 1945 was certainly recent enough) did little to help Jews melt back into the fabric of Austrian society, however: there are about 10,000 Jews in Austria today, but in an opinion poll taken in October 1991, 50 per cent of respondents thought 'Jews are responsible for their past persecution', 31 per cent said they did not want a Jew as a neighbour and 20 per cent said they wanted no Jews in the country.[26]

---

24 According to Joseph Rothschild, in inter-war eastern Europe 'the only really potent international ideology...was antisemitism based on both conviction and experience', *East–Central Europe between the two wars* (Seattle: University of Washington Press, 1974) 9.

25 See Istvan Deák, 'Could the Hungarian Jews have survived?' *New York Review of Books*, 29, 1 (4 February 1982); Randolph L. Braham, *The Politics of Genocide: The Holocaust in Hungary* (New York: Columbia University Press, 1981); György Ránki, 'The Germans and the destruction of the Hungarian Jewry', in Randolph L. Braham and Belá Vago (eds.), *The Holocaust in Hungary: Forty Years Later*, Social Science Monographs (New York: Columbia University Press, 1985); and András Kovács, 'Could Genocide have been averted?' *Budapest Review of Books*, 1, 1(1991), 20–5.

26 On post-war Austrian handling of indigenous antisemitism and the memory of local enthusiasm for the Nazis, see Bruce F. Pauley, *From Prejudice to Persecution:*

Further west still, in France, returning Jewish survivors of the camps were tacitly invited to merge into the general category of 'deportees'. Only men and women deported for acts of anti-Nazi resistance received special recognition – indeed, in the 1948 parliamentary discussions of a law defining the status and rights of former deportees no-one made any reference to Jews. It has taken some forty years for the distinctive experience of Jews in occupied France and the manner in which Vichy singled them out for punishment to become a central part of the debate over the memory of the Occupation. In France, too, this neglect was in some measure the responsibility of the Jewish community, which sought to reclaim for itself an (invisible) place in the universal Republic and had little interest in inviting further discrimination by arousing unpleasant memories – its own and those of its persecutors. This stance only began to alter with the next generation of French Jews, their consciousness 'raised' by the Six-Day War of June 1967, and de Gaulle's ill-starred remarks. It is for this reason that the special responsibilities of the Vichy regime, which lie in its autonomous and thoroughly French reasons for seeking out and disadvantaging Jews in particular, were for so long shrouded in ambiguity.[27] If Helmut Kohl could in the 1990s speak of the extermination of Jews as a crime 'committed in the name of Germany' (and thus not by any particular Germans), it is not surprising that for the best part of half a century French politicians saw little reason to arouse any sense of guilt among the French for crimes committed 'in their name'.

Goodbye to all that?

And now? Goodbye to all that? The revolutions of 1989 have forced open the east European past, just as the historiographical transformations in the West have removed decades-long taboos on parts of wartime memory. There will be infinite revisions and re-interpretations, but the recent past will never look the same again, anywhere. However, even the most superficial survey of the 1990s reveals new myths and new pasts already in the making.

To begin with, there is something to be said, socially speaking, for taboos. In western Europe, for forty years after the end of the Second World War, no respectable scholar or public figure would have thought to attempt a rehabilitation of fascism, antisemitism or the hyper-collaborationist regimes and their doings. In return for the myth of an ethically respectable

---

A History of Austrian Anti-Semitism (Chapel Hill: University of North Carolina Press, 1991), 301–10.

[27] See Annette Wievorka, *Déportation et Génocide: Entre la mémoire et l'oubli* (Paris: Plon, 1992), notably 19–159, 329–433; Serge Klarsfeld, *Vichy-Auschwitz: Le rôle de Vichy dans la solution finale de la question juive en France*, 2 vols. (Paris: Fayard, 1983).

past and an impeccably untainted identification with a reborn Europe, we have been spared the sorts of language and attitudes which so polluted and degraded the public realm between the wars. In eastern Europe the brutal, intolerant, authoritarian and mutually antagonistic regimes which spread over almost all the region in the years following the Second World War were cast into the dustbin of History. The many unpleasant truths about that part of the world were replaced by a single beautiful lie. For it must not be forgotten that communism was constrained by its own self-description to pay steady lip service to equality, freedom, rights, cultural values, ethnic fraternity and international unity. By its end few questioned the hypocrisy of the affair; but in public at least there were certain things no longer said and done which had once been the common currency of hatred throughout the area.[28]

What we are witnessing, so it seems to me, is a sort of interregnum, a moment between myths when the old versions of the past are either redundant or unacceptable, and new ones have yet to surface. The outlines of the latter are already beginning to form, however. Whereas for the purposes of European moral reconstruction it was necessary to tell a highly stylised story about the war and the immediate post-war trauma, the crucial reference point for Europe now will be the years immediately preceding the events of 1989. This is not to say that the earlier mis-memories will henceforth be recast in tranquility into objective and univerally recognised histories. As I have suggested, east Europeans in particular have not yet begun to sort through and understand the multi-layered pasts to which they are the unfortunate heirs, including the past which began in 1948 and ended in 1989. The war and especially the post-war years are still largely unexplored territory in the historiography of this region (in any language), and Leszek Kolakowski is doubtless correct when he predicts that eastern Europe is in for a painful *Historikerstreit* of its own. But the crucial new myths will be about something else.

Western Europe is already afloat in a sea of mis-memories about its own pre-1989 attitude towards communism. Whatever they now say, the architects and advocates of a unified Europe à la Maastricht never wanted to include a whole group of have-not nations from the east; they had yet fully to digest and integrate an earlier Mediterranean assortment. The Soviet grip on eastern Europe had the double virtue of keeping that region away from the prosperous west while at the same time allowing the latter the luxury of lamenting the very circumstances from which it was benefiting.

---

[28] The glaring exception of course was the ugly outbreak of officially condoned antisemitism in Poland in the years 1967–8. But for many people this has already been cosmetically reshaped as the work of a few hotheads in the political apparatus, with no support or roots in the Party or the nation at large.

In a like manner, the non-communist European left is already forgetting just how very defensive it had been for the previous two decades on the subject of Soviet rule. Between Willy Brandt's Ostpolitik and the fantasies of the extreme disarmers, the western left not only discouraged criticism of the communist regimes but was often quite energetic in their defence, especially in the later Brezhnev era. Even now there are suggestions of an attempt to cast *perestroika* as the missed occasion for a renewal and rebirth of the communist project, with Gorbachev as the would-be Bukharin of a different road to socialism. The history and memory of western political and cultural attitudes towards the east is an embarrassing one; if Václav Havel and others do not allude to it as often or as acerbically as they once did, this is because they must needs look ahead and to their immdiate interests. But they have not forgotten that the western left played *no* role in their own liberation, nor are they insensible to the manifest lack of enthusiasm displayed by French and other statesmen at the fall of the Wall and its consequences. If the west forgets its own immediate past, the east will not.[29]

But eastern Europe, too, is in thrall to a freshly minted version of its own recent history. Of these the most disturbing may be, as I have already noted, a denial of the communist experience. That the years 1948–89 were an ugly parenthesis in the history of central and eastern Europe is of course true; their legacy is mostly ashes, their impact mostly negative. But they did not come from nowhere, and even ashes leave their mark. That is why the ongoing debates over collaboration and collusion in Germany, Czechoslovakia and elsewhere are so crucial and difficult. But these very debates and the revelations surrounding them risk repeating the experience of the French post-war *épurations*: the whole episode was so shot through with private score-settling and bad faith that within a few months no one any longer believed in the undertaking and it became difficult (and eventually unfashionable) to distinguish between good and evil in such matters. To avoid this result – to avert the danger of arousing sympathy for communist 'victims' of revenge and public cynicism as to

[29] Nor should it be forgotten that socialists in Italy, especially, were happy to join with communists in applauding the East European show trials of the forties and fifties, a subject over which they and their heirs now prefer to maintain a discreet silence. Even Aneurin Bevan in Britain's Labour Party was not exempt from temptation; in 1959, reiterating his faith in the future of the Soviet Union, he declared that 'the challenge is going to come from those nations who, however wrong they may be – and I think they are wrong in many fundamental respects – nevertheless are at long last being able to reap the material fruits of economic planning and of public ownership'. Quoted in Michael Foot, *Aneurin Bevan: A Biography, Volume II 1945–1960* (New York: Atheneum, 1974). All in all, it is hard to dissent from the bitter conclusion of Paolo Flores d'Arcais: 'nel comunismo la sinistra europea è stata coinvolta quasi tutta, direttamente o indirettamente. Per scelta, per calcolo, per omissione'. See his editorial in *Micro-Mega*, 4 (1991), 17.

the motives of the revengers – some political leaders in the region have already begun to suggest that it might be best just to draw a veil over the whole uncomfortable communist episode.

But that same veil would also blur our understanding of the place of communism, for good or ill, in the modern transformation of eastern Europe. This would be a mistake: communism in eastern Europe has some achievements to its name, paradoxal though these may now appear; it industrialised certain backward regions (Slovakia being a notable case) and, it destroyed old castes and structures which had survived earlier wars and revolutions, which will not now return. Moreover, the communists pursued and accelerated programmes of urbanisation, literacy and education which were sadly lacking in this part of Europe before 1939;[30] their drive to nationalise production and services was consistent in form, if not in manner, with a process which had begun in Poland and Czechoslovakia before 1939, was pursued by the Nazis and maintained and extended by the coalition governments of the post-war years before the communists seized power. To insist, as many now do, that communism in Eastern Europe was an alien and utterly dysfunctional imposition of Soviet interests is as misleading as to claim that the Marshall Plan and NATO were forced upon an unwilling and supine western Europe (one of the more enduring myths of an earlier generation of western critics).

Finally, the very events of 1989 themselves may be about to enter the no-man's-land of mythical and preferable pasts. It will be hard to claim that any of the liberations of eastern Europe, even those of Poland or Hungary, would have been possible without at least the benign neglect of the Soviet Union; indeed there is some reason to believe that in Czechoslovakia and perhaps Berlin the Soviets played an active part in bringing down their own puppet regimes. This is not a very appealing or heroic version of a crucial historical turning-point; it is as though Louis XVI had engineered the fall of the Bastille, a course of events which would have had detrimental consequences for the identity of nineteenth-century republicanism in France. It is also a sequence of developments humiliatingly familiar in eastern European memory, where the wheel of history has all too often been turned by outsiders. The temptation to tell the story in a different and more comforting way may become overwhelming.

The new Europe is thus being built upon historical sands at least as shifting in nature as those upon which the post-war edifice was mounted. To the extent that collective identities, whether ethnic, national or continental, are always complex compositions of myth, memory and political

[30] In 1939, illiteracy levels were still 32 per cent in Bulgaria, 40 per cent in Yugoslavia and nearly 50 per cent in Romania. See Barbara Jelavich, *History of the Balkans: Twentieth Century* (Cambridge and New York: Cambridge University Press, 1983), 242.

convenience this need not surprise us. From Spain to Lithuania the transition from past to present is being recalibrated in the name of a 'European' idea which is itself a historical and illusory product, with different meanings in different places. In the western and central regions of the continent (including Poland, the Czech Lands, Hungary and Slovenia, but not their eastern neighbours) the dream of economic unity may or may not be achieved in due course.

But what will not necessarily follow is anything remotely resembling continental political homogeneity and supra-national stability – note the pertinent counter-example of the last years of the Habsburg monarchy, where economic modernisation, a common market and the free movement of peoples was accompanied by a steady increase in mutual suspicion and regional and ethnic particularism.[31] As for eastern Europe, the 'third' Europe from Estonia to Bulgaria, the idea of European identity there is fast becoming the substitute political discourse of an embattled minority of intellectuals, occupying the space which in other circumstances would be taken up by liberal and democratic projects, and facing the same formidable opponents and antipathies which have weakened such projects on past occasions. At a time when Euro-chat has turned to the happy topic of disappearing customs barriers and single currencies, the frontiers of memory remain solidly in place.

[31] See David F. Good, *The Economic Rise of the Habsburg Empire, 1750–1914* (Berkeley: University of California Press, 1984).

8   The emergence and legacies of divided
     memory: Germany and the Holocaust
     since 1945

Jeffrey Herf

In the large literature on *Vergangenheitsbewaeltigung* or 'coming to terms with the (Nazi) past' in the two post-war Germanys, silence, avoidance and repression have received more attention than have memory and justice.[1] This is an imbalance which reflects the actual state of affairs. Yet, given the extent of support for the Nazi regime up to its bitter end, the explanatory burden of accounting for silence and the paucity of memory is a light one: many people had a great deal to hide and thus to be silent about.[2] Moreover, the historical experiences of other countries before and after the Nazi regime suggests that silence, avoidance, repression of the memory of past crimes is the norm rather than the exception.

Hence it is not difficult to understand why so few Nazis were convicted by German courts and why so many former Nazi officials managed to retain their former positions. What does require more reflection is why, in light of the extent of support for Nazism in German society up to 8 May 1945, there was any public memory at all in the post-war era of Nazi criminality and the Holocaust in the two post-Nazi German states. How and why did memory divide along the political fault lines in the way it did? That is, why was the memory of the Holocaust and what many contemporaries called 'the Jewish question' repressed in 'anti-fascist' East Germany and why did it find a place in the era often and justly called one of political and economic restoration, historical amnesia and judicial delay in West Germany? What was the relationship between memory of the crimes of the Nazi era and the establishment of a liberal democracy in West Germany and a communist dictatorship in East Germany?

In this chapter, I ask these question in the process of writing the history of an often unpopular yet morally significant and historically distinctive

---

[1] I have explored these issues in Jeffrey Herf, *Divided Memory: The Nazi Past in the Two Germanys* (Cambridge, MA: Harvard University Press, 1997).

[2] For important recent examinations of the avoidance of punishment, premature amnesty and rapid re-integration of former Nazis into West German society see Norbert Frei, *Vergangenheitspolitik: Die Anfänge der Bundesrepublik und die NS-Vergangenheit* (Munich: C. H. Beck, 1996); and Ulrich Herbert, *Best: Biographische Studien über Radikalismus, Weltanschauung und Vernunft, 1903–1989* (Bonn: J. H. W. Dietz, 1996).

tradition of public political memory of past state criminality. I trace German political interpretation and then memory of the Nazi era and its crimes from the 1930s up to the establishment in January 1996 of a national day of remembrance for the victims of National Socialism. My focus is on the publicly articulated views of the most prominent national political figures regarding anti-Jewish persecution and the Holocaust, especially during the late 1940s and early 1950s, when these leaders helped to shape the political culture of the two post-war German states. The post-war decade is also important because it is then that we see most clearly the discontinuities but also the continuities that connect German political traditions defeated in 1933 to the shaping of political memory after 1945; the connections between democracy, dictatorship and memory; and the impact of rapidly shifting international alliances on how the two Germanys faced and avoided Nazi criminality.

In recent years, whether due to the influence of Foucault and the place of discourse in public life, post-Marxist notions of ideology or liberal scepticism about national celebrations, historians have focused on how power shapes memory. For German historians, the domination of the present over the past was one of the central issues to emerge from the *Historikerstreit* of the mid-1980s. Yet however much we focus on how power shapes ideas, we ought not to and cannot escape from the historian's task of thinking about both ideology and interest, traditions and instrumentalisation. Rather than treat the realms of meaning and power as independent of one another, we ought to focus on that middle ground on which their intersection takes place. The history of the memory of the Holocaust in occupied Germany after 1945, in the two Germanys after 1949, and in unified Germany after 1989 is one shaped by both the endurance and autonomous impact of political and intellectual traditions.

The necessary, but not sufficient, condition for the emergence of some, rather than no memory of the Holocaust and other crimes committed on the orders of the Nazi regime was Allied military victory and then the Nuremberg trials and de-Nazification procedures of the occupation years. Total victory, overwhelming Allied power, and with it the definitive destruction of Nazism as a major movement and political force was indispensable. (The more typical muddied efforts to prosecute crimes against humanity in Bosnia and Rwanda remind us how unusual and atypical the link between power and memory in 1945 was.)

Allied power made it possible for anti-Nazi German political memories of Nazism to reemerge. Post-war German political culture and with it the memory of the Holocaust rested both on Allied power as well as on what I have called multiple restorations of past defeated German political traditions. These multiple restorations were brought about by a generation of non- and anti-Nazi German politicians who *re*-entered political life in 1945 having survived the Nazi era in concentrations camps, through withdrawal from public life in Germany – what the Germans called 'innere Emigration' – or having had the good luck to find refuge abroad, especially in Britain, Mexico, the Soviet Union, Sweden, Turkey or the United States. All of the leading political figures of early post-war political life in West and East Germany came of political age between 1900 and 1930. They experienced Nazism, the Second World War and the Holocaust in their mature, not their young and formative, years, and interpreted it after the war on the basis of long-held beliefs. The power or 'hegemony' of the victors lay partly in the ability to impose their own interpretations on the Germans. Yet even more importantly for the shaping of post-war memory, power meant the ability to encourage some to speak and repress other, in this case, Nazi voices. To understand how and when the memory of the Holocaust entered into German political discourse we must look beyond the dominating figures of Adenauer and Ulbricht to the partly successful efforts of the democratic left and liberals in West Germany, especially Kurt Schumacher and Theodor Heuss, and to the failed attempts by dissident communists in East Germany, notably Paul Merker.

Konrad Adenauer (1876–1967), the leader of the post-war Christian Democrats (CDU) and chancellor of the Federal Republic of Germany from 1949 to 1963, had been mayor of Cologne from 1917 to 1933. Kurt Schumacher (1895–1952), the leader of the post-war Social Democrats (SPD), served as a member of the Reichstag in the Weimar Republic. Theodor Heuss (1884–1963), the first president of the Federal Republic, worked as a journalist and a professor of politics, and was active in liberal politics in the Weimar years as well. Ernst Reuter (1889–1953), the mayor of West Berlin during the crucial early years of the Cold War, had been a Social Democratic politician in Weimar; after being held prisoner in a Nazi concentration camp, he went into political exile in Ankara, Turkey. The communist leadership in East Germany also came of political age before 1933 and drew on an intact German political tradition. Walter Ulbricht, the effective head of the East German government, was born in 1893. Otto Grotewohl, co-chair of the Socialist Unity Party, and Wilhelm Pieck, a comrade and friend of Rosa Luxembourg and the first president of the German Democratic Republic, were born in 1894 and 1876 respectively. Paul Merker, a leading figure of the German Communist Party since 1920 whose unsuccessful efforts to raise the Jewish question in East Berlin led to his political downfall in 1950, was also born in 1894.

From 6 May 1945, two days before the Nazi surrender, until his death at the age of fifty-seven on 20 August 1952, Kurt Schumacher urged his fellow Germans to face the Nazi past, including the mass murder of European Jewry. Among post-war German political leaders he was the first to emphatically support *Wiedergutmachung* or restitution to the Jewish survivors of the Holocaust, and to urge close and warm relations with the new state of Israel. A democratic socialist, Schumacher believed that overcoming the Nazi past meant breaking with German capitalism. However, his Marxism notwithstanding, Schumacher stressed that Nazism had been more than a plot by a small group of capitalists and Nazi leaders and that it had a mass base of support, that the Germans fought for Hitler to the bitter end, and that the Nazi regime was destroyed only as a result of Allied arms.

He rejected the idea of a collective guilt of the German people because doing so neglected the anti-Nazi resistance, and helped those who had committed crimes to escape justice. If all were guilty, none was responsible. Yet Schumacher was blunt in his criticism of German passivity in the face of Nazi criminality. In 1945 he said that the Germans knew what was taking place in their midst. They 'saw with their own eyes, with what common bestiality, the Nazis tortured, robbed, and hunted the Jews. Not only did they remain silent, but they would have preferred that Germany had won the Second World War thus guaranteeing them peace and quiet and also a small profit'. They had believed in dictatorship and violence, and thus were occupied by others after 1945. 'This political insight', he said, was 'the precondition for a spiritual–intellectual and moral repentance and change'.[3] In his post-war speeches, Schumacher supported the removal of former Nazis from positions of power and influence, the continuation of war crimes trials, the payment of financial restitution to Jews, and honesty about the Nazi past. In the election of 1949, the West Germans opted instead for Adenauer's very different view of the relationship between democratisation and the Nazi past.

Schumacher's post-war statements drew on personal conviction combined with enduring solidarity between German Social Democrats and German Jews. These solidarities had their origins in pre-Nazi Germany and deepened during the anti-Nazi emigration, when many German Social Democrats found refuge in Britain and the United States. Schumacher was the first German politician to be invited to the United States after 1945. The invitation came from the Jewish Labor Committee, an umbrella organisation representing 500,000 members of the labour

---

[3] Kurt Schumacher, 'Wir verzweifeln nicht', in *Kurt Schumacher: Reden-Schriften-Korrespondenz, 1945–1952*, ed. Willy Albrecht (Berlin: J. J. W. Dietz, 1985), 217.

movement in New York City, as well as from leaders of the American Federation of Labor (AFL) such as William Green and especially David Dubinsky. In September and October 1947, Schumacher travelled to New York and San Francisco. In San Francisco, he spoke at the annual meeting of the AFL where he repeated his support for restitution to Jewish survivors. He was the first nationally prominent German politician to take this position. Bonds formed in New York City between Social Democratic exiles and American Jewish labour leaders during the Nazi era endured after 1945. In West Germany, the core of support for the arguments of Jewish survivors came from the social democratic left, a political force which for a variety of reasons remained a minority, opposition party in the crucial post-war years. Given the amount of antisemitism which the Allies found in their post-war polling data, it seems a reasonable assumption (one which deserves to be researched further) that the post-war SPD lost votes due to Schumacher's emphatic public support for Jewish-related issues. His kind of public memory conflicted with his interests in the electoral struggle for power.

More than any other figure, founding Chancellor Konrad Adenauer shaped West German policy towards the Nazi past. Although not a member of the anti-Nazi resistance, he opposed the Nazis and had been briefly imprisoned by the Gestapo. His wife's early death after the war at the age of fifty-seven stemmed from her two suicide attempts due to her despair over having divulged information about his whereabouts in a Gestapo interrogation. Adenauer believed that Nazism was the result of deep ills in German history and society: above all Prussian authoritarianism, the weakness of individualism, the 'materialist world view of Marxism' which eroded religious faith and fostered nihilism, and an ideology of racial superiority which filled the vacuum left by the erosion of the dignity of all human beings grounded in Christian natural right. For Adenauer, a political leader of the Catholic Zentrum party of the Weimar era, the antidote to these ills was democracy resting on the basis of Christian natural right, and the belief that flowed from it in the dignity and value of every individual. However, Adenauer did not examine the role of Christianity in the history of European antisemitism.

Adenauer's pessimism about the breadth and depth of Nazism within German history and society did not lead him to adopt the pose of the avenging angel. Rather, his view of the depth of Nazi support led him to pursue a strategy of democratisation by integration of former and hopefully disillusioned followers of Nazism or, in the terms of this book, of pursuing power by de-emphasising memory of the crimes of the Nazi era. As early as spring and summer 1946, when the major Nuremberg trial was still going on and thousands of suspects had yet to be charged, Adenauer repeatedly told audiences in his election speeches in the British zone of occupation that 'we *finally* [endlich–emphasis added] should leave in peace the followers, those who did not oppress others, who did not enrich themselves, and who broke no laws'.[4] For Adenauer, liberal democracy in post-Nazi Germany could not be established against the will of the majority. More accurately, he did not want to risk offending the will of crucial minorities who could make the difference between electoral victory and defeat. Equating the fortunes of the CDU with the fate of democracy per se, Adenauer's strategy gave to the West German 'amnesty lobby' of the 1950s a de facto veto over aggressive post-war judicial procedures. His view of the power–memory link contributed to victory in national elections but at the high price of delay and denial of justice. In view of the fact that any democratic politician intent on winning a national election in the post-war decade was seeking the votes of citizens many of whom were emphatically opposed to timely trials for war crimes and crimes against humanity, the Western decision to grant sovereignty to the new West German democracy in these matters came with the very high cost of the delay and denial of justice.

Within these limits, Adenauer took a clear and unchanging position in favour of offering restitution payments to Jewish survivors and to the state of Israel. He publicly declared his willingness to do so in the Bundestag in September 1951, and pushed the restitution agreement through in the face of considerable opposition within his own party. Although Adenauer supported the *Wiedergutmachung* agreement with Israel and Jewish survivors, he also restored pension rights to former members of the Wehrmacht and Nazi regime. As Thomas Schwartz has shown, in his contact with US High Commissioner John J. McCloy, he pleaded for amnesty and leniency towards those who had already been convicted of crimes by the Allies in the occupation period.[5] Integration of ex-Nazi Germans took priority over justice. When Theodor Adorno in 1959 said that suppression of the Nazi past was far less the product of unconscious processes or deficient memory than it was 'the product of an all too wide awake consciousness', he captured the actual practice of the Adenauer years. 'In the house of the hangman', he continued, 'it is best not to talk

[4] Konrad Adenauer, 'Grundsatzrede des 1. Vorsitzenden der Christlich-Demokratischen Union für die Britische Zone in der Aula der Kölner Universität', in *Konrad Adenauer: Reden, 1917–1967: Eine Auswahl*, ed. Hans-Peter Schwarz (Stuttgart: Deutsche Verlags-Anstalt, 1975), 92.
[5] Thomas Schwartz, *America's Germany: John J. McCloy and the Federal Republic of Germany* (Cambridge, MA: Harvard University Press, 1991).

about the rope.'[6] In the Adenauer era those who won national elections in the Federal Republic and had a democratic mandate opposed a vigorous programme of justice for past crimes and supported a programme of premature and undeserved amnesty. This tension between justice and early democratisation is a major theme of post-war West German history, as well as of the transition from dictatorship to democracy in the twentieth century in general. Daring more democracy with an electorate which included crucial voting blocs opposed to putting the past on trial meant attaining less justice.

The distinctive West German government tradition of remembering the crimes of the Nazi past began as elite tradition that sounded a soft dissonant note in the larger West German silence. It was inaugurated by Theodor Heuss, the first occupant of the largely honorific position of *Bundespräsident* of the Federal Republic. He used the office of president, and its insulation from the electoral struggle for political power, to remember publicly the crimes of the Nazi era, and to define the office as a repository of the nation's conscience and memory. To his critics, he was the cultured veneer of the Adenauer restoration, and an advocate of eloquent memory separated from politically consequential justice. Yet in speeches about German history and in extensive private correspondence with Jewish survivors, resistance veterans, and West German and foreign intellectuals, Heuss began an elite tradition of political recollection that would eventually contribute to broader public discussion and action. He could have done much more. Others in his position would have done, and later did do, much less.

Heuss delivered his most important speech regarding the Nazi past at memorial ceremonies held at the former Nazi concentration camp at Bergen-Belsen on 29–30 November 1952. Officials of the Federal Republic and representatives of many governments and of Jewish organisations gathered to dedicate a memorial to those persecuted at the Nazi concentration camp at Bergen-Belsen. The ceremonies were a decidedly Western event which reflected the realities of the Cold War and divided memory. Attending were government representatives from Britain, the United States, Denmark, Belgium, the Netherlands, Switzerland, Sweden, France, Yugoslavia, Israel and the Jewish communities in Germany, Europe and the United States. None of the communist states was represented.

---

[6] Theodor Adorno, 'Was bedeutet Aufarbeitung der Vergangenheit', in *Theodor Adorno: Gesammelte Schriften*, 10, 2 (Frankfurt am Main: Suhrkamp Verlag, 1977), 558.

Nahum Goldmann spoke on behalf of the World Jewish Congress.[7] He described the destruction of European Jewry in detail and recalled 'the millions who found their tragic end in Auschwitz, Treblinka, Dachau, and in Warsaw, and Vilna and Bialistock and in countless other places".[8] In this very Western ceremony at the height of the Cold War, Goldmann drew attention to the *eastern geography* of the Holocaust. In so doing, he implicitly pointed out that the geography of memory did not coincide with the fault lines in the West of the Cold War. The Holocaust had largely taken place in a part of Europe that during the Cold War was 'behind the Iron Curtain'. Goldmann's recounting of the Holocaust inevitably called to mind German aggression on the Eastern Front during the Second World War, an invasion which eventually led to the presence of the Red Army in the centre of Europe in May 1945. This was an uncomfortable and inconvenient recollection of causality when Western memory of the Second World War often gave short shrift to the attack on 'Jewish Bolshevism' on the Eastern Front. To be sure there were efforts to separate the memory of the Holocaust from memory of the attack on the Soviet Union, but on the whole it did not fit well into the discourse of the Cold War.

Heuss's speech in Bergen-Belsen, 'No one will lift this shame from us' (*Diese Scham nimmt uns niemand ab!*), was the most extensive statement up to that date of national West German reflection on the mass murder of European Jewry. It was broadcast on the radio and was the subject of reports in the West German press, especially the liberal press.[9] Heuss took issue with those who sought to avoid the crimes of the Nazi past by pointing to alleged misdeeds of others.

It seems to me that the tariffs of virtue [*Tugendtarif*] with which the peoples rig themselves out, is a corrupting and banal affair... Violence and injustice are not things for which one should or may resort to reciprocal compensation... Every people has in reserve its poets of revenge or, when they get tired, its calculated publicists.[10]

---

[7] Theodor Heuss, 'Diese Scham nimmt uns niemand ab: Der Bundespräsident sprach bei der Weihe des Mahnmals in Bergen-Belsen', *Bulletin des Presse- und Informationsamtes der Bundesregierung*, 189 (1 Dec. 1952), 1655–6. An abridged version appeared as 'Das Mahnmal', in Theodor Heuss, *Die Grossen Reden: Der Staatsmann* (Tübingen: Rainer Wunderlich Verlag, 1965), 224–30. See also Bundesarchiv Koblenz, NL Heuss B122, 2082.

[8] Nahum Goldmann, speech at Bergen-Belsen, 30 November 1952, BA Koblenz NL Theodor Heuss B122 2082, 1–2.

[9] Theodor Heuss, 'Diese Scham nimmt uns niemand ab!' *Bulletin des Presse- und Informationsamtes der Bundesregierung*, 189 (2 Dec.1952), 1655–6; 'Heuss weiht Mahnmal in Belsen ein: Der Bundespräsident gedenkt der Opfer des ehemaligen Kz', *Frankfurter Rundschau* (1 Dec. 1952), 1.

[10] Ibid.

Heuss evoked a patriotism self-confident enough to face honestly an evil past rather than seek to balance past crimes by pointing to communist misdeeds. He placed the language of patriotism in the service of memory rather than avoidance and resentment. For Heuss, the moral imperative to remember the past was not a burden imposed by the occupiers and victors but a legacy passed on by German history. Hence, by 1953 public memory of the Holocaust had become a part of official West German political culture. Until the early 1960s this Heussian tradition of public memory and expression of collective shame did not translate into effective judicial action.

Past political convictions shaped the memory of the Holocaust in East Germany no less than in West Germany. Those convictions included a Marxist orthodoxy which placed the Jewish question on the margins of the class struggle, viewed antisemitism primarily as a tool to divide the working class (rather than as a belief system with autonomous and widespread impact) and fascism as a product of capitalism. Worse, many communists, beginning with Marx himself, identified Jews with hated capitalism, while Stalin, in his canonical 1913 essay on the national question, denied that the Jews were a nation, not to mention a persecuted nation. Yet, especially under the extreme pressures of the Second World War, even communism in its totalitarian form displayed latitude regarding the Jewish question. Under the pressure of the Nazi attack on 'Jewish Bolshevism', wartime communist sympathy for the oppressed at times extended to persecuted Jewry. Moreover, and very importantly, during the Second World War many communists – both in the Soviet Union and in Western emigration – nurtured hopes that shared experience of persecution and struggle on the Eastern Front in the Second World War would lead to a turning away from communist orthodoxy regarding Jewish matters. Yet after 1945, and especially after 1948, the power of the dominant traditions of German and European communist orthodoxy were reinforced by the shifting power political interests of the Soviet Union. The result was the suppression of the memory of the Holocaust for the entire post-war period and the end of those hopes for a communist–Jewish rapprochement which had flickered during the war and the Holocaust.

The dominant German communist views found a home in Moscow during the war and were expressed immediately after the war in Walter Ulbricht's canonical *Die Legende vom 'Deutschen Sozialismus'* (*The Legend of 'German Socialism'*).[11] Ulbricht stressed the memory of Soviet suffering, heroism, redemption and victory while he marginalised the memory of the Jewish catastrophe. The wartime radio addresses and propaganda

---

[11] Walter Ulbricht, *Die Legende vom 'Deutschen Sozialismus'* (Berlin: Dietz Verlag, 1945).

efforts of the German communist exiles in wartime Moscow shed important and intriguing insights into the connection between memory and dictatorship. Spokesmen of the National Committee for a Free Germany, such as Wilhelm Pieck, along with Ulbricht the leading figure of the German communist exile in Moscow, and the writer Erich Weinert, urged German soldiers and citizens to turn against the Nazi political leaders and generals. As these repeated and increasingly desperate pleas failed to result in a German revolution against Nazism, a tone of bitterness and rage against the German people is unmistakable in the exiles' statements.

For these returning exiles memory of the Nazi past and its crimes, and of the absence of an anti-Nazi German revolt reinforced their already powerful communist-bred suspicions of liberal democracy. As one can see from their 'Appeal to the German People' in June 1945, their memory of the past included memory of their past rejection by the German people. Despite public declarations of support for a democratic, anti-fascist government in the early post-war months and years, their texts contain abundant evidence of fear and distrust of their fellow Germans. The more they remembered their own past persecution by the Nazi regime and its popular support in German society, as well as its attack on the homeland of revolution, the more they were inclined to impose another dictatorship on this dangerous people. Both past ideological commitments and the power of the Soviet Union placed the story of Soviet suffering and victory at the centre of orthodox Communist memory.

A minority view among the communists found expression in Western, specifically in Mexican exile. In wartime Mexico City the Jewish question moved from the periphery to the centre of the struggle against Nazism. Paul Merker (1894–1969) was it leading exponent. The Doctors' Plot in Moscow in 1953, and the Slansky trial in Prague in 1952 have entered into the major narratives of post-war European history.[12] Before 1989 the Merker affair and the anti-cosmopolitan and anti-Jewish purge of 1949 to 1956 in East Germany were either forgotten or remained largely unknown outside the circles of quietly dissenting historians in the former East Germany, Jewish émigrés from East Germany, and East German experts in West Germany.[13] Documents from the recently opened archives of

[12] On the Jews, communism and antisemitism after 1945 in Europe see François Fejto, *Les Juifs et l'Antisemitisme dans les Pays Communistes* (Paris: Librairie Plon, 1960); German edition, *Judentum und Kommunismus in Osteuropa* (Vienna, Frankfurt/Main and Zurich: Europa Verlag, 1967). On the Jewish question and East German communists see the essays by Olaf Groehler and Mario Kessler in Jürgen Kocka (ed.), *Historische DDR-Forschung: Aufsätze und Studien* (Berlin: Akademie Verlag, 1994).

[13] On the Merker case see Karl Wilhelm Fricke, *Warten auf Gerechtigkeit: Kommunistische Säuberungen und Rehabilitierungen, Bericht und Dokumentation* (Cologne: Verlag Wissenschaft und Politik, 1971); Karl Wilhelm Fricke, *Politik und Justiz in der*

the former ruling Socialist Unity Party (SED) and of the East German Ministry of State Security, the Stasi, indicate that the Merker case and the anti-cosmopolitan purge of winter 1952/3 were the decisive turning-points in the history of the Jewish question in East Germany. They constituted the decisive blow to hopes for a distinctively East German communist confrontation with the Jewish catastrophe, for East German restitution to Jewish survivors, for close relations with Israel, or for continuation of wartime solidarities into the post-war era.[14]

In exile in Mexico, Merker, who was not Jewish, together with Jewish communists including Otto Katz, Rudolf Feistmann and Leo Zuckermann, conducted the most extensive discussion of the Jewish question in the history of German communism.[15] Merker was the only member of the German Communist Party Politburo in Mexico City. From autumn 1942 to December 1945 he was a leading figure of the Bewegung Freies Deutschland (Movement for a Free Germany). He contributed regularly to *Freies Deutschland*, the bi-weekly journal of the German communists in Mexico City, assuming responsibility for its general political line. In contrast to the writings of the Moscow group, Merker's books and essays on Nazism and the Second World War placed antisemitism and the Jewish catastrophe at the centre of the anti-fascist struggle. In essays such as 'Antisemitism and Us'[16] he stressed the commonality of the interests of Jews and communists, supported restitution for the Jewish survivors, and expressed understanding for the growth of Jewish national feeling and the desire for a Jewish state. He envisaged a post-war Germany with a restored Jewish community. He supported practical, financial assistance to help bring this result about. He also pointed to differences between the persecution of Jews and of communists. The former were persecuted because of who they were and thus had the same right as did 'all of the nations

---

DDR: Zur Geschichte der politischen Verfolgung 1945–1968, Bericht und Dokumentation (Cologne: Verlag Wissenschaft und Politik, 1979); Rudi Beckert and Karl Wilhelm Fricke, 'Auf Weisung des Politbüros: Aus den Geheimprozeßakten des Obersten DDR-Gerichts, Teil III: Der Fall Paul Merker', *Zur Diskussion/Geschichte Aktuell*, broadcast by Deutschlandfunk, Hamburg, 10 Jan. 1992; George Hermann Hodos, *Schauprozesse: Stalinistische Säuberungen in Osteuropa 1948–1954* (Frankfurt/Main: Campus Verlag, 1988).

[14] On East German historians and the Jewish question, see Helmut Eschwege, *Fremd unter meinesgleichen: Erinnerungen eines Dresdner Juden* (Berlin: Ch. Links Verlag, 1991). On East Germany and Israel see Inge Deutschkron, *Israel und die Deutschen: Das besondere Verhältnis* (Cologne: Wissenschaft und Politik, 1983).

[15] On this see Jeffrey Herf, 'German Communism, the Discourse of "Antifascist Resistance," and the Jewish Catastrophe,' in Michael Geyer and John W. Boyer, eds. *Resistance Against the Third Reich: 1933–1990* (Chicago: University of Chicago Press, 1994), 257–94; and especially Fritz Pohle, *Das Mexikanische Exil* (Stuttgart: J.B. Metzler, 1986).

[16] Paul Merker, 'Antisemitismus und wir', *Freies Deutschland*, 1, 12 (October 1942), 9–11.

Hitler invaded and oppressed'. The latter were persecuted because of what they believed and did. They had voluntarily taken up the struggle against the Nazis and thus could not 'expect material compensation for the sacrifices that result'. For the communists, he argued, victory over Nazism was more than adequate compensation. Merker was supported in his efforts by Leo Zuckermann, another member of the KPD, who was Jewish.

When Merker and Zuckermann returned to East Berlin, in 1946 and 1947 respectively, they brought with them the concern for Jewish matters which had flourished in Mexican exile. They argued within the emerging communist government in favour of *Wiedergutmachung*, close relations with Israel and an anti-fascist discourse which made ample room for the Jewish catastrophe. In bitter political and bureaucratic disputes within the emergent communist governing apparatus, Merker argued for placing the claims of the Jewish *victims* on the same – elevated – moral and political level as those of former communist 'anti-fascist resistance fighters'.[17]

Stalin, however, believed that communist émigrés returning from the West to the Soviet bloc after 1945 were a dangerous source of subversive ideas about democracy, and probably harboured lingering sympathies for the counterparts of his own wartime 'Western Alliance' with the 'Anglo-American imperialists', Roosevelt and Churchill. In East Germany, the attack on the West and the association of Jews with capitalism in East Germany overlapped with older anti-Western currents in German nationalism.[18] Memory of the Holocaust also carried with it memories of Stalin's own now quite embarrassing 'Western Alliance' with the United States and Great Britain. In both East and West, the forgetting of the Holocaust was an integral aspect of the forgetting of the full dimensions of the Second World War.

In August 1950, Merker was expelled from the Central Committee and the SED itself, because of espionage accusations stemming from his wartime contact with Noel H. Field, an American leftist, perhaps also a communist, who helped him and others escape from Vichy to Mexico City. According to the denunciation, Merker and his associates in France and Mexico had erroneously 'imagined that the goal of American,

---

[17] See Stiftung Archiv für Parteien und Massenorganisationen der DDR im Bundesarchiv, Zentrales Parteiarchiv (henceforth SAPMO-BA, ZPA), Sekretariat Lehmann IV/2027/29–33 (Wiedergutmachung gegenüber den Verfolgten des Naziregimes, 1945–1950).

[18] Sigrid Meuschel, 'Die nationale Frage zwischen Antifaschismus, Sozialismus und Antizionismus', in *eadem*, *Legitimation und Parteiherrschaft in der DDR* (Frankfurt/Main: Suhrkamp, 1992), 101–16. On the Weimar right and the West, see among much else, Jeffrey Herf, *Reactionary Modernism: Technology, Culture and Politics in Weimar and the Third Reich* (New York: Cambridge University Press, 1984).

English and French imperialism consisted in the liberation of Europe from fascism'. In asserting that Britain and the United States were motivated more by a desire to create an anti-Soviet bulwark in Europe than to the 'liberation of Europe from fascism', the Field denunciation projected the antagonisms of the Cold War back into the war years. It, and the 'anti-cosmopolitan purge' in general, are textbook examples of the placement of memory and official history in the service of current political goals.

Zuckermann, who in 1949 and 1950 was chief of East German President Wilhelm Pieck's office, resigned under pressure to take a position teaching law at the Walter Ulbricht academy in law and international affairs at Potsdam. On 18 July 1951, presumably in response to increasing pressure, he wrote a second, far more extensive letter of resignation to the SED Central Committee.[19] He wrote that he had been deeply shaken by the murder of many of his relatives and friends in the camps, as well as by what he described as 'the population's widespread lack of interest' and at times 'open antisemitic sentiments', despite all that had happened. Thus he joined the Jewish community in East Berlin as 'an act of solidarity with persecuted Jews', that is, as a political, not a religious act. 'Looking back on this now, I see that this decision was a false and sentimental reaction. I will not excuse or justify it in any way but I do want to try to make it understandable.'[20] Ironically, the fact that Zuckermann was Jewish and that many of his relatives had perished in the Holocaust made it possible for him to offer a plausible alternative explanation for his decision other than that he was US or British spy. Zuckermann believed that he could save his political career, and perhaps more than that, only by describing his perfectly human and humane responses to the Holocaust as 'false and sentimental reactions'.

The Noel Field affair in 1950 and Merker's expulsion from the SED formed only the beginning of the anti-cosmopolitan purge in East Germany. Merker's fate was sealed by the outcome of the show trial against Rudolf Slansky and other high-ranking communist, mostly Jewish, defendants in Prague in November 1952. On 3 December 1952, four days after Stasi agents arrested Paul Merker in Berlin, Rudolf Slansky, the second most powerful figure in the Communist Party of Czechoslovakia and the Czechoslovak government, Otto Fischl, the

---

[19] 'Leo Zuckermann, Abschrift: Lebensbericht' (Berlin, 18 July 1951), SAPMO-BA, ZPA Kaderfragen IV 2/11/V 5248, 27–30.

[20] Ibid. 'I come from an East European Jewish family, in which Yiddish and Russian were spoken, and in which certain Jewish traditions and national residues were much more present than they were among Jews in Germany. The social development which has taken place in the GDR since that time [1947] has also solved this problem [of post-war antisemitism and the place of the Jewish community in Germany].'

former Czechoslovak ambassador to East Germany, and Merker's friend and former Mexico City comrade, Otto Katz ('Andre Simone'), were among the eleven, mostly Jewish, defendants to be executed in Prague by hanging. In the trial, confessions of extremely dubious origins from the accused included accusations that Merker was linked to the Slansky defendants in an international conspiracy to destroy communism in eastern and central Europe.

On 20 December 1952, with the publication of 'Lehren aus dem Prozess gegen das Verschwörerzentrum Slansky' ('Lessons of the trial against the Slansky conspiracy center') the SED leaders in East Germany struck the decisive blow against Merker.[21] The author of the statement, Herman Matern, denounced a vast espionage conspiracy of American imperialists, Zionists, Jewish capitalists and some members of communist parties, such as Slansky. Matern's 1952 denunciation rested on an old antisemitic stereotype, namely the pejorative connection between the Jews and capitalism as well as the association of European Jews with vast, international power. In Mexico, Matern argued, Merker defended 'the interests of Zionist monopoly capitalists'. Merker was a 'subject of the USA financial oligarchy who called for compensation for Jewish property in order to facilitate the penetration of USA finance capital into [post-war] Germany. This is the real basis of his [Merker's] Zionism.' Merker's support for restitution concerned 'above all . . . wealthy Jewish economic emigrants'.[22]

With such arguments, Matern retrospectively reinterpreted the wartime cooperation and solidarity between some German communists in exile in the West, on the one hand, and German-Jewish emigrants, American Jewish and non-Jewish communists, leftists and liberals on the other, into an enormous and powerful international conspiracy of American imperialists and Jewish capitalists. 'Lessons of the trial against the Slansky conspiracy centre' presented the old international Jewish conspiracy, this time, in a Communist discourse. In Matern's statement, the Jews ceased to be 'victims of fascism'. Instead they emerge as the active and powerful perpetrators of an international and anti-German conspiracy. Once again a German government attacked the Jews as cosmopolitans, rather than true members of the nation. Once again German nationalists, this time of a communist variant, defined themselves in opposition to a Western, capitalist, international, liberal, Jewish conspiracy.[23] Remarkably, at a

---

[21] Herman Matern, 'Lehren aus dem Prozess gegen das Verschwörerzentrum Slansky', *Dokumente der Sozialistische Einheitspartei, Band IV* ([East] Berlin: Dietz Verlag, 1954), 199–219.

[22] Ibid., 206–7.

[23] See Meuschel, *Legitimation und Parteiherrschaft*, 101–16.

moment of extreme Jewish weakness, Germany's anti-fascist regime denounced the Jews for their supposed power.

December 1952/January 1953 was the turning-point in the history of the Jewish question in East Germany. In January and February 1953 fear spread through the tiny East German Jewish community and among the Jewish members of the SED, all of whom were now potential targets of espionage accusations. Hundreds fled to the West. East German communists who knew Merker and who agreed with his views on the Jewish question understood the dangers of continuing to remain in the DDR. Leo Zuckermann and his family fled to West Berlin in January 1953.[24] In December 1952 the SED Central Committee demanded that the leaders of the Jewish communities in East Germany publicly denounce the restitution agreement between West Germany and Israel and also publicly state that the Joint Distribution Committee, which was sending relief supplies to Jews in Germany, was a tool of US espionage; Zionism was the same as fascism and Israeli President Ben Gurion was an agent of US imperialism; US justice was criminal because it condemned the Rosenbergs to death; restitution for the injustice done to the Jews amounted to exploitation of the German people.[25] Julius Meyer, the head of the organised Jewish Community in East Berlin, and Leo Löwenkopf, the chairman of the organised Jewish community in Dresden, both of whom were SED party members, decided to flee. They did so, in Meyer's words, due to 'fear of a repetition of the pogrom of 1938'.[26] The arrest of Merker, followed by the flight of Zuckermann, Löwenkopf and Meyer, removed from the East German political scene the leading advocates for Jewish interests within the SED and the government.[27]

---

[24] Zuckermann had been last seen in East Berlin on 13 December 1952. 'Aktennotiz' (20 Dec. 1952), 'Aktenvermerk' (20 Dec. 1952), 'Abschluss-Bericht' (15 April 1953), Bundesbeauftragte der Bundesregierung für die personenbezogenen Unterlagen des ehemaligen Staatssicherheitsdienst (henceforth BStU), Ministerium für Staatssicherheit (henceforth MFS), Archiv 147/53 Leo Zuckermann, BStU, 000037–41. See also Nathan Margolin, 'East German Jews Don't Say Good-bye; They Silently Vanish to the West,' *Look*, 10 March 1953, 73–4.

[25] 'Moskauer Antizionismus in der DDR: Interview mit geflüchtetem Leiter der Jüdischen Gemeinde der Sowjetzone', *Die Neue Zeitung*, 24 Jan. 1953. On the flight of the Jewish leaders from East Germany see also 'Four Jewish Leaders in East Zone Flee', *New York Times*, 16 Jan. 1953, 3; and Mario Kessler, 'Zwischen Repression und Toleranz: Die SED Politik und die Juden', in Jürgen Kocka (ed.), *Historische DDR Forschung* (Berlin: Akademie Verlag, 1993), 149–67.

[26] Julius Meyer, quoted in 'Moskauer Antizionismus in der DDR: Interview mit geflüchteten Leiter der Jüdischen Gemeinde der Sowjetzone', *Die Neue Zeitung*, 24 Jan. 1953, 1.

[27] Meyer contrasted Hitler's racially motivated persecution to the purely political motives behind the SED anti-Jewish measures. He saw four grounds for the purge: to gain sympathy among the Arab countries, to break the links between Jews in the Soviet

There were non-religious, genuinely non-Jewish-Jews who survived the purge and later played significant roles in the East German government. The case of Alexander Abusch, a leading cultural functionary of the East German regime, illustrates how those who have been cast into the wilderness could crawl their way back to redemption and salvation. In December 1950 Abusch had been relieved of all his party functions, in part because, as the Central Party control commission (*Zentralparteikontrollkommission* or *ZPKK*, hereafter Control Commission) put it, as the editor of *Freies Deutschland* in Mexico City, 'he published Merker's false views on the question of Jewish emigration', on the nationalities question, and on restitution towards the Jews.[28] In his exchanges with officials of the control commission, Abusch insisted that, although born into a Jewish family, he had no interest at all in Jewish matters.[29]

On 31 May 1952 Abusch agreed to work as an informant for the Stasi.[30] He did so until 26 October 1956.[31] As a past official of the Kulturbund zur demokratischen Erneuung Deutschland (Cultural Association for Germany's Democratic Renewal), Abusch knew all the prominent intellectuals in East Germany and offered Ulbricht and Erich Mielke, a member of the SED Central Committee from 1950 and head of the Stasi from 1957, a window into the world of elite intellectuals. He also testified against Merker to the control commission and the Stasi, and in the secret political trial of 1955. Yet testifying against others alone would not have brought Abusch redemption. His 'My Errors in Mexico and Their Lessons for the Present', written between January and March 1953, documents the terms on which communists 'of Jewish origin' were able to

zone and friends and relatives in the West, to use the Jews as a collective scapegoat for economic problems, and to exclude potential critics of Ulbricht's policies, ibid. See also Walter Sullivan, 'Jewish Fugitives Reveal Pressures By East Germans: Eight Leaders Say They Were Asked to Back Slansky Case and Denounce Zionism', *New York Times*, 8 Feb. 1953, 1, 13.

28 See 'Betr.: Alexander Abusch, Berlin' (11 Dec. 1950), SAPMO-BA, ZPA ZPKK IV 2/4/111, p. 54.

29 See Alexander Abusch, 'Ergänzungen zu meinen mündlichen Aussagen vom 10. 11. 1950', 42–5, and 'Skizze der innerparteilichen politischen Diskussionen in Mexiko 1942/45', 47–51, SAPMO-BA, ZPA ZPKK IV 2/4/111.

30 'Verpflichtung' (30 May 1951), BStU, MfS-Archiv 5079/53 Alexander Abusch, Arbeitsvorgang 2282/53, Band I, Teil I, 000082. Abusch had to assume that Merker's mail would be read, and his telephone tapped so that the Stasi would know immediately that he had tried to contact Abusch. Had he not brought the letter and telephone call to Ulbricht's attention immediately, the control commission and the Stasi would assume that Abusch's protestations of innocence of genuine friendship or agreement with 'the agent Merker' were themselves lies.

31 Abusch's code name was 'Ernst'. His category was 'geheimen Informator' (secret informer) or 'GI'. See 'Aktenspiegel' (23 July 1953), BStU, MfS-Archiv 5079/56 Alexander Abusch, Band I, Teil I, 000027–28, 000031; 'Schlussbericht' (26 Oct. 1956), BStU, MfS-Archiv 5079/56 Alexander Abusch, Band I, Teil II, 000224.

remain within the SED leadership.[32] He admitted to having failed to 'quickly recognise and to decisively fight against the enemy nature of Merker's theories on the Jewish question', and to apply the 'Lenin–Stalin theory of imperialism in this context'.[33] He confessed to having 'allowed concessions to Jewish chauvinism' in Mexico. Abusch started on the path to his sought-after political rehabilitation in summer 1951. From 1958 to 1961, when the memorials to the victims of fascism in Buchenwald and Sachsenhausen were being built by the East German Ministry of Culture, Abusch was the East German Minister of Culture.

The entry, or, as the case may be, re-entry, ticket into the East German political elite for those Jews who remained or recovered prominent posi-tions in the SED, such as Abusch, entailed saying little or nothing publicly about the murder of European Jewry, accepting without protest the Soviet bloc diplomatic attack on Israel, and focusing anti-fascist energies on attacking developments in West Germany. As of December 1952–January 1953, it was clear that inadequacies and silences concerning the Jewish question in East Germany were no longer only a result of the inadequacies of Marxist-Leninist theories of fascism and anti-fascism. At this point at the latest, East German communists, Jews and non-Jews, understood that sympathy for the Jews as expressed by Merker was not only 'incorrect'. It was dangerous.[34]

The political survival of non-Jewish Jews such as Abusch or Albert Norden, the head of the East German office charged with propaganda offensives against West Germany, is historically important beyond the drama of courage, opportunism and survival under dictatorship. For both Abusch and Norden illustrate a chapter in the history of German-Jewish assimilation as radical if not more so than any of the much more famil-iar episodes of the much studied nineteenth and early twentieth century. Indeed, if one wishes to speak of a dialectic of enlightenment, a rage of ra-tionality against the stubborn particular which refuses to succumb, then it seems to me appropriate to see this dialectic at work in the communist suppression of the particulars of the Jewish question. Both Abusch and Norden presented the DDR as representing a progressive Germany, a fully enlightened nation in which there was no more room for what they regarded as religious obscurantism of any kind. The power of communist

---

[32] Alexander Abusch, 'Meine Fehler in Mexiko und ihre aktuellen Lehren', BStU, Archiv-MfS 5079/56 Alexander Abusch, Arbeitsvorgang 2282/53 Band I, Teil II, 000075–83.

[33] Ibid., 000078.

[34] A full discussion of 'non-Jewish Jews' in the East German government must include discussion of Albert Norden. In no other East German communist's work does the contrast between celebration of a communist variant of 'the German nation' coincide so sharply with refusal to raise the Jewish question. See Albert Norden, *Um die Nation* ([East] Berlin: Dietz Verlag, 1952).

tradition and a reading of German national identity reinforced one another to marginalise Jewish concerns.

Merker was imprisoned in East Berlin from December 1952 to January 1956. During that time he was interrogated by agents of the Stasi and by Soviet NKVD (secret police) agents. His Stasi file comprises over a thousand typed and handwritten pages.[35] In an eerie echo of the famous question of the US House of Representatives Un-American Activities Committee, he was repeatedly asked if he had been or 'was a member of Jewish-Zionist organisations'.[36] According to the conversations Merker had with his cell-mate, who was a Stasi informant during the early months of his imprisonment in winter and spring 1953, the NKVD and Stasi agents threatened to kill him, and made threats against his family. They told him that his 1942 article, 'Antisemitism and Us', showed that he was a '*Judenknecht*', that is, a 'servant of the Jews'. They ridiculed him as 'the king of the Jews', as one who 'had been bought by the Jews' and whose intention was to 'sell the DDR off to the Jews'.[37] Again and again they probed into his contact with and assistance from Jews, both communists and non-communists, during the French and Mexican emigration for further evidence of his participation in an espionage conspiracy.

Merker was tried in the East German Supreme Court in March 1955. The trial remained a secret until the collapse of the DDR in 1989 and the opening of access to the archives of the Oberste Gericht, which had been transferred to the Stasi archives. On 30 March 1955 the judges of the East German Supreme Court sentenced Merker to eight years in prison.[38] The court's verdict[39] closely followed the political indictment Matern had voiced in December 1952. The court explained Merker's engagement on

[35] For the Merker file see BStU MfS Archiv No. 192/56, Untersuchungsvorgang über Paul Merker No. 294/52, Band I–III; and BStU, pp. 000156–000410.

[36] See 'Vernehmungsprotokoll des Häftlings, Merker, Paul Friedrich' (3 March 1953), BStU MfS Archiv Nr. 192/56 Untersuchungsvorgang Nr. 294/52 Paul Merker, Band II, p. 000122.

[37] Paul Merker, 'An die Zentrale Kontrollkommission des ZK. der SED: Stellungnahme zur Judenfrage', (1 June 1956), Paul Merker NL 102/27, SAPMO-BA, ZPA, 1. Most of this important statement is reprinted in the orginal German with other documents from the Merker case in Jeffrey Herf, 'Dokument 3: An Paul Merker, "An die Zentrale Kontrollkommission des ZK. der SED", in "Dokumentation: Antisemitismus in der SED: Geheime Dokumente zum Fall Paul Merker aus SED- und MfS-Archiven"', *Vierteljahrshefte für Zeitgeschichte* 42, 4 (Oct. 1994), 635–67.

[38] The records of the political trials in the East German Oberste Gericht were placed in the Stasi files. For the court's judgment in Merker's case, see 'Oberste Gericht der Deutschen Demokratischen Republik I. Strafsenat I Zst. (I) 1/55: Im Namen des Volkes in der Strafsache gegen den Kellner Paul Merker' (March 29–30, 1955), BStU M.f.S, Untersuchungsvorgang Nr. 294/52 Band III, Archiv Nr. 192/56, pp. 000138–000152.

[39] Reprinted in the original German in *Vierteljahrshefte für Zeitgeschichte* (autumn 1994).

behalf of the Jewish people as a result of corrupting Jewish influences. In Mexico, according to the court, Merker's base in the emigrant community did not lie in 'the political but rather in the racial emigration' especially 'emigrant, capitalist, Jewish circles'. The court saw in Merker's views on Jewish-related matters as proof of his involvement in an international, anti-communist, espionage conspiracy. In placing the link between Jews, capitalism and financial corruption at its core, the verdict stands alongside Matern's denunciation of December 1952 as an important document of post-war East German antisemitism.

Ten months later, on 27 January 1956, shortly before Khrushchev's Secret Speech and a period of de-Stalinisation, Merker was released from prison. In July 1956, Ulbricht wrote elliptically to Merker that 'the re-examination undertaken under new points of view led to the conclusion that the accusations made against you in the most important matters were of a political nature and do not justify judicial prosecution'.[40] Yet Merker's request for a full political rehabilitation and return to a leading position in the party and government was unsuccessful. The same court that had convicted him now declared him innocent of all charges.[41] Although Merker had been released from prison, Ulbricht's letter made it clear, however, that his views remained politically incorrect.

The SED archives reveal further evidence that the 'political reasons' for Merker's downfall were centred on the Jewish question. On his release, and in response to his efforts at full political rehabilitation, the Party control commission asked Merker to write a statement responding to the accusations made by Matern and the Central Committee against him in December 1952. On 1 June 1956 Merker submitted a remarkable thirty-eight-page statement on his 'position on the Jewish question'.[42] He wrote that his Soviet and German interrogators were convinced that he must have been an agent for the United States, Israel, or 'Zionist organisations' because he had taken such a strong position on the Jewish question during the Second World War. They found no evidence that he was Jewish. Why, they reasoned, would any non-Jewish German communist pay so much attention to the Jewish question unless he was an agent of American imperialists, or Zionists and Jewish capitalists? Merker responded as follows:

[40] 'Walter Ulbricht to Paul Merker, 31 July 1956', SAPMO-BA, ZPA NL Paul Merker 102/27, p. 84.
[41] 'Oberste Gericht der Deutschen Demokratischen Republik 1. Strafsenat 1 Zst (I) 1/55, In der Strafsache gegen Merker, Paul Friedrich, 13 July 1956', BStU, MfS, Untersuchungsvorgang No. 294/52 Merker, Paul Band III Archiv No. 192/56, 000206.
[42] Paul Merker, 'An die Zentrale Kontrollkommission des ZK. der SED: Stellungnahme zur Judenfrage' (1 June 1956), SAPMO-BA, ZPA NL Paul Merker 102/27, 16.

I am neither Jewish, nor a Zionist, though it would be no crime to be either. I have never had the intent to flee to Palestine. I have not supported the efforts of Zionism... Moreover: Hitler fascism emerged among us. We [Germans] did not succeed through the actions of the working masses in preventing the erection of its rule and hence the commission of its crimes. Therefore, especially we Germans must not and ought not ignore or fight against what I call this strengthening of Jewish national feeling.[43]

He recalled Soviet support for Israel, as well as the opposition of 'English and American imperialism'. 'No-one', Merker wrote, 'will want to claim that the Soviet government was an "agent of American imperialism".'[44] Merker's defence of the bonds between communists and Jews and his argument that these bonds should continue into the 1950s was sufficient to ensure that he would not again play a leading role in East German communist politics. Zuckermann quietly practised law in Mexico City.

Conclusion

Several factors contributed to the marginalisation of the memory of the Holocaust in East Germany. First, Soviet policy during the Cold War brought it about. In the Soviet empire, the memory of the Second World War constituted first and foremost the memory of the suffering and victory of the Soviet Union. There was to be no competition for attention and empathy from weak claimants such as the Jews. Communist orthodoxy had long excluded the Jews from those Europeans defined as constituting a nation. Second, however, some of the same cultural trends were at work among German as among Soviet communists. In the Cold War, the older anti-Western legacies of the German *Sonderweg* found new expression in the communist ideological assaults on the West, assaults which evoked older antisemitic currents within German, east European and Russian nationalisms that came to the fore in the conspiracy theories aimed at supposedly powerful Jews during the anti-cosmopolitan purges. Although the record of East German persecution of the Jews pales into insignificance compared with that of the Nazi regime, the important moral and historical point is that such a record exists at all – and existed in a self-described anti-fascist regime in the decade following the Holocaust.

Although the memory of the Holocaust emerged in the Federal Republic, the famous power of the Jews was never so potent as to connect memory with justice. The most adamant advocates of the memory of the Holocaust were not clever conservatives eager to enhance West Germany's reputation and prospects for integration into the West by bringing up

[43] Ibid., 16.   [44] Ibid., 18.

the Holocaust and eagerly offering financial restitution. On the contrary, in the Federal Republic, with a few moderate conservative exceptions in the formative years, it was liberals in the Heussian tradition and Social Democrats who brought these issues to the fore. The West German experience indicated that the claims of memory of the Jewish catastrophe were not much stronger than the pangs of conscience of that minority of Germans who like Schumacher and Heuss articulated 'collective shame'. As a result, in the early years of the Adenauer's Federal Republic, daring more democracy meant seeking less justice, and speaking less, not more, about the destruction of European Jewry. In 1950s West Germany, the memory of the destruction of European Jewry entered into national political discourse above all because liberals, Social Democrats, and a few atypical moderate conservatives placed moral considerations above electoral expediency. It was not until the 1960s, when a successor generation asked difficult questions about the Nazi past, that the minority political traditions of memory of the first post-war decades for the first time found a broad audience.

In neither West nor East Germany did the Holocaust fit into anyone's happy narrative of victory and redemption. In both East and West, as Goldmann's speech in Bergen-Belsen indicated, the memory of the Holocaust crossed the fault lines of provincial and divided memory of the Cold War. In both West and East, forgetting and repressing the memory of the Jewish catastrophe was inseparable from forgetting the full dimensions of the Second World War as well as the embarrassing fact that Cold War enemies had only recently been anti-Nazi allies.

Nevertheless, and despite the great shortcomings in the matter of judicial confrontation with the Nazi past, the leaders of the Bonn republic, in the Heussian tradition, made acceptance of this burden of German history a key element of national self-definition. Conversely, despite years of anti-fascist discourse, the East German regime repressed the memory of the Jewish catastrophe and then moved on to anti-Zionist, at times antisemitic, ideology and policy, both at home and in the Middle East. The communist normalcy that was established in the anti-cosmopolitan purge of winter 1952–3 remained intact until 1989. The consequences of multiple restorations and the post-war division of memory remained intact until April 1990, when in its first act the short-lived East German post-communist parliament acknowledged East German responsibility for assuming the burden of the Nazi past. There was a striking historical symmetry to the parliament's action. Just as the suppression of the memory of the Jewish catastrophe accompanied the consolidation of the power of the East German communist dictatorship, so memory's return accompanied the return of democratic political life in East Germany.

Some have argued that postponement of justice and weakness of memory contributed to successful democratisation in West Germany. Such a conclusion wrongly assumes that democratisation had to come about in the way that it did. A different path to democratisation, one which encompassed timely justice, was conceivable, but in my view it would have required a much slower extension of sovereignty to the post-Nazi democracy in West Germany. Justice was at odds with the rapidity of the shift from the anti-Hitler coalition to the fronts of the Cold War. The era of forgetfulness and justice delayed were two of the costs of the early collapse of the anti-Hitler coalition and the emergence of the Cold War. The ongoing struggle for power between East and West overwhelmed the comparatively powerless claims of memory of the Holocaust. Yet given the state of West German public opinion and the political influence of groups interested in avoiding and postponing judicial confrontation with the past, daring more democracy at this early stage meant producing less justice.

In the light of the combined weight of popular will, domestic political interest and international politics favouring forgetfulness, the emergence and persistence of a distinctive post-war West German tradition of political memory of the Holocaust testifies to the, distinctly limited but nevertheless significant, power and impact of the cultural traditions of 'the other Germany' which reemerged from the ruins of Nazi Germany. This precious, often unpopular, tradition constituted the foundation on which a broader tradition of public memory emerged in the 1960s. It persisted even after German unification in 1989, when again many voices have been raised seeking 'finally' to put the past behind. To what extent and in what form it will persist now that the generation of 1968 has won power at the national level remains to be seen.[45]

---

[45] Current debates over a proposed memorial in Berlin indicate that issues concerning memory and politics confound simple left–right dichotomies. For a provisional opinion see Jeffrey Herf, 'Traditionsbruch: Rollenaustausch zwischen SPD und CDU', *Die Zeit*, 13 Aug. 1998.

9   Unimagined communities: the power of memory and the conflict in the former Yugoslavia

Ilana R. Bet-El

There is a power to the words 'I remember': the power of an event long past, exerting itself upon the present, the power of an individual over a collective, the power of opinion over fact. It is not one that can simply be included in academic theory or quantified by statistics, nor can it easily be discredited as untrue. Often enough, 'I remember' is not an exchange – it is an authoritative statement, based on the stark power of personal conviction, seemingly resistant to contestation by others. When the words begin a flow of warmth or love, it is a positive, binding power, but it is the most divisive and negative one possible when they lead on to events of death and destruction, allocating blame and defining justice in terms of personal and national memories. For as the dark recollections swirl around, enforced by the personal pain of the speaker, the statements join together into a weapon of hate and fear.

In the former Yugoslavia, it was this divisive, negative power which underlay the collapse into the wars. From nationalist leaders to village paupers, as of the mid-1980s memories seemingly poured out in an incessant stream: some personal, others personalised, some no more than a myth, others specific recollections – but all reflecting on pain and past ills. Large chunks of verbal agony, beginning with the words 'I remember', and often ending with a sharp admonition: Remember! These were memories of aggressive acts committed by the others: Croats upon Serbs and Muslims; Muslims upon Croats and Serbs; Serbs upon Croats and Muslims and Albanian Kosovars; Albanian Kosovars upon Serbs. Sin upon sin, national memories conjured up as if they were real, personal memories, locking each ethnicity into itself, making all the others abhorrent, unjust and fearful. Words of the past became weapons of war.

The power of memory was not unique to the Yugoslavs. As the wars unfolded, they drew in many and various elements of the international

While specific sources and relevant bibliography are given in the footnotes, this chapter is no less based on personal reflections and countless professional interviews conducted by me throughout 1995–7 and 1999 – first as political analyst with UN missions in the region (UNPROFOR and UNMIBH), then as Senior Advisor on the Balkans in the UN Department of Political Affairs.

community, from mandated organisations such as the UN to tiny religious non-governmental organisations (NGOs), from every significant state in the world to caring individuals and curious intellectuals. And all of these arrived well armed with their own memories. At the one end were those derived from history – the derisive ones of 'another Balkan war', closely followed by the romantic ones inspired by literature, especially the work of Rebecca West, and the actions of a distant intelligentsia. At the other end were the relatively modern memories of tourism in the multi-ethnic Yugoslavia, both the inter-war kingdom and the communist state, and the very new memories of individuals who were part of the ongoing international intervention in the conflict – those who went home and wrote histories and memoirs. But the bulk of what one might call 'international memories', and those which ultimately compelled any action, were undoubtedly rooted in the Second World War: the memories of policy, especially appeasement; the memories that defined the ethnic groups, especially the Serbs and Croats, as either good or bad; and, most crucially, the memories of genocide on European soil.

The international memories were forged with those of the warring factions, and together they shaped the modern Balkan wars: the swift and relatively bloodless departure of Slovenia in 1991, followed by the extended bitterness and brutality of the Croatian conflict and the horrors of the Bosnian war. These both ended in 1995, and once the Dayton Agreement had been signed, the region moved into an uneasy state of non-war – which ultimately ended in 1999, when the Kosovo conflict flared. And by this time it was not only the distant memories of past sins which compelled all sides, but also those of the more recent battles. Most crucially, the extended memory of Serb victimisation was embellished by the expulsion and killings of the Croatian Serbs from the Krajina region in 1995; while the spectre of prolonged inaction during the Bosnian carnage undoubtedly galvanised the international community to strong intervention. In other words, within a decade the modern Balkan wars had generated their own powerful cycle of memories, that is, a contained unit of inter-referential words and images.

Cycles of Yugoslav memory

The origins of the cycle are no less disputed than is the responsibility for the actual wars. However, there is one event in the Yugoslav past on which all the peoples and ethnicities seemingly concur: the crucial impact of Slobodan Milosevic's speech to angry Serbs in the historically resonant town of Kosovo Polje on 24 April 1987. Whether supporting Serbs and Montenegrins, horrified Albanian Kosovars, or watchful Croats, Muslims,

Slovenes and Macedonians, it is commonly recalled as the point after which a unified Yugoslavia could be no more:

First I want to tell you, comrades, that you should stay here. This is your country, these are your houses, your fields and gardens, your memories... You should stay here... Otherwise you would shame your ancestors and disappoint your descendants. But I do not suggest you stay here suffering and enduring a situation with which you are not satisfied. On the contrary! It should be changed...[1]

It was the death-knell of Yugoslavia, sounded upon memory, carefully chosen words that commenced the manipulation of memories into weapons of destruction, through a process of distortion and radicalisation.[2] For Milosevic was invoking a specific collective, national memory – the battle of Kosovo in 1389, in which the Serbs were defeated by the Ottomans – as a rallying call to the Serbs. But to the other ethnicities it was configured as a threat, of resilient Serb nationalism, which in itself competed with their own distinct memories of past achieved glory or inflicted indignity. The Croats harked back to brave Teutonic conquests and the sophistication of Habsburg culture, alongside twentieth-century images of Serb oppression between the wars and in Tito's Yugoslavia; the (mostly Bosnian) Muslims brought long memories of both Ottoman supremacy and religious oppression since the empire was shattered; and the Albanian Kosovars had a heritage of brutal conflict with the Serbs in the region, dating back at least to the seventeenth century. However, at another level, the Serbs and the Croats shared memories of harsh Ottoman rule, which united them against the Muslims; yet these last also joined with the Serbs in cruel memories of the Croat Ustashe in the Second World War, and especially the horrors of the Jasenovac concentration camp.

One of the most potent principles imposed by Tito in Yugoslavia was the suppression of all these memories: 'to throw the hatred into history's deep freeze', as Misha Glenny put it.[3] Yet even then, words were undoubtedly spoken, handed down from generation to generation as precious notes of identity. Words such as: 'I remember being a Partisan and fighting the Croats', or 'I remember when the Ustashe came to the village and took everyone away'. These were private words, delivered while fields were tilled or over a family meal, painful personal experiences slowly transmuted into collective, but still largely private memory. But in 1980,

---

[1] Quoted in Tim Judah, *The Serbs: History, Myth and the Destruction of Yugoslavia* (London: Yale University Press, 1987), 29.

[2] On the manner in which Milosevic stage managed the speech and its impact, see Tim Judah, *Kosovo: War and Revenge* (London: Yale University Press, 2000), 52–4.

[3] Misha Glenny, *The Fall of Yugoslavia: The Third Balkan War* (Harmondsworth: Penguin, 1993), 148.

with Tito's death, they slowly began to become public and nationalised. And as a result, they were distorted: the personal context of the memories, their narrative coherence, was eliminated; all that was left was the pain of the past, and anger at its suppression.

As time passed, this raw emotion became a tool in the crumbling Yugoslavia. For a worsening economic situation slowly encroached on the fragile common life, driving the republics apart, and the memories turned into a flood, driving the ethnicities apart.[4] They were radicalised – into separate monolithic ethnic memories, each ethnic group unto itself. Milosevic's speech was a crucial and legitimising point in this process: sanctifying the power of memory, endorsing it as a tool of difference. Worse still, it heralded an open competition between the ethnicities, for a single true version of a memorialised past. And this culminated in the decade of wars; wars which sought to annihilate the weakest competitors and their memories. But instead, it was the basic sense of humanity or humanism that was destroyed, along with Yugoslavia, ensuring that 'I remember' could only mean pain, division and a stronger fear of all the 'others'.

Myth, memory and Messianic time

References to the Battle of Kosovo or to the Ottoman Empire may suggest a confusion between myth and memory, or between national memory and individual memory. But in fact that is not the case: part of the power invested in the words 'I remember' is precisely in their ability to reconfigure any event, however long past or collective, into a seemingly real personal memory. Moreover, as is apparent to anyone who has travelled around the former Yugoslavia, especially during the conflict, the oral tradition is the strongest one among all the peoples. And the combination of the two can produce truly startling results. As Peter Maas put it:

Time travelling in Bosnia is an involuntary event that can occur at any moment. It happens, for instance, when a Serb farmer invites you to his house, serves a glass of slivovitz, homemade plum brandy, and then serenades you with a lecture on the Battle of Kosovo Polje... The brandy is the same stuff that was drunk back then, the Serb who is your host carries the same genes of the warriors he evokes... If you ignore the refrigerator in the kitchen and the running water in the bathroom, you are back in 1389.[5]

Elevated to a more theoretical level, this concept of memory is somewhat akin to Walter Benjamin's definition of Messianic time, as 'a simultaneity

---

[4] On the economic theory of the collapse of Yugoslavia, see Susan L. Woodward, *Balkan Tragedy* (Washington, DC: Brookings Institution, 1995).

[5] Peter Maass, *Love Thy Neighbour: A Story of War* (London: Papermac, 1996), 15.

of past and future in an instantaneous present'.[6] In the Balkans, both this simultaneity and a general Messianic vision was – and to a large extent still is – exceptionally apparent in Serb self-conceptions, both in history and as evoked in the collapse of Yugoslavia. Tim Judah has chronicled this consistent tendency, commencing with the sanctification of the mediaeval king Nemanja, who was depicted by contemporaries as a 'new Israel', which meant that his Serb descendants became the 'elected people'. And in 1848, with the wave of national awakening that swept through Europe, Ilija Garasanin, a prominent Serbian politician, wrote that 'our present will not be without a tie with our past, but it will bring into being a connected, coherent and congruous whole, and for this Serbdom . . . stands under the protection of sacred historic right'.[7] Milosevic's references to ancestors and descendants were therefore not merely a rhetorical measure linking past and future in a viable, near-active time, they were also an appeal to longstanding notions of Serb identity.

But it was not merely the Serbs. Political leaderships on all sides used the same notion of simultaneity to inflame the passions of different ethnicities, in order to instil hatred of the other; and it was no less apparent during the war, in order to justify both the events and their prolongation. There are five distinct components of historical time – and memory – which could appear within this simultaneity, without any consistent scheme. The oldest and longest one stretches from the Battle of Kosovo to the end of the nineteenth century, thus during the time of the Ottoman and Habsburg empires, when none of the ethnicities was allowed independent definition, save for short periods and in confined spaces – although, as in many other parts of Europe, here too the nineteenth century saw the development of distinctive national identities among each group. This extended period provided memories of both great glory and ancient ills, used at random in the collapsing Yugoslavia as proof of coherent ethnic histories and an absence of any common past.[8]

The next distinct component covers the First World War and the resulting inter-war Kingdom of Serbs, Croats and Slovenes, later renamed

---

[6] Walter Benjamin, 'Theses on the Philosophy of History', in idem, *Illuminations* (London: Pimlico, 1999 [1968]), 246. For a select bibliography on the unique conception of time in the Balkans, see Wolfgang Hoepken, 'War, Memory, and Education in a Fragmented Society: The Case of Yugoslavia', *East European Politics and Society*, 13, 1 (Winter 1999), 191–227, nn. 3–4.

[7] Judah, *The Serbs*, 21, 58; on the wider theme of Serb self-conceptions of a sacred nation, see chs. 1–5, esp. 48–72.

[8] On the actual historical chronologies, and their perceptions by the ethnicities, see for example Judah, *The Serbs*, chs. 1–5, passim; Marcus Tanner, *Croatia: A Nation Forged in War* (London: Yale University Press, 1997), chs. 1–8, passim; Noel Malcolm, *Bosnia: A Short History* (London: Macmillan, 1994), chs. 1–7, passim; idem, *Kosovo: A Short History* (London: Macmillan; 1998), chs. 1–12, passim.

Yugoslavia. Thus a period in which the empires collapsed, and the various ethnic groups received international recognition. But the kingdom was a compromise, dominated by the Serbs at the expense of the Croats, the Muslims and the Albanian Kosovars, and as such it inspired new hatreds. Moreover, since these were created in the twentieth century, their surrounding memories did not have to be adapted from the misty collective past: there were still people alive in the 1980s who personally experienced the events, people who could, for example, tell younger generations of the prevailing Croat perceptions of the Serbs in the late 1920s: 'Every post is reserved for the predominant [Serb] race, despite the fact that the Croatian people are by common consent a century ahead of the Serbs in civilisation'.[9] When whispered over decades into the ears of younger generations, prefaced by the words 'I remember', such opinion becomes implanted as collective memory: a real tableau of a loved one's past.

The third and in many ways most relevant and painful component of historical time is that of the Second World War: the initial inadequate neutrality of the Kingdom and the subsequent capitulation to the Nazis; the rule of the Croat Ustashe and the rise of the Serb-dominated Partisans; and the horrific struggle to death between these two. This was the first dissolution of Yugoslavia into an internal bloody war, and it created the most pervasive, and divisive, personal and collective memories: of Croat cruelty to all other ethnicities, but especially the Serbs; of some Muslim cooperation with the Ustashe; of Serb heroism in conquering the Croats and saving the region – but also of Serb violence against the defeated Croats at the end of the war. As already noted, in Tito's Yugoslavia all such memories were officially banned, save for those relating to Partisan heroism. Ostensibly, this was meant to stop any further antagonism between the different ethnicities, in the name of the overarching principle of 'Brotherhood and Unity' upon which the Titoist state was founded. In fact, the elimination of all but the positive Partisan past was a 'policy of memory', as an historian recently put it, designed to legitimate the ruling Communist Party by recreating the Second World War solely and officially as a 'national liberation war and a socialist revolution', rather than 'a war of each against everybody'.[10] It was the ultimate manipulation: forging a single memory as a basis for a single identity in a single, unified state. But ironically, by enshrining a monolithic collective memory, the variety became no less apparent. For example, each district in Bosnia-Hercegovina has a war memorial listing the Partisan fighters who died, yet as Misha Glenny has reflected, 'in most regions four Serbs died

[9] H. Tiltman, *Peasant Europe* (London: Jarrolds, 1934), 59; quoted in Tanner, *Croatia*, 127.
[10] Hoepken, 'War, Memory, and Education', 196, 201–2.

for every Muslim'.[11] In other words, by default the preserved memory was one of difference.

But of more significance was the pain of the memories – which even after years of suppression could be easily evoked, and used to the utmost divisive nationalist effect. To the Serbs, memories of the cruel, systematic actions of the Ustashe became both a currency of justified self-determination – largely, as noted, based upon notions of victimhood – and an anti-Croat one. And in this latter scheme they were very much aided by the Croats themselves, headed by Franjo Tudjman, who both refused to apologise for the existence of these horrific memories, especially of Jasenovac, and ultimately also came to redefine them as crucial steps on the way to nationhood. Thus in his 1990 election campaign Tudjman clearly stated:

Our opponents see nothing in our programme but the claim for the restoration of the independent Croatian Ustashi state. These people fail to see that the state was not the creation of fascist criminals; it also stood for the historic aspirations of the Croatian people for an independent state. They knew that Hitler planned to build a new European order.[12]

The power of such words is immeasurable – as fuel to both Croat nationalism based on heritage and Serb nationalism based upon fear. They are words that actively recreate the past, giving public meaning to every whispered memory that was kept private over fifty years. They are words that make memory into currency of war.

The fourth component of time is that of Yugoslavia as Tito's state and the early phase of disintegration that followed him – to 1987. There are three types of memory from this period. The first was common to all: the vacuum of memory imposed by the Communist Party. In other words, everyone remembered that any form of ethnic or personal memory was illegal. The second type was similar to that of the Kingdom of Yugoslavia: for all other ethnicities the main memory instilled from this period is that of Serb domination at the expense of all others. Indeed, as the state fell apart it was this issue which the other republics used as justification for independence. Conversely, the Serbs claim a memory of deprivation in the Titoist state, by being divided among three republics and limited in the sovereignty of their own by the autonomous provinces of Kosovo and Vojvojdina. And then there was the third type of memories, those that became increasingly banned in the harsh and disintegrating state: memories of people living together amicably as neighbours, of agreeable

---

[11] Glenny, *Fall of Yugoslavia*, 120.

[12] Laura Silber and Allan Little, *The Death of Yugoslavia* (Harmondsworth: Penguin, 1996), 86.

co-existence. As a Serb of the town recalled: 'We all lived in Visegrad like a big family, the Muslims and Serbs ... We didn't look for differences.'[13]

These individual recollections also fuse with those from the fifth component of time: the downward spiral into war, between 1987 and 1991. It was then that these 'families' began to fall apart, through rumours of death lists or amassed weapons held by each ethnicity against the other.[14] These are memories of disorientation and hurt, compounded by those of deep hardship: the economic situation in Yugoslavia had deteriorated to the degree of breadlines, defaulting banks and inflation. Indeed, once the Dayton Agreement ended the war in 1995, it was not uncommon in the following year for Bosnians to compare favourably the produce in the shops – with that not only during the war, but also during the years preceding it, emphasising their bad memories of that period. But, nonetheless, then came war.

Fuelled and armed with all these radicalised memories and components of time, the ethnicities strode on to the battlefield, striving to wipe out all 'others': the Muslims in Bosnia, the Krajina Serbs in Croatia, the Albanians in Kosovo. These were brutal contests, that sought to destroy centuries-old mosques and churches, to eliminate people as if they were not established local descendants, to ethnically cleanse villages, towns and ultimately an entire province; to delete the others, and then recreate the landscape in the image of the winning sacred memories. And in each horrific case there was initial success, but then failure – and irony: for those who survived, on all sides, had new and tangible memories of hate and fear, distinct images of cruelty, brutality and death – delivered by the neighbours and friends of yesterday. The battlefield had eliminated the present, but not the past, people, but not memories: 'In order to kill a people, you must kill memory, you must destroy everything that belongs to that people. But if two people stay alive, they can remember.'[15]

International memories

Much as the attitudes to and involvement of the sides in the Balkan conflicts were driven by memory, so the international interventions were largely defined by memorialised images and analogies. And while the actual policies contrived by the international community were ultimately a poor composite of differing opinions drawn together by the line of least resistance, the implications of the images and precedents that compelled

---

[13] Maass, *Love thy Neighbour*, 11.
[14] On such rumours in Foca, for example, see Glenny, *Fall of Yugoslavia*, 170; Malcolm, *Bosnia*, 237.
[15] Maass, *Love thy Neighbour*, 238.

them were far from anaemic: these were true passions from the past. And there were many of them, intertwined in a complex web of disorientation, indifference and guilt.

A central image of the decade of wars was Sarajevo, besieged and pathetic, in the heart of the conflict – especially as it unfolded in the press and on television screens – just like the other Sarajevo: the place in which Archduke Franz Ferdinand was shot, the source of the First World War. It was the story taught in schoolrooms around the world, a learned collective memory of a place and an event.[16] And it was one that undoubtedly shaped international perceptions of the conflict, if only because it tied into another, more historic memory that stemmed from the Balkan wars of the nineteenth century, which apparently erupted with alarming regularity among the local ethnic groups, dragging in the international powers of the age. The fact that these were basically imperial conflicts between the Habsburg and Ottoman empires – occasionally aided and abetted by Britain, France and Russia – never made much impression on Western onlookers. For the overriding, longstanding image of the Balkans in the West seems to have been of a region whose inhabitants had a natural inclination for violent and frequent wars among themselves, at their own instigation:[17]

I'm sure one's dreadfully sorry for poor Serbia – she does seem to be having a bad time; but I'm not sure that our men ought to be sent out to those parts. They're all so wild out there; it seems as if, in a way, they rather *like* fighting each other; anyhow they've always been at it since I can remember, and I think they'd much better be left to fight it out among themselves . . . [18]

Rose Macaulay wrote these words in 1916, yet they are an excellent summary of the attitude of 'another Balkan war' in the 1990s. For in replacing Serbia with Bosnia, it would become an absolute precis of the opinion voiced by many when the former Yugoslavia collapsed into war in 1991, and for at least two years later – if not longer. More crucially, as David Owen reflected in the memoir of his role as European Union (EU) negotiator in the conflict, it was an attitude pervasive among all the key governments dealing with the conflict. In real terms, this translated into a minimalist humanitarian intervention within a bloody war, backed up by poorly armed troops devoid of any power of enforcement. And this

---

[16] A classic example of the memorialised prominence of Sarajevo as the source of the war is Richard Holbrooke's memoir of his Dayton mission, that commences with his visit as a young student to the site of the Archduke's murder, in 1960. *To End a War* (New York: Random House, 1998), xix.

[17] On the history of all the Balkan wars and international involvement, see Misha Glenny, *The Balkans 1804–1999* (London: Granta, 1999).

[18] Rose Macaulay, *Non-Combatants and Others* (London: Methuen, 1986 [1916]), 132, emphasis in the original.

'ensured that international diplomacy without military power was the hallmark of every attitude and action towards the former Yugoslavia'.[19] In turn, however, it was the memory of this disastrous approach which compelled action in the next war, Kosovo – as many politicians and editorial writers reiterated. For example, the following appeared in the *Sunday Times* of 4 April 1999: 'Let me remind you of what someone you revere said just six years ago: "We have been a little like an accomplice to massacre. We cannot carry on like that." That was Lady Thatcher on Bosnia.' It was clear that the modern Balkan wars had created their own cycle of memory, locking in the international community no less than the warring factions. And while this may have ensured speedier action, it was not necessarily more effective – simply inverse. In other words, speeded on by the memory of Bosnia, the international community intervened swiftly in Kosovo – with massive military power but very little diplomacy.

Macaulay wrote a relatively unknown Great War novel, but there is no doubt that literature about, and from within, the Balkans was immensely influential in creating a strong image of the region and its people. Largely a bleak one, reflecting both a long sense of history and deep underlying emotions of past miscarriages of justice – on all sides, but mostly the Serbs – it was this image that became a memorialised filter through which many Westerners perceived the conflict. Ivo Andric was probably the best known of Balkan writers with this perspective, having won the 1961 Nobel Prize for *The Bridge over the Drina*, but he was far overshadowed by the English writer Rebecca West, author of *Black Lamb and Grey Falcon*.[20] First published in 1941, it is a beautifully written account of a journey made in 1937 that has rarely been out of print. However, like Andric's, her narrative enshrines the historic role of the Serbs in the region – an attitude that influenced the many readers who imbibed it over the next half century, including those who intervened in the wars of the former Yugoslavia and wrote of them. Thus Robert Kaplan partially incorporated West's themes into his bestselling *Balkan Ghosts* (1993), a book apparently highly popular with US president Bill Clinton and many members of his administration. Unfortunately, as Richard Holbrooke notes, the Kaplan/West combination was undoubtedly instrumental in creating the

[19] David Owen, *Balkan Odyssey* (London: Indigo, 1996), 18.
[20] As the war progressed, other works by Andric also gained a modest international following, most notably *Bosnian Chronicle*, also known as *The Days of the Consuls* (London: Harvill Press, 1996 [1945]). Apart from West, two other Western books were probably influential, both establishing an image of the region based in the Second World War: Sir Fitzroy Maclean, *Eastern Approaches* (London: Macmillan, 1949), and Evelyn Waugh, *Unconditional Surrender* (London: Chapman & Hall, 1961). Maclean, one of the founder members of the Special Air Services regiment (SAS) and head of the 1944 mission to Yugoslavia, was imbibed by many soldiers and diplomats; while Waugh covers the same territory from the perspective of a lowly officer on the ground.

'ancient hatreds' approach to the Balkans, which dismissed any external intervention as pointless.[21] Closely related to 'another Balkan war', it basically defined the conflict as inevitable in the region, due to embedded disputes between the ethnicities, which had been kept under control by the communism of old Yugoslavia. And in the analysis of John Major, the UK prime minister who made the phrase current during the Bosnian and Croat wars: 'Once that discipline had disappeared, those ancient hatreds reappeared, and we began to see their consequences when the fighting occurred.'[22]

Diametrically opposed to the 'ancient hatreds' approach was one held by many Western intellectuals, who advocated intervention at practically any cost. Although undoubtedly stemming from sound fact and reason, their attitude was clearly also informed by the warming memories of meaningful times past, such as the Russian Revolution, Cuba or the events of 1968. For after decades of relative prosperity that dampened any true radicalism, the significance of intellectuals as a relevant vanguard had seemingly become reduced. In this light, the modern Balkan wars – especially that in Bosnia-Hercegovina – became a redeeming *cause célèbre*, in line with the most dramatic and romantic images of the century, that of the Spanish Civil War. And indeed, between 1992 and 1995, and then in 1999, an endless succession of writers, 'thinkers' and campaigners visited the combat zone, apparently to understand the conflicts better, to identify with the population, to try and bring rationality to an irrational situation. This all resulted in a truly impressive mountain of books, magazine essays and newspaper columns, mostly devoted to criticism of the woefully inadequate international interventions. Yet its underlying theme was no less the authors themselves – as a reincarnation of people who personally intervene not through the power of organisations or conventions, but rather through the power of thought and campaigning. Ultimately, however, it was an attempt to become relevant. In this way, David Rieff, an author who visited Bosnia frequently, could write that 'They – we – tried. They – we – failed', when referring to the attempts of the press and individuals such as himself to influence the war, in preference to the failed attempts of the UN. Similarly, Bianca Jagger, a celebrity human rights campaigner, noted angrily that in 'June 1993 I denounced the safe areas . . . and the so-called experts frowned at me'. Shades of Orwell's *Homage to Catalonia* or Hemingway's *For Whom the Bell Tolls* resonate from

---

[21] Holbrooke, *To End a War*, 22; Robert Kaplan, *Balkan Ghosts: A Journey Through History* (New York: Vintage, 1993). See also Brian Hall, 'Rebecca West's War', *New Yorker*, 15 April 1996.

[22] *Hansard*, 23 June 1993, col. 324.

this approach: it was the rebirth of the intelligentsia as a band of brave individuals, morally superior to the Establishment and therefore its light in the darkness.[23]

Much the same is true of the Kosovo conflict, which sent the Western intelligentsia flocking to the massive refugee camps erected in the states bordering the province. But to an extent their efforts were overshadowed by those of international politicians. In early May 1999, for example, the 'prime ministers of France and Britain ... the Canadian foreign minister, the most recent [US] congressional delegation and some prominent Greeks' all toured the camps – and they had been preceded by four other US congressional delegations, Queen Noor of Jordan and George Bush Jr. Given the prominence of the war in the media, there is no doubt that the visits were an opportunity for 'televised attention-grabbing'.[24] But it was no less obvious that these prominent people, and their image makers, were mindful of the appalling memory of the international approach to Bosnia, and thus eager in this event to be seen as caring and active.

For all the self-serving attitude of many intellectuals during the Bosnian conflict, there is no doubt that their moralising stance was also rooted in the horrific, overtly reprehensible reality of a genocidal war – one which seemingly recreated in detail acts committed in this particular region, and throughout Europe, fifty years before. For it was this group, together with the press, that forced the world to realise that the Bosnian war was covering the same ground, literally and figuratively, as the Second World War, thereby inducing memories long since buried as unrepeatable and untenable, or, as Mark Danner put it, 'consigned to the century's horde of images'.[25] However, once uncovered, these memories became the most dominant ones within the West, compelling both debate and ultimately intervention when all else failed. The memories became indictments.

In the broadest of terms, the accusing memories fell into two categories: appeasement and the Holocaust. Both were problematic, relevant and clearly linked. For the inept handling of the conflict by the international community gained deeper significance and urgency once the discovery of Serb concentration camps in Bosnia was made by the press in

---

[23] David Rieff, *Slaughterhouse: Bosnia and the Failure of the West* (New York: Vintage, 1996), 222; Bianca Jagger, 'The Betrayal', *The European*, 25 Sept. 1997, 14. Michael Ignatieff has damningly reflected that the actions of the intellectuals were aimed, at rescuing not Bosnia, but rather 'the image of the committed intellectuals of the Left'. 'Virtue by Proxy', in Alex Danchev and Thomas Halverson (eds.), *International Perspectives on the Yugoslav Conflict* (London: Macmillan, 1996), xiii.

[24] *International Herald Tribune*, 6 May 1999, 2.

[25] Mark Danner, 'America and the Bosnia Genocide', *New York Review of Books*, Dec. 4 1997, 55.

August 1992.[26] Up to that point, it was possible to distance the Yugoslav wars from having any immediate importance to the West or a clear linkage to a memorable past, even if they were occurring in Europe. In other words, until the discovery it was possible to remain within the distant collective memory of 'another Balkan war'. But the camps catapulted the event into direct correlation with the Second World War, imposing clear recognition both of war on European soil and of the Holocaust. And to the Western world, that had spent fifty years with a notion that war and genocide now occurred only in other continents, among non-Western people, this forced confrontation with its own past was undoubtedly a 'mnemonic shock'.

The memory of appeasement in Bosnia was well defined by Martin Bell as 'history gone into fast rewind... flashing back to 1914, only pausing along the way to fail to absorb the lessons of 1938'.[27] To all those on the ground, like him, and to many observing from afar, it seemed that the international community at large, and the United Nations more specifically, constantly attempted to reconcile the Serbs, rather than stop their murderous activities, and to achieve a settlement on the basis of the Serb conquests, rather than to punish those who made them. In essence, this was actually a simplistic view, being rooted in the notion that swift resolution could be achieved through justice – without actually taking into account the price, in civilian lives and troops, that such justice would demand. But it was also a sound moral view, no less firmly rooted in the knowledge of the huge price paid in the past for appeasement. Ultimately, the international community attempted to straddle both views, but without serious intent: the UN mission, UNPROFOR, was deployed with no more than a humanitarian mandate – but the International Criminal Tribunal for the former Yugoslavia (ICTY) was created to pursue the war criminals in the region (although for several years it was woefully under-staffed and underfunded); a safe area regime was created by UN Security Council Resolution 836 (1993) to protect the besieged enclaves – but of the 40,000 troops needed to uphold it, only 7,000 were dispatched. Pragmatism costs less than morality, but it also amounts to appeasement.

As already noted, the memory of appeasement only gained real currency with the revelation of the concentration camps: it was the horror of genocide that made the policy a relevant issue. But the genocide itself also

---

[26] Roy Guttman first reported the existence of the camps in the US *Newsday*, 2 Aug. 1992. Ed Vulliamy reported an eye-witness account of the Omarska camp in the UK *Guardian* on 5 August, and on the following day the UK's ITN broadcast the first pictures.

[27] Martin Bell, *In Harm's Way: Reflections of a War-Zone Thug* (Harmondsworth: Penguin, 1996), 38.

posed problems of memory, not least in its definition. While everything from the camps to the obvious attempt to annihilate a group of people on the basis of race evoked specific parallels with the Holocaust, there was rightly a reluctance – indeed refusal – to use the specific term. Ed Vuillamy summarised both issues well in noting that the day after his discovery of the camps there were many headlines such as '"Belsen 1992". The reaction was so tumultuous that, to my annoyance, I was obliged to spend more time emphasising that Omarska was not Belsen or Auschwitz than detailing the abomination of what we had found'.[28] Ultimately, the genocide committed in Bosnia was defined as 'ethnic cleansing', but, regardless of title, it was clear the images did indeed invoke the darkest of the twentieth century, leaving all who saw them horrified.

The horror was also deeply apparent during the Kosovo conflict, in which the ethnic cleansing centred on mass deportations rather than concentration camps:

At 4 a.m., the family and their neighbours were given one hour to get out . . . The soldiers stood in a line along the road, ten yards apart . . . The overwhelming impression was of an ethnic cleansing operation carried out with such clinical efficiency, calculated menace and ruthless speed that it must have been meticulously planned in advance.[29]

Once again, these were images that directly evoked the worst of the Second World War – but this time both in the victims, and the perpetrators. Moreover, while in the Bosnian war the images of the camps were relatively limited, in the case of Kosovo the written descriptions were far overshadowed by the endless live footage of the deportations. Memory was invoked not only by association, but by reality. And the reality, it seems, was of the basic Balkan war paradigm: 'The Serbs even stripped them of their identity, seizing birth certificates, passports and car registration plates in an attempt to ensure that those who left would never be permitted to return'.[30] In other words, it was an attempt to delete a people – and their memory.

To the general public, inasmuch as it really cared about the wars in the Balkans – although doses of it were delivered daily on television and in the written press – the situation was truly perplexing, especially during the Croat and Bosnian wars: beyond the Holocaust, the relevant memories of the Second World War were those of the Serb Partisans and the Croat Ustashe. As such, they were of the 'good Serbs' who saved the

[28] Ed Vuillamy, *Seasons in Hell: Understanding Bosnia's War* (New York: St. Martin's Press, 1994), xii.
[29] *International Herald Tribune*, May 9, 1999.
[30] *Sunday Times*, 4 April 1999, 14.

Allies and the 'bad Croats' aligned with the Nazis (the Muslims barely figured in these memories, other than as floating between Partisans and Ustashe, or, more frequently, as a rather exotic presence in the region). Marcus Tanner, claiming that this memory of the ethnic groups influenced national leaderships no less than the public, has defined it as the 'bitter hostility of so many British writers and politicians to Croatia and the mawkish, sentimental tone so often adopted to "much misunderstood Serbia"'.[31]

Even if this approach is somewhat extreme, it is not entirely incorrect – nor necessarily relevant only to Britain – and serves to emphasise the confusion felt by many with the dissolution of the former Yugoslavia into war, since the Serbs were apparently the villains of the piece, the Muslims the pathetic victims, with the Croats more aligned to the latter rather than the former image. It was a cognitive dissonance and one, moreover, strongly compounded by a near-monolithic memory of the former Yugoslavia as a truly multi-ethnic state. This had actually originated in the inter-war period of the Kingdom of Yugoslavia, when the newly created tourist authority defined it as 'romantic, it is thrilling, it is cheap . . . and above all it is different'. More interesting was the manner in which the authority specifically promoted multi-ethnicity as a selling point. Sarajevo, for example, was described as 'a town unique in its oriental and western contrasts . . . white-bearded Moslems who seem to embody the dreamy east, and young beauties in the latest western fashion . . . all live here together, mingle, and blend in a curious shrill harmony of their own'. Equally, 'all the country meet and mingle in Belgrade to create what could only now have been created: the new Yugoslav type'.[32] The positive image of the Partisans and the emergence of Tito's Yugoslavia as a non-aligned state rather than part of the Soviet bloc made it relatively simple for Western tourism to resume a few years after the Second World War. Both these conducive factors, and the imagery established in the earlier period were greatly exploited in 1963, when the Yugoslav authorities set up a Ministry of Tourism, and dropped all visa requirements for foreign visitors. As a result, hordes of West European tourists visited the region from the mid-1960s, enjoying a cheap holiday in splendid scenery. To such people, Yugoslavia had been a patchwork of ancient villages nestling side by side, populated by 'people [who] are everything you imagine yourselves to be and are not. They are hospitable, good-humoured and very good-looking', as George Bernard Shaw once

---

[31] Tanner, *Croatia*, 273.
[32] *Yugoslavia* (Putnik Tourist Office, Belgrade, n.d., presumably between 1934 and 1939), 2, 60, 9.

described them.[33] But these were images incompatible with the beamed pictures of the modern Balkan wars: pictures of destruction, mutilated bodies and ethnic cleansing. Yet the images were real.

The warring sides entered the battlefield armed with memories, whereas the international intervention was merely defined by them. The international community – the complex yet amorphous combination of states, politicians and diplomats that ultimately decides on such issues as international interventions – rather than learn from these images of the past, chose in Bosnia-Hercegovina first to use them as a reason to dismiss the conflict, and then, when the awful reality of 'ethnic cleansing' became evident, as a bland moral weapon that ultimately trivialised the events they recalled. It would take three years for any decisive action to be taken. Until that time, all leaders and spokesmen of the international community preferred the path of condemnation based upon horrified memory – emphasising the moral indictment it invoked, rather acting upon it.[34] But even after the Bosnian intervention, the international community paid little heed to the meaning and power of memory in the Balkans. For while the Kosovo conflict compelled much swifter and stronger action, it was to little avail: the perpetrators had apparently surprised it again, in the systematic barbarity of their actions. In other words, the community remembered the guilt of not intervening, but not the actual dynamics of the conflict: the ability of the sides, especially the Serbs, to use memory as both a legitimising tool of destruction and as a defensive barrier of self-justification. Moreover, given that this was Kosovo – the most crucial source of all Serb national memories, dating back at least to the fourteenth century, but equally, an ancient site of collectively memorialised national humiliations, including the most recent ones under the Milosevic regime – it was to be expected that memory would play a large part in the conflict, that it would be constantly invoked in all forms of media available to each side, and especially the state-owned Serbian one, and that it would be preached to soldiers of all units and factions by their commanders. All of this had already happened just a few years before – in the earlier Balkan wars of the 1990s, yet these precedents were ignored.

[33] Ibid., front cover.
[34] There is an argument – rather rooted in the United Kingdom – that suggests that the US leadership was much influenced by the Jewish reaction to the existence of the concentration camps. Thus a very senior British diplomat who served at the United Nations throughout most of the war claimed that the Jewish leadership acted out of continuing guilt about not intervening in the Second World War (private interview, 9 Jan. 1998). General Sir Michael Rose, commander of the UN forces in Bosnia in 1994, also noted that 'the Jewish influence on current events was to play a significant role in shaping US policy towards Bosnia'. See *Fighting for Peace: Bosnia 1994* (London: Harvill Press, 1998), 5.

A senior British diplomat noted that 'there was a failure of imagination in Europe, given the Bosnian experience'.[35] But there was no need for imagination: just recognition and acceptance of the overpowering role of memory in the Balkan wars – and sincere efforts to stem it, at least by countermanding the media as had subsequently been done in Bosnia, as Monroe Price describes in his chapter. But that never happened, because, throughout all the modern Balkan wars, the international community basically understood the power of memory to be no more than the power of rhetoric. Louis Gentile, UNHCR representative in Banja Luka in 1994, put it well:

To those who said to themselves after seeing *Schindler's List*, 'Never again': it is happening again. The so-called leaders of the Western world have known what is happening here for the last year and a half. They receive play-by-play reports. They talk of prosecuting war criminals, but do nothing to stop the crimes. May God forgive them. May God forgive us all.[36]

---

[35] *Sunday Times*, 4 April 1999, 4.   [36] *New York Times*, 14 Jan. 1994.

10 Translating memories of war and co-belligerency into politics: the Italian post-war experience

Ilaria Poggiolini

The 1940s were the formative years for conflicting memories in post-war Italy. During the second half of that decade different sets of memories were linked to different political choices and translated into the exclusive heritage of various political forces. The multiplicity of conflicting memories remained intact because a general, that is, national, process of recasting collective memories, as in the case of other defeated countries, did not take place. This chapter provides an interpretation of why no unifying national memory emerged in Italy after the Second World War. It also suggests that a pattern of national amnesia versus the 'counter-cultural' left-wing form of remembrance of the Resistance took its place.

The main argument of this chapter revolves around the question of how the post-war Italian split between a political system dominated by the Christian Democrats and a civil society penetrated by the communists operated on the level of memory. Indeed, the rebirth of the new democratic Italy was based on both amnesia and remembrance of the Resistance. The latter inspired the Italian constitution and the former, at the cost of fifty years of Christian Democratic hegemony, made possible economic prosperity and Italy's military security in NATO.

While the moderate Italian governments capitalised first on the shock of defeat and later on the 'communist danger' for their pragmatic political usefulness, the left cultivated memories of the anti-Fascism experience in the form of an almost exclusive heritage and, as a result, it was very slow in re-examining them.

This chapter shows how, in a country where, arguably, a process of nation-building has yet to be completed, conflicting memories of the Second World War and the Resistance did not prevent a long-term process of political reconciliation, but the myths remained separate, deepening cultural and national divisions even further.

Memories and politics

Can the formation and persistence of multiple memories in Italy be explained analytically? One possibility is to look at memories of the transition from war to peace, as I intend to do in this chapter, in order to trace their impact on the choices of individuals as well as political groups. These were conflictive memories among the right and the left of defeat, of the failure of fascism to fulfil its promises, of the struggle to liberate the country, and of US economic and military power. Pre-war memories had almost been swept away by those of the aftermath of the Second World War. What remained were scattered traces of a peculiar, populist nationalism. This appeared to entitle all political forces to believe, even after the defeat, that Italy should maintain a role in north Africa, that Trieste must remain Italian and that a favourable settlement of the dispute with Yugoslavia over the eastern border could be achieved. Politicians, diplomats and the public shared these beliefs as well as the many memories from the recent past.

By the late 1940s the first major attempt at translating mass personal memories and national ambitions into politics was completed and the government coalition was in a position to put an end to the period of political cooperation with the left. Almost at the same time, the gap between the state and civic society began to deepen.

The moderate outcome of the anti-Fascist political collaboration was largely due to the political success of the Christian Democratic Party (DC) and to the US project to stabilise Western Europe. However, the duel between the two main translators of memories into politics in Italy, the DC and the Italian Communist Party (PCI), took place in a new internal and international context. Neither party had been part of the formation of the pre-war liberal Italian nation. In fact, Catholic and socialist forces had grown in opposition to it. After the Second World War the PCI and the DC became the main protagonists of an attempt at laying down the constitutional foundations of the new state. The Italian constitution did reflect many aspirations of those who had fought to liberate the country, but it was based on a delicate compromise between anti-Fascist social values, moderate political ideas, the interests of the Vatican, and a new strong commitment to internationalism and European cooperation. The end of the anti-Fascist cooperation in 1947 and the beginning of the hegemony of the Christian Democratic Party brought this experiment to an end. The constitutional framework remained. However, as a result of the radical fracture between moderate forces and the left, it seemed to large sectors of the public that the process of renovation of the Italian nation, which they had hoped for during the Resistance, could not be pursued any further by democratic means. At the same time, instead of choosing ideological retrenchment in the fashion of the French Communist Party (PCF), the PCI aimed at broadening its doctrine and strategy in order to regain a role within the progressive debate in the areas of both politics and culture.

Selective memories

Having identified the transition from war to peace as the crucial phase for the formation of individual and collective memories in Italy, it is important to discuss how a myth of national renewal emerged from the experience of defeat and occupation.

Among the various long-lasting memories, losing the war as one of the Axis powers was only one and perhaps not the most shocking memory of those years. Most Italians knew that defeat could have hardly been avoided, given the circumstances of Mussolini's decision to ignore Italy's lack of preparation and resources and enter the war in 1940 instead of keeping out until 1942 as expected. Most Italians came to this realisation very soon, which is why, once neutrality was abandoned, the erosion of political consensus towards the Fascist regime grew day by day and spread across all circles of Italian society. To most, the declaration of war sounded like a death-knell. They foresaw the conflict ahead as the final disaster for the Fascist regime and the country, and feared the return of pre-Fascist political chaos.

The war turned out to be even more disastrous than these expectations had envisaged, but finally led to the dismissal of Mussolini by the king and the dissident Fascists in July 1943. The king was actually 'bombed' into this decision by the Allies, having lost the opportunity to make up his mind during the previous months of secret contacts with the British and the Americans. Most Italians welcomed Mussolini's dismissal as the first good news in years, and went so far as to expect that they would soon be out of the war.

The fracture between civil society and the Fascist regime was by this time complete and the joy caused by the end of Fascism grew out of the illusion that the transition to peace and democracy would begin very soon. The general expectation was that the bombing of Italy would stop and that the king – after twenty years of abdicating his institutional re-sponsibilities – would regain his role.[1]

But this rosy dream was followed by the most dramatic awakening, and the memory of it was long-lasting. In order to achieve unconditional surrender, the Allies intensified the bombing of Italian territory. The

---

[1] B. Arcidiacono, *Le 'précedent italien' et les origines de la guerre froide: les alliés et l'occupation de l'Italie 1943–1944* (Brussels: Bruylant, 1984).

bombing, coupled with hunger and fears of what could be expected in the near future, did not help the Italian public to understand the slow pace of negotiations for the armistice. But the worst of all memories was still to be shaped: on 8 September 1943 the armistice was announced and the most painful phase of the war on Italian soil began.

The announcement of the armistice swept away all illusions: Italy would pay for having changed sides, both the Germans and the Allies invaded the country, and the king left Rome to take refuge under the protection of the Allies in the south. As a result, the army was abandoned to its fate of facing the consequences of the armistice. Acts of heroism such as that of Cefalonia, where the Italian contingent resisted and was massacred by the Germans, coexisted with a general sense that nothing was left to fight for. These feelings were shared by many officers, who had received no orders from their superiors and therefore had no expectation of receiving moral or material support while abroad, or indeed on Italian territory.[2]

The Italian soldiers who had learned to fend for themselves during a war fought in the worst material and psychological circumstances did not, in most cases, feel any allegiance to their country: they only wanted to go home, and home meant their town, village or family, not Italy. The officers felt betrayed and torn between their oath to the king and the impossible task of confronting the power vacuum which had followed the armistice. Indeed, nothing seemed to have been planned at the top, by the king or the Allies, in order to avoid the complete disintegration of the Italian army.

The circumstances of the war contributed to this situation, because the Italians had not been able to persuade the Allies to deploy, before the announcement of the armistice, large forces for the defence of Rome against the Germans. This meant that the Italian civilians and what was left of the military forces were exposed to their former ally's revenge and that the Germans had to be fought by the Allies all along the peninsula in order to liberate it.[3]

This was definitely the most shocking memory of the war, not only because of the material consequences which derived from the armistice but even more because it generated long-lasting feelings of loss. Indeed, the destiny of the military class and that of most Italians after the armistice had one central trait in common: many felt that no sense of honour or

---

[2] E. Aga Rossi, *l'Italia nella sconfitta: politica interna e situazione internazionale durante la seconda guerra mondiale* (Rome: Istituto della Enciclopedia Italiana, 1983); N. Kogan, *Italy and the Allies* (Cambridge, MA: Harvard University Press, 1956); A. Varsori and I. Poggiolini, 'Une ou des occupations anglo-américaines? Les cas de l'Italie et du Japon', *Relations internationales*, 79 (1994), 347–366.

[3] R. Lamb, *War in Italy 1943–1945: A Brutal Story* (London: Murray, 1993).

allegiance could be rescued from the ruins of the recent past; only personal honour and personal allegiances remained. In other words, honour and allegiance, once closely associated with Italian nation-building, became entirely privatised. The memory of this realisation and the sense of deprivation which could not be separated from it had long-lasting repercussions on Italian post-war politics and society.

Memories and allegiances

Such a tragic transition from war to peace and its memory deepened the gulf which had always separated the Italians from the Italian nation. After the war, no common feeling of allegiance seemed to re-emerge. Remembrance – and amnesia – were parcelled out according to partisan political allegiances. Instead of creating a common national memory – as part of a nation-building process – an exercise in transferring to the superpowers or to Europe a variety of demands and expectations was carried out, at different levels and with different motivations, by the government, the opposition and the public. This process, which resembled what Tony Judt describes for other European countries in chapter 7, started after the armistice and continued during the years 1945 to 1948.

However, the experience of the Resistance can be seen as one of the moments – together with the 1948 pre-electoral confrontation – of most intense political involvement which stand on their own within a panorama characterised by the reluctance of civil society to be involved in major political struggles. Already by summer 1944 the number of partisans fighting on the side of the Allies to liberate the country was in the thousands. They were coming from the most diverse ways of life and their motivations were equally diverse. This crowd had no centre, but fought in the name of one common unifying idea: the need to overcome the past of national division and move on towards the renovation of the Italian state and society.

It has been pointed out that one of the most vivid literary accounts of this reality, an account which is almost the literary translation of the *resistenza*, is the novel by Italo Calvino, *Il Sentiero dei nidi di ragno*.[4] In the preface to the edition of 1964, Calvino himself argued that the Resistance was possible because the aspirations to redeem the country from its recent, tragic past and the determination to bring about radical social changes were two faces of the same coin. Given this unity, social or political differences in the ranks of the partisans did not matter much. What did matter was the commitment to that central idea.

[4] E. Di Nolfo, *La Repubblica delle speranze e degli inganni* (Florence: Ponte alle Grazie, 1996), 108.

In the north, even more than in the south of Italy, radical choices had to be made very early on: one was whether to join the puppet government of the Germans, the 'Republic of Salo', with Mussolini reinstated after his rescue and return orchestrated by the Germans. This choice was made by some in the name of the past and was supposedly dictated by a sense of allegiance, even honour. The alternative was to fight against the former ally in the name of another vision of honour: that of making possible the return of freedom and democracy and start a process of radical internal economic and political renovation.

This dramatic choice had to be made in the name of one interpretation or another of what honour or loyalty to the homeland dictated, and therefore generated a sense of sharp division within Italian society and even within groups of close friends or families. Collaboration with, or resistance against, the Germans during the Second World War in France is probably the case that comes closest to this memory of division in Italian history. Lucien Febvre in a series of lectures only recently published has debated this issue at length. He poses a central question: were radically different choices made on the basis of what honour and allegiance to the homeland dictated to different groups? Could this be explained by tracing the historical evolution of three notions: honour, homeland and nation?

In France, the passage from the medieval idea of honour to that of homeland and, finally, nation, in the course of the eighteenth century, led to the creation of a national conscience which could be described as the sum of history and ideals. The Nation, Febvre argues, is a fact both inevitable and welcomed. History lived in common determines the consciousness of being a nation and this realisation itself gives direction to history. *Patrie* was the idea at the heart of the French Revolution: it brought about a clear separation between the struggle in the name of the homeland and the defence of the aristocratic sense of honour. Napoleon subsequently claimed *honneur* for himself. The Restoration, however, proved that the previous dichotomy could not be overcome but only modernised.

According to Febvre, *honneur* and *patrie* once again posed radically different choices in France at the end of the Second World War. He recalls how one morning in 1942 he was told by a friend that one of her two sons, a naval officer, had died at sea in order to defend what his brother, an officer of the French colonial army under Leclerc, was fighting against. In the name of the very same two words, honour and homeland, two brothers lost their lives fighting for France but against each other.[5]

[5] L. Febvre, *Honneur et Patrie* (Paris: Perrim, 1996).

The historical evolution of the idea of honour, homeland and nation was far less linear in Italy than in France and, therefore, even more ambiguous. The late unification of the country meant that different allegiances to different homelands remained even after territorial unity was achieved. In other words, the Italian State and the Italian nation did not develop along parallel paths and did not become a unit with which all Italians could identify. During the Risorgimento, the struggle to create an Italian homeland and nation was not pursued on the basis of one single project. How many formerly independent Italian states would the new nation include and which form of government would be finally chosen? These remained open questions up to the end of the unification process. Only the Piedmontese king, after national unity, could claim allegiance on the basis of what honour should dictate first of all to the aristocrats and the officers, but this allegiance had been built – except in the case of the Piedmontese themselves – on breaking similar allegiances to the monarchs of the former independent states, not all of whom were foreign and loathed as much as the Austrians. Giuseppe Tomasi di Lampedusa's novel *The Leopard* shows extremely well how weak a Sicilian aristocrat's feeling of allegiance towards the new Italian king could be in the aftermath of unification. The First World War turned out to be a unifying but very trying experience. During that war military discipline was harshly enforced, and after the war the liberal state failed to reward this tremendous national effort. Finally, within this scenario, violent confrontation between a new left and right brought Mussolini to power. Subsequently, the events of 1943 brought about another dramatic split in national allegiances. The armistice, the continuity of government represented by the king under the protection of the Allies in the south, and, on the other side, the comeback of Mussolini with the help of the Germans in the north, forced the Italians to choose between two homelands – or hide. In the post-war period, the Italians faced yet another major national confrontation: that of the 1948 general election. The choice was now between East and West, between renovation and stabilisation, between remembrance and amnesia.

Memories of the end and new myths

Between 1947 and 1948, with the country on the verge of civil war, once again no unifying idea of the Italian nation could provide a rallying point or a source of consensus for the Italians. One could argue that by that time an already weakly integrated Italian nation had became even weaker, and maybe ceased to exist altogether. Alternatively, one could argue that what had disintegrated in 1943 had been only the Fascist nation. Indeed, the symbols of Fascism were violently torn to pieces or at least exposed and humiliated.[6]

Memories of shameful revenge include the exhibition of the most emblematic among those symbols: Mussolini's body hanging from a pole on Piazzale Loreto in Milan alongside that of his lover, Clara Petacci. This act of revenge on the remains of the Duce took place in the same square where a group of partisans had previously been executed. After many more attempts at deleting the memory of the regime, a sense of passivity swept through the Italian society. Dependence on the American model became material as well as psychological: all Italians now suddenly discovered the United States, a mythic land of opportunities which was now exporting its way of life and not only welcoming Italian immigrants.

The struggle of the Resistance and that for mere survival, the celebration of the death of the regime and the American dream had long-lasting repercussions on Italian politics in the form of both myths and political inspiration. From 1946 to 1948 Italy became a laboratory for testing Cold War strategies and American plans of economic and political stabilisation. In 1948, at the peak of internal polarisation between pro-American moderate forces and the coalition of the left (the Popular Front), the US commitment in favour of the DC government became decisive. Certainly the victory of the DC in Italy was greatly helped by the support of the Vatican and by the giant propaganda machine set up by Washington in order to prevent the victory of the left. While the PCI moved slowly towards the social democratic option, because of the internal repercussions of the Cold War all the moderate Italian parties agreed that the communists should be kept out of government long after the PCI had actually distanced itself from Moscow. Indeed, even without the five million Italians who went every week to see the film *Ninotcha* (the film with Greta Garbo which had been released in 1939 but was made available in Italy by the Americans only in April 1948), the Stalinist option could hardly exercise greater appeal to Italian public opinion than the Marshall Plan.[7]

In 1948 a new fundamental memory was shaped: that of the 'grande paura' (great fear) of a communist take-over, of a struggle between two models of civilisation, of the defeat of the innovative ideas of the Resistance. The 'great fear' of communism, coinciding with a turning-point in economic

---

[6] On the present debate on Italian national identity see E. Galli Della Loggia, *L'identitá italiana* (Bologna: Il Mulino, 1998); M. Isnenghi, *Breve storia dell'Italia unita a uso dei perplessi* (Milan: Rizzoli, 1998). On the question of symbols see M. Dondi, 'Piazzale Loreto', in M. Isnenghi (ed.), *I luoghi della memoria: Simboli e miti dell'Italia Unita* (Bari: Laterza, 1996), 487–99.

[7] Di Nolfo, *La Repubblica*, 349.

reconstruction and with emerging from the tunnel of hunger and uncertainties about the future, had the effect of consolidating the moderate block and of strengthening amnesia against remembrance.

The overwhelming majority obtained by the DC in 1948 gave Prime Minister De Gasperi and his coalition the political leverage to translate freely into politics only useful memories. One could point out that this process of translation had large gaps. However, the suspension of the debate on the heritage of the Resistance, particularly as far as the renovation of the economic, institutional and administrative structure of the state were concerned, seemed justified by the urgency of achieving national reconstruction and security. The Marshall Plan paved the way for the economic boom of the 1950s and the Atlantic alliance made it possible to ignore the weakness of the Italian military structure. Finally, as Guido Piovene, one of the most well-known Italian writers of the time, argued in his *Viaggio in Italia*, wealth and modernisation brought about precisely that radical change in Italian society which the DC leadership had at first resisted.[8]

However, lack of renovation seriously affected the area of public administration. The Catholic model was superimposed on the existing weak, laic ethic of government with the result of creating a system of clienteles (the so called *assistenzialismo*) which slowed the process of modernisation of the state and contributed to maintaining and reproducing a system of massive corruption.[9]

It has also to be pointed out that, during the years of De Gasperi's leadership, between 1945 and 1953, civil society and political society remained split. One unifying myth was that of the unification of Europe. The post-war governments had apparently rescued it from the memories of the Resistance in order to legitimate some of the most difficult decisions to be taken in foreign policy: the ratification of the peace treaty and the signing of the Atlantic Pact. The Europe that the Italian government pursued was a pragmatic choice born of necessity and certainly did not coincide with the idea of a European federation which most of the groups within the Resistance had believed in. However, it was the pragmatic European project of the DC governments that most of the Italian public supported. Italian foreign policy was now solidly based on two pillars: NATO and the European Economic Community (EEC). This had a strong self-congratulatory dimension: thanks to the Atlantic Alliance and

[8] G. Piovene, *Viaggio in Italia* (Milan: Mondadori, 1963).
[9] M. Salvati, *Stato e industria nella Ricostruzione: Alle origini del potere democristiano (1944–1949)* (Milan: Feltrinelli, 1982).

Europe, Italy had been accepted as an equal by the rest of the Western world. Amnesia could now be justified.[10]

A regime of national amnesia

Having emerged from the tunnel of poverty and destruction, the new Italy aimed at securing her security, stability and wealth. Even the debate on productivity became marginal as compared with the capacity to export the new Italian industrial design, for example, the Alfa Romeo Giulietta car and Olivetti's Lexicon and Lettera 22 typewriters. Films such as Comencini's *Pane, amore e fantasia* and Fellini's *I Vitelloni* were also examples of this new hedonism.[11]

Over the years, the Christian Democrats developed a formidable machine of government based on clienteles, but large sectors of civil society remained quite independent. The attempt of the PCI to develop an Italian road to socialism moved from the political area of society, where it had been defeated in 1948, into the area of civil society. The PCI now essentially organised its own society of press networks, research institutions and cultural, recreational and sporting structures, and produced a high-level cultural debate and cultural life which came to be shared by very many non-communist 'fellow travellers'.

During the 1940s the DC had capitalised on a particular set of memories and translated them into political consensus. Memories of Italy's defeat, isolation and post-war economic and international weakness justified pro-Western economic and military choices. They also provided a very rich source of legitimacy in internal politics by showing that the moderate coalition could stabilise the country and make possible a successful economic reconstruction. At the time of the economic boom in the 1950s, however, a sort of collective amnesia replaced this pragmatic use of memory. On the other hand the PCI, but also what was left of the democratic left, cultivated and almost made a cult of their own memories of the Resistance and early post-war period, particularly after being politically defeated. Therefore the left, even when engulfed by the debate on keeping its distance from Moscow, contributed in a decisive way to challenging the official culture by keeping memories alive.

[10] I. Poggiolini, 'Italy', in D. Reynolds (ed.), *The Origins of the Cold War in Europe: International Perspectives* (New Haven and London: Yale University Press, 1994); E. Di Nolfo (ed.), *The Atlantic Pact Forty Years Later* (Berlin and New York: De Gruyter, 1992); A. Varsori, 'Italy's Policy towards European Integration (1947–58)', in C. Duggan and C. Wagstaff (eds.), *Italy in the Cold War: Politics, Culture and Society 1948–1958* (Oxford: Berg, 1995).

[11] Di Nolfo, *La Repubblica*, 383–7.

In Italy the Soviet model had been defeated at the elections of 1948. The national past, the heritage of the Risorgimento and the Resistenza, and a new third way to socialism which would lead the Italian socialists to put an end to their collaboration with the communists, contributed to the creation of a new positive model which attracted large sectors of civil society. Neorealism in Italian cinema represented very well the attempt of the left at not forgetting. On the other hand, the comedies of the 1950s, with Sophia Loren, Gina Lollobrigida and Marcello Mastroianni, projected the notion that at a time of economic success ordinariness and beauty could blend positively.[12]

One could argue that, in the Italian case, the winning political side seemed willing to let the losers create a monopoly of memories to pass on to other generations. One could further argue that this division of labour made it possible for conflicting memories to live together. But in the early years after Stalin's death, the official silence over the past and the leftist debate on it had ceased to be examples of culture and counter-culture. They had come to represent yet another Italian mediation between the suppression of the truth and the exposure of it. This is true to the point that, consistently after 1968, but even before then, the heritage of the Resistance surfaced again and again as a myth among all political parties, including the DC.

During the 1960s, with the formation in Italy of centre-left governments and the legitimate entry of the socialists into the system of power created by the DC, the monopoly of remembrance by the opposition was left in the hands of the PCI. The heirs of De Gasperi struggled in order to elaborate new relations with the Western bloc by revisiting their Atlanticism, and also to shape a new Italian role in the Mediterranean. Now more actors had entered the policy-making process in Italy. Alongside the government, a stronger state presidency, more assertive private economic forces and even a manager of the public sector such as Enrico Mattei competed for the initiative in international relations. The centre-left coalition governments were indeed the expression of an attempt at reinventing a solid political basis and at distancing the country from a past of ideological confrontation.

Great expectations of economic growth had been sustained by plans for the creation of a common market after the birth of the EEC. Italy had undergone a process of dramatic change during the post-war years, and the pace of change had accelerated at the end of the 1950s and the beginning of the 1960s. Industrial growth, the dying out of the agrarian society, internal emigration and the disproportionate size of the public

[12] Ibid., 387.

sector, were the central characteristics of this change. Indeed, a parasitic, state-controlled industrial sector grew out of all proportion during these years. Political nepotism, which had been the expression of agrarian power during the nineteenth century, now evolved into the creation of a bloc protecting the interests of public capital and of the various layers of clienteles around it.[13]

In the early 1960s, with Federico Fellini's *La dolce vita* and *8 ½*, Dino Risi's *I mostri* and *Il sorpasso* and, even more, Michelangelo Antonioni's early productions, the most perverted aspects of the economic boom and the loss of values which was felt to go hand in hand with it, were taken up by Italian cinema. The rosy, happy but naive image of previous films was now abandoned in order to describe the costs of living in a much more complex and less reassuring society. Along with this sense of disillusion grew an increasingly strong feeling of detachment from the implications of the opening to the left in politics. It was felt that the system of power created by the DC had not been challenged but accepted – and reproduced – by the socialists and even by the PCI at local level.[14]

A 'historic compromise of memories'?

Enrico Berlinguer launched the idea of 'a historic compromise' with the moderate forces in 1973. By 1975 the Fourteenth Congress of the PCI had accepted Italy's membership of NATO. The general election of June 1976 sanctioned the approval of the electorate for Berlinguer's line and for the DC's willingness to move in the same direction. The Socialist Party (PSI) and the PCI abstained when the new Andreotti government, composed only of Christian Democrats, was presented in parliament. For the PCI, to abstain was supposed to be the first step towards the goal of sharing the responsibility of government, a goal supported by large sectors of society, including Confindustria, the association of Italian private entrepreneurs.[15]

Aldo Moro, one of the leading figures in the Christian Democratic Party, had given an interview to Eugenio Scalfari, the editor of the new progressive daily *La Repubblica* in February 1978. The interview was released only in October, after the Red Brigades had murdered Moro. The substance of the interview centred on the necessity of working out some form of collaboration with the PCI, but appeared very obscure when it came to the basis of this collaboration. A government negotiated with the PCI and led by Andreotti was ready to be presented in parliament on

---

[13] G. De Rosa, *Da Sturzo ad Aldo Moro* (Brescia: Morcelliana 1988), 39–42.
[14] G. Galli, *L'Italia sotterranea: Storia, politica, scandali* (Bari: Laterza, 1983).
[15] P. Craveri, *La Repubblica dal 1958 al 1992* (Rome: UTET, 1995).

the morning of Moro's kidnapping on 16 March 1978. The Red Brigades kept him imprisoned until May 9, when he was killed.[16]

The kidnapping and murder turned into one of the most traumatic memories of recent Italian history. The 1970s had been plagued by terrorism of the extreme right and of the extreme left. However, Moro's kidnapping was perceived as an act of unprecedented violence even in the context of the so-called 'strategy of tension'. A key personality in politics, Moro was very reserved, a political figure quite distant from the public. However, the attack by the Red Brigades was particularly shocking because it appeared as a demonstration of power on a grand scale, and it was followed by seven weeks of pressure on the public, marked almost daily by Moro's open letters to other politicians or members of government. Finally, there was the discovery of his body in a car parked in the centre of Rome. Moro wrote his revelations, accusations and requests to the government. He demanded that the government, while he was declared on trial by the Red Brigades, accept negotiations with the terrorists in order to secure his release. However, even considering the circumstances, what emerged from Moro's writing did expose the many divisions existing within the party and the only common feature was the ambition to remain in power. Moro's letters, published daily and, even more, the picture of his dead body on the front-pages of the newspapers on 9 May, form the most vivid memories of that era. Those images became almost a symbol, or a negative myth, of the degeneration of Italian political life.

The blow to the image of the DC was only one of the consequences of what turned out to be an almost desperate last attempt by the Red Brigades to destabilise the Italian state and to challenge Berlinguer's position. One can argue that the challenge to the PCI was indeed successful, because at the end of the 1970s and in the early 1980s, the communists shifted their position away from their ambition to join the government and stressed their difference from the other parties. But this difference was not based on ideological grounds as in the past, but rather on Berlinguer's critique of the Italian political parties, described as 'machines of power and clienteles', distant from civil society and empty of ideals.

The ethical difference between the PCI and the other Italian parties claimed by Berlinguer could only be sustained against the many examples of communist acceptance of the existing style of government, because the moral and political charisma of the communist leader gave it a certain credibility. With the death of Berlinguer in 1984, the internal

---

[16] De Rosa, *Da Sturzo*; F. Traniello, *Da Gioberti a Moro: Percorsi di una cultura politica* (Milan: Feltrinelli, 1990).

crisis of the PCI emerged in all its complexity and eventually led to open parliamentary opposition and to a process of internal, radical transformation of the party itself.[17]

Political reconciliation between the moderate parties and the left was going to be channelled through the transformation of the Socialist Party under Craxi. His rise and fall between the early 1980s and beginning of the 1990s was for many, even those who never were or became socialists, the memory of a great illusion. Finally it seemed that a political alternative to the DC could emerge and reform the Italian political system. It was an illusion that transformed itself into a memory of having failed, once again, to overcome the split memories and myth of the post-war period.

Indeed, for the first time since 1945, the Socialist Party was given an opportunity to lead the government and to contribute to the legitimisation of the left in power.[18] While Craxi's PSI was emerging, the Christian Democrats were losing their control on the governmental coalition and the PCI was experiencing a very difficult post-Berlinguer period. Thus the new socialist leadership could count on the crisis in both the PCI and the DC and aim at becoming the new element of stability on the Italian political scene. Indeed, the duration of the government led by Craxi was unprecedented: from August 1983 to April 1987.

Not only the public but also a large sector of the intelligentsia believed that new ideas and a new style of government could improve the level of Italy's governability. It also became increasingly urgent to open a debate on constitutional reforms. This could have meant the relaunching of the political debate on Italian post-war institutions, which had been frozen in 1947–8 and, therefore, the end of a period of political amnesia within the moderate forces and of almost forced remembrance of the anti-Fascist political debate within the left.

However, these expectations were not fulfilled. Craxi made use of his political leverage on the DC to obtain as many positions of power as possible and to achieve the formation of non-DC-led governments. As a result, during the 1980s, Italian politics was still perceived as decadent. Once again, one of Fellini's films, *E la nave va*, perfectly epitomised this view. In reviewing the film at the end of 1983, the political journalist Giorgio Bocca commented that even Felini's genius should not get away with a metaphor of society which suggested only grotesque inertia or death. But one can argue that the metaphor seemed appropriate to describe how

[17] An interview with Berlinguer regarding the debate on the ethical dimension of politics was published in *La Repubblica* of 28 July 1981.
[18] S. Colarizi, *Storia dei partiti nell'Italia repubblicana* (Bari: Laterza, 1994).

hopeless the task of reinventing political life in Italy could appear to a large sector of the public.[19]

Reclaiming memories

The electoral results in 1992 were a negative signal for the PSI, the DC and also the new Democratic Party of the Left (PDS, the non-communist successor of the PCI after its split in 1991, which also led to the creation of a new communist party, the Rifondazione Comunista). The political success of the Northern League in the 1992 elections was another signal of opposition to the leadership of the traditional parties and in favour of regional interests. By this time the final crisis of the post-war political system had come close: corruption charges against businessmen and politicians of the socialist circle put in motion an avalanche which revealed the role of all parties in government, but particularly of the DC and the PSI, in creating and maintaining a massive system of clienteles and bribery which pervaded almost all levels of society.

One can argue that from Moro's declarations in 1978 to the launch of the 'clean hands' operation in 1992 by Judge Antonio Di Pietro in Milan, Italian political life had consistently declined to the point of relegating to a marginal role the debate on ideas. This explains how the most recent Italian collective memory is centred on a flow of revelations of what most Italians were already aware of, but had previously accepted as a reality which could not be changed. This fatalistic approach had pushed public opinion away from wanting a direct involvement in politics. The images of the hitherto untouchables being taken to prison now received full attention, because the public could identify with the 'cleansing' role of the judges and finally act, even if indirectly, against the political class. This 'revolutionary' spirit almost naturally seemed to reconnect many Italians with the memories of the years 1943 to 1945, because it swept away half a century of DC hegemony and of the forgetting of the resistance.

The changes in the international scenario at the end of the 1980s and the beginning of the 1990s also contributed to the end of an era of passivity in Italy. In a country where the beginning of the Cold War had been experienced so dramatically, the end of bipolarism was a great source of hope. At the same time the Yugoslav crisis posed a potential threat to Italian territory, which reemphasised the need of an international backup for national security. Finally, the Gulf crisis exposed the traditionally minor Italian role in the Atlantic alliance. Continuity and change in Italian

[19] G. Bocca, 'Processo a Fellini. La parola all'accusa', *La Repubblica*, 24 Nov. 1983; quoted in G. Brunetta, *Spari nel buio* (Venice: Marsilio 1994).

foreign policy merged, again, over the debate on European integration. During negotiations over the Maastricht Treaty, Italy took the side of Britain in the debate on security, choosing once again NATO as opposed to plans of transforming the Western European Union (WEU) into a new model of European defence.

But the ending of the Cold War meant that the translation of memories into politics, which had been carried out at the beginning of the years of East–West confrontation, could now be reversed or revised. After the signing of the Maastricht Treaty and the beginning of the post-clean hands Italian political life, the government of the new right led by media mogul Silvio Berlusconi in 1994 seemed a prelude to a shift in Italian foreign policy away from the previous commitment in favour of Europe. However, Berlusconi's movement Forza Italia, Umberto Bossi's autonomist Northern League and Gianfranco Fini's post-Fascist National Alliance, could hardly express a coherent foreign policy, particularly as far as Bossi's attitude was concerned, and indeed it was he who caused the fall of the government in December 1994. A caretaker government of technocrats led by Lamberto Dini replaced that led by Forza Italia.

The pace of political change accelerated in Italy with the general election of 1996, which brought to power the center-left Olive Tree coalition and made possible the formation of Romano Prodi's government. Prodi, to become the President of the European Commission in 1999, was the protagonist of the remarkable effort which allowed Italy to join the process of monetary union and improved its economic and financial credibility. Italy's foreign policy remained linked to the post-war tradition of alliance with the United States, but it has also taken concrete steps in the direction of a more active participation in European and regional collaboration.

In internal politics Prodi's Olive Tree project and his government of the centre-left offered a 'third way' political option which had never been convincingly available before in Italian post-war political life. In the course of an interview in *Time* magazine published on 21 April 1997, Prodi – with a brief experience in politics and a longer one as professor of economics at Bologna University, senior adviser for Goldman-Sachs and head of the state holding company IRI – remarked that 'it's really not so strange that I am the leader of a centre-left government. The strange thing is our history, but I want to get out of that history'. What Prodi probably meant was 'to get out' of an internal logic based on political polarisation and to move, finally, into a more pragmatic and efficient dimension of politics.

However, Fausto Bertinotti's Communist Refoundation turned out to be the most uncomfortable symbol of the past to obstruct Prodi, contributing in the end to his resignation in 1998. Pressure from Bertinotti's party brought to an end Prodi's government, but did not reverse the most remarkable achievements of the 'clean hands' experience and of the ending of the Cold War, namely the formation of a consensus in Italy around the centre-left political project. Prodi's achievements in internal economic policy and in Europe were the heritage entrusted to the hands of the first Italian government led by a former communist, Massimo D'Alema, the leader of the Democratici di Sinistra (DS, the successor of the PDS).

D'Alema's leadership marked the end of the long march of the post-Second World War Italian communist party towards government. However, the strength of the parties of the right and their forceful opposition to the leader of the DS, show that memories of the 'communist danger' could still be kept alive. It has to be pointed out that the transition from Prodi to D'Alema was marked by a change in the government coalition away from the majority grouping which followed the 1996 elections. This was due partly to Bertinotti's decision to oppose the last Prodi government to the end and partly to D'Alema's flexibility in making alliances with political groups outside the previous coalition. One can argue that D'Alema showed from the very beginning an inclination for compromise that made him a far less innovative leader than Prodi in Italian political life. Certainly, Prodi was able to dismiss history much more easily than D'Alema could ever dream of doing because the latter is the product of the cultural environment of the left which had monopolised, together with the laic parties, the memories of the Resistance and of the early post-Second World War political struggle.

D'Alema's resignation as prime minister, following the poor result for his coalition in regional elections, seemed to prove his inability to capitalise on the original Olive Tree project and to reinforce and expand the idea of an Italian 'third way'. Giuliano Amato followed, his new government supported by a wide parliamentary majority of the centre-left. Amato is an academic by training with much high-level political experience, including the post of finance minister in D'Alema's government.

His main task was, from the point of view of the centre-left, to prevent the general election, due by April 2001, being held very early, because this was likely to usher Berlusconi into government for the second time. Indeed, Amato gained respect within and outside Italy for his competent and effective style of government. However, the general election held on 13 May 2001 did sanction the success of Berlusconi and his political allies on the right of the Italian political spectrum.

Not surprisingly, the 1996 electoral victory of the centre-left coalition as well as the shift to the centre-right in 2001, contributed to a remarkable revival of the debate on national identity in Italy. At the core of this debate were the views of the Italian nation and state as perceived by the left and the right. Italy's modernity has been described as a 'modernity with a lot of politics and very little state, necessarily a modernity subservient to society'.[20] This could explain the weakness of the state and the dominance of party politics, the difficulty of creating an independent class of administrators, the slow pace towards modernisation, the absence of a mature political class, the preponderance of religious or ideological thinking. Two questions can be asked: is Italian national identity really different from that of other countries or simply the product of conflicting sets of memories? and how much national memory is needed to operate as a national collectivity?

The Italian nation has rarely seemed to act on the basis of collective national memories, and the years 1943 to the present have been characterised by the formation of different sets of memories and their translation into partisan politics. Memories have been and still are in competition and are constantly reinvented in politics. However, in the Italian case this process of competition and reinvention has, at least until the early 1990s, further fragmented an already fragmented national identity. It has also exacerbated the separation between state and society, to the point of making it very difficult for any government to operate on the basis of a coherent national project. According to this interpretation, the civic dimension has been particularly weak in Italy, compared with allegiance to the family or to local groups.

If the state is weak in Italy because society has never entrusted it with all its most deeply felt values, the reason can be found in how one reads Italian history; however, the role of memory in providing Italian society with a collective sense of itself is no less central.[21] At the end of the Second World War and during the post-war period, relevant sets of collective memories were shaped and superimposed on the historical experience as a result of Cold War internal and international political confrontation, and almost became official history. The two more striking examples are, first, the mythic experience of the Resistance, which has proved to be stronger than most attempts at reassessing its role; and second, the memory of the 1948 political election, another memory of polarisation – almost civil war – that lasted for half a century.

The reinvention of memories in Italy has in the past been very much linked to the state of international relations and to its reflection on internal political debates. After the end of the Cold War and the 'clean hands' operation, memories of the Second World War have been translated more convincingly than in the past into the moderate project of the new left, and directed towards a more pragmatic European design.

[20] Galli Della Loggia, *L'identitá italiana*, 148.
[21] Isnenghi, *Breve storia dell'Italia*, 12.

However, the renewal of the political struggle between left and right has been an issue in Italy at least since 1996. A post-Cold War division, between those who wanted to rewrite history and those who defended its anti-fascist origins, has been substituted for the dichotomy of amnesia and nostalgic remembrance that characterised the previous era. Memories of the Resistance are at the centre of the debate as much as before, but the camps of the supporters and detractors have widened.

Carlo Ciampi, president of Italy since 1999, has shown a strong commitment to his role of ensuring balance in national politics, something he has been able to do because he is perceived as having no personal political bias or agenda. Among the forms this commitment has taken has been his approach to the celebration of national symbols in the form of remembering the liberation of Italy and reviving in 2000 the celebration of National Day on 2 June. In 1946 the Italians had on that date made their choice between the monarchy and the republic, and it had then been celebrated annually until 1977.

In 2000 Ciampi paid the customary visit on 25 April, the anniversary of the liberation of Italy, to the tomb of the Unknown Soldier and to the Fosse Ardeatine (where in March 1944 more than 300 Italians were executed by the Germans as a reprisal for an attack on them by Roman resistance fighters). More unusually, he also went to the village of Sant'Anna di Stazzema in the Apuane Alps, where 560 civilians were massacred by the Germans in 1944, and was the first president do so in his official capacity. Previously, such a gesture would have been seen as clashing with the desire to normalise Germany's position in Europe and within the Western bloc.

The following day Giorgio Bocca, a well-known Italian columnist and himself a protagonist in the war of liberation, wrote against dishonest historical revisionism in the daily *La Repubblica*. The headline of his article, 'Italy without Memory Forgets the Partisans', confirms a revival of the debate on the Resistance whose tone non-Italians may find very difficult to understand. Bocca has decided to remind the public of the role played by the Resistance in 'bridging the gap between fascism and democracy' and to recommend that this role should not again be forgotten or subjected to unfair revisionism. The revival of the historical–political debate on what prompted Italians in 1943 to choose either in favour of Mussolini and his 'Republic of Salo' or against him and for the liberation of Italy, does contribute to a reassessment of the complexity of such a choice. Indeed, both groups made their choice in the name of allegiance to the Italian nation.[22]

[22] See Paolo Mieli, *Storia e Politica: Risorgimento, fascismo e comunismo* (Milan: Rizzoli, 2001), and R. Vivarelli, *La fine di una stagione: Memoria 1943–1945* (Bologna: Il Mulino, 2000).

President Ciampi may think that reopening old wounds may not be in the interest of the nation today. The second National Day celebration included the revival of a military parade on the Fori Imperiali in Rome in 2001, but with the idea that it could be 'a history lesson on the road'. It aimed at illustrating Italy's struggle to create a nation from the Risorgimento to the world wars to a new European identity. One hundred and fifty thousand people attended this peculiar 'history lesson', which included for the first time women officers of the Italian army, contingents of foreign NATO forces and those Italian contingents which had taken part in peace-keeping operations in Kosovo, Bosnia-Hercegovina and East Timor.

Such a day of reconcilation and, perhaps, of pride without inflated rhetoric, could not have been more necessary, coming as it did soon after the polemics of an electoral campaign and the general election victory of the centre-right coalition led by Berlusconi, the Forza Italia leader.

The peculiarity of the Italian case is that the multiplicity of collective memories which characterised the early post-war period can still inflame internal political debate. Possibly never since April 1948 has the confrontation between two opposed political sides been felt so strongly by the electorate as in May 2001. The incumbent centre-left coalition and the challenging centre-right parties confronted each other not so much on current issues as on memories, images and views of the past and the future.

As regards the right, the many unanswered questions about the origins of Berlusconi's media empire and its future, the aggressive regionalism of the Northern League and the fascist political origins of Alleanza Nazionale evoked memories of the past and worries about the future cohesion and commitments of the Italian republic.

On the other hand, after the end of communism the new Italian left, which has been part of the international 'Third Way' debate and which brought Italy into the single European currency, openly claimed for itself the political right to reconcile past and present around its project. Its lack of cohesion and the response of the electorate in May 2001 have forced it into rethinking its strategy and goals.

Quite independently of all this, Ciampi is determined to play his role as guarantor of fairness in internal political life. He believes that the resistance at the end of the Second World War, as well as the many acts of heroism of the Italian army against the Germans, should be celebrated because they were central episodes in a 'people's war'. This struggle was inspired by love of the homeland and by the desire to overcome the tragic experiences of Fascism and defeat. Would this view of the origins of the Italian republic, as being a continuous process from the Risorgimento to the pro-republican referendum of 1946, become the collective memory of future generations of Italians?

One can argue that this view, if combined with a mature understanding of the complexity of Italian modern history, could provide Italians with a stronger feeling of national belonging at a time of globalisation. However, success depends on how far the Italian people will move away from ideological divisions and provincialism and will reinvent their local and national allegiance with pride – but not inflated rhetoric – on the basis of the difficult heritage of its past.

11 Institutionalising the past: shifting memories of nationhood in German education and immigration legislation

Daniel Levy and Julian Dierkes

This chapter explores the relationship between memory and politics in the articulation of national identity in post-war Germany. We study attempts by the two post-war states to legislate and reform dominant perceptions of nationhood. More specifically, we focus on the institutionalisation of memory in two realms: first, we analyse educational policies and the ways in which they are expressed in secondary history instruction in the Federal Republic of Germany (FRG or West Germany) and the German Democratic Republic (GDR or East Germany); second, we examine the differential effects policies and perceptions about ethnic German immigrants have had on national self-understanding in West Germany since 1945.

Rather than presuppose the persistence of national identities, we explore the conditions under which nationhood has been negotiated and how distinctive memories and institutional practices became entwined at specific historical junctures. We treat the nation as a contested terrain on which groups with competing memories struggle to generalise their ideal conceptions of society. Our study is based on the premise that collective memories inform institutional arrangements as the past is 'stored and interpreted by social institutions'[1] and that these institutional arrangements structure the subsequent understanding of collective memories.[2] Hence our empirical focus is on state practices. We do not assume that politicians, legislators and administrators are the sole powers determining the shape of national memories, but that state actors are a dominant force that supplies categories to articulate and legitimise nationhood. As is evidenced in numerous contributions to this book, the nexus of memory and power manifests itself in a variety of realms and forms. Our analysis shows that collective memories are shaped in specific institutional contexts and

---

[1] Maurice Halbwachs, *On Collective Memory* (Chicago: Chicago University Press, 1992), 24.

[2] For a theoretical discussion of memory and political culture analysis see Jeffrey K. Olick and Daniel Levy, 'Mechanisms of Cultural Constraint: Holocaust Myth and Rationality in German Politics', *American Sociological Review*, 62 (December, 1997), 921–36.

are contingent on political developments. Moreover, the dominance of specific group memories is circumscribed by historical junctures and carried by emerging generational shifts.

The portrayal of the nation in educational policies

The state-centred institutionalisation of nationhood

In the project of modern nation-building the state has played a formative role. The institutional arena of education legislation has been of particular importance for this project. In the aftermath of the Second World War, the German nation was discredited by the experiences of Nazism. Under pressure from the Allies, the two post-war German states had to reform their history schooling and purge narratives of nationalistic elements.

National identity and the professionalisation of pedagogues in West Germany

The significance of education for matters of national identity and collective memory was a central concern for the Allies after the German surrender in 1945. One of the primary goals of the three Western Allies was to prevent a resurgence of nationalism. Allied reforms were aimed largely at the democratisation and demilitarisation of education. Democratisation meant different things to different occupying authorities, but all officials agreed on the need for the reform of the rigid, three-tiered educational system and of the teaching materials that remained from the Nazi period. The degree to which this commitment was acted upon varied greatly, not only by occupational sector, but even by locality. All three Allied authorities had initial aims to restructure education along the lines of their own educational systems. The French occupation authorities emphasised federalism and supported quick efforts at changes in teaching materials and personnel.[3] Policies regarding the accessibility of the top tier of German secondary education were largely unsuccessful due to the concerted opposition of teachers and parents. British educational officials were much more keen on German participation in educational reform than their French counterparts. Their planning was focused mostly on the rewriting of teaching materials in cooperation with German educators deemed untainted by national socialism.[4] Meanwhile, American officials made

[3] Angelika Ruge-Schatz, *Umerziehung und Schulpolitik in der Französischen Besatzungszone 1945–1949* (Frankfurt am Main: Peter Lang, 1977).

[4] Maria Halbritter, *Schulreformpolitik in der Britischen Zone von 1945 bis 1949* (Weinheim: Beltz Verlag, 1979).

perhaps the strongest effort at changing the three-tiered German educational system. However, they met with strong local opposition, as had British and French attempts, and abandoned this reform project in the light of their own support for some sort of self-determination, especially in the education sector.[5]

The federalist structure of education in the FRG complicates analyses and comparisons with the GDR, as there is a fair amount of variance between states on questions of the portrayal of the nation in education. We limit ourselves to exemplary illustrations drawn from the textbooks and curricula for *Realschulen* (the middle tier of the three-tiered educational system) of Bavaria, Hesse and North Rhine-Westphalia. The earliest curriculum for Bavarian 'middle schools' completely omits discussions of German history after the establishment of the League of Nations, even though the elementary school curriculum for age 14 includes a heading 'On the most recent past'.[6] By the time the next complete set of guidelines is issued in 1961, the Second World War has appeared as a section of its own.[7] As is the case with almost all West German curricula, the content of teaching in the curriculum is described schematically at best, but the 1961 section includes mention of 'inhumanity', but also of the displacement of 'German *Volksgruppen*'.

In contrast to these Bavarian guidelines, the early curricula of North Rhine-Westphalia are more extensive and include discussions of the period of National Socialism. The first guidelines, published in 1949, include a section on violent policies of the National Socialists and on the Second World War.[8] However, no mention is made of genocide, persecution or concentration camps. Attention to the recent German past intensifies by the time of the next guidelines in 1966.[9]

Textbooks offer more substance for the analysis of collective memories in that they spell out national histories in far greater detail than the more schematic West German curricula. For example, one textbook which was first approved by occupation authorities and later by the ministries of culture in Hesse and North Rhine-Westphalia, devotes nineteen pages to the period 1933–45.[10] In comparison, the Weimar Republic is covered

---

[5] Jutta Lange-Quassowski, *Neuordnung oder Restauration?* (Opladen: Leske & Budrich, 1979).

[6] *Amtsblatt des Staatsministers für Unterricht und Kultus*, 49, 17 (30 Aug. 1949), 154–5.

[7] *Amtsblatt des Bayerischen Staatsministeriums für Unterricht und Kultus*, 1961, 10 (20 March 1961), 252–5.

[8] *Geschichtsstoffplan für Volks- und Mittelschulen – Nach den ministeriellen Richtlinien des Landes Nordrhein-Westfalen* (Dortmund: Verlag Lambert Lensing, 1949).

[9] 'Heft 27 – Richtlinien für den Unterricht in der Realschule', in *Die Schule in Nordrhein-Westfalen* (Düsseldorf: Henn Verlag, 1966).

[10] *Deutsche Geschichte in Kurzfassung* (Frankfurt: Hirschgraben-Verlag, 1950).

in only nine pages. Although much of the portrayal is focused on Hitler and his associates under the heading 'National Socialists over Germany', the textbook seems to implicate the German population at large through questions such as '1. National Socialism is still frequently portrayed as solely the creation of Hitler and the circumstances. However, its roots are to be found at a deeper level. Where are these roots to be found?'[11] The textbook makes multiple explicit mentions of concentration camps and of the Nazi goal of the extermination of Jews.[12] Of course, anecdotal evidence suggests that these sections of textbooks were often omitted by teachers. As such, their inclusion primarily signals attempts at the production of identity and the reshaping of collective memories.

Despite Allied attempts to reform education, the most striking feature of the FRG's educational system is that it remained largely unchanged from before the Second World War. The ideological commitment to re-educate Germans often conflicted with the necessity to maintain a functioning educational system in general. Change in terms of the structure of secondary education was not to come until the late 1960s with the introduction of general high schools. One continuity from the Weimar Republic stands out despite Nazi attempts to dismantle it: federalism and the state-level control over education. This was intended by the Allies as a bulwark against totalitarianism in education and has remained largely intact throughout the post-war era, despite occasional calls for greater coordination among the states.

After the assumption of policy-making control over education by the state governments of the FRG, a variety of actors competed to generalise their views of national identity. Throughout the post-war era, political parties remained curiously absent from this process. To be sure, parties were decisively involved in the restructuring of the educational system and pushed for some major initiatives in this area. For instance, the introduction of general high schools in various Länder in the late 1960s and early 70s, and the integration of social science subjects into a project-based curriculum were spearheaded by the Hessian Social Democrats in the early 1970s. However, political parties and thus state parliaments for the most part did not engage in debates about the specific content of curricula or teaching materials. For one thing, demands for the professionalisation of knowledge by representatives of teachers led to the increasingly schematic nature of West German curricula which only provide teaching guidelines and no specifics on the emphases to be put on certain periods or subjects. Secondly, approval of teaching materials rested in bureaucratic hands with the state ministries of culture,

[11] Ibid., 243; all translations are ours.   [12] Ibid., 245–6, 255–6.

further blocking attempts by parties to determine teaching content. But this process was dominated by issues of professionalisation of pedagogical knowledge rather than ideological concerns per se. Following general trends towards the professionalisation of knowledge, pedagogues successfully wrested from the state substantive control over education, although some members of the bureaucracies in the various ministries of culture acted as agents of this professionalisation.

In the portrayal of the German nation in textbooks and curricula this professionalisation is perhaps most visible in the close coupling of trends in academic historiography and changes in depictions of the nation. Particularly from the early 1970s onwards, a strong trend towards a representation of history as social and structural history is in evidence in all pedagogical writings. This emphasis comes at the expense of a presentation of the 'great men' of history and – in some cases concomitantly – of the primordial character of the nation.

For illustrative purposes we compare two different editions of a textbook series[13] in order to show some of these differences occurring along with a general professionalisation and following developments in academic historiography. The first several pages of the chapter on the Weimar Republic differ greatly in the types of pictures which they offer, even though only twenty years passed between the publication dates and the intended audiences do not vary much. The 1958 edition offers pictures of President Friedrich Ebert, an organisational chart of the Weimar government, and a picture of Ebert and other leading politicians offering a toast to the new constitution.[14] In contrast, the 1978 edition offers reproductions of Otto Dix and George Grosz paintings (*The matchbox seller* and *The pillars of society*, respectively), a picture of a French soldier guarding a shipment of coal from the Ruhr area and a poster advocating passive resistance to the occupation of the Ruhr area.[15] Whereas the historical narrative in the older edition is dominated by a succession of renegotiations of war reparations (e.g. the treaty of Rapallo), the more recent book focuses on the plight of common people during the years of hyperinflation and offers tables and pictures illustrating this plight.

Developments in the societal environment of educational policies overshadow these professionalisation processes especially with regard to the presentation of the Third Reich. Generational shifts in the make-up of teaching cadres in response to the expansion of education in the 1960s brought a new cohort of teachers into schools in the 1970s. This new

---

[13] *Spiegel der Zeiten, Band V – Die Neueste Zeit* (Frankfurt: Diesterweg Verlag, 1958), approved in Hesse, and *Band 4 – Von der russischen Revolution bis zur Gegenwart* (Frankfurt: Diesterweg Verlag, 1978), approved in Bavaria, Hesse and North Rhine-Westphalia).
[14] *Band V*, 62–4.   [15] *Band 4*, 32–7.

generation was part of the inter-generational debate about educational policies and the pervasive support of their parents for the Nazi regime. Textbooks as well as curricula devoted increasing attention to recent German history, and portrayals of the nation, even in prior historical episodes such as national unification in 1871, were reevaluated. The debate about the teaching of recent German history serves as an example of wider societal influences on textbooks and thus on the construction of national identity. Although this debate is mediated by professional concerns, it clearly has an influence independent of these.[16]

Whereas the 1958 edition of *Spiegel der Zeiten* opens its chapter 'Germany under Hitler's dictatorship' with a fact-oriented biography of Hitler, in the chapter 'The National Socialist dictatorship and its consequences' in the 1978 edition the biography is prefaced by a statement of the social factors that made Hitler's popularity and rise possible in the early 1930s. Hitler's biography is placed in a much wider political context here and shown to interact with a number of developments. Early quotes from Hitler's *Mein Kampf* immediately portray Hitler as a violent anti-semite and anti-communist. Such contrasts abound particularly between books published before and after the early 1970s. On the whole, textbook authors devoted increasing resources to the depiction of the Nazi period, in terms both of the space allocated as well as the historical detail offered.

The portrayal of the German nation in West German textbooks thus changed in the course of post-war history, reflecting processes of professionalisation and generational shifts. Teachers reoriented history instruction in line with changes in academic historiography. These changes reflected academic trends such as the emphasis on previously neglected groups in history writing and a reexamination of recent German history demanded by younger cohorts of historians in the late 1960s.

National identity and macro-political developments in East Germany

From the formal establishment of the Soviet Military Administration in Germany under Marshal Zhukov on 6 June 1945 until the proclamation of the German Democratic Republic on 7 October 1949, the occupation was characterised politically by a gradual passing of power into German hands. This applied to educational policies as well as to other sectors. The period of the Soviet occupation of eastern Germany can be divided

---

[16] More recently, the environment and women's history have been introduced into the history curriculum through similar channels.

roughly into two phases of educational policy:[17] the first lasted until approximately 1947 and was dominated by a reaction to fascism and the establishment of 'anti-fascist, democratic' schools; the second phase encompassed the last two years of the occupation, which were increasingly dominated by the model of Soviet education and by attempts to instrumentalize education in the creation of a socialist society. The two periods were punctuated by the passing of the Gesetz zur Demokratisierung der deutschen Schule (Law for the Democratisation of the German School) in 1946. This phase was a turning-point in the period of Soviet occupation and marked the increasing consolidation of party power.

By the mid-1950s the educational system was structured very differently from that of Weimar Germany or Nazi Germany. The three-tiered structure of education had been abolished and had been converted to a system of general high schools. The groundwork for such structural changes was laid in the period of the Soviet occupation of eastern Germany. However, even during the occupation educational reform was in flux and the precise structure of the educational system did not emerge until the founding of the GDR. From October 1949 until the demise of the GDR, education remained under the direct control of the ruling Socialist Unity Party of Germany (SED) and specifically under the control of Margot Honecker, who controlled the educational apparatus from 1963. All aspects of educational policy-making were coordinated centrally and final approval of policies lay with party committees, although policy proposals for high school education were drafted formally outside the party. Central coordination of educational policy implied a close link between curriculum and textbook writing, as some of the same authors usually worked on both tasks simultaneously. Despite this apparently monolithic body of party control, educational policy did undergo significant changes during the post-war era.

Soviet occupation forces together with German communist cadres were perhaps fastest among the Allies in drafting new curricula and textbooks for use in schools. They were aided in these efforts by pre-surrender deliberations about the content of teaching in post-war Germany. In some subjects, such as history, guidelines for teaching were issued as early as autumn 1945. These guidelines provided the basis for the drafting of fully fledged curricula and textbooks only a few months later. Like the Western Allies, the Soviet occupation forces were particularly keen on revisions of existing teaching materials. As Nazi textbooks had been rewritten to

---

[17] Uwe Henning, Gerhard Kluchert and Achim Leschinsky, 'Erziehungskonzeption und ihre Umsetzung in den Schulen der SBZ und der frühen DDR', in Dietrich Benner, Hans Merkens and Folker Schmidt (eds.), *Bildung und Schule im Transformationsprozeß von SBZ, DDR und neuen Ländern – Untersuchungen zu Kontinuität und Wandel* (Berlin: Institut für Allgemeine Pädagogik, Freie Universität Berlin, 1996), 104.

reflect ideological priorities, the occupation authorities wanted to make sure that they would be able to exert control over new constructions of collective memories, both distant and near.

Even in early post-war curricula, German history under National Socialism already played a significant role in East German educational materials. In the curriculum for age 14 as of 1 July 1946, twelve hours (out of 120 for the year) were to be devoted to the Second World War.[18] As the Russian Revolution of 1917 was treated in eight hours and the Weimar Republic in seven hours, this was a significant commitment. The curriculum for age 18 reviewed the same time period and devoted fourteen hours (out of 120 for the year) to 'Die Gewaltherrschaft Hitlers und der zweite Weltkrieg'. An early textbook includes an explicit discussion of concentration camps, also in connection with National Socialist racial legislation and the genocide of Jews.[19] However, curricula and textbooks are careful to attribute wrongdoing during the Second World War to the fairly abstract 'fascists' or 'fascist clique with the support of imperialist capitalists'. The textbook includes the summary statement that 'this monstrous, never before witnessed terror against the German working class and the entire German people revealed the true face of fascism'.[20] As this entire section views German history through the prism of class conflict, the Second World War is portrayed as an outgrowth of imperialism, and this abstraction indirectly seems to exonerate large parts of the German populace from association with National Socialist crimes, including, of course, the population of the GDR. The history of the military conflict in the Second World War in these early East German portrayals is largely focused on the heroic role of the Soviet army and the Soviet population, and thus also does not hold implications for the self-identification of Germans. German resistance and particularly communist resistance is highlighted, even though a summary statement concludes clearly that 'The German people did not liberate themselves'.[21]

The two towering post-war leaders of the GDR, Walter Ulbricht and Erich Honecker, both moved over time from internationalism to a particularism stressing the distinctive traits of GDR nationhood. Having started out as a staunch internationalist and faithful junior partner to the Soviet Union, Ulbricht increasingly became interested in the peculiarly German aspects of socialism in general and of the GDR's variety in

---

[18] Deutsche Zentralverwaltung für Volksbildung in der sowjetischen Besatzungszone Deutschlands, *Lehrpläne für die Grund- und Oberschulen in der sowjetischen Besatzungszone Deutschlands – Geschichte* (1946).

[19] *Lehrbuch für den Geschichtsunterricht 8. Schuljahr IV. Teil* (Berlin: Verlag Volk und Wissen, 1951), 9–10, 51–3.

[20] Ibid., 10.   [21] Ibid., 69.

particular.[22] Perhaps more than in any other field this view was implemented in education. Although Honecker had engineered Ulbricht's ouster with Moscow's support, on the grounds that Ulbricht had strayed from the accepted path towards communism, Honecker in time also succumbed to a view that celebrated the GDR's national traits and its economic efficiency. The renewed interest in the 1980s in Prussia and the GDR's historical heritage was clearly approved by the party leadership. Honecker's wife, the minister of education, implemented this view in educational materials. Pedagogical issues or attempts by teachers to professionalise educational knowledge were subject to these transformations in officially imposed memories.

Perhaps the most poignant example of these developments in East German educational materials is the treatment of the *Grosser Deutscher Bauernkrieg* (Great German Peasant War) of 1525 in textbooks and curricula and the role this war played in the development of German nationhood. Portrayals of the nation vis-à-vis the agrarian uprising vacillated between stressing the class conflict aspect of such uprisings (especially during the immediate post-war era) and emphasising that this uprising was inspired by Luther and his translation of the Bible and thus represents one of the first moments of a German national consciousness among a collective movement. Whereas portrayals of the uprising emphasised class conflict in the immediate post-war portrayal, this emphasis was replaced throughout the 1950s and 60s by that on the particularly German character of the uprising, to be revived in the mid-1970s, that is, after Honecker assumed leadership positions.

To summarise, we can see how the respective occupational powers influenced both the organisational structure of the educational system (federalist versus centralised) as well as the general orientations of the new states. While historical explanations of Nazism in the FRG were subject to generational shifts and the professionalisation of the educational field, the GDR simply adopted a Marxist explanation of fascism. This officially prescribed anti-fascism displaced the responsibility for the Second World War to capitalist Germany and portrayed the East German people as victims of fascist seduction. The portrayal of the German nation in East German textbooks, on the other hand, was subject to changes. Initially, the nation was commemorated in terms of class politics. Later, under the leadership of Honecker, particular episodes from German history were recovered and memories of a socialist class nation were replaced with more traditional historical memories.

---

[22] Hermann Weber, *Geschichte der DDR* (Munich: Deutscher Taschenbuch Verlag, 1985), 393–8.

The politics of immigration

In recent decades, matters of national identity in western European countries have been problematised through the cultural, economic and political effects of immigration, giving rise to a politics of belonging and the reassessments of collective boundaries.[23] No longer are these debates confined to questions of the labour market. Citizenship debates convey how strangers are perceived and simultaneously express the self-understanding of a polity setting the boundaries between 'us' and 'them'.[24] The FRG's citizenship legislation has until recently defined members of the national community exclusively in ethnic terms, awarding citizenship to those who prove according to certain criteria that they are German by descent.[25] Consequently, it has granted so-called ethnic Germans from east and central Europe full access to citizenship. They are descendants of Germans who had settled in Eastern Europe since the eighteenth century. After the war, the Potsdam Treaty sanctioned large population transfers, which led to the flight and expulsion of about ten million ethnic Germans from states under Soviet influence. They are commonly referred to as 'expellees' (*Vertriebene*). About eight million ethnic German expellees from eastern and central Europe came to West Germany in the immediate aftermath of the Second World War. Another two million ethnic German resettlers (*Aussiedler*) followed between 1950 and 1988. Nearly one fifth of the early Federal Republic's population consisted of refugees.[26]

Different public memories of ethnic Germans' expulsion and their subsequent integration into West Germany have been appropriated for various political agendas and played a prominent role in the reconfiguration

---

[23] Andrew Geddes and Adrian Favell (eds.), *The Politics of Belonging: Migrants and Minorities in Contemporary Europe* (Aldershot: Ashgate, 1999).

[24] Rogers Brubaker, *Citizenship and Nationhood in France and Germany* (Cambridge, MA: Harvard University Press, 1992).

[25] The GDR essentially sought to replace the national with a socialist conception. Initially, however, it also perpetuated, at least implicitly, the idea of 'a socialist state of the German nation'. This phrase was replaced by a 'socialist state of workers and peasants' in Article 1 of a constitutional revision in 1974 (John Breuilly, 'The National Idea in modern German history', in Mary Fulbrook (ed.), *German History since 1800* (New York: Arnold, 1997). Despite these attempts to create a class-based internationalist conception where the GDR constituted a separate nation-state, 'the underlying assumption of a common German nation defined in ethnic terms proved remarkably resilient among the population', Mary Fulbrook, 'Germany for the Germans? Citizenship and Nationality in a Divided Nation', in Mary Fulbrook and David Cesarani (eds.), *Citizenship, Nationality and Migration in Europe* (New York: Routledge, 1996). This also supports the broader claim that it is inappropriate to imply a congruence between official definitions of citizenship and popular conceptions of national belonging. As the case of the Federal Republic shows, the formal persistence of the ethnic idiom is not inevitably reflected in a popular self-understanding as an ethno-cultural nation.

[26] Klaus Bade, *Ausländer, Aussiedler, Asyl* (Munich: Beck'sche Verlagshandlung, 1994).

of national identity in the Federal Republic. As we demonstrate in this essay, changing perceptions of ethnic Germans had differential impacts on how the nation was publicly narrated: in the first post-war decade, perceptions of ethnic Germans' suffering played a significant role in the reproduction of an ethno-cultural self-understanding; in subsequent years, negative public perceptions of ethnic Germans contributed to the gradual discrediting of this ethno-cultural idiom. This shift shows that we cannot assume that automatic citizenship rights for ethnic Germans necessarily correspond to an ethno-cultural understanding of nationhood. Instead, we show how changing memories and perceptions of ethnic Germans, rather than some primordial commitment to the ethnic nation, have contributed to both ethnic and civic conceptions of national self-understanding in post-war Germany.

The post-war years

The reconstruction of German national identity in the immediate aftermath of the Second World War and the first decade of the Federal Republic constitute a formative period. This decade comprises an important backdrop to an understanding of how Germany's national idiom was reformed and how it has subsequently operated as a frame of reference for the articulation of domestic and foreign policy agendas. The ways in which this early period is being remembered in the FRG supplies a vocabulary with which the post-Cold War integration of *Aussiedler* has been assessed.

Below we briefly illustrate how the public representation of the expulsion of ethnic Germans and their ensuing hardship were inscribed into the public memory during the first post-war decade in order to recreate a legitimate sense of collectivity.[27] The national experience of these years was marked by two central and often related aspects. One was the tense encounter with the Allied occupation forces; the other was the public and political debate about how to compensate expellees and other groups for their war losses. Perceptions of German suffering and the context of occupation were decisive for the moral and political justification of German nationhood and the emergence of policy measures on behalf of ethnic Germans. The institutionalisation of victimhood, on both the domestic and the international front, in conjunction with gradual economic reconstruction, played a prominent role in reassessing the meaning of nationhood.

[27] For a lengthier analysis of ethnic German immigration see Daniel Levy, 'Coming Home? Ethnic Germans and the Transformation of National Identity in the Federal Republic of Germany' in Geddes and Favell (eds.), *Politics of Belonging*, 93–108.

Expellees comprised the largest and most important group around which this discourse of suffering and victimhood was constructed, mostly in reference to the often violent mass expulsions from Eastern Europe. But these narratives of victimhood were also constructed in opposition to the Western Allies. Politicians from all parties blamed economic hardship on the Allies, and resistance to their policies became a unifying practice. Another significant cornerstone in the reconstruction of national identity was established through a widespread anti-communist consensus. The Allies as well as Adenauer perceived the expellees as a bulwark of anti-communism and were eager to exploit experiences of expulsion as a reminder of Soviet aggression. Adenauer had no illusions about the irreversibility of the territorial settlements that followed the Potsdam Treaty, but he recognised the political potential of a revisionist rhetoric as it coincided with his policy to integrate the Federal Republic into the Western Alliance. Memories of the fate of expellees were instrumental in sustaining the legitimacy of West Germany's claim to embody German unity, despite its actual division and the permanent loss of some of its territory.

The salience of these memories of expulsion was underscored by the widespread institutional and public impact ethnic Germans had at the time. They were a pervasive presence in all realms of German politics and society. Many expellees joined existing parties and acted as a political pressure group. After the second election to the Bundestag in 1953, 18 per cent of all members of the federal parliament were ethnic Germans. Shared memories of expulsion often transcended the ideological differences of their respective political parties. Expellees also formed their own party, the Bloc of Expellees and Disenfranchised (Bund der Heimatvertriebenen und Entrechteten – BHE). The BHE focused its electoral platform on compensation for the property losses of ethnic Germans. In 1953 the BHE became a junior partner in the governing coalition with Adenauer's Christian Democratic Union (CDU), bolstering their public visibility. They were a powerful voice in the articulation of refugee policies (mostly through their control of the Ministry for Expellees and Refugees). The identities of a significant portion of West Germans were shaped by their memories of expulsion, and the public narration of these memories played a decisive role for the rehabilitation of national identity after 1945.

These memories of suffering were underscored through legislative measures pertaining to the immigration of ethnic Germans. An analysis of parliamentary debates reveals a broad consensus with regard to the memory of their suffering and a legal recognition of their status as victims. The refugee problem was a major concern for the new state.

Expellees' automatic right to citizenship goes back to the 1913 Reichs-und Staatsangehörigkeitsrecht (Imperial and State Citizenship Law).[28] Entitlement to full citizenship was reinforced in the Preamble and Article 116 of the Grundgesetz (Basic Law) which expresses the ethnic understanding of German nationhood. The distinction between citizens of the Federal Republic of Germany (*Staatsangehörige*) and those who do not possess German citizenship but belong to the community by virtue of descent (*Volkszugehörige*) has constituted the foundation for the continuous migration of *Aussiedler* ever since.

However, the perpetuation of this ethno-cultural understanding did not emerge from some primordial ethnic sense of nationality. It was primarily the result of social and political considerations. Our analysis of legislative debates shows that the adoption of a descent-based citizenship owed more to questions of political legitimacy than to an essentialist ethno-cultural notion. Article 116 emerged against the background of three central considerations generated by the confusion that expulsion, flight and population transfers created after the Second World War. First, the law was anchored in a moral obligation to compensate ethnic Germans for their suffering. They were also viewed as victims of Nazism, inasmuch as the reprisals against them came in response to acts perpetrated by the Nazis in eastern and central Europe. Second, it was agreed that only a generous interpretation of German citizenship law could provide legal equality between *Volkszugehörige* and *Einheimische* (native population). This was a necessary precondition for the political solution of expellees' integration into the Federal Republic. Third, there was a strong ideological incentive. The emerging Federal Republic insisted that it was the legal successor of the German Reich of 1871. Facing the division of Germany, this claim played an important role in creating legitimacy for a unified Germany and conversely not recognising the GDR as a sovereign entity. As a result of these political considerations, rather than an essentially primordial commitment to the ethnic nation, the imperial law of 1913 retained its validity and German citizenship legislation continued to rely on the principle of descent. This, of course, provided the legal and ideological foundation for the continuous immigration of ethnic Germans.

The decline of ethnos

However, the significance of ethnic Germans for the articulation of national identity was not static. The Adenauer government as well as

---

[28] Kay Hailbronner, 'Citizenship and Nationhood in Germany', in Rogers Brubaker (ed.), *Immigration and the Politics of Citizenship in Europe and North America* (Lanham: University Press of America, 1989).

politicians from opposition parties celebrated the integration of ethnic Germans and their contributions to the burgeoning economy, and gradually the ethno-national idiom in Germany was reconfigured into an economic identity. National identity was no longer articulated with regard to conventional symbols of nationhood (e.g. flag, anthem) but through references to the economic prowess of the new Germany.[29] The contributions of expellees to this process were particularly significant as they encountered more exacting conditions and faced more obstacles and hardship than the natives. Consequently, their accomplishments were valorised during public commemorations on their behalf and they came to epitomise this new source of collective identification. Once this economic pride became the foundation for collective identification it made little sense to subscribe to primordial attachments.

The political leadership of ethnic Germans quickly realised the implications of socio-economic integration and subsequently shifted their attention away from issues of relative deprivation and focused instead on matters pertaining to the 'lost territories' in the east. Ultimately, this shift further aggravated the decline of ethno-national perceptions in public discourse. In the early years of the Cold War, expellees' hardline approach towards the communist bloc, the uncompromising attitude with respect to the Oder-Neisse border and their demands for the return of and to their old homes was in tune with the rhetoric of Adenauer's governments. However, during the 1960s the government took a more conciliatory approach towards the East, and the government now perceived the expellee organisations' foreign policy stance as disruptive and retrograde. During the 1950s and until Kiesinger became chancellor in 1966 it had been standard political practice for politicians to pay public tribute to the concerns of expellee organisations. On becoming chancellor in 1969 Willy Brandt ended this courtship with his decision to dismantle the Ministry for Expellees.

Several scandals involving leading expellee politicians and the discovery of their Nazi past also added to a growing public association of ethno-national values with Nazi ideology. To be sure, discoveries about the Nazi past of public figures were not new, but in contrast to the 1950s they now resonated with public sensibilities that were marked by the political maturation of Germany's first post-war generation. The generational conflicts of the 1960s found their expression in the confrontation of the post-war generation with their parents' role during the Nazi period.

---

[29] Erica Carter, *How German is She? Postwar West German Reconstruction and the Consuming Woman* (Ann Arbor: University of Michigan Press, 1997); Harold James, *A German Identity 1770–1990* (New York: Routledge, 1989). It is striking that for both Germanys economic achievement became the primary source of national pride.

The emphasis on German victims' suffering – manifested mostly through the experiences of expulsion and displacement of ethnic Germans – was replaced with the suffering of victims of Germans.[30] This new political culture viewed the Holocaust as an integral part of Germany's history. No subsequent national identification could exclude it (which is, of course, at the core of several debates about the role of public memory in the Federal Republic, from the *Historikerstreit* up to the more recent Bubis-Walser controversy). Gradually, nationalism became synonymous with the excesses of Nazism and other undemocratic traditions in the history of Germany.

The return of the nation?

The marginal role of ethnic Germans in West Germany's political–cultural discourse became evident during the 1980s. Helmut Kohl's assumption of the chancellorship in 1982 provided a broad public arena for an attempted recovery of Germany's ethno-cultural self-understanding. Memories of ethnic Germans' suffering and their economic accomplishment in the formative years of the Federal Republic were an important part of what Kohl termed *Geschichtspolitik* (history with politics). Kohl's explicit and self-conscious employment of memories for political purposes presents a particularly interesting subject to students of West German political culture.[31] His *Geschichtspolitik* was based on the assumption that whoever controls the images of the past, controls the future. Or as the historian Michael Stürmer, a former adviser of Kohl, put it, 'in a land without history whoever supplies memory, shapes concepts, and interprets the past will win the future'.[32] In other words, *Geschichtspolitik* tells us something about how memories can be recovered for political purposes.

The memory of ethnic Germans' fate played a central role in Kohl's attempt to revive and rehabilitate old notions such as the '*Vaterland*' and the '*Volk*'. He sought to dissociate the ethno-cultural idiom from its Nazi connotations. In his inaugural address Kohl emphasised the suffering of ethnic Germans during the Second World War. At the same time, he stressed their contribution to the reconstruction of the Federal Republic

---

[30] Robert G. Moeller, 'War Stories: The Search for a Usable Past in the Federal Republic of Germany', *American Historical Review*, 101(1996), 1008–48.

[31] For a general discussion about the relationship of historiography, memory and national identity formation, see Daniel Levy, 'The Future of the Past: Historiographical Disputes and Competing Memories in Germany and Israel', *History and Theory*, 38, 1(1999), 51–66.

[32] *Frankfurter Allgemeine Zeitung*, 25 April 1986.

and used expellees' resilience during the 1950s as exemplary for the new spirit in Germany. Once again, albeit under changed circumstances and mediated through periods of oblivion and differential memories, the postwar history of ethnic Germans became relevant for the reordering of the German nation. But this time it did not have the same resonance as during the 1950s. Memories of the expellee fate were no longer uncontested.

A central aspect of reviving the memory of ethnic Germans consisted of Kohl's symbolic endorsement of expellee organisations. As discussed earlier, Brandt had ended the standard political practice of attending the annual meetings of expellees. Kohl decided to revive this long-forgotten tradition and he started publicly addressing expellee organisations in 1984. His decision in June 1985 to attend the annual meeting of Silesians – by far the largest expellee organisation in Germany – reflected the continuous effort to present the experience of German suffering as a legitimate trope for Germany's national self-understanding. Or, as *Der Spiegel* noted in January 1985, 'Without any hesitation Kohl courted the expellees with the result that their annual meeting, which had long become a marginal folkloristic event, again assumes significance.'[33] In contrast to the 1950s, Kohl's interest in and acknowledgment of these groups had little to do with their substantial political claims and foreign policy concerns, most of which conflicted with Kohl's continuation of Brandt's Ostpolitik. The GDR was long recognised, and cooperation between the two German states was shaped by economic and political considerations that left little room for the heated ideological battles that characterised their relationship throughout the 1950s and early 1960s. Ultimately, it was clear that Kohl rejected the expellees' political demands, but his public endorsement of their symbolic status as victims stood firm.[34]

However, Kohl's decision to make a public appearance at the expellee meeting created controversy. Both the decision itself and its timing – one month after the Bitburg scandal (which erupted after the decision of US President Ronald Reagan to visit a military cemetery in Germany where members of the Nazi SS and SA were buried alongside regular soldiers of the German army) – caused negative reactions across the political spectrum. The publicised portrayal of expellee organisations positioned them at the far right of German politics. Kohl's embrace of their concerns was

---

[33] *Spiegel*, 7 Jan. 1985.
[34] Kohl perceived the expellees as one of the few authentic agents for the ethno-cultural conceptions he was trying to reintroduce into public discourse. The history and fate of the expellees in the aftermath of the Second World War provided Kohl with concrete examples of a German tradition that he thought were immune to the imperatives and codes of the 'Holocaust nation' and in several ways could serve as a symbolic counterweight to the centrality of the suffering of victims of Germans.

further complicated by the fact that the organisers of the Hannover rally in June 1985 wanted to use a slogan for the convention which unmistakably implied territorial demands ('40 years expulsion – Silesia remains ours'), a position to which Kohl could not subscribe. Intense negotiations between Kohl's staff and expellee representatives over the wording of the slogan began. In the end, a compromise was reached and it proclaimed that 'Silesia remains our future in a Europe of free people'.

The scandal surrounding the slogan and Kohl's attendance ultimately served as confirmation for a broad rejection of ethno-cultural values. The controversial slogan reinforced the view that expellee organisations were anachronistic remnants from the 1950s and Cold War rhetoric, characterised by radical statements that were a far cry from the political realities of the day and to some extent even construed as reminders of Nazi expansionism. One of the unintended consequences of this episode then was the longstanding confirmation of the equation between nationalism and extremism.

However, public perceptions of ethnic Germans were not confined to symbolic politics alone, and their immigration became increasingly controversial after 1989. The opening of the Iron Curtain precipitated large-scale migrations of ethnic Germans from Eastern Europe.[35] Economic and political considerations led to the restriction of certain privileges for *Aussiedler*. The Kohl government found itself in a bind. On the rhetorical level, it continued to insist on the entitlement of *Aussiedler* to German citizenship, thus preserving the notion that the German nation is based on descent. On the other hand, it faced mounting criticism of this ethnic understanding of nationhood. This critique emanated mostly from the left, but also from some Free Democrats, who were part of the governing coalition. They dismissed the ethnic principle as an anachronistic relic and an obstacle to the naturalisation and full integration of Germany's large migrant labour population.

Our analysis of public and official debates after unification shows how the 'national' has been reconfigured as a social problem. The immigration of ethnic Germans was no longer a mere symbolic reminder, but primarily a policy problem creating social envy between newcomers and natives. It also intensified the debate about the ethnic and civic foundations of German citizenship laws, juxtaposing the automatic right

[35] Between 1965 and 1979 the number of *Aussiedler* totalled 488,312. During the 1980s the average yearly number grew slightly, to about 40,000. In 1988 this number jumped to 202, 673, with another significant increase in 1989–90 to 377,055 and 397,073 respectively. Since 1991, the number has declined to fewer than 100,000 by 1999 (Source: *Info-Dienst Deutsche Aussiedler*).

for ethnic Germans and the reluctance to give full citizenship rights to Germany's extensive second- and third-generation foreign population, which persisted until the end of the 1990s. By then, the main political frame of reference revolved around questions of integration. Not only were memories of expellees a peripheral feature of Germany's political culture, but ethnic German immigrants (who by 1993 were officially referred to as *Spätaussiedler*) themselves were now perceived as an increasingly marginal group.

In this context, memories of the expulsion and integration of ethnic Germans during the 1950s were increasingly subjected to competing interpretations. During the 1980s the formative period of the post-war decade had often been invoked as an exemplary social and political experiment, referring mostly to the successful integration of ethnic Germans. But after reunification, a reassessment of this success story emerged. While politicians used to celebrate the integration of expellees as one of the most important accomplishments of the young FRG, many of them, from both the left and the right, are presenting a more complex story since the early 1990s. Horst Waffenschmidt (CDU), who was appointed as Commissioner of the Federal Government for Outsettler Affairs (*Beauftragter der Bundesregierung für Aussiedlerfragen*), invoked memories of early tensions between natives and newcomers to demonstrate how even the widely celebrated integration of expellees was not accomplished without frictions. The central aim of this revision has been to create more tolerance for the post-Cold War situation, at a time when integration has been hampered by a variety of socioeconomic problems and cultural differences resulting in a growing reluctance among the resident population to welcome additional ethnic Germans. Public reactions toward *Aussiedler* are increasingly negative and more people simply identify them as strangers. This new situation has also affected the legal status of ethnic Germans in reunified Germany. The government has curtailed their legal privileges, and new laws effectively put an end to future citizenship applications for ethnic Germans from east–central Europe by the year 2010.

Much of the governmental rhetoric defending the continuous immigration of *Aussiedler* was couched no longer in national but rather in utilitarian terms of economic contributions. The ethno-national vocabulary was gradually replaced by a focus on ethnic German immigration as a social and economic problem. This dynamic has been underscored through the frequent conflation of *Aussiedler* and foreigners in public discourse. Collective identities are increasingly justified in universal rather than particularistic terms. Thus, for instance, many of the more recent defenders of ethnic Germans invoke the right to difference. *Aussiedler* no longer represent nationhood but rather the perils of immigration. They are now often perceived as yet another ethnic group in a multicultural society. By focusing on the problems strangers encounter in a society that subscribes to the myth of ethnic homogeneity, they serve as illustration that Germany, after all, is 'a country of immigration'.

Politicians frequently framed their condition as immigrants in human rights rather than ethno-national terms. The strongest manifestation of this rhetorical change emanates from the Green party. However, the universalisation of nationhood is evident in the Europeanisation of the *Aussiedler* theme by both the right and the left. After the Second World War, memories of expellees' political pacification were exploited to ascribe a distinctive role to ethnic Germans for bridging the gaps between Western and Eastern Europe. The instrumental value of these memories for Germany's foreign policy agenda persisted, even when expellee organisations continuously disrupted official attempts of reconciliation with east and central European states.

During the 1990s, the persistence of ethnic German enclaves and their general situation in the former Soviet Union were addressed in terms of minority rights. This universalising trend was once again reinforced through the idea of a united Europe with ethnic Germans enjoying a bridging role between West and East. This appeal to minority rights and the invocation for a united Europe also bequeathed a vocabulary that resonated with several government objectives, namely: the eastern enlargement of NATO, the incorporation of new members into the European Union, and the ongoing financial incentives for ethnic Germans to stay in their current *Heimat*. The domestic discourse on ethnic German immigrants during this period, however, has been dominated by their fate as an increasingly marginalised social group.

Concluding remarks

In this chapter we have explored the relationship of memory and national identity in post-war Germany. Forms of national belonging are primarily problematised by how the nation is collectively remembered at different times. We have illustrated that memories of a nation's past and institutional practices are mutually constitutive and shaped by political contingencies. The German case is of particular interest since it thematises the effects of historical ruptures in the context of two different political regimes. Furthermore, it illustrates how conceptions of nationhood are contingent on changing generational memories.

Our analysis of educational policies, expressed in the form of high school history books, shows that both the success of organisational efforts by respective groups and the organisational structure itself determined which memory would dominate at a given period of time. Developments in West Germany have been characterised by the professionalisation of pedagogical knowledge and by demographic shifts in policy-making and teaching cadres. As a result, a new generation of teachers approached German nationhood through the lens of critical historiographical paradigms. Changes in East German education have been overshadowed by macro-political developments and attitudes of the East German party leadership. Educational policies remained under the centralised control of the state. Nazism was explained in terms of Marxist historiography, focusing on the structural affinities of capitalism and fascism. Conversely, the GDR presented itself, through the personification of its leaders, as a model of anti-fascism. However, as we have shown here, prevalent images of the German nation did change in the context of new political leadership. A class-based understanding of the nation was gradually complemented by the recovery of memories of German national traditions.

Differential memories have also informed debates on immigration in the Federal Republic. Memories of ethnic German immigration have structured debates on citizenship, both confirming and undermining its ethno-cultural self-understanding. Early legislative efforts on behalf of ethnic Germans institutionalised and thus inscribed their suffering into public memory. However, as we have demonstrated, changing political configurations and different generational memories led to a marginalisation of the ethno-cultural idiom in the public sphere. Official attempts to revive memories of ethnic Germans during the 1980s remained insignificant. This became apparent in the aftermath of unification, when the ethno-national idiom was challenged by the ongoing tension between West and East Germans and the growing reluctance to welcome ethnic German *Aussiedler*.

The post-Cold War period constitutes a historical juncture during which memories of the nation are being reconfigured once again. So far, no new educational guidelines about teaching history have been issued in unified Germany, but such changes might be forthcoming in the context of an increasing Europeanisation of educational policies and/or with a reevaluation of Germany's role in the post-Cold War world. The impact of political contingencies on citizenship legislation was immediately revealed after the election of a Red–Green coalition in autumn 1998. The first policy measure by the new coalition of Social Democrats and the Greens was to propose a change to Germany's citizenship laws which has since been enacted.[36] With the move of Germany's capital to Berlin the 'Bonn Republic' itself is becoming history. Another assessment of Germany's past is required as the new slogan that 'Berlin is not Bonn' seeks to replace the collective memory of the old slogan that 'Bonn is not Weimar'.

[36] The new legislation, in effect since 1 Jan. 2000, is expected to affect up to three million of the seven million resident 'foreigners'. Immigrant children born in Germany now qualify for a passport if one parent was under fourteen on entering the country and has remained a resident. In addition, foreigners resident for eight years, or five years if under sixteen, will get citizenship. The agreement also provides for 'dual citizenship', allowing new Germans to keep their other passports until the age of twenty-three, when they have to choose one or the other. For a more detailed discussion of this new law and the controversies surrounding its dual citizenship provision, see Daniel Levy, 'The Politicization of Ethnic German Immigrants: The Transformation of State Priorities', in Rainer Münz and Rainer Ohliger (eds.), *Ethnic Migration in Twentieth-Century Europe: Germany, Israel and Russia in Comparative Perspective* (London: Frank Cass, 2002).

12   Trials, purges and history lessons: treating a difficult past in post-communist Europe

Timothy Garton Ash

The question of what nations should do about a difficult past is one of the great subjects of our time. Countries across the world have faced this problem: Chile, Argentina, Uruguay, El Savador, Spain after Franco, Greece after the Colonels, Ethiopia, Cambodia, all the post-communist states of central and eastern Europe today. There is already a vast literature, mostly written by political scientists, lawyers and human rights activists rather than historians, and mainly looking at treating the past as an element in 'transitions' from dictatorship to – it is hoped – consolidated democracy. Three invaluable, thick volumes, too narrowly entitled *Transitional Justice*, document the worldwide story up to 1995. The material for a fourth volume is even now being prepared in South Africa, Rwanda, Bosnia and The Hague.[1]

Yet what exactly are we talking about? There is no single word for it in the English language. German, however, has two long ones in regular use: *Geschichtsaufarbeitung* and *Vergangenheitsbewältigung*. These may be translated as 'treating' the past, 'working over' the past, 'confronting' it, 'coping, dealing or coming to terms with' it; even – in the case of *Vergangenheitsbewältigung* – 'overcoming' the past. The variety of possible translations indicates the complexity of the matter in hand. Of course the absence of a word in a language does not necessarily indicate the absence of the thing it describes. Byron remarks somewhere that while the English do not have the word *longeurs* they have the thing in some profusion. But the presence of not just one but two German terms does indicate that this is something of a German specialty.

To be sure, many rivers flow into this ocean, and everyone comes to the subject in their own particular way. The lawyer and human rights activist Aryeh Neier, for example, traces what he calls the 'movement for accountability' back to Argentina in the early 1980s, and there is no doubt that a major impulse did come from Latin America, with its various models of

---

[1] Neil J. Kritz (ed.), *Transitional Justice: How Emerging Democracies Reckon with Former Regimes*, I, *General Considerations*; II, *Country Studies*; III, *Laws, Rulings, and Reports*, (Washington, DC: United States Institute of Peace Press, 1995).

a 'truth commission'. An article reprinted in *Transitional Justice* identifies no fewer than fifteen 'truth commissions' established between 1974 and 1994; the present tally is probably close to twenty.[2] Yet Germany is the only country (so far) to have tried it not once but twice: after Nazism and after communism.

In this chapter I shall concentrate on how central European countries have coped – or not coped – with the legacy of communism since the end of the Cold War. In particular, I want to compare the very special case of Germany with those of its east central European neighbours, and draw some conclusions which may usefully be read together with Jan-Werner Müller's remarks about the 'ethics of memory' in the introduction.

In doing so, I pose four basic questions: *whether* to remember and treat the past at all, in any of the diverse available ways, or simply to try to forget and look to the future; *when* to address it, if it is to be addressed; *who* should do it; and, last but not least, *how*?

I

The answer given to the first question – *whether?* – in Germany since 1989 has been unequivocal: 'Of course we must remember! Of course we must confront the history of the communist dictatorship in Germany in every possible way!' And Germany has set a new standard of comprehensiveness in the attempt.

The arguments made for tackling the past like this are moral, psychological and political. Interestingly, the moral imperative, the commandment to remember, is often quoted in Germany in forms that come from the Jewish tradition: 'to remember is the secret of redemption'. Then there is the psychological notion, spelled out in an influential book by Alexander and Margarete Mitscherlich, that it is bad for nations, as it is for individual people, to supress the memory of sad or evil things in their past, and good for them to go through the hard work of mourning, *Trauerarbeit*. Above all, there is the political idea that this will help to prevent a recurrence of the evil. How many times has one heard repeated in Germany George Santayana's remark that those who forget the past are condemned to repeat it?

You can see at once why it is regarded in Germany as Politically Incorrect, to say the least, to question this received wisdom. After the Holocaust, how dare anyone talk of forgetting? Yet the basic premiss has in fact been rejected in many other times and places. Historically,

---

[2] The article is by Priscilla B. Hayner, who is currently working on a book about truth commissions. I am grateful to her for confirming my estimate of some twenty truth commissions to date.

the advocates of forgetting are numerous and weighty. Just two days after the murder of Caesar, for example, Cicero declared in the Roman senate that all memory of the murderous discord should be consigned to eternal oblivion: *oblivione sempiterna delendam*. European peace treaties, from one between Lothar, Ludwig of Germany and Charles of France in 851 to the Treaty of Lausanne in 1923, called specifically for an act of forgetting. So did the French constitutions of 1814 and 1830. The English Civil War ended with an Act of Idemnity and Oblivion.

Even since 1945, there have been many examples in Europe of a policy of forgetting. The post-war French republic was built, after the first frenzy of the *épuration*, upon a more or less conscious policy of supplanting the painful memory of collaboration in Vichy and occupied France with de Gaulle's unifying national myth of a single, eternally resistant, fighting France. In fact, as Tony Judt argues in his chapter, much of post-war West European democracy was constructed on a foundation of forgetting: think of the Italian case, as described by Ilaria Poggiolini in this volume, or of Kurt Waldheim's Austria – happily restyled, with the help of the Allies, as the innocent victim of Nazi aggression. Think, too, of West Germany in the 1950s.

The examples do not stop there. The transition to democracy in Spain after 1975 was made with a conscious strategy of not looking back, not confronting or 'treating' the past. Jorgé Semprun speaks of 'a collective and willed amnesia'. To be sure, there was an initial explosion of interest in recent history, but there were no trials of Francoist leaders, no purges, no truth commissions. On the fiftieth anniversary of the beginning of the Spanish Civil War, the prime minister, Felipe González, issued a statement saying that the civil war was 'finally history' and 'no longer present and alive in the reality of the country'.

What is more, we find something similar in Poland after the end of communism. Poland's first non-communist prime minister for more than forty years, Tadeusz Mazowiecki, declared in his opening statement to parliament: 'we draw a thick line [*gruba linia*] under the past'. He has since repeatedly insisted that all he meant by this was what he went on to say in the next sentence: that his government should only be held responsible for what it would do itself. Yet the phrase 'thick line', often quoted in the slightly different form *gruba kreska*, rapidly became proverbial and was understood to stand for a whole 'Spanish' approach to the difficult past. While this was unfair to the original context in which Mazowiecki first used the phrase, it was not unfair as a shorthand characterisation of the general attitude of Mazowiecki and his colleagues.

As I well remember from conversations at that time, their general attitude was: let bygones be bygones; no trials, no recriminations; look to the future, to democracy and 'Europe', as Spain had done. Partly this was because Poland in 1989 had a negotiated revolution, and representatives of the old regime were still in high places – including the government itself. Partly it was because by 1990 they simply could not imagine the post-communist party being voted back into power in free elections. So there seemed no pressing political need to remind people of the horrors of the communist past, and many, many more urgent things to do – such as transforming the economy with the so-called Balcerowicz Plan. Yet it also reflected a deeper philosophy, one that Mazowiecki, a liberal Catholic and veteran Solidarity adviser, shared with many from the former opposition movements in central Europe.

In Germany it was the former East German dissidents who pressed for a radical and comprehensive reckoning. Elsewhere in east central Europe it was the dissidents – those who had suffered most directly under the old regime – who were often most ready to draw that 'thick line' under the past. Václav Havel in Czechoslovakia was a classic example, and his policy in his first year as president, like that of Mazowiecki, could be described as one of preemptive forgiveness. The Hungarian case was rather different. Here the conservative government of József Antall, composed of people who had not been in the front line of opposition to communism, indulged a vivid rhetoric of reckoning – but their purgative words were not matched by purgative deeds. The sharpest contrast, as so often, was between Germany and Poland.

II

This brings me to my second basic question: *when?* For there is an intermediate position which says: 'yes, but not yet'. An intellectual argument for this is the neo-Rankean one made against any attempt to write the history of the very recent past: we don't have sufficient distance from the events to understand their meaning, we are emotionally involved, and the sources are not fully available. Better wait thirty years for the relevant official papers to be available in the archives. In post-communist central Europe, however, the last part of the argument is circular, since those who say 'the sources are not available' are often the same people who are keeping the archives shut.

Beyond this, the arguments are political. What is supposed to strengthen the new democracy might actually undermine it. To examine the difficult past too closely will reopen old wounds and tear the society apart. You need to integrate the functionaries, collaborators and merely supporters of the dictatorship into the new democracy. Thus Hermann Lübbe has suggested that it was precisely the fact that Adenauer's West Germany in the 1950s suppressed the memory of the Nazi past, with both amnesty and amnesia, that permitted the social consolidation of democracy in West Germany. It helped Nazis to become democrats.[3]

Against this it can be argued, I think powerfully, as follows. First, the purely historiographical loss is as large as any gain in evidence or detachment. The witnesses die; others forget, or at least, rearrange their memories; and it is the worst horrors that are often the least well documented in the archives. Second, the victims and their relatives have a moral right to know at whose hands they or their loved ones suffered. Third, delay and suppression have their own psychological and political price. The fact that the torturers or the commanders go unpunished, even remain in high office, compromises the new regime in the eyes of those who should be its strongest supporters. Dirty fragments of the past constantly resurface and are used, often dirtily, in current political disputes.

Many among the hugely influential West German 'class of '68' also thought that the suppression of the Nazi past and the anti-communism of the older generation were two sides of the same coin. In reaction, they produced sympathetic, even rose-tinted accounts of communist East Germany, with, for example, no mention of the Stasi secret police. There is an interesting if perverse connection here. Their revolt against their fathers' failure to treat fully the past of the previous German dictatorship contributed to their own failure to see clearly the evils of the current one.

In any event, a sense of the high price of that delay in addressing the Nazi past is one reason why the demand for an immediate, comprehensive 'treatment' of the communist past was so swiftly accepted in Germany after 1989.

III

The German case also raises my third question: *who?* Before the long silence of the fifties there had, of course, been the attempt at denazification, carried out by the occupying powers, and the Nuremberg trials, conducted by the victorious allies. Both Nuremberg and denazification have ever since been basic reference points for all such discussions. Having it done from outside, after a total defeat, does have obvious advantages. There are no domestic political constraints to compare with putsch-happy militaries in Latin America or the still functioning security services in today's Russia. Something gets done. But it also shows the disadvantages. Indeed, one could argue that the suppression of the Adenauer years was itself, in part, a reaction to what had been seen as 'victors' justice' – and victors' history.

---

[3] Herman Lübbe, 'Es ist nichts vergessen, aber einiges ausgeheilt: Der Nationalsozialismus im Bewußtsein der deutschen Gegenwart', *Frankfurter Allgemeine Zeitung*, 24 Jan. 1983.

In most of post-communist Europe we have the opposite position to that of post-1945 Germany. Far from being newly occupied, most post-communist countries see themselves as newly emerged from occupation. Moreover, only in five countries – Poland, Hungary, Romania, Bulgaria and Albania – is the communist past being faced (or not faced) within the same state boundaries as those in which it occurred. Everywhere else, in the former Soviet Union, the former Yugoslavia and the former Czechoslovakia, you have a number of new, smaller successor states. Or rather, they might and do say, *not* successors – not heirs to that past. In a country like Lithuania, genuinely emerging from an oppressive occupation, and struggling to build up a new national and state identity, the temptation to say 'that was them, not us', is almost irresistible. Yet even for the Russians there is a large temptation to say: 'that was the Soviet Union, not Russia'.

The German position is, once again, unique. Whereas Poles and Hungarians are, so to speak, alone with their own past, East and West Germans have to work it through together. Disgruntled East Germans, mixing their historical metaphors, talk of an *Anschluss* followed by 'victors' justice'. But this was a voluntary *Anschluss*, voted for by a majority of East Germans in a free election, and the boldest steps of confronting the past were actually pressed for by East Germans. Still, the resentment is understandable. In many cases, West Germans do sit in judgement, whether in courts of law or simply by executive decision, over East Germans.

This extraordinary German self-occupation, or half-occupation, poses in a singular form the issues always raised by outside participation in the process. There is the practical issue of popular acceptance. But there is also the moral issue. What right have we, who never faced the dilemmas of living in a dictatorship, to sit in judgement on those who did? Do we know how we would we have behaved? Perhaps we, too, would have become party functionaries or secret police informers? So what right have we to condemn? But equally, what right have we to forgive? 'Do not forgive,' writes Zbigniew Herbert, the great poet of Polish resistance,

> Do not forgive, for truly it is not in your power to forgive
> In the name of those who were betrayed at dawn.

Only the victims have the right to forgive.

IV

This is a problem for those inside a country too. Even inside, the question remains: who has the right to judge? Parliament? Judges? Special commissions or tribunals? The media? Or perhaps historians? At this point, the question of *who* shades into the question of *how*. In my title I have indicated three main paths: trials, purges or history lessons. (I leave aside here the very important but also very complex issues of rehabilitation, compensation and restitution for the victims or their relatives.)

The choice of path, and the extent to which each can be followed, depends on the character of the preceding dictatorship, the manner of the transition and the particular situation of the succeeding democracy – if that is what it becomes. Thus, for example, the political constraints in central Europe are far less acute than in Latin America. But the preceding repression was also very different.

The American writer Tina Rosenberg has put it simply but well: in Latin America, repression was deep, in central Europe it was broad. In Latin America, there was a group of people who were clearly victims – tortured, murdered or, in that awkward but strangely powerful locution, 'disappeared' – by a group of people – army and police officers, members of death squads – who were clearly perpetrators. In central Europe, since the high Stalinist period, and with a few major exceptions, the regime was generally kept in power by a much larger number of people exerting less violent or explicit pressure on a much larger number. Many people were on both sides. Society was kept down by millions of Lilliputian threads of everyday mendacity, conformity and compromise. This is a point Václav Havel has constantly stressed. In these late or post-totalitarian regimes, he says, the line did not run clearly between 'them' and 'us', but through each individual. No one was simply a victim, everyone was in some measure co-responsible.

If that is true, it is much less clear who, if anyone, should be put on trial. Havel's implicit answer is: everyone, and therefore none. The Polish writer Adam Michnik has made this answer explicit. Exceptions to prove the rule are individual cases of abnormal brutality, such as the Polish secret police officers directly responsible for the murder of the Solidarity priest, Father Jerzy Popieluszko.

The record of trials in post-communist central Europe is, in fact, a very chequered one. In what was then still Czechoslovakia, two senior functionaries were convicted for their part in the repression of anti-regime demonstrations in 1988 and early 1989. In 1993, the Czech Republic's Law on the Illegal Character of the Communist Regime lifted the statute of limitations for crimes which 'for political reasons' had not been prosecuted in the communist period. An Office for the Documentation and Investigation of the Crimes of Communism was established, and in December 2001 three former communist party leaders were indicted for their role in assisting the Warsaw Pact invasion of Czechoslovakia in 1968. In Poland, General Jaruzelski was investigated for ordering the destruction of Politburo records and then, more substantially, indicted on charges relating to the shooting of protesting workers on the Baltic coast in 1970/1. A number of senior figures were charged with causing the deaths of striking workers during martial law in 1981–2. But altogether, the judicial proceedings have been fitful, fragmentary and usually inconclusive.

Germany has, unsuprisingly, been the most systematic. Border guards have been tried and convicted for shooting people who were trying to escape from East Germany. More recently, the country's last communist leader, Egon Krenz, was sentenced to six and a half years' imprisonment for his co-responsibility for the 'shoot to kill' policy at the frontier. Several other senior figures were found guilty with him. Yet even in Germany, the results are very mixed, to say the least.

The arguments generally made for trials are that they go at least some way to doing justice for the victims; that they help to deter future transgressions by the military or security forces; that they exemplify and strengthen the rule of law; and, finally, that they contribute to public knowledge and some sense of a wider catharsis. The first consideration – justice for the victims – certainly applies in some of these cases; the second applies to a much smaller degree, since, broadly speaking, where such deterrence might still be important (as in Russia) there have been no such trials, and where there have been trials (as in Germany) the deterrence is hardly needed.

Have these trials exemplified and strengthened the rule of law? It is very hard to say that they have. Equality before the law is a fundamental principle: but even in Germany, still more elsewhere, there has been a radical, arbitrary and political selection of the accused. Then there is the familiar problem of trying people for crimes that were not crimes on the statute books of their countries at the time. How to avoid violating the time-honoured principle of *nulla poena sine lege*?

Determined to avoid such a 'Nuremberg' procedure, German prosecutors have therefore tried to identify crimes that were offences in East German law at the time. However this has involved a highly selective application of East German law, thus violating another basic principle. (Yet otherwise, the prosecutors should themselves be prosecuted for defaming the East German state, which was an offence under East German law!) And when the case could still not quite be made to stick, they bridged the gap with an awkward invocation of 'natural law'. Meanwhile, the former Minister for State Security, Erich Mielke, was convicted not for his heavy responsibility in the regime but for his part in the murder of a policeman as a young street-fighting communist in 1931. The central trial of Erich Honecker, the Party leader from 1971 to 1989, was finally abandoned on the grounds of his ill-health. He then flew off to spend his last months quietly in Chile.

None of this contributed much to any sense of popular catharsis. As for public knowledge: the thousands of pages of legal argument did little to illuminate the true history of the regime, certainly not for the general reader. Nor will future students of communism, I think, use the records of these trials as we do still use those of the Nuremberg trials to understand Nazism.

The Hungarian case is an interesting contrast. Here parliament initially passed a law which, like the Czech one, lifted the statute of limitations for acts of treason, murder and manslaughter during the communist period, but the Constitutional Court struck that down on the grounds that it was retroactive justice. A new law was then passed specifically on Crimes Committed During the 1956 Revolution. This took a different tack, and applied the Geneva and New York conventions on 'war crimes' and 'crimes against humanity' to what happened in 1956. Unlike the German prosecutors, and uniquely in central Europe, they therefore claimed that some things done in the communist period did qualify for those Nuremberg trial categories – 'crimes against humanity', 'war crimes' – and that these provisions had at least notionally been in force in international law at the time.

The second way is that of purges. Or, to put it more neutrally: the path of administrative disqualification. In this field alone it was not Germany that set the pace. Partly in reaction against Havel's policy of preemptive forgiveness, the Czechoslovak parliament passed a draconian law in the autumn of 1991. It laid down that whole categories of people – including high party functionaries, members of the People's Militia, agents and what it termed 'conscious collaborators' of the state security service – should be banned from whole, widely drawn categories of job in the public service. In Czech, the process was called not 'purge' (a somewhat compromised term) but *lustrace*, a word derived from the Latin and implying both 'illumination' and 'ritual purification'. Thanks to the Czechs, we can therefore revive an old English word: lustration. Among the meanings given by the *Oxford English Dictionary*, with supporting quotations from the seventeenth to the nineteenth centuries, are 'purification *esp.* spiritual or moral' and 'the performance of an expiatory sacrifice or a purificatory rite'.

The Czechoslovak lustration was fully effective in its original form for little more than a year, since Czechoslovakia then broke into two. While the Czech Republic continued with a slightly modified version, Slovakia virtually dropped it. Yet there is no doubt that it did keep a number of highly compromised persons out of public life in the Czech lands (while such persons remained in Slovakia). However, the original legislation was also so crude and procedurally unjust that President Havel publicly expressed deep reluctance to sign the law, and the Council of Europe protested against it. Disqualification by category meant that any particular individual circumstances could not be taken into account. A commission determined, on the basis of a sometimes cursory examination of secret police and other official records, whether someone had belonged to one of the categories. The person thus publicly branded often did not see all the evidence and had only limited rights of appeal. In effect, they were assumed guilty until found innocent.

The German law on the Stasi files is more scrupulous. Employers receive a summary of the evidence on the individual's file from the so-called Gauck Authority – the extraordinary ministry set up to administer the 111 miles of Stasi files, and colloquially named after its head, Joachim Gauck, an East German priest. The employer then makes an individual decision, case by case. Even in the public service, some two-thirds of those negatively vetted have remained in their jobs. The employee can also appeal to the labour courts. Yet here, too, there clearly have been cases of injustice – even when denunciatory media coverage has not ruined the person's life. And the sheer numbers are extraordinary: to the end of May 1999 some 2.4 million vetting enquiries had been answered by the Gauck Authority. In other words, something approaching one in every seven East Germans has been, to use the colloquial term, 'gaucked'. Here the strict, procedural equality may, in fact, conceal a deeper structural inequality: between the treatment of East as opposed to West German employees.

Yet one also has to consider the cost of not purging. In Poland, that was the original 'Spanish' intent. Within a year, however, the continuance of former communists in high places became a hotly disputed subject in Polish politics. In summer 1992 the interior minister of a strongly anti-communist government supplied to parliament summaries of files identifying prominent politicians as secret police collaborators. Of course the names were leaked to the press. This so-called *noc teczek* – or night of the long files – shook the new democracy and actually resulted in the fall of the government. In December 1995 the outgoing interior minister, with the consent of the outgoing president, accused his own post-communist prime minister of being an agent for Russian intelligence. The prime minister subsequently resigned, and the affair still rumbles on. In the latest parliamentary election campaign, it was suggested that the current post-communist president of Poland, Aleksander Kwaśniewski, himself had close contacts with the Russian agent who allegedly 'ran' the former prime minister.

So in the absence of an agreed, public, legal procedure, Poland has not enjoyed Spanish-style consensus but bitter, recurrent mud-slinging and crude political exploitation of the files. As a long-overdue antidote to all this, the Polish parliament finally passed a carefully drafted lustration law in 1997. It obliges people in senior positions in public life, including in the state-owned media, to sign, at the time they stand for elected office or are appointed to the job, a declaration as to whether they did or did not 'consciously collaborate' with the security services in the period June 1944 to May 1990. At the recent parliamentary elections, I saw polling stations plastered with long lists of the candidates, and under each name the appropriate declaration. The admitted fact of collaboration does not in itself disqualify you from standing for public office. Indeed, several candidates on the post-communist list stood admitting their past collaboration. Only if you lie, saying you did not collaborate when in fact you did, are you disqualified for ten years. The declarations of innocence are to be checked, in secret, by a Lustration Court, for which it has proved rather difficult to find judges. However, since more 'decommunisation' was a major demand of several of the parties gathered in the Solidarity Electoral Action coalition, now the senior partner in Poland's new government, we can expect these difficulties to be overcome.

Hungary passed a lustration law in 1997, which is slowly being implemented. Here, a commission vets senior figures in public life, but exposes them publicly only if they refuse to resign quietly. The prime minister Gyula Horn admitted in September 1997 that he had been negatively assessed in the terms of the law, both on account of his service in the militia assembled to help crush the 1956 revolution and because, as foreign minister, he had been the recipient of secret police information. However, he declined to resign and said he now regards the matter as closed. In both the Polish and the Hungarian cases, the circle of persons to be vetted is – wisely in my view – drawn much more closely than in the German case.

Some analysts have taken the argument for purges a step further. Where there was no lustration, they say, as in Poland and Hungary – and elsewhere in eastern and south-eastern Europe – the post-communist parties returned to power. Only where there was lustration, in Czechoslovakia and Germany, did this not occur. To deduce causality from correlation is an old historian's fallacy – *cum hoc, ergo propter hoc*. On closer examination, you find that in eastern Germany the post-communist party has done very well in elections, and one reason for this is, precisely, resentment of what are seen as West German occupation purges and victors' justice. In fact, the number of votes the post-communist Party of Democratic Socialism (PDS) received in East Germany at the last Bundestag election, in October 1994, is remarkably similar to the number of people who have been 'gaucked'. (Not that I would deduce causality from this correlation, but still . . .)

Putting Germany aside leaves the single, Czechoslovak, and by now only Czech, exception, for which other reasons can also be adduced. Moreover, one should by no means simply assume that the return to power of post-communist parties with impeccably social democratic programmes has been bad for the consolidation of democracy. Yet it is true that in Poland and Hungary, the new democracy has been shaken by issues arising from the lack of lustration, including the current activities of the security services. And the return to power not just of the post-communist parties but of historically compromised persons within them has furnished the populist, nationalist right with arguments against the working of the new parliamentary democracy altogether: 'If such people are elected, there must be something wrong with elections.'

Finally, there are what I call 'history lessons'. These can be of several kinds: state or independent, public or private. The classic model of a state, public history lesson is that of the 'truth commission', first developed in Latin America and then used in South Africa. As José Zalaquett has noted, the point is not only to find out as much as possible of the truth about the past dictatorship but also that this truth be 'officially proclaimed and publicly exposed'. Not just knowledge but acknowledgement is the goal. It is also a matter of what in his chapter Tim Snyder describes as establishing 'sovereignty over memory' and rewriting a collective, national memory for the sake of reconciliation. In truth commissions, there is a strong element of political theatre; they are a kind of public morality play. Bishop Tutu has shown himself well aware of this. He leads others in weeping as the survivors tell their tales of suffering and the secret policemen confess their brutality. The object is not judicial punishment: in South Africa, full confession leads not to trial but to amnesty. It is formally to establish the truth, insofar as it can ever be established; if possible, to achieve a collective catharsis, very much as Aristotle envisaged catharsis in a Greek tragedy; and then to move on. In South Africa, as in Chile, it is a commission for 'Truth and Reconciliation', and the hope is to move through the one to the other.

You might think that this model would be particularly well suited to the communist world, where the regimes were kept in place less by direct coercion than by the everyday tissue of lies. But again, only in Germany has it really been tried, and even there, they somehow did not dare to use the word 'truth'. Instead, the parliamentary commission, chaired by an East German former dissident priest, was cumbersomely called the 'Enquete Commission in the German Bundestag [for the] Treatment [*Aufarbeitung*] of the Past and Consequences of the SED-Dictatorship in Germany (SED being the initials of the East German communist party). Hundreds of witnesses were heard, expert reports commissioned, proceedings covered in the media. We now have a report of 15,378 pages. There are problems with this report. The language is often ponderous. Some of the historical judgements represent compromises between the West German political parties, worried about their own pasts. Yet as documentation it is invaluable. For students of the East German dictatorship this may yet be what the records of the Nuremberg trials are for the student of the Third Reich.

In Poland and Czechoslovakia, by contrast, the national commissions of enquiry have concentrated on major crises in the history of the communist state: Solidarity and the Prague Spring respectively. In each case, the focus has been on the Soviet connection: who 'invited' the Red Army to invade Czechoslovakia in August 1968? Who was responsible for martial law in Poland in 1981? In Hungary, too, official enquires have concentrated on the 1956 revolution, and the Soviet invasion that crushed it. So instead of exploring what Poles did to Poles, Czechs and Slovaks to Czechs and Slovaks, Hungarians to Hungarians, each nation dwells on the wrongs done to it by the Soviet Union. Instead of quietly reflecting, as Havel suggested, on the personal responsibility which each and everyone had for sustaining the communist regime, people unite in righteous indignation at the traitors who invited the Russians in.

Any explanation for the absence of wider truth commissions must be speculative. I would speculate that part of the explanation, at least, lies in this combination of the historically defensible but also comfortable conviction that the dictatorship was ultimately imposed from outside and, on the other hand, the uneasy knowledge that almost everyone had done something to sustain the dictatorial system.

Another kind of history lesson is less formal and ritualistic, but requires permissive state action. This is to open the archives of the preceding regime to scholars, journalists, writers, filmmakers – and then to let a hundred documentaries bloom. Yet again, Germany has gone furthest, much helped by the fact that the East German state ceased to exist on 3 October 1990. Virtually all the archives of the former DDR are open, and provide a marvellous treasure-trove for the study of a communist state. I say 'virtually all' because a notable exception is the archive of the East German foreign ministry, in which are held most of the records of the often sycophantic conversations that West German politicians conducted with East German leaders. In opening the archives, West German politicians have thus fearlessly spared nobody – except themselves.

It has also helped that Germany has such a strong tradition of writing contemporary history. The research department of the Gauck Authority, for example, is partly staffed by younger historians from the Munich Institute for Contemporary History, famous for its studies of Nazism. Theirs are strange careers: progressing smoothly from the study of one German dictatorship to another, while all the time living in a peaceful, prosperous German democracy. The results are impressive. Whereas a West German schoolchild in the 1950s could learn precious little about Nazi Germany, every German schoolchild today can already learn a great deal about the history of communist Germany. Whether they are interested is another question.

Elsewhere in central Europe, the opening of the archives has been more uneven, partly because of the political attitudes I have described, partly for simple lack of resources and trained personnel. Yet here, too, there have been some interesting publications based on the new archive material, and school textbooks have significantly improved. In Poland there has been a lively intellectual and political debate about the nature, achievements and (il)legitimacy of the Polish People's Republic. In Prague, a new Institute for Contemporary History concerns itself with the history of Czechoslovakia from 1939 to 1992. In Hungary, a whole institute has been established solely to study the history of the 1956 revolution. It has roughly one staff member per day of the revolution.

Beyond this, what Germany has uniquely pioneered is the systematic opening of the secret police files, administered by the Gauck Authority, not just for vetting and purging purposes, but also to everyone – whether spied upon or spying – who has a file and still wants to know. The power is in the hands of the individual citizen: You can choose to read your file, or not to read it. The informers on your file are identified only by codenames, but you can request formal confirmation of their true identity. Then you have to decide whether to confront them, or not to confront them; to say something publicly, just to tell close friends, or to close it in your heart. This is the most deep and personal kind of history lesson.

Thus far, some 500,000 people have seen their Stasi files, over 200,000 are still waiting to do so, and more than 500,000 have learned with relief – or was it with disappointment? – that they had no file. I can think of no remotely scientific way to assess this unique experiment. People have made terrible personal discoveries: the East German peace activist Vera Wollenberger, for example, found that her husband had been informing on her throughout their married life. Only they can say if it is better that they know.

There has also been highly irresponsible, sensationalist media coverage: denouncing people as informers without any of the due caution about the sources or circumstances. In German, such exposure is revealingly called 'outing'. Here is a structural problem of treating the past in societies with free and sensation-hungry media. Against this, however, one has to

put the many cases where people have emerged from the experience with
gnawing suspicions laid to rest, enhanced understanding and a more solid
footing for their present lives.

Elsewhere in central Europe, the German experiment was at first
strongly criticised and resisted, on the grounds that it would reopen old
wounds, unjustly destroy reputations, and that the Polish or Hungarian
secret police records are much more unreliable than the German ones.
(This last comment is made with a kind of inverted national pride.)
Officers put innocent people down as informers, or simply invented
them – the so-called 'dead souls' – in order to meet their assigned plan
targets for the number of informers. Many files were later destroyed, others tampered with, and so on. So, instead, the secret police files have
remained in the hands of the current interior ministry or still active security service, and been used selectively by them and their political masters.
Limited access has been given to just a few individual scholars.

Yet, interestingly, this is now changing. Hungary has provided for individuals to request copies of their own file. The precedent is clearly the
German one, although the Hungarian rules demand even more extensive 'anonymisation' – that is, blacking-out of the names on the copies.
The Hungarian Gauck Authority is called simply, and rather sinisterly, the
Historical Office. In sanctioning this access, the Hungarian constitutional court drew heavily on the judgements of the German constitutional court, notably in using the interesting concept of 'informational
self-determination'. In plain English, I have a right to know what information the state has collected on me and, within limits, to determine what
is done with it. Altogether, it is remarkable to see how, in this of all areas,
Germany has been not just a pioneer but also, in the end, something of
a model for its eastern neighbours.

The Czech Republic has passed a law which provides for people who
were Czechoslovak citizens at any time between 1948 and 1990 to read
their own files, under similar conditions. The first applications were accepted in June 1997. Thus far there has been remarkably little debate
about individual cases, and few prominent former dissidents have applied to see their files. Perhaps this will change when sensational material
is found and published, but at the moment one is told in Prague that there
seems to be little public interest. There is a strong sense that the Czechs
have already 'been through all this' with the great lustration debate of the
early 1990s.

V

There are no easy generalisations and certainly no universal laws. So
much depends on the character of the preceding regime and the nature

of the transition. Even my first, basic question – *whether?* – does not have a simple answer. The ancient case for forgetting is much stronger than it is quite comfortable for historians to recall. Successful democracies have been built on a conscious policy of forgetting, although at a cost, which often has not appeared until a generation later.

In central Europe after communism, Germany's policy of systematic, unprecedentedly comprehensive past-treating contrasted with the Polish, post-Solidarity government's proclaimed policy of drawing a 'thick line' under the past. But the Polish attempt to follow the Spanish example did not work as it did in Spain. Within a year, the issue of the communist past had come back to bedevil Polish politics, and continues to be used in a messy, partisan way. My conclusion is that if it is to be done it should be done quickly, in an orderly, explicit and legal way. This also has the great advantage of allowing people then to move on, not necessarily to forget, perhaps not even to forgive, but simply to go forward with that knowledge behind them.

If the questions *'whether?'* and *'when?'* are thus closely connected, so are the questions *'who?'* and *'how?'* In Germany, the process has been made both easier and more difficult by West German participation: easier administratively, more difficult psychologically. Yet doing it among themselves, Hungarians, Poles, Czechs and Slovaks have all too humanly inclined to focus on the responsibility of others rather than their own.

There are places in the world where trials have been both necessary and effective. In central Europe, trials have been – with a few important exceptions – of only questionable necessity and even more dubious efficacy. The attempt to use existing national laws has been contorted, selective and often ended in simple failure. It has hardly exemplified or strengthened the rule of law. This is one area in which the international component may be a real advantage. Difficult though it is, the least bad way forward must be to try establish a firm international framework of law on 'crimes against humanity' or 'war crimes'. Building on the Hague tribunals on Bosnia and Rwanda, we need to move towards the permanent international criminal court for which Richard Goldstone and others have eloquently argued – a court to which all dictators, everywhere, should know that they may one day have to answer. Meanwhile, the Hungarian path of writing the existing international law into domestic law is an interesting one. But it was confined to just one event, the Hungarian revolution of 1956, now more than forty years past, and its implementation has been plagued by all the problems of evidence that we know so well from the trials of Nazi criminals in recent decades.

As for purges, there is probably no such thing as a good purge, even if it is politely called a lustration. The Czechoslovak lustration was prompt and crudely effective, but deeply flawed by procedural injustice. The German 'gaucking' has been procedurally more just: careful, individual, appealable. But it has often been perverted by media abuse and has suffered from elephantiasis. Did postmen and train-drivers really need to be gaucked? Again we come back to the question of who is doing it: for would the West Germans ever have done this to themselves?

Yet Poland has shown the price of not purging. The Hungarians, with their nice habit of taking the German model and then improving on it, came up with a defensible refinement: careful individual scrutiny, confined strictly to those in senior positions in public life. But this was seven years late. Now Poland has finally followed suit, with a law that is probably the most scrupulous of them all.

I personally believe the third path, that of history lessons, is the most promising. Much of the comparative literature comes to a similar conclusion for other countries: what is somewhat biblically called 'truth-telling' is both the most desirable and the most feasible way to grapple with a difficult past. This is what West Germany did best in relation to Nazism, at least from the 1960s on. What united Germany has done in this regard since 1990 has been exemplary: the parliamentary commission, the open archives, the unique opportunity for a very personal history lesson given by access to the Stasi files. Some of this has been done elsewhere in central Europe, but nothing like as much. I have suggested an explanation for why Poland, Hungary and Czechoslovakia did not have comparable national commissions of enquiry, but an explanation is not the same as a good reason.

This endorsement of the third path does, of course, assign a very special place to contemporary historians. In fact I do think that if you ask 'who is best equipped to do justice to the past?' the answer is, or at least should be, historians. But this is also a heavy responsibility. Truth is a big word, so often abused in central Europe during the short, rotten twentieth century that people there have grown wary of it – and perhaps not so often heard even in our own universities. Studying the legacy of a dictatorship, one is vividly reminded how difficult it is to establish any historical truth. In particular, across such a change of regime, you discover how deeply unreliable is any retrospective testimony. In Robert Louis Stevenson's words, people 'have a grand memory for forgetting'.

Yet studying this subject also strengthens one's allergy to some of the bottomless, ludicrous frivolities of post-modernist historiography. Carelessly used, the records of a state that worked by organised lying, and especially the poisonous, intrusive files of a secret police, can ruin lives. Memory in this sense of knowledge of the past can also be a form of pernicious power. To use the files properly tests the critical skills that historians routinely apply to a mediaeval charter or an eighteenth-century pamphlet. But having worked intensively with such material, and read much else based on it, I know that it can be done. It is not true, as is often claimed, that these records are so corrupted that one cannot write reliable history on the basis of them. The evidence has to be weighed with very special care. The text must be put in the historical context. Interpretation needs both intellectual distance and the essential imaginative sympathy with all the men and women involved, even the oppressors. But with these old familiar disciplines, there is a truth that can be found. Not a single, absolute Truth with a capital T, but still a real and important one.

Index